Get the eBook FREE!

(PDF, ePub, Kindle, and liveBook all included)

We believe that once you buy a book from us, you should be able to read it in any format we have available. To get electronic versions of this book at no additional cost to you, purchase and then register this book at the Manning website.

Go to https://www.manning.com/freebook and follow the instructions to complete your pBook registration.

That's it!
Thanks from Manning!

ScyllaDB in Action

ScyllaDB in Action

BO INGRAM

MANNING
SHELTER ISLAND

Manning Publications Co.
20 Baldwin Road
PO Box 761
Shelter Island, NY 11964

Development editor:	Connor O'Brien
Technical editor:	Piotr Wiktor Sarna
Review editor:	Kishor Rit
Production editor:	Keri Hales
Copy editor:	Tiffany Taylor
Proofreader:	Olga Milanko
Technical proofreader:	Alex Ott
Typesetter:	Dennis Dalinnik
Cover designer:	Marija Tudor

ISBN: 9781633437265
Printed in the United States of America

to Ernie, the best

brief contents

contents

preface

It was 2021, and I had a week off before starting a new job at Discord. They told me I'd be working with the distributed database Apache Cassandra to start, but they were in the midst of switching to ScyllaDB—a more performant rewrite of Cassandra. That week, I went hunting for resources to learn about ScyllaDB, but resources outside of the official docs were few and far between. I ended up mostly studying Cassandra and pretending that every time I saw the word Cassandra, it actually said ScyllaDB. This approach wasn't the worst option, but it left some definite gaps in my knowledge that I had to work to fill in later.

Because we were running both databases together when I started, I was able to compare their behaviors. I immediately was a big fan of how, by distributing their data, they provide scalability and fault tolerance. Coming from a relational database background, I'd seen how a single database node going offline due to a cloud-provider problem could wreck an application's availability. ScyllaDB's and Cassandra's more gradual degradation paradigm brings immediate benefits. The catch lies in their comparative performance. The Cassandra database felt like it was always alerting, paging someone to fix a failure or mitigate an overwhelmed cluster. But the ScyllaDB databases were quiet; they rarely paged, and they exhibited better performance. We finished the ScyllaDB migration a few months later, and the barrage of Cassandra alerts ceased.

In 2023, Jonathan Gennick from Manning Publications reached out to me and asked if I would be interested in writing a book on ScyllaDB. I've always wanted to write a book, and this cold email out of the blue found an incredibly willing participant. I immediately had flashbacks to 2021 when I was trying to find a book about ScyllaDB. *ScyllaDB in Action* is the book I desperately wanted all those years ago (if any of you ever build a time machine, I wouldn't say no to Past Bo being handed a copy). I wanted something that not only covered ScyllaDB-specific features but also was practical and would explain why I was getting paged at 3 a.m. Also, with a dreamer's arrogance, I thought that if I ever wrote a technical book, I'd want it to be in Manning's *in Action* series; as a reader, I love Manning's focus on practical and actionable teaching. Accordingly, I've focused this book on teaching the database from the basics and preparing you to run the database in production so you'll know what a hot partition is, what queries are likely to cause it, and why it can cause performance degradation in your cluster.

I'm excited to share this work with you, and I hope you find it as instructive and helpful for you as it was enjoyable and rewarding for me to assemble. Happy reading!

acknowledgments

I can't begin anywhere else than by thanking my best friend, accomplice, and wife, Emily. Without her support, encouragement, and willingness to listen to me blather about writing challenges, we'd never have gotten past page 1. I must also thank one very good dog: my writing muse, Ernie. His inclusion as the proprietor of Ernie's Eats reflects the immensity of his contributions. He passed away just as I finished writing, and I miss him terribly. I would also like to thank my teammates at Discord. Our experiences operating ScyllaDB have been invaluable when writing this book, and I'm hoping that our lessons learned can spare readers from some late-night alerts. I'd like to especially thank Mike Sun, my manager, who encouraged me to write this book after my shock from the initial reach-out from Manning.

I thank all the Manning staff for their tremendous help in getting this book to print: Jonathan Gennick, acquisitions editor, Connor O'Brien, developmental editor, Kishor Rit, review editor, Alex Ott, technical proofreader, and Piotr Wiktor Sarna, a long-time contributor and former maintainer of ScyllaDB, the Seastar framework, and libSQL who worked as my technical editor. I'd like to also thank Toni Arritola, my original developmental editor on the book, for her help in the first few chapters. In addition, thanks to all the behind-the-scenes production staff who whipped this book into shape.

Thanks also to all the reviewers: Albert Leung, Ali Shakiba, Andres Sacco, Ankit Virmani, Dirk Gómez, Eder Andrés Ávila Niño, Ganesh Swaminathan, Giampiero Granatella, Greg Kreiter, Heng Zhang, Iyabo Sindiku, Jeff Smith, Jens Christian Bredahl Madsen, John McCormack, Jose San Leandro, Nadir Doctor, Ozay Duman, Piotr

Jastrzebski, Rui Liu, Sasha Sankova, Sergio Britos Arévalo, Simone Sguazza, Sumit Pal, Valerie Parham-Thompson, and Victor Duran. Your suggestions helped make this a better book.

about this book

ScyllaDB in Action was written to teach you how to operate and build applications on ScyllaDB. Throughout the book, you'll be considering a small design problem as a tool to learn about ScyllaDB: a restaurant review application. It begins by grounding you in the database's basics—how to read and write data—through building some simple tables for your application. You'll then learn how to design a database schema by taking the requirements for your restaurant review app and performing query-first design: determining what queries your database needs to support and building the schema from that. Having created your schema, you'll learn how reads and writes work and perform efficiently in Scylla. The book continues by examining Scylla's architecture, building an API on top of Scylla in Python, examining how to run and monitor Scylla in production, and learning how to move data in bulk in and out of your database.

Who should read this book

ScyllaDB in Action is written for anyone looking to learn ScyllaDB or work with it. To get the best out of it, you should have some basic familiarity with SQL. You've probably written a SELECT statement before, and that knowledge will assist you throughout the book as you learn about Scylla. If you're a database expert, that's okay too! You'll get to break some habits and pick up some new ones to effectively use ScyllaDB. You should also have some experience with a programming language—preferably Python, as you'll use it to build the sample application to learn about the database driver and its client-side features.

How this book is organized: A road map

Like many books, this one has chapters. I've divided it into 4 parts totaling 12 chapters. Part 1 begins you on your ScyllaDB journey, introducing the database and letting you play with it locally:

- Chapter 1 provides an overview of ScyllaDB, sharing its benefits and comparing and contrasting it with different databases.
- Chapter 2 shows you how to build a small ScyllaDB cluster on your laptop and run some basic queries against it.

In Part 2, you'll learn how to design a database schema that best fits ScyllaDB through a practice called query-first design:

- Chapter 3 discusses how to gather application requirements and, by looking at the queries that fulfill those requirements, ultimately translate them into database tables.
- Chapter 4 uses your application requirements, queries, and tables to teach ScyllaDB's data types by determining the types needed to meet those requirements.
- Chapter 5 finishes your design by polishing it up and transforming it into correctly configured tables in a database.

Part 3 takes a close look at querying Scylla, using the database schema created in part 2:

- Chapter 6 is all about writes—inserting, updating, and deleting data.
- Chapter 7 is the companion chapter to the previous one; you'll learn all about reads, their performance, and the various tools Scylla provides to help you read data efficiently.

The last part of the book, part 4, covers running Scylla:

- Chapter 8 teaches you about ScyllaDB's architecture by examining its design goals and how each feature of the database exists to fulfill at least one of them.
- Chapter 9 covers running ScyllaDB in production, discussing configuring, sizing, and operating a Scylla cluster.
- Chapter 10 guides you through connecting a Python application to a ScyllaDB cluster using a database driver.
- Chapter 11 demonstrates how you monitor a ScyllaDB cluster running in production and assess its performance via observability and load-testing, as well as what to do when the graphs tell you that your cluster isn't having a great time.
- Chapter 12 ends the book by examining data migrations in ScyllaDB, both into the cluster and out of it.

About the code

This book contains source code and code output throughout, through both inline examples and numbered listings. In all cases, code is identified by using `this fixed-width font`. Output is also potentially formatted or abridged when necessary; although we can always horizontally scroll terminal windows, we can't do that in a book. Occasionally, a line-continuation marker (➥) has been added to indicate that a command or output continues onto a new line.

For commands the reader should execute, I've attempted to notate where they should be run using the following conventions:

- Lines beginning with a $ should be executed in your local terminal.
- Lines beginning with (scylla-reviews) $ should be executed in the terminal of the Docker container in parentheses (scylla-reviews in this example).
- Lines beginning with cqlsh:> should be executed within a cqlsh session inside a Docker container.

You can get executable snippets of code from the liveBook (online) version of this book at https://livebook.manning.com/book/scylladb-in-action. The complete code for the examples in the book is available for download from the Manning website at https://www.manning.com/books/scylladb-in-action and in the book's GitHub code repo at https://github.com/scylladb-in-action/code.

liveBook discussion forum

Purchase of *ScyllaDB in Action* includes free access to liveBook, Manning's online reading platform. Using liveBook's exclusive discussion features, you can attach comments to the book globally or to specific sections or paragraphs. It's a snap to make notes for yourself, ask and answer technical questions, and receive help from the author and other users. To access the forum, go to https://livebook.manning.com/book/scylladb -in-action/discussion. You can also learn more about Manning's forums and the rules of conduct at https://livebook.manning.com/discussion.

Manning's commitment to our readers is to provide a venue where a meaningful dialogue between individual readers and between readers and the author can take place. It is not a commitment to any specific amount of participation on the part of the author, whose contribution to the forum remains voluntary (and unpaid). We suggest you try asking the author some challenging questions lest his interest stray! The forum and the archives of previous discussions will be accessible from the publisher's website as long as the book is in print.

about the author

BO INGRAM is a staff software engineer at Discord, working in database infrastructure. He has extensive experience working with ScyllaDB as both an operator and an application developer.

about the cover illustration

The figure on the cover of *ScyllaDB in Action*, titled "La Figurante," is taken from a book by Louis Curmer published in 1841. Each illustration is finely drawn and colored by hand.

In those days, it was easy to identify where people lived and what their trade or station in life was just by their dress. Manning celebrates the inventiveness and initiative of the computer business with book covers based on the rich diversity of regional culture centuries ago, brought back to life by pictures from collections such as this one.

Part 1

Getting started

The first part of the book focuses on introducing you to ScyllaDB. In chapter 1, you'll begin by learning about this distributed database and seeing what it is and why it's useful to you. In chapter 2, you'll get your hands dirty by spinning up a local Scylla cluster and playing with some basic queries to get the data flowing.

Introducing ScyllaDB

1

This chapter covers

- ScyllaDB and what it is
- ScyllaDB versus other databases
- How ScyllaDB takes advantage of being a distributed system

ScyllaDB is a distributed NoSQL database designed to be a more-performant rewrite of Apache Cassandra. Although it rhymes with "Godzilla" and has an adorable creature as a mascot, it's designed not to be monstrous to operate.

Compared with relational databases, ScyllaDB brings two big weapons to the Great Database Battle Royale: scalability and fault tolerance. It is a distributed database that runs multiple nodes to store and serve data. This distribution simplifies scalability; to add additional capacity, operators only need to add more nodes. By providing users with the capability to tune how many nodes respond to a query, ScyllaDB also provides fault tolerance because the system can handle the loss of a configurable number of nodes before being unable to serve requests, as seen in figure 1.1.

This distributed design impacts everything around it: how you design applications, how you query data, how you monitor the database, and how you recover the

3

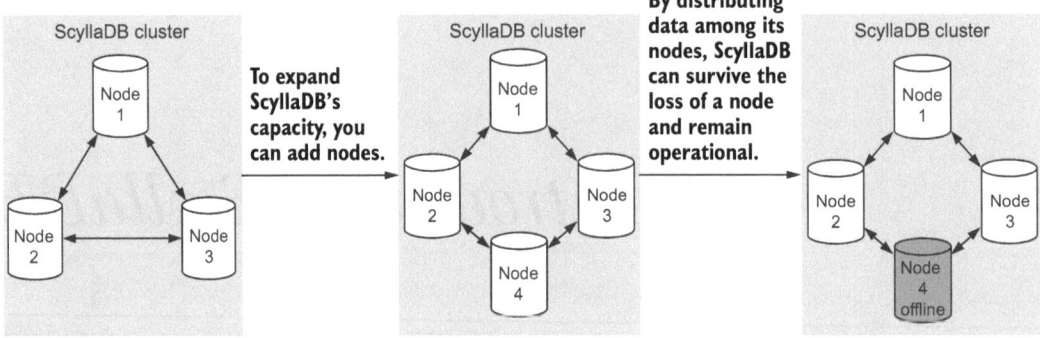

Figure 1.1   ScyllaDB is a distributed database that provides scalability and fault tolerance.

system during an outage. We'll explore all of these areas, showing how ScyllaDB can be the practical distributed database for any application. Let's dive in!

1.1   ScyllaDB, a different database

ScyllaDB is a database—it says so in its name! Users give it data; the database gives the data back when asked. This very basic and oversimplified interface isn't too dissimilar from popular relational databases like PostgreSQL and MySQL. ScyllaDB, however, is not a relational database; it eschews joins and relational data modeling to provide a different set of benefits. To illustrate these, let's look at a fictitious example.

1.1.1   Hypothetical databases

Let's imagine you've just moved to a new town, and when you go to restaurants, you want to remember what you ate so that you can order it again or avoid it next time. You could write your order in a journal or save it in the Notes app on your phone, but you hear about a new business model that has people remember information you send them. Your friend Robert has just started a similar venture: *Robert's Rememberings*.

ROBERT'S REMEMBERINGS

Robert's business (figure 1.2) is straightforward: you can text Robert's phone number, and he will remember whatever information you send him. He'll also retrieve information for you, so you won't need to remember everything you've eaten in your new town. That's Robert's job.

   The plan works swimmingly at first, but problems begin to appear. Once, you text Robert and he doesn't respond. He apologizes later and says he had a doctor's appointment. Not unreasonable—you want your friend to be healthy. Another time, you text him about a new meal, and it takes him several minutes to reply instead of his usual instant response. He says that business is booming, and he's been inundated with requests—so response time has suffered. He reassures you and says not to worry; he has a plan (figure 1.3).

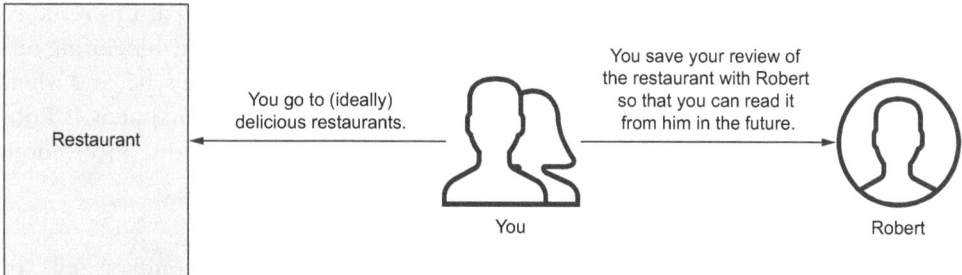

Figure 1.2   Robert's Rememberings has a seemingly simple plan.

When Robert's business gets overwhelmed due to its popularity, he adds Rosa to serve read requests. Although this addition does reduce the individual number of requests, it also introduces additional ways the system can fail.

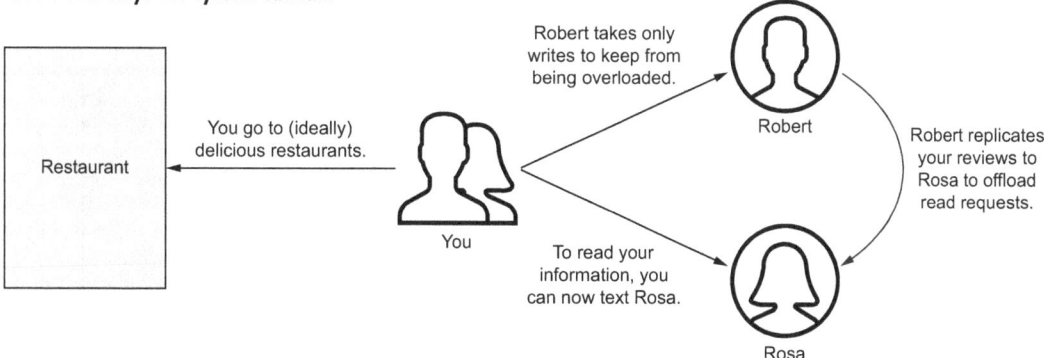

Figure 1.3   Robert adds a friend to his system to solve problems, but doing so introduces complications.

Robert has hired a friend to help him out. He sends you the new updated rules for his system. If you only want to ask a question, you can text his friend, Rosa. All updates are still sent to Robert; he will send everything you save to Rosa so she'll have an up-to-date copy. At first, you slip up and continue to ask Robert questions, but the system seems to work well. Robert is no longer overwhelmed with read requests, and Rosa's responses are prompt.

One day, you realize that when you asked Rosa a question, she texted back an old review that you had previously overwritten. You message Robert about this discrepancy, worried that your review of the much-improved tacos at Main Street Tacos is lost forever. Robert tells you there was a problem in the system so Rosa didn't receive messages from Robert but was still able to get requests from customers. Your request hasn't been lost, and they're reconciling to get back in sync.

You wanted to be able to answer one question: is the food at this restaurant good or not? Now you're worrying about contacting multiple people depending on whether you're reading a review or writing a review, whether data is in sync, and whether your friend's system can scale to satisfy all users' requests. What happens if Robert can't even handle every save request? When you begin brainstorming intravenous energy drink solutions, you realize it's time to consider other options.

ABC DATA: A DIFFERENT APPROACH

Your research leads you to another business: ABC Data. The company tells you that its system is a little different: it employs three people—Alice, Bob, and Charlotte—and any of them can save information or answer questions. They communicate with each other to ensure that each of them has the latest data, as shown in figure 1.4. You're curious what happens if one of them is unavailable, and the company says it provides a cool feature: because there are multiple employees, they coordinate among themselves to provide redundancy for your data as well as increased availability. If Charlotte is unavailable, Alice and Bob will receive the request and answer. If Charlotte returns later, Alice and Bob will get Charlotte back up to speed on the latest changes.

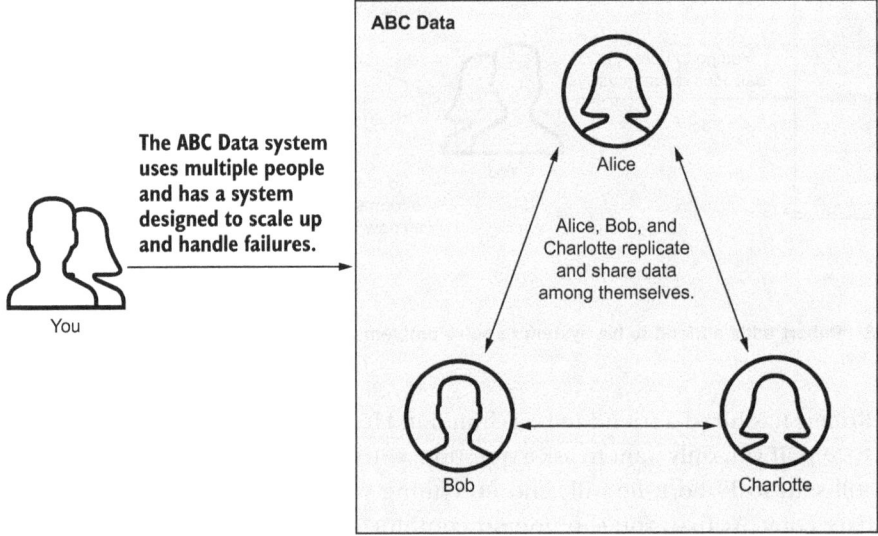

Figure 1.4 ABC Data's approach is designed to meet the scaling challenges that Robert encountered.

This setup is impressive, but because each request can lead to additional requests, you're worried that the system may be overwhelmed even more easily than Robert's. This distribution, ABC Data tells you, is the beauty of its system. It creates multiple copies of the data set. The employees then divide this redundant data among themselves. If the company needs to expand, it only needs to add additional people, who take over some of the existing slices of data. When a hypothetical fourth person, Diego, joins, one customer's data may be owned by Alice, Charlotte, and Diego, whereas Bob, Charlotte, and Diego may own other data.

Because it allows you to choose how many people should respond internally for a successful request, ABC Data gives you control over availability and correctness (figure 1.5). If you want to always have the most up-to-date data, you can require all three holders to coordinate to give you the answer. If you want to prioritize getting an answer, even if it isn't the most recent one, you can require only one holder to respond, skipping any internal coordination and returning immediately. You can balance these properties by requiring two holders to respond—you can tolerate the loss of one, but you can ensure that a majority of them have seen the most up-to-date data, so you should get the most recent information.

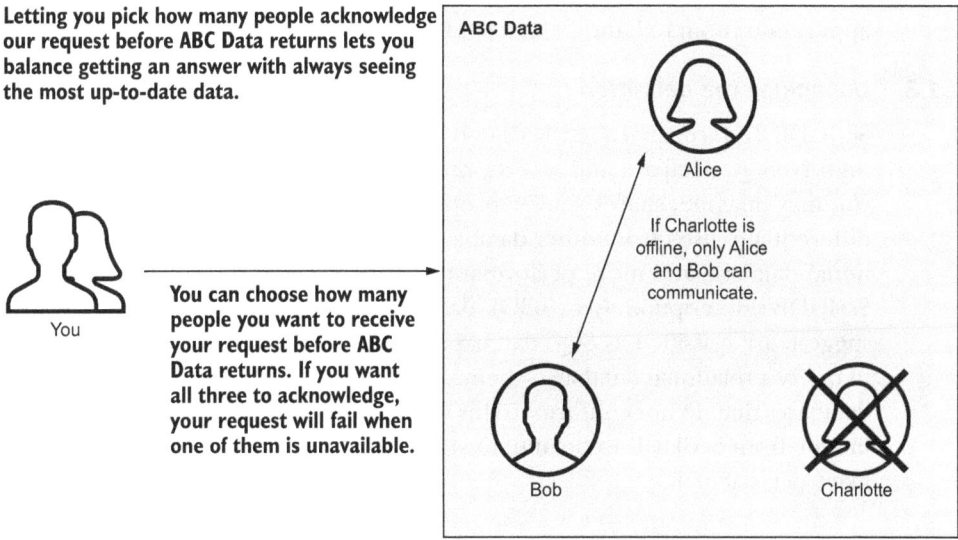

Letting you pick how many people acknowledge our request before ABC Data returns lets you balance getting an answer with always seeing the most up-to-date data.

ABC Data

You

You can choose how many people you want to receive your request before ABC Data returns. If you want all three to acknowledge, your request will fail when one of them is unavailable.

Alice

If Charlotte is offline, only Alice and Bob can communicate.

Bob

Charlotte

Figure 1.5   ABC Data's approach gives you control over availability and correctness.

You've learned about two imaginary databases here: one that seems straightforward but introduces complexity as requests increase, and another with a more complex implementation that attempts to handle the drawbacks of the first system. Before contemplating the awkwardness of telling a friend you're leaving his business for a competitor, let's snap back to reality and translate these hypothetical databases to the real world.

1.1.2 Real-world databases

Robert's database is a metaphorical relational database like PostgreSQL or MySQL. These are relatively straightforward to run, fit a multitude of use cases, and are performant, and their relational data model has been used in practice for more than 50 years. Very often, a relational database is a safe and strong option. Accordingly, developers tend to default toward these systems. But as demonstrated, they also have drawbacks. Availability is often all or nothing. Even if you run with a read replica, which in Robert's database is his friend Rosa, you would potentially be able to do reads only if you lost your primary instance. Scalability can also be tricky: a server has a maximum amount of compute resources and memory. Once you hit that limit, you're out of room to grow. ScyllaDB differentiates itself by addressing these drawbacks.

The ABC Data system is ScyllaDB. Like ABC Data, ScyllaDB is a distributed database that replicates data across its nodes to provide both scalability and fault tolerance. Scaling is straightforward; with a well-designed data model, you only need to add more nodes. This elasticity in node count extends to queries. ScyllaDB lets you decide how many replicas are required to respond for a successful query, giving your application room to handle the loss of a server.

1.1.3   *Unpacking the definition*

ScyllaDB (informally called Scylla) is commonly described as a distributed wide-column NoSQL database and is a rewrite of the popular Cassandra database, which, as you may imagine, shares similar properties. This definition demonstrates how Scylla differentiates itself from other databases. It aims to be both more scalable than a relational database and more performant than Cassandra. This positioning is typified by ScyllaDB's description as a NoSQL database. PostgreSQL and MySQL, as their names suggest, are classified as SQL databases. They use SQL (Structured Query Language) to query a relational database schema. *NoSQL* has become a catch-all term to describe databases that do not conform to this model. A broad array of databases fall under this model, from ScyllaDB to document stores like MongoDB to "not-only SQL" databases like CockroachDB.

> **What's a wide-column database?**
> ScyllaDB and Cassandra are often called *wide-column databases*. In this type of database, data can be thought of as a multidimensional map or a key-key-value store, where tables have columns but aren't required to have values for every column. These tables, or *column families*, as they were originally called in Cassandra, are stored together on disk. This approach contrasts with a columnar database, where all values of a given column are stored together.
>
> In a columnar database, storing all values for a given column together allows you to easily perform aggregations on all values in a column. The database can easily calculate the average value of a column that stores numbers because all the values are stored together and co-located, so it doesn't need to locate and read every row in the database to aggregate that data. The following figure illustrates how the columnar approach differs from a wide-column database.

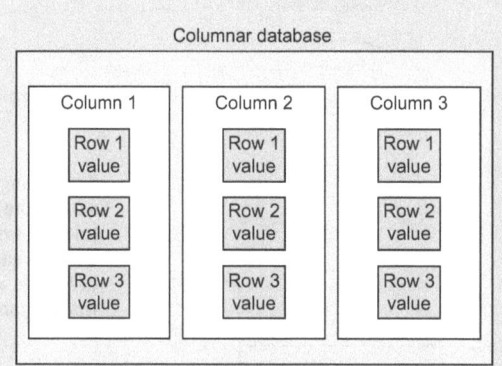

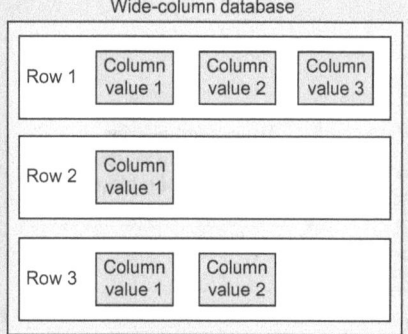

In a columnar database, values are stored together by columns, enabling easy aggregation of per-column data.

In a wide-column database, data is stored together by rows, but each row can contain any number of columns.

Although they have similar names, columnar and wide-column databases differ significantly in their storage paradigms. ScyllaDB is a wide-column database.

The way I remember the difference is that in ScyllaDB and Cassandra, tables—they're not called column families anymore—can be arbitrarily wide. Therefore, ScyllaDB is a wide-column store. The rows in these tables can be distributed across the database—another example of width. I find *wide-column* to be a superfluous term, so I encourage you to focus on the rest of the definition: ScyllaDB is a distributed NoSQL database that accentuates fault tolerance and scalability compared to other databases.

NoSQL databases tend to emphasize scalability and fault tolerance over total correctness and accuracy of the data in the database, a property called *consistency*. This tradeoff may sound ridiculous at first, but you'll examine it closely throughout the book. In practice, Scylla works to be *eventually consistent*, converging toward correctness over time. To achieve its desired scalability and fault tolerance, ScyllaDB runs multiple instances of itself in a cluster.

There is no overarching, all-powerful leader; each node is just as important as any other node. Not only are there multiple nodes in the system, but data is distributed across all these nodes. ScyllaDB isn't a distributed database because distributed systems are cool; it's distributed because it was designed to make a more reliable and scalable database. If you distribute data across all nodes in a cluster, what happens if you lose one node? ScyllaDB stores multiple copies of the data, and by letting you choose how many replicas are required to respond to a query, picking any number fewer than the maximum lets the database tolerate node failure. This distribution also helps with scalability. If one node is taking a large amount of traffic, the rest of the cluster won't be affected. Requests that don't hit your one heavily trafficked node won't be affected by any overburdening of another node. This fault tolerance is criti-

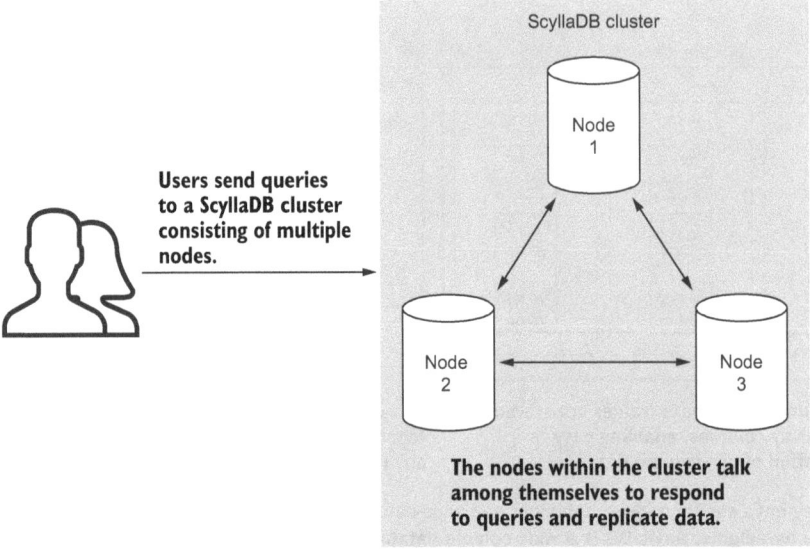

Figure 1.6   ScyllaDB is a distributed database that provides scalability and fault tolerance.

cal to ScyllaDB's design. Instead of putting all your eggs in one basket, you can have many eggs in many baskets. If you lose a basket, you still have lots of eggs!

1.2   *ScyllaDB, a distributed database*

ScyllaDB runs multiple nodes, making it a distributed system. By spreading its data across its deployment, it achieves its desired availability and consistency, which, when combined, differentiates the database from other systems.

1.2.1   *Distributing data*

All distributed systems have a bar to meet: they must deliver enough value to overcome the introduced complexity. ScyllaDB, designed to be a distributed system, achieves its scalability and fault tolerance through this design.

When users write data to ScyllaDB, they start by contacting any node. Many systems follow a leader-follower topology, where one node is designated as a leader, giving it special responsibilities in the system. If the leader dies, a new leader is elected, and the system continues operating.

ScyllaDB does not follow this model; each node is as special as any other. Without a centralized coordinator deciding who stores what, each node must know where any given piece of data should be stored. Internally, Scylla can map a given row to the node that owns it, forwarding requests to the appropriate nodes by calculating its owner using the hash ring that you'll learn about in chapter 3.

To provide fault tolerance, ScyllaDB not only distributes data but also replicates it across multiple nodes. The database stores a row in multiple locations—the number depends on the configured replication factor. In a perfect world, each node acknowledges every request instantly every time, but what happens if they don't? To help with unexpected trouble, the database provides tunable consistency.

How you query data depends on what degree of consistency you're looking to get. ScyllaDB is an eventually consistent database, and you may see inconsistent data as the system converges toward consistency. Developers must keep this eventual consistency in mind when working with the database. To facilitate the various needs of consistency, ScyllaDB provides a variety of consistency levels for queries, including those listed in table 1.1.

Table 1.1 Sample of consistency level options, assuming a cluster with three replicas

Consistency level	Description	Number required to succeed	Failures tolerated
ALL	Requires all replicas to succeed	3	0
QUORUM	Requires a majority of replicas to succeed	2	1
ONE	Requires a single replica to succeed	1	2

With a consistency level of ALL, you can require that all replicas for a key acknowledge a query, but this setting harms availability. You can no longer tolerate the loss of a node. With a consistency level of ONE, you require a single replica for a key to acknowledge a query, but this greatly increases the chances of inconsistent results.

Luckily, some options aren't as extreme. ScyllaDB lets you tune consistency via the concept of quorums. A group that includes a majority of members is a *quorum*. Legislative bodies, such as the US Senate, do not operate when the number of members present is below the quorum threshold. When this concept is applied to ScyllaDB, you can achieve intermediate forms of consistency.

With a QUORUM consistency level, the database requires a majority of replicas for a key to acknowledge a query. If you have three replicas, two of them must accept every read and every write. If you lose one node, you can still rely on the other two to keep serving traffic. You additionally guarantee that a majority of your nodes get every update, preventing inconsistent data if you use the same consistency level when reading.

Once you have picked your consistency level, you know how many replicas you need to execute a successful query. A client sends a request to a node, which serves as the coordinator for that query. Your coordinator node reaches out to the replicas for the given key, including itself if it is a replica. Those replicas return results to the coordinator, and the coordinator evaluates them according to your consistency. If it finds that the result satisfies the consistency requirements, it returns the result to the caller.

The CAP theorem (www.scylladb.com/glossary/cap-theorem) classifies distributed systems by saying that they cannot provide all three of these properties: *c*onsistency, *a*vailability, and network *p*artition tolerance, as shown in figure 1.7. For the CAP theorem's purposes, we define *consistency* as every request reading the most recent write; it's a measure of correctness in the database. *Availability* is whether the system can serve requests, and network *partition tolerance* is the ability to handle a disconnected node.

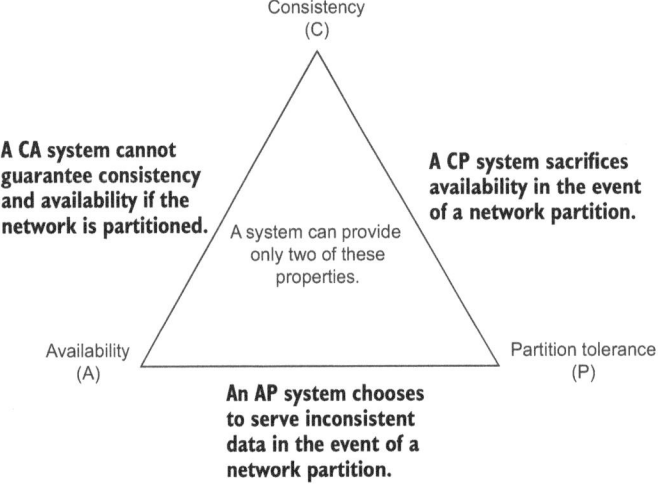

Figure 1.7   The CAP theorem says a database can only provide two of these three properties: consistency, availability, and partition tolerance. ScyllaDB is classified as an AP system.

According to the CAP theorem, a distributed system must have partition tolerance, so it ultimately chooses between consistency and availability. If a system is consistent, it must be impossible to read inconsistent data. To achieve consistency, it must ensure that all nodes receive all necessary copies of data. This requirement means it cannot tolerate the loss of a node, therefore losing availability.

> **NOTE**   In practice, systems aren't as rigidly classified as the CAP theorem suggests. For a more nuanced discussion of these properties, you can research the PACELC theorem (https://www.scylladb.com/glossary/pacelc-theorem/), which illustrates how systems make partial tradeoffs between latency and consistency.

ScyllaDB is typically classified as an AP system. When it encounters a network partition, it chooses to sacrifice consistency and maintain availability. You can see this in its design: ScyllaDB repeatedly makes choices, via quorums and eventual consistency, to keep the system up and running in exchange for potentially weaker consistency. In its emphasis on availability, you see one of ScyllaDB's differentiators against its most popular competition—relational databases.

1.2.2 ScyllaDB vs. relational databases

I've introduced ScyllaDB by describing its features in comparison with relational databases, but we'll examine the differences in closer detail here. Relational databases such as PostgreSQL and MySQL are the standard for data storage in software applications, and they're almost always the default choice for a new developer looking to build an application. Relational databases are a very strong option for many use cases, but that doesn't mean they're suitable for every use case.

ScyllaDB is a distributed NoSQL database. By distributing data across a cluster, ScyllaDB unlocks better availability when nodes go awry than a single-node all-or-nothing relational database. PostgreSQL and MySQL can run in a distributed mode, but that is powered through extensions or newer storage engines and is not the primary native mode of the database. This distribution is native to ScyllaDB and is the bedrock of its design.

By running as a distributed system, ScyllaDB empowers horizontal scalability. Many relational databases are only vertically scalable—you can add more resources only by running the database on a bigger server. With horizontal scalability, you can add nodes to a system to increase its capacity. ScyllaDB supports this expansion; administrators can add more nodes, and the cluster will rebalance itself, offloading data to the new cluster member. In a relational database, horizontal scaling is possible, but it's often manual. Operators need to manually shard data between multiple nodes to achieve this behavior.

ScyllaDB does not provide a relational database's *ACID* (atomicity, consistency, isolation, and durability) guarantees, instead opting for a softer model called *BASE* (*b*asic *a*vailability, *s*oft-state, and *e*ventual consistency), where the database has basic availability and is eventually consistent. This decision leads to faster writes than a relational database, which has to validate the consistency of the database after every write; ScyllaDB only needs to save the write because it doesn't promise that degree of correctness. The tradeoff, though, is that developers need to consider ScyllaDB's weaker consistency.

ACID vs. BASE

ACID provides a set of guarantees for *transactions*. A transaction is one or more statements applied to a database. When developers refer to a transaction in a database, they are almost always referring to ACID transactions. ACID provides the following:

- *Atomicity*—All statements in the transaction succeed together or fail together.
- *Consistency*—The database is in a valid state after every transaction.
- *Isolation*—A transaction cannot interfere with a concurrently executing transaction.
- *Durability*—Any change in a transaction will be persisted.

I like to think of ACID as how you would expect a database to run. You want a consistent database, and you'd like your writes to be durable. You'd be dismayed if you wrote data to the database and it didn't persist.

(continued)

ScyllaDB provides a softer set of guarantees called BASE. Softer isn't bad, though; these guarantees let ScyllaDB more easily provide scalability and fault tolerance. BASE provides the following:

- *Basic availability*—The database is basically available. Some portions of the database may be down, but overall, the system is available.
- *Soft state*—Every node in the database doesn't have to be consistent at every moment in time.
- *Eventually consistent*—The database converges toward consistency over time.

Although I remain convinced that the designer of BASE named the property "soft state" to make the acronym work, it does accurately describe ScyllaDB's benefits. It can tolerate the loss of a node and remain available, but to do this, it has to weaken consistency. Nevertheless, it should strive and converge toward consistency. In upcoming chapters, we'll discuss these properties, how they affect ScyllaDB and your usage of it, and how the system's architecture provides them.

Ultimately, ScyllaDB versus relational databases is a foundational and philosophical decision. They operate so differently and provide such varying guarantees to their clients that picking one over the other has large effects on an application. If you're looking for availability and scalability in your database, ScyllaDB is a strong option.

1.2.3 *ScyllaDB vs. Cassandra*

ScyllaDB is a rewrite of Apache Cassandra. It is frequently described as "a more performant Cassandra" or "Cassandra but in C++." ScyllaDB is designed to be compatible with Cassandra: it uses a compatible API, query language, on-disk storage format, and hash-ring architecture. "Like Cassandra, but better," is ScyllaDB's goal; it makes some improvements to accomplish this.

The choice of language in the rewrite immediately unlocks better performance. Cassandra is written in Java, which uses a garbage collector to perform memory management. Because objects are loaded into memory, at some point they need to be removed. Java's garbage-collection algorithms handle this removal, but it comes at the cost of compute. Time spent garbage collecting is time Cassandra can't spend executing queries. If garbage collection reaches a certain threshold, the Java Virtual Machine will briefly pause all execution while it cleans up memory, referred to as a "stop the world" pause. Even if it's just for milliseconds, that pause can be painful to clients. Although Java exposes many configuration knobs and improves the garbage collector with each release, it's a tax that all Java-based applications have to pay—whether in garbage-collection time or time spent mitigating it.

ScyllaDB avoids this tax because it is implemented in C++ and provides more granular controls for memory management. By having full control over memory allocation and cleanup, ScyllaDB doesn't need to let a garbage collector perform this functionality on an application-wide scale. It avoids "stop the world" pauses and can dedicate its compute time to executing queries.

ScyllaDB's biggest architectural difference is its shard-per-core architecture (figure 1.8). Both Cassandra and ScyllaDB shard a data set across various nodes via placement in a hash ring, which you'll learn more about in chapter 3. ScyllaDB takes this further by using the Seastar framework (https://seastar.io) to shard data within a node, splitting it per CPU core and giving each shard its own CPU, memory, and network bandwidth allocation.

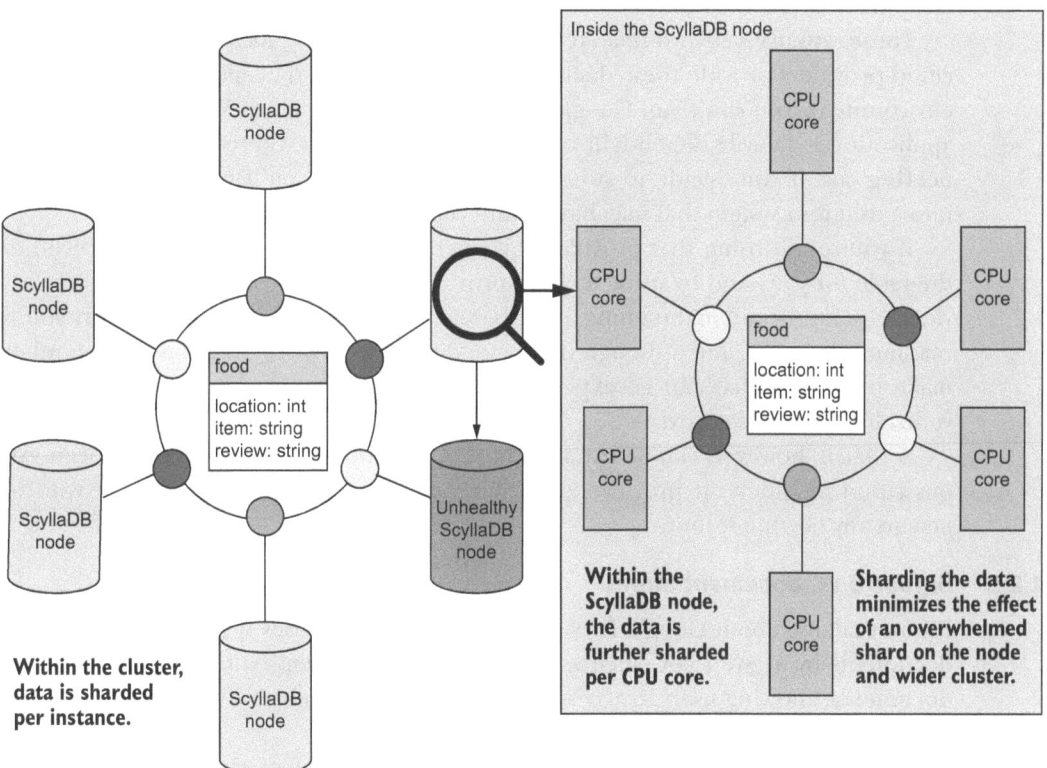

Figure 1.8 ScyllaDB shards data not only within the cluster but also within each instance.

This sharding further limits the blast radius due to hot traffic patterns—the damage is limited to just that shard on that node. Cassandra does not follow this paradigm, however, and limits the sharding to only per node. If a data partition receives a large number of requests, they can overwhelm the node, leading to cluster-wide struggles.

Performance justifies the rewrite. Both in benchmarks (see "Benchmarking Apache Cassandra (40 Nodes) vs. ScyllaDB (4 Nodes)" at https://mng.bz/1a6g) and in the wild (see "How Discord stores trillions of messages" at https://mng.bz/PNmP), ScyllaDB is faster and more consistent and requires fewer servers to operate than Cassandra.

1.2.4   *ScyllaDB vs. Amazon Aurora, Amazon DynamoDB, Google Cloud Spanner, and Google AlloyDB*

I've lumped a few similar systems together here: Amazon Aurora, Amazon DynamoDB, Google Cloud Spanner, and Google AlloyDB. They can be generally described as scalable cloud-hosted databases. They aim to take a relational data model and provide greater scalability than out-of-the-box PostgreSQL or MySQL. This effort accentuates a need in the market for scalable databases, showing the value of ScyllaDB.

These systems have two related drawbacks: cloud vendor lock-in and cost. Because cloud providers provide these databases, they run only in that specific vendor's cloud environment. You can't run Google Cloud Spanner in Amazon Web Services. If your application is heavily dependent on one of these systems, there can be a high engineering cost if you decide to switch cloud providers, as you'll need to migrate data into a different system that may have a different storage paradigm.

If you're not using that provider (or any provider), these options aren't even on the table for you. And by using a cloud provider, companies pay money for these services. Operating and maintaining a database is challenging (which is partly why you're reading this book), and although these cloud vendors provide solutions to potentially make it simpler, that can be expensive for clients. Of course, operating a database yourself can also be costly.

ScyllaDB, however, can be run anywhere. Companies run it on-premises or in various cloud providers. It provides a scalable and fault-tolerant database that you can take to any hosting solution.

1.2.5   *ScyllaDB vs. document stores*

I'm not talking about Google Drive here but rather databases that store unstructured documents by a given key, such as MongoDB. Such systems support querying these documents, allowing users to access arbitrary document fields without defining a database schema.

ScyllaDB eschews this flexibility to provide (relatively) predictable performance. By requiring users to define their schema up front, it clarifies to both users and the system how data is distributed across the cluster. By forcing users to query data in patterns that match this distribution, ScyllaDB can limit the number of nodes involved in a query, preventing surprisingly expensive queries.

Document stores, on the other hand, tend to be biased toward initial ease of use. In MongoDB, no schema definition is required, but users still need to consider the design of their data to query it effectively. MongoDB runs as a distributed system, but unlike ScyllaDB, it doesn't attempt out of the box to minimize inefficient queries that hit more than the expected number of nodes, leading to potential performance surprises.

In the CAP theorem, MongoDB is a CP (consistent and partition-tolerant) system. Writes require the presence of a primary node and are blocked until a new primary is elected in the event of a network partition. But ScyllaDB prioritizes availability in its query path, keeping the system up and relying on its tunable consistency.

1.2.6 ScyllaDB vs. distributed relational databases

One interesting development for databases over the past few years has been the growth of distributed transactional databases. These systems—such as CockroachDB, TiDB, and YugabyteDB—focus on improving the availability of a traditional relational database like PostgreSQL while still offering strong consistency. In the CAP theorem's classifications, they're CP systems; they prefer consistency over availability. By emphasizing correctness, they need a quorum of nodes to respond to successfully complete a query; if a quorum is lost, the database loses availability. ScyllaDB, however, provides tunable consistency to dodge this problem. By allowing weaker consistency levels, such as ONE, Scylla can handle a greater loss of availability to preserve functionality.

In a relational database, writes are a computationally intensive operation. The database needs to validate its consistency on every write. Scylla, on the other hand, skips this verification, opting for speed and simplicity when writing data. The tradeoff, however, is that reads in Scylla will be slower than writes, as you need to gather data from multiple nodes that have data stored in different places on disk. You'll learn a lot more about this behavior in chapters 6 and 7, but the big takeaway is that writes in Scylla will be faster than in these systems.

1.2.7 When to prefer other databases

I've described ScyllaDB's benefits relative to other databases, but sometimes, I admit, it's not the best tool for the job. I can't describe it as a unique database because of the Cassandra rewrite approach, but it does trade operational and design complexity for more graceful failure modes. Choosing Scylla requires you to design applications differently because it has specific data-modeling needs to best use its capabilities and adds more complexity than something like a cloud-hosted PostgreSQL server. If you don't need ScyllaDB's horizontal scalability and nuanced availability, the increased operational overhead may not be worth it. If your application is small, makes few requests, and isn't expected to grow over time, ScyllaDB may be overkill. A database backing comments on your blog probably doesn't need a ScyllaDB cluster unless, like many of us, you're wanting that as an excuse to try it out.

Operating and maintaining a ScyllaDB cluster isn't a hands-off exercise. If you can't dedicate time to operating and maintaining a cluster, that is another signal that a managed offering may be preferable for you. Teams must choose wisely about how they spend their time and money on what they do; choosing a less hands-on is a valid decision.

One thing you'll see about Scylla in upcoming chapters is that with data modeling, it can be inflexible to change your database's design. Adding new query patterns that don't fit in with your initial design can be challenging. Although there are ways to work around this, other databases can potentially give you more flexibility when you're in the prototyping and learning stage of building features for an application.

Finally, some use cases may prefer a stronger transactional model like ACID. If you're working with financial data, you may want to use a relational database so you can have isolation in your operations. One popular example to demonstrate the importance of ACID transactions is concurrent access to bank accounts. Without isolation, you run the risk of concurrent operations causing a mismatch between how much money the database thinks you have and how much money you actually have. Accountants traditionally prefer accuracy in these areas, so you may prefer a relational database when working with something that needs stronger database transactions. Although scaling a relational database has its challenges, dealing with them may be preferable to surrendering ACID's guarantees. Scylla can get closer to ACID through careful design and the use of some more advanced features you'll learn about in chapter 6, but it's not as "out-of-the-box" an experience as a relational database.

1.3   ScyllaDB, a practical database

We've talked about what exactly ScyllaDB is and how it differs from other systems, but how does it run in practice? In this section, we'll look at it as a real, deployed system and show that ScyllaDB isn't just a distributed database but a practical one, too.

1.3.1   Fault tolerance

If you're on call for a database, you want it to handle failures gracefully so you can avoid the dreaded 3:00 a.m. alert and get a night of undisturbed rest. ScyllaDB is designed to be a fault-tolerant database to give you a good night's sleep. Through its tunable consistency model, it can survive spontaneous downtime without any effect on queries. By using quorum consistency, not every node needs to be up and running to serve traffic. A server can crash, and if the underlying hardware self-recovers, the ScyllaDB process can start, rejoin the cluster, receive any data it missed, and return to serving traffic, with you asleep and none the wiser.

If for some unfortunate reason a node is unable to recover, you don't need to execute a complicated operation like restoring from backups. You can provision a new node and tell the cluster that the new node is a replacement for the old node. Because ScyllaDB replicates data across the cluster, your new node takes the place of the old node, and other replicas stream data to it until the node has caught up and joined the cluster, serving traffic.

1.3.2   Scalability

If you're hitting the limits of your existing data store or if handling growth is important to you, scalability is one of the prime reasons people choose ScyllaDB. Fortunately, in ScyllaDB, scalability is often straightforward—in a well-designed cluster, you add more nodes! Even with terabytes of data, adding a node should take no more than a few hours.

> **NOTE** With apologies to Spider-Man, with greater nodes comes greater responsibility. Upgrading to a new version of Scylla or rolling out an operating system patch means updating all of your nodes, which can be time-intensive if you've got a lot of them.

Similar to when you replace a node in the cluster, adding a node involves joining the cluster, signing up for what slices of data the node will own, and then receiving data from other replicas until the node is caught up. Although this bootstrapping process is limited to one node at a time, it is a simple operation to execute.

1.3.3 *Production usage*

Software developers tend to be conservative in their choice of data store, and with good reason: a database is the base for all of your data. A database may meet all the requirements, but it's scary to be the only one running something. As a field, software development moves forward as more people use things, discovering bugs and finding pain points and solutions to them. A big question you'll frequently hear when considering a less-ubiquitous solution is "Does anyone actually use this thing?"

Yes! ScyllaDB is a database used in real-life production systems and is growing in popularity. Several companies use it today:

- Discord stores their trillions of messages in ScyllaDB.
- Epic Games uses ScyllaDB as a cache for binary assets.
- Comcast stores DVR data for its X1 cable platform in ScyllaDB.

They've built systems that use Scylla because they want a scalable and fault-tolerant database. Each of these use cases involves highly distributed reads serving important functionality to their systems.

As a reader of this book, you may be considering building a similar system using ScyllaDB. My goal is to get to that point by the end of this book: by learning how to structure schemas, query the database, and operate it, you will gain the knowledge to go off and build your own system. I've spent a lot of time introducing ScyllaDB; let's dive in and query the thing!

Summary

- ScyllaDB is a distributed NoSQL database compatible with Apache Cassandra's API, providing scalability and fault tolerance by distributing its data across multiple nodes.
- Contrasting with a relational database, Scylla allows you to scale your database by adding nodes.
- To provide for the loss of a node, Scylla lets you tune how many nodes need to be online to serve a request so you can balance correctness and availability.

- ScyllaDB favors scalability and fault tolerance over consistency—the total correctness and accuracy of the database. It prefers eventual consistency, converging to correctness over time.

- The `ALL` consistency level requires every node to respond, whereas the `ONE` level requires a single node. With `QUORUM`, a majority of nodes must respond, balancing consistency and availability.

- The CAP theorem says that a distributed system must sacrifice one of the following properties: consistency, availability, and partition tolerance. ScyllaDB is classified as an available and partition-tolerant system, sacrificing consistency.

- Scylla's horizontal scalability—adding nodes—contrasts with a relational database's single-node approach, which can often only scale vertically by adding additional resources.

- As opposed to a relational database's ACID (atomicity, consistency, isolation, and durability) guarantees, Scylla offers a BASE guarantee: basic availability, soft state, and eventual consistency.

- ScyllaDB is a rewrite of Cassandra in a non-memory-managed language and extends Cassandra's replication by further sharding its data set in a node-per-CPU core.

- When a node crashes, Scylla self-heals, streaming data from other nodes to help the cluster recover.

- Scylla is used in production by many companies today; it is a tested and proven storage solution.

Touring ScyllaDB

This chapter covers

- Running ScyllaDB locally with Docker
- Using `nodetool` to view operational details of the cluster at the command line
- Creating a table and reading and writing data
- Experimenting with failures and changing consistency levels

Users use a database to store data. Whether it's blog posts, text messages, or image metadata, the use case for every database begins with "I want to store data for later consumption." Spending pages and pages discussing consistency, fault tolerance, and comparative benefits, although it's useful information, gets away from this goal. I've written a lot about ScyllaDB in theory, but here, it's time to delve into practice. In this chapter, you'll launch your first ScyllaDB cluster, getting dirty with the database as you run your first queries and examine Scylla's fault-tolerance guarantees.

2.1   *Launching your first cluster*

ScyllaDB is an application written to run on Linux. Unfortunately for people at home, there is no support for running it directly on Windows or MacOS. Do not despair, though, for there is a solution. ScyllaDB provides a Docker image! Docker is an application that lets us run packaged applications called *containers* via a friendly interface to a virtual machine. If you'd like some guidance configuring Docker, you can learn more about it and get it installed in appendix A.

> **NOTE**   If you'd like to learn more about Docker, Manning's *Docker in Action* by Jeff Nickoloff and Stephen Kuenzli is an excellent resource (www.manning .com/books/docker-in-action-second-edition)!

To facilitate learning and experimenting with ScyllaDB, you will use Docker to spin up a three-node cluster on a local machine (figure 2.1). You'll start up three containers that we'll call `scylla-1`, `scylla-2`, and `scylla-3`. By running three nodes, ScyllaDB can demonstrate its distributed benefits. Later in the chapter, you'll take one node offline and see how tuning consistency lets the cluster continue operating and serving traffic.

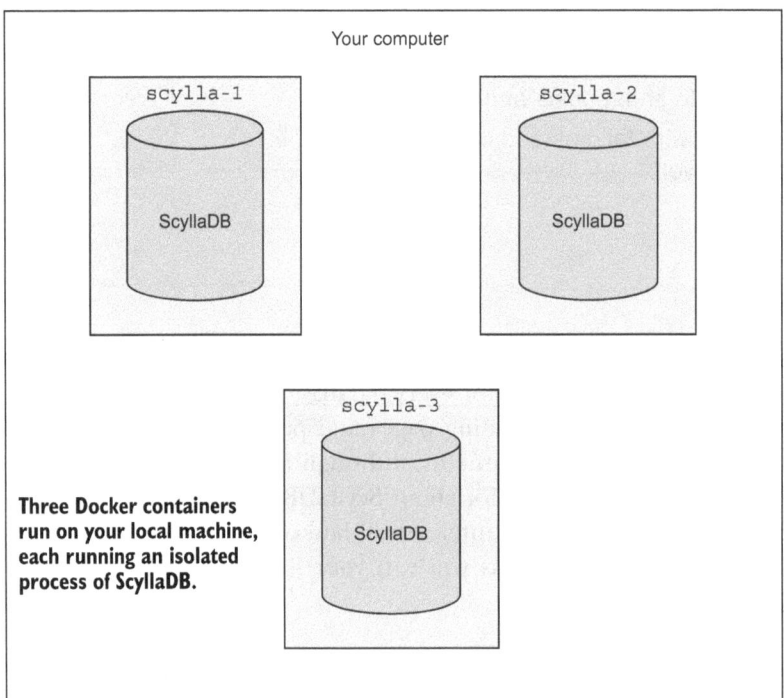

Figure 2.1   Launching three Scylla nodes in Docker containers lets you test a cluster on a local machine.

Why do you run three nodes? You want to be able to tolerate the loss of a single node, so you need at least two. In the previous chapter, you learned that ScyllaDB provides the capability of changing a query's consistency levels. By choosing quorum consistency, operators can guarantee that a majority of the nodes must respond to a query to be successful. In a two-node cluster, what's the majority? You need greater than half, so the operation would require two nodes to respond—the entire cluster. That's not ideal! By adding a third node, you can use quorum consistency and not lose availability if a node dies. Before you can have three nodes, though, you need to have one, so let's go ahead and get the first node started.

2.1.1 The first node

There is an initial bit of infrastructure work to do before you can create your first node. You need to provision a network for the containers, which can be accomplished by a command built into Docker. By creating your own specific network, the cluster can reference other nodes by their DNS names, skipping using IP addresses directly.

Run the following command in a command-line prompt to create a network called `scylla-network`, allowing the nodes in the cluster to communicate over a dedicated network on your computer. This command will create the network and output its ID, a blob of hexadecimal text:

```
$ docker network create scylla-network
```

Now that the networking is set up, you're clear to begin building the cluster. A ScyllaDB cluster consists of one or more ScyllaDB nodes. The database necessitates three nodes to derive its benefits, so you will build a three-node cluster. Scylla doesn't have a "give me a cluster" executable (because it would need to connect potentially multiple nodes running on separate machines), so you must build your cluster one node at a time.

> **NOTE** For examples in this book, you'll be running ScyllaDB 5.4, the current version as of this writing. Docker lets you select a specific version, so you can verify the same behavior here. Scylla may add patches as time goes by, but the core functionality should remain the same in this version.

To start, run the following `docker run` command. It tells Docker that you want to run a container. It has a friendly name, `scylla-1`, instead of the giant hash Docker wants to give it by default. You also specify the hostname, as you'll need other nodes to connect to it to build the cluster. The `--detach` flag specifies that you want to run in detached mode, meaning the container will continue running in the background when the command returns. The `-p` flag specifies port forwardings, starting with the port you'd like to assign to from your local machine, followed by the port it should forward to in the container. Although you won't use this for several chapters, it will be very helpful when building an application that connects to your Scylla cluster. Next you specify the *container image* you want to run, which identifies the application—in this case, ScyllaDB:

```
$ docker run --name scylla-1 --hostname scylla-1 \
 --network scylla-network --detach -p 9241:9042 \
 -p 19241:9042 scylladb/scylla:5.4 --reactor-backend=epoll
```

When you run this command, Docker starts your container, which is prepackaged by ScyllaDB to run a ScyllaDB node.

> **NOTE**   I included an additional argument to your container: `--reactor-backend=epoll`. This argument tells Scylla to use a legacy implementation for async I/O internally, avoiding potential resource contention problems that may stop your development clusters from running.

Docker provides access to the logs via a `docker logs` command, which takes a container name as an argument. To check on the first ScyllaDB node, you can tail its logs to see if it started successfully by passing the `--follow` flag. When you run this command, that container's logs are printed to the command line:

```
$ docker logs scylla-1 --follow
```

For now, you're looking for the two following messages in the output, which read `serving` and `Scylla … initialization completed`. These messages signal that ScyllaDB is initialized and ready to serve traffic:

```
...
INFO  2023-10-05 12:36:37,166 [shard 0] init - serving          ⟵  Indicates ScyllaDB is
INFO  2023-10-05 12:36:37,167 [shard 0] init - Scylla              ready to serve traffic
⟹   version Scylla version 5.4.1-0.20231231.
⟹   3d22f42cf9c3 initialization completed.    ⟵  Indicates ScyllaDB
                                                  initialization is complete
```

> **NOTE**   Startup can take a couple of minutes, so be patient!

If something had gone awry, these messages might not be there. Throughout startup and while it's running, ScyllaDB logs messages to describe what it's doing as well as what errors it's encountering. It's a decent tool to analyze a node. For quicker debugging, you can use a tool packaged with ScyllaDB that can inspect the node and the cluster—called, appropriately enough, `nodetool`.

2.1.2   *Your new friend, nodetool*

`nodetool` is a command-line tool shipped with ScyllaDB that contains a variety of commands to analyze the cluster and interact with it as a maintainer and operator. It's an indispensable part of running ScyllaDB: you can see all the nodes in the cluster, view per-table performance, and even remove nodes from the cluster, all via a terminal.

`nodetool` runs by connecting to the cluster. It can do this over a network, or it can communicate locally. The most straightforward option here is to open a shell in the container and run it there. To run commands in the container the node is running on, you can use docker exec to open bash in the container. Pass in the -it flags—i for interactive, meaning it won't exit immediately, and -t to allocate a pseudoterminal. The exec command then takes a container to run the command in, as well as the command you want to run. By passing /bin/bash with the preceding arguments, you get a bash shell in your designated container:

```
$ docker exec -it scylla-1 /bin/bash
```

As an operator and one who has recently begun launching a cluster, the first question you probably have is "What's the status of this thing?" Coincidentally, the nodetool command you'll run most frequently helps you answer that. To get an overview of the state of the cluster, you can run nodetool status, which lists each node, its state, how much data it owns, and where it lives in the cluster. If you pass in --resolve-ip, you'll also resolve the IP address of the nodes, seeing friendlier DNS names and not IP addresses.

> **NOTE** To indicate when a command is running in a container, I've elected to prefix the shell session's $ with the session's container name:
>
> ```
> (scylla-1) $ nodetool status --resolve-ip
> ```

nodetool status correctly identifies that there is one node in the cluster, but it contains a lot of information that, at the moment, lacks meaning. It says something about UN—does that mean the node is part of the United Nations? Let's learn how to analyze the output:

```
Datacenter: datacenter1
=======================
Status=Up/Down
|/ State=Normal/Leaving/Joining/Moving
--  Address   Load    Tokens Owns Host ID                               Rack
UN  scylla-1  572 KB  256    ?    75ddfa00-9624-4137-b926-429dff20e516  rack1
```

The first line lists the node's *datacenter*, which refers to a grouping of nodes. If you're running on a single local machine or in the cloud, this can be a logical grouping, but if you're running on-premises, this can also be an actual physical grouping. A cluster can comprise multiple datacenters, each with its own replication configuration. It provides an abstraction for a separation of groups of nodes to enable redundancy, cluster migrations, or maybe even a multiregional setup.

Peeking ahead, the last column in the output lists the node's *rack*, a further grouping within the datacenter. Just like the datacenter, it can be a logical-only grouping, or it may correspond to an actual server rack in a real-life datacenter or availability zone in the cloud. You're using only the defaults here, but you'll learn more about how ScyllaDB uses datacenters and racks in future chapters.

The first column contains a two-letter abbreviation indicating what `nodetool` calls the *status* (table 2.1) and *state* of the cluster (table 2.2). Status refers to the node being *U*p or *D*own. It's either up and healthy, or it isn't. State, meanwhile, is about the node's lifecycle state in the cluster. A node begins as *J*oining, which is a quick process initially but grows longer as your cluster gains more data. Once it's joined, it becomes *N*ormal, marking it as a full member of the cluster. If you want to remove a node and hand off its data, the node is in the *L*eaving status. If you explicitly move a node to a different location in the cluster, the node gets the *M*oving status.

Table 2.1 Possible values for the node's status

Status letter	Meaning	Description
U	Up	Node is taking traffic
D	Down	Node is unhealthy and not taking traffic

Table 2.2 Possible values for the node's state

State letter	Meaning	Description
N	Normal	Node is in the normal state, having successfully joined the cluster previously
J	Joining	Node is in the process of joining the cluster
L	Leaving	Node is in the process of leaving the cluster
M	Moving	Node is moving datacenters or racks in the cluster

TIP If you forget which letter means what, run the command `nodetool status` at the prompt. It provides a helpful key before listing the nodes.

When a node is ready to go, healthy, and taking traffic, `nodetool status` lists it as UN. Seeing other values here is an indication that the cluster is in an unusual state. Perhaps this is intentional—you may be adding additional nodes to the cluster, causing a node to be in the `Joining` state. It could also be unplanned—a server may have gone offline. By checking the status, you can get high-level insight into what's happening in the cluster.

After the status, `nodetool` lists the node's address as follows:

```
Status=Up/Down
|/ State=Normal/Leaving/Joining/Moving
--  Address    Load    Tokens Owns Host ID                               Rack
UN  scylla-1   572 KB  256     ?    75ddfa00-9624-4137-b926-429dff20e516 rack1
```

By passing in the `--resolve-ip` flag (or `-r`), `nodetool status` resolves IP addresses and prints the DNS name. If that flag wasn't present, you would see an IP address here. Next in the row is information about the data stored on that node.

Load tells you the size of the data stored on that node. The Tokens field contains information about the allocation of data for this node. You'll learn more about tokens when we discuss *vnodes*, or virtual nodes, and dive into the hash ring.

Owns tells you what percentage of the data in the cluster this node owns. Depending on how tables are configured, however, nodetool is often unable to accurately compute this information and prints only a ?. Last, the Host ID is a node identifier in the cluster. Put together, you get a broad overview of the cluster's status.

Right now, when you run nodetool status, you get a very short list of nodes because one node alone doesn't make a cluster. Let's add a couple more.

2.1.3 Building the cluster

Adding nodes is similar to starting the first node, but additional configuration is required so the second node can talk to the first and form a cluster. When ScyllaDB starts up, it assumes that it is either the first node in a brand-new cluster or an additional node in an existing cluster. When joining an existing cluster, operators must provide *seed nodes* as configuration to the joining node so that it can have a point of contact to learn about the rest of the cluster. A seed node is another already-running node in the cluster. It's up to date, takes traffic, and can help get a newly joined node introduced into the cluster.

It's similar to starting a new job: you're introduced to your manager on the first day, and they put you in touch with the rest of the team and get you up to speed on how they operate (figure 2.2). When a node joins a Scylla cluster, it reaches out to a seed node. The seed node and the joining node exchange information about the cluster via Scylla's *gossip* protocol, where nodes communicate cluster membership with each other. The other nodes stream data to the newly joining node based on the data the node has signed up to own.

By providing a seeds argument, the second node can know about the first node, learn about the other nodes in the cluster, and begin receiving data. You can spin up your second node via an updated docker run command with new values for your new node and the new seeds argument so it knows how to find the first node in your cluster. Additionally, note the new ports used. Because you've already used 9241 and 19241 for your first container on your host machine, you need to forward different ports here:

```
$ docker run --name scylla-2  --hostname scylla-2 --network scylla-network \
 -d -p 9242:9042 -p 19242:9042 scylladb/scylla:5.4 --seeds=scylla-1 \
 --reactor-backend=epoll
```

> **NOTE** Scylla only allows you to add one node at a time. If you want to expand your cluster by five nodes, you can't add all five simultaneously. You are limited to adding one node, waiting for it to finish joining, then adding the second, and so on, until you have your desired cluster size. If you're expanding due to an incident, you'll have to wait patiently as each node is added. Because a node isn't finished joining until data is done streaming, this process scales

Figure 2.2 Joining a Scylla cluster isn't too dissimilar from joining a team at work.

by the total size of the data in the cluster. However, features in upcoming versions of Scylla make this expansion faster, as you'll learn more about in chapter 8.

When you set scylla-1, the hostname you gave the first node, as the seed argument, your new node will reach out to scylla-1 on startup and attempt to join the cluster. This joining can be a long process (and it gets longer as your cluster stores more data); if you run nodetool status --resolve-ip again, you can view the node joining. If you prefix it with watch, the command will run every few seconds, updating after each interval. Be sure to run this on scylla-1 because scylla-2 isn't live yet:

```
(scylla-1) $ watch nodetool status --resolve-ip
```

If you run this command before joining is complete, you'll see scylla-2 with a status of UJ (for *up and joining*), indicating it's joining the cluster:

```
Datacenter: datacenter1
=======================
```

```
Status=Up/Down
|/ State=Normal/Leaving/Joining/Moving
--  Address    Load    Tokens Owns Host ID                                Rack
UN  scylla-1 ?         256      ?    75ddfa00-9624-4137-b926-429dff20e516 rack1
UJ  scylla-2 944 KB    256      ?    2b38db3b-1b00-41f8-a3d5-1e66afc31db8 rack1
```

If scylla-2 is marked as UN (for *up and normal*), it has completed joining and is now a fully fledged member of the cluster. Otherwise, the node is going through the join procedure, getting copies of the data it is now responsible for from other nodes.

When the node has joined the cluster, it prints the same messages as scylla-1 to indicate that initialization is complete. At this point, nodetool status will also show both nodes with the status UN:

```
(scylla-1) $ nodetool status --resolve-ip
Datacenter: datacenter1
=======================
Status=Up/Down
|/ State=Normal/Leaving/Joining/Moving

--  Address    Load      Tokens Owns Host ID                              Rack
UN  scylla-1 1008 KB 256        ?    75ddfa00-9624-4137-b926-429dff20e516 rack1
UN  scylla-2 944 KB  256        ?    2b38db3b-1b00-41f8-a3d5-1e66afc31db8 rack1
```

You now have a two-node cluster, but ultimately you desire three nodes for your cluster (in production systems, you want to always have at least three nodes so that you can use quorum consistency and tolerate the failure of a single node), so let's go ahead and create the last node. Similar to scylla-2, run another docker run command, swapping the 2s in scylla-2 for 3s:

```
$ docker run --name scylla-3  --hostname scylla-3 --network scylla-network \
 -d -p 9243:9042 -p 19243:9043 scylladb/scylla:5.4 --seeds=scylla-1 \
 --reactor-backend=epoll
```

This command launches a third Scylla node and tells it to use your friend scylla-1 as a seed. Once the node has joined, you can observe via nodetool status the complete cluster with all nodes up and normal:

```
(scylla-1) $ nodetool status --resolve-ip
```

You can see all three nodes here; they are all marked as UN and are healthy members of your first ScyllaDB cluster:

```
Datacenter: datacenter1
=======================
Status=Up/Down
|/ State=Normal/Leaving/Joining/Moving
--  Address    Load    Tokens Owns Host ID                                Rack
UN  scylla-2 944 KB    256      ?    2b38db3b-1b00-41f8-a3d5-1e66afc31db8 rack1
UN  scylla-1 572 KB    256      ?    75ddfa00-9624-4137-b926-429dff20e516 rack1
UN  scylla-3 1.11 MB   256      ?    2b769a73-1119-4981-ba82-5a5b92af61b9 rack1
```

> **Rebuilding your cluster**
>
> If something happens to your cluster, you can either follow the steps in this chapter or use Docker Compose to rebuild it. In the book's sample code, available on the book's website (www.manning.com/books/scylladb-in-action) and in the GitHub repo (https://github.com/scylladb-in-action/code), I've included a Docker compose.yaml file; you can use it to re-create your cluster by running the following command in the ch02 directory:
>
> ```
> $ docker compose up --detach
> ```

With your three-node cluster, by using quorum queries, where a majority of nodes are required to respond, the cluster can tolerate the loss of a node. Databases exist to store data, not to start up and discuss hypothetical failure scenarios, so let's dive in and put some data in your brand-new cluster.

2.2 Creating your first table

When adding data to ScyllaDB, it has to go somewhere. Before you can read or write data, you need to tell ScyllaDB how it should store data and what that data should look like. To define how the database stores data, you construct a *schema*, a modeling of your data that describes how it is organized in a database.

In the previous chapter, you ordered food at a restaurant at a specific date and time, and you listed the food and your review of it—a very basic schema for a hypo-thetical database. In that example, you used a company called ABC Data, but you've decided to run your own database. You want a system that is scalable and fault-toler-ant, and your research has led you to ScyllaDB. Let's create a schema and try it out!

2.2.1 Keyspaces and tables

ScyllaDB stores data in *tables*, a grouping of zero or more *rows* in the database. A row is a collection of data signifying a complete entry into the database. When you store data, it has some structure to it. You don't send a random number and a random list of words; you assign meaning to those values via a label or name. In Scylla, these labels and their associated values are called *columns*. Columns are uniquely identified in the database by a *primary key*: a collection of one or more of these columns that uniquely identify this grouping of data. No two rows can have the same primary key; it always uniquely identifies one row per table. Tables are grouped in *keyspaces*, which provide not only a grouping but the configuration for replicating data across the cluster.

In your food reviews, you define a location, a time, a meal, and a review. Each of these four things is a column—a piece of data given a name to identify it. Columns have types: you can store the time you ate the meal as a timestamp, but your review could be text or even a score stored as an integer. Column types are per-table, so all values for a given column have the same type. A row's primary key also determines where the row lives in the cluster. ScyllaDB groups rows into *partitions* based on the primary key. You decide on these partitions; when you design your tables, your primary key determines how Scylla groups these rows—a critical part of ensuring good performance, which you'll learn about in upcoming chapters (a Scylla cluster performs best when data is distributed evenly throughout the cluster and partitions are similarly sized). Each partition is assigned to a node. These relationships are modeled in figure 2.3, showing how Scylla stores data using a "nesting doll" of concepts.

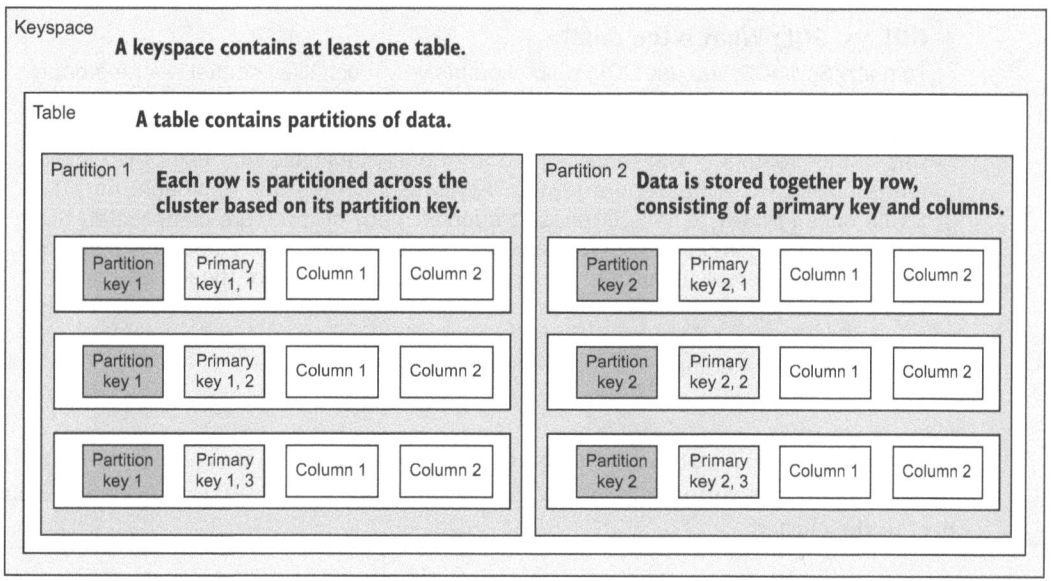

Figure 2.3 ScyllaDB consists of rows, identified by primary keys and grouped into partitions, which are grouped into tables, which are grouped into keyspaces.

> **NOTE** If you've worked with relational databases, these concepts are very familiar; relational databases also have tables, rows, columns, and primary keys. What ScyllaDB calls keyspaces, relational databases tend to also call databases (or schemas), which I've always found to be a little confusing. This automatic partitioning, however, is a wholly ScyllaDB (and similar distributed databases) concept; relational databases either shard data manually across multiple nodes or replicate the entire data set. Partitioning is not a concept typically native to a relational database; you often need to manually implement this partitioning in a relational database.

By putting all these concepts together—keyspaces, tables, columns, primary keys, and partitions—ScyllaDB can store and serve data. Let's use them in action: it's finally time to start working with the database.

2.2.2   *Creating a schema*

To create the schema, you can use a tool called `cqlsh`, an abbreviated form of a Cassandra Query Language (CQL) shell. This application provides a command-line interface to run queries against the cluster. Because ScyllaDB uses the same protocol that Cassandra does, it can reuse Cassandra's `cqlsh` to connect to the database, which ScyllaDB does by default.

> ### CQL vs. SQL: What's the deal?
> To query ScyllaDB, you use CQL, which sounds very much like "sequel"—one pronunciation of the ubiquitous SQL from relational databases. This similarity is intentional: CQL not only sounds like SQL but also looks like SQL! Instead of reinventing the wheel, the creators of Cassandra opted for a query language that uses the simpler forms of SQL. As a Cassandra rewrite, ScyllaDB inherited this approach. Because Scylla doesn't have `JOIN`s, it doesn't support many of the more complicated SQL queries and operations. To model and query these one-to-many relationships, you have to use different techniques, such as storing both sides of these relationships together in an approach called *denormalization*, which you'll learn more about in chapter 3. Syntax-wise, if you're coming from a relational database background, you should be right at home.

Similar to `nodetool`, `cqlsh` is already installed in the Docker image and running in your container. By running a `docker exec` command, you can open `cqlsh` and connect to the cluster:

```
$ docker exec -it scylla-1 cqlsh
```

You now have a shell open that you can run CQL statements against. It tells you which node it's connected to, as well as information about the various versions of the components in play:

```
Connected to  at 172.18.0.2:9042
[cqlsh 6.2.0 | Scylla 5.4.1-0.20231231.3d22f42cf9c3 | CQL spec 3.3.1
➡ | Native protocol v4]
Use HELP for help.
cqlsh>
```

Your shell can be used to run commands against your Scylla cluster. When starting from scratch, you first create a keyspace to house your tables, and then you create tables and add data to them. You have to begin with a keyspace because otherwise your tables have nowhere to live.

CREATING A KEYSPACE

To create a keyspace, you run a `CREATE KEYSPACE` statement. You follow that with the name of the keyspace—we'll use `initial`. After the keyspace name, you define the keyspace's options, beginning with WITH. Subsequent options are added to the statement using AND instead of WITH (you'll see an example of this soon). You set only one option here—replication—defining how the keyspace should replicate data across the cluster. This command uses a class of SimpleStrategy, which assigns each row to a number of nodes configured by the replication_factor: in this case, 3. Finally, you terminate your command with a semicolon:

```
cqlsh> CREATE KEYSPACE initial WITH replication =
   ⇒ {'class': 'SimpleStrategy', 'replication_factor': 3};
```

> **TIP** If you press Tab, cqlsh will autocomplete where possible.

> **Warning!**
> If you're so excited to use ScyllaDB that you go to use it in production immediately, don't use SimpleStrategy for your replication configuration. Other strategies, which you'll learn about later, are more nuanced and bring greater safety to systems.

To view the newly created keyspace, you can use the DESCRIBE command, passing in your keyspace. Be sure to terminate your command with a semicolon!

```
cqlsh> DESCRIBE initial;
```

Running the DESCRIBE command prints out the full CQL statement to recreate the table. You'll immediately see that it's very similar to your CREATE KEYSPACE command—it begins the same but with additional information at the end. Scylla has added durable_writes = true. Keyspaces and tables have many configuration options—if one is not set in your statement, ScyllaDB will set it to its default value and define it explicitly when you run DESCRIBE. Having durable writes defaulted to true is very good (it ensures that your writes always make it to disk); you'd be quite surprised if you woke up and this wasn't the case, so Scylla assumes it's true if not set:

```
CREATE KEYSPACE initial                                    Your previous
   WITH replication = {'class': 'SimpleStrategy',          CREATE KEYSPACE
     'replication_factor': '3'}                            statement
   AND durable_writes = true;                              Additional options you omitted
                                                           that Scylla is making explicit
```

You now have a keyspace: its name is initial, it replicates data to three nodes per partition, and it has durable writes. What do you do with the new keyspace? It's empty, so it needs to be filled with something. A keyspace contains tables—so let's create a table!

CREATING A TABLE

Creating a table involves running a CREATE TABLE statement. You specify the keyspace you want to create the table in along with the table name in the format keyspace_name

.table_name, where keyspace_name refers to an existing keyspace and table_name refers to your new table.

Follow the table name with parentheses, inside which are the columns you want to store. Scylla has many types to represent data—from simple types like text and numbers to more complex types like timestamps and collection types. What does storing a restaurant review entail? You need to know where you ate, which you can store as the name of the restaurant. You ate the meal at a specific time, so you can store the date and time you ate, as well as what you ate. You also need the review so you know how good (or not good) the food was. To accomplish these, you can use two types here: text and timestamps.

What about IDs?

If you're familiar with relational databases, you may notice an absence of autoincrementing integer-based IDs in this example. PostgreSQL and MySQL let you use numbers that automatically set and increase when used as primary keys, letting you skip the logic of creating a unique identifier for a row. This feature is unsupported in ScyllaDB. Which node would handle creating these IDs? How would it guarantee uniqueness without sacrificing speed and needing to do a quorum call to calculate it? What would happen if a node crashed?

This means you'll need to bring your own IDs to the party (or to the database). Later we'll discuss some approaches that make for a good ID in ScyllaDB.

Finally, to create your table, you need to specify the primary key. A primary key uniquely identifies a row in the table. What will make a food review unique? The restaurant alone is insufficient; you could always visit multiple times. The date and the restaurant also may not be enough; you may get dessert or other additional foods sometimes. To ensure a row's uniqueness, you can make the primary key the restaurant, the time you ordered, and a food item.

ScyllaDB uses the primary key to group rows into partitions and spreads data across the cluster based on the partition key. What is the partition key? It's the first part of the primary key; here, it's restaurant. Now that you know what you're about to do, you can combine these into a CREATE TABLE statement, as shown in the following listing. Run that, and you'll have your first table!

Listing 2.1 First table, which stores food reviews

```
CREATE TABLE initial.food_reviews (        ◁──┐ Creates a table in the initial
    restaurant text,                       ◁──┘ keyspace called food_reviews
    ordered_at timestamp,
    food text,                                 Defines the various columns
    review text,                               and their data types
    PRIMARY KEY (restaurant, ordered_at, food)   ◁──┐ Specifies the primary key to
);                                                  └─ uniquely identify the row
```

Run the DESCRIBE command again for the keyspace, and you'll see the new table with some additional settings added with their default values. Not only is the initial keyspace there, but you also see the CREATE TABLE statement:

```
cqlsh> DESCRIBE initial;                      The previous CREATE
                                              KEYSPACE command
CREATE KEYSPACE initial             ◄──┘
    WITH replication =
        {'class': 'SimpleStrategy', 'replication_factor': '3'}
    AND durable_writes = true;

CREATE TABLE initial.food_reviews (   ◄──┐  The new CREATE
    restaurant text,                         TABLE command
    ordered_at timestamp,                             Scylla inferred a
    food text,                                        sorting order from
    review text,                                      your primary key
    PRIMARY KEY (restaurant, ordered_at, food)        because you didn't
) WITH CLUSTERING ORDER BY (ordered_at ASC, food ASC) ◄──┘ make it explicit.
    AND bloom_filter_fp_chance = 0.01             ◄──┐
    AND caching = {'keys': 'ALL', 'rows_per_partition': 'ALL'}  Additional
    AND comment = ''                                            inferred options
    AND compaction = {'class': 'SizeTieredCompactionStrategy'}  on the table
    AND compression = {                                         made explicit.
        'sstable_compression':
            'org.apache.cassandra.io.compress.LZ4Compressor'
    }
    AND crc_check_chance = 1.0
    AND dclocal_read_repair_chance = 0.0
    AND default_time_to_live = 0
    AND gc_grace_seconds = 864000
    AND max_index_interval = 2048
    AND memtable_flush_period_in_ms = 0
    AND min_index_interval = 128
    AND read_repair_chance = 0.0
    AND speculative_retry = '99.0PERCENTILE';
```

The DESCRIBE command makes all the various table options explicit; we'll discuss many of them in the future. Another thing added is WITH CLUSTERING ORDER BY (ordered_at ASC, food ASC). The columns in a primary key that aren't the partition key (the ones after the first column) are referred to as *clustering keys,* and they are responsible for sorting your rows within their partition.

> NOTE   You'll learn about selecting the correct partitioning and clustering keys for your tables in the next few chapters as you design a schema for ScyllaDB.

The DESCRIBE command also makes the sorting explicit. It defaults to ascending order in the order in which the columns were specified. For your table, this means it sorts by the earliest ordered, followed by the food alphabetically. Depending on how you want to query your data, you may choose to change this. For example, you may want recent meals listed first. We'll also discuss the various ordering concepts and data modeling approaches in a later chapter.

You now have a table, but it's empty. Like an empty house, you need to fill it with something. Because it's a database table, instead of chairs, couches, and beds, you'll fill it with data. Let's run some queries!

2.3 *Running your first queries*

You've built your schema for your database, and it's time to start running queries. For the remainder of the chapter, you'll add three new reviews from two restaurants: *Ernie's Eats* and *Really Good Ramen*. You went there and had good meals, and now, with the shiny new Scylla database, you can store those reviews.

2.3.1 *Inserting data*

Finally, let's insert some data! Just like the `CREATE KEYSPACE` and `CREATE TABLE` commands, you can apply writes in `cqlsh`. An insert command in CQL is extremely similar to SQL's one: it uses the same syntax. You name the table and list the columns you're writing to, followed by the values for those columns. You had an excellent grilled cheese at Ernie's Eats, so let's save that. You're telling ScyllaDB that you want to insert into `initial.food_reviews` and that you're writing to the `restaurant`, `ordered_at`, `food`, and `review` columns. You then specify the values for these columns. Ernie's Eats needs an extra apostrophe to escape the inner possessive apostrophe, as CQL uses single-quoted strings. Your `ordered_at` timestamp is specified as a time string, but you can also use milliseconds since the Unix epoch or choose among several other formatting options.

To save your grilled cheese review from Ernie's Eats, run the following statement in `cqlsh`:

```
cqlsh> INSERT INTO initial.food_reviews(
    restaurant,
    ordered_at,
    food,
    review
) VALUES (
    'Ernie''s Eats',
    '2023-05-09 12:00:00',
    'Grilled cheese',
    'Outstanding'
);
```

You returned to Ernie's Eats later that week and tried the fried chicken. You found it to be tasty, and you had some leftovers, so you were able to save some for later. The values in the primary key columns determine the uniqueness of the row. For this table, that's `restaurant`, `ordered_at`, and `food`. Despite returning to Ernie's Eats, you have different values for `ordered_at` and `food`, so Scylla sees this as a separate row and inserts it into the database. Go ahead and insert your review:

```
cqlsh> INSERT INTO initial.food_reviews(
    restaurant,
    ordered_at,
    food,
    review
) VALUES (
    'Ernie''s Eats',
    '2023-05-13 11:30:00',
    'Fried chicken',
    'Tasty, saved some for later'
);
```

You now have two rows—one for each of your trips to Ernie's Eats. You may update this review in the future after trying the leftovers.

You were also craving some ramen, so you tried a place that hopefully lived up to its name—Really Good Ramen. When you created your table, Scylla used the first part of the primary key, `restaurant`, as the partition key. This key drives the distribution of data across the cluster. The Ernie's Eats rows are stored together, and when you add a review from a new restaurant, the Really Good Ramen row is stored separately. Each of these rows could be stored in separate nodes or on the same node, but they are in different locations on disk. It turned out to be good ramen, so add this review to the database as well:

```
cqlsh> INSERT INTO initial.food_reviews(
    restaurant,
    ordered_at,
    food,
    review
) VALUES (
    'Really Good Ramen',
    '2023-05-11 18:00:00',
    'Ramen',
    'it really was good'
);
```

You now have three rows in the database—two for Ernie's Eats and one for Really Good Ramen. You don't have to take my word for it; you can see them in the database for yourself via a read query.

2.3.2 Reading data

Like inserts, the reading syntax for CQL is very similar to that of SQL. You specify a SELECT statement, enumerate the columns you want to read (or add a wildcard, *, to indicate all columns), say what table you're reading from, and filter the data via a WHERE clause. To begin, run a SELECT but skip the WHERE clause:

```
cqlsh> SELECT * FROM initial.food_reviews;
```

By running this query without filtering the data, you can see all the rows in the database. They have the values you previously set, and they're sorted by the ordering you implicitly provided:

```
cqlsh> SELECT * FROM initial.food_reviews;

@ Row 1
------------+---------------------------------------------
 restaurant | Really Good Ramen
 ordered_at | 2023-05-11 18:00:00.000000+0000
 food       | Ramen
 review     | it really was good

@ Row 2
------------+---------------------------------------------
 restaurant | Ernie's Eats
 ordered_at | 2023-05-09 12:00:00.000000+0000
 food       | Grilled cheese
 review     | Outstanding

@ Row 3
------------+---------------------------------------------
 restaurant | Ernie's Eats
 ordered_at | 2023-05-13 11:30:00.000000+0000
 food       | Fried chicken
 review     | Tasty, saved some for later

(3 rows)
```

> **On formatting**
>
> For formatting reasons, I've set my `cqlsh` session to use EXPAND ON, which displays rows vertically:
>
> ```
> cqlsh> EXPAND ON;
> ```

However, you queried the entire database. Doing this in a real production system is, to use a technical term, a "big no-no." When you read data, the *coordinator node*, the node servicing the request, reaches out to other nodes that potentially hold that data. When you read within a partition, this is usually efficient—there are only a few nodes in a request. When you read across every partition, the coordinator needs to send requests to each node for every partition. This approach doesn't scale well and, if run in a production system, is liable to cause big performance problems. This is why, with ScyllaDB, *you want a single query to read within a single partition*.

In this book, you'll learn how to design your system to always do this, but if you take away one thing from here, it's this principle: Scylla performs best when querying by the partition key, so you should structure your data to facilitate this query pattern (figure 2.4).

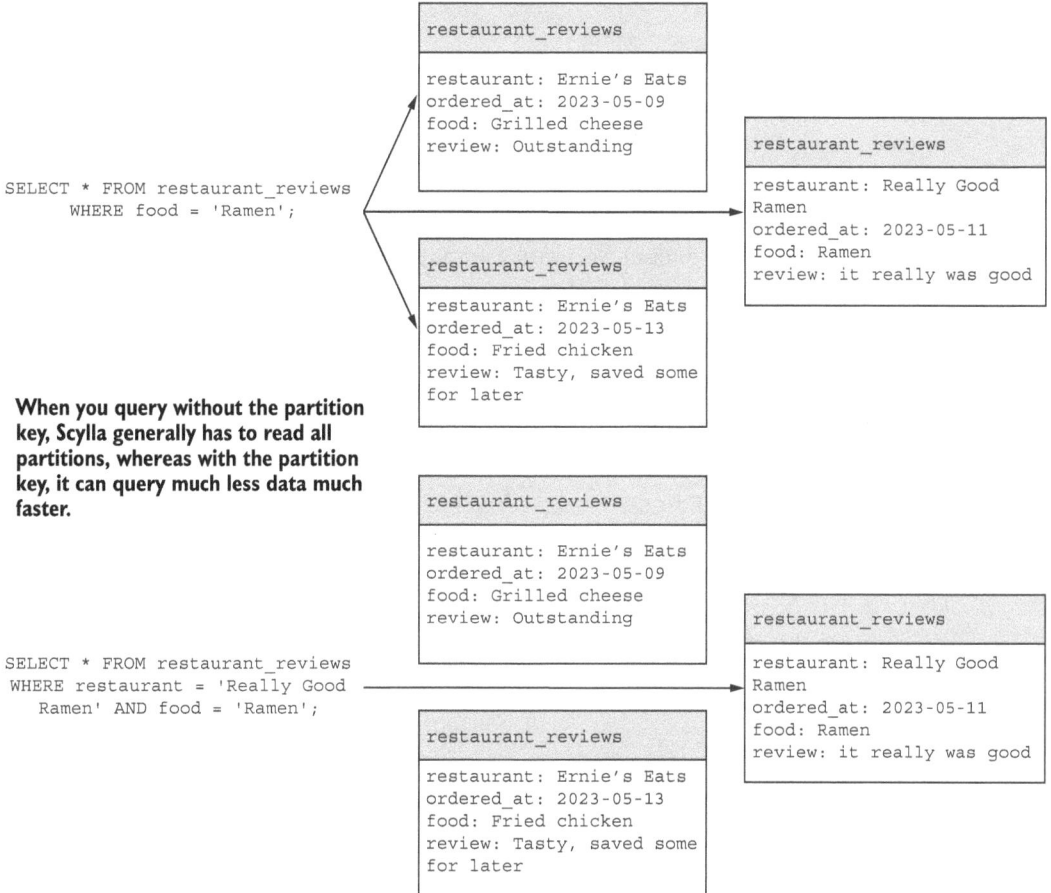

SELECT * FROM restaurant_reviews
    WHERE food = 'Ramen';

When you query without the partition key, Scylla generally has to read all partitions, whereas with the partition key, it can query much less data much faster.

SELECT * FROM restaurant_reviews
WHERE restaurant = 'Really Good
    Ramen' AND food = 'Ramen';

Figure 2.4 Querying by the partition key queries less data faster and is what you always want to do.

To illustrate a happier pattern, query the food reviews for Ernie's Eats. Querying by the partition key—the restaurant—is much friendlier to the database. You can add a WHERE clause to the previous query, which restricts your results to only reviews for Ernie's Eats:

```
cqlsh> SELECT * FROM initial.food_reviews WHERE restaurant = 'Ernie''s Eats';
```

As expected, you only see reviews from Ernie's Eats:

```
@ Row 1
-----------+---------------------------------------------
 restaurant | Ernie's Eats
 ordered_at | 2023-05-09 12:00:00.000000+0000
 food       | Grilled cheese
 review     | Outstanding
```

```
@ Row 2
------------+----------------------------------------------
 restaurant | Ernie's Eats
 ordered_at | 2023-05-13 11:30:00.000000+0000
 food       | Fried chicken
 review     | Tasty, saved some for later

(2 rows)
```

With such a minuscule dataset, you won't see much performance difference when you get two rows instead of three, but the database can be much more efficient in its query execution. Scylla recognizes that you're querying by the partition key, so it determines who owns that partition by hashing the provided value and determining its owner. It then sends the queries to the owner and replica nodes to attempt to achieve the desired consistency. Querying by the partition key is straightforward and database-friendly, but what happens when you filter a query, but not by the partition key? You can test this by querying by ordered_at for the date you ate at Really Good Ramen:

```
cqlsh> SELECT * FROM initial.food_reviews
  WHERE ordered_at = '2023-05-11 18:00:00';
```

You only see the review from Really Good Ramen, which was what you expected, but you also see an ominous warning after your results:

```
@ Row 1
------------+---------------------------------
 restaurant | Really Good Ramen
 ordered_at | 2023-05-11 18:00:00.000000+0000
 food       | Ramen
 review     | it really was good

(1 rows)

Warnings :
This query should use ALLOW FILTERING and will be rejected in future versions.
```

What does Scylla do if it can't route a query directly to the appropriate nodes by the partition key? It scans all partitions! Once again, this can be very heavyweight for performance; hence the warning. Because you have three rows, you can get away with it for now (imagine ominous music playing as you read this sentence).

If you want to further filter the data within a partition, you can expand your WHERE clause by adding an AND to it and setting another value. To get all reviews from Really Good Ramen on a certain date, you can run the following query, specifying both the restaurant and the date you ordered:

```
cqlsh> SELECT * FROM initial.food_reviews
  WHERE restaurant = 'Really Good Ramen'
    AND ordered_at = '2023-05-11 18:00:00';
```

There are no warnings; Scylla is much happier with your query. Scylla uses the partition key to query the partition directly and then further filter the data based on the condition you provided. This pattern is one you'll come back to time and time again—querying within the partition via the partition key and filtering that down via extensions to your WHERE clause:

```
@ Row 1
------------+--------------------------------
 restaurant | Really Good Ramen
 ordered_at | 2023-05-11 18:00:00.000000+0000
 food       | Ramen
 review     | it really was good

(1 rows)
```

When you inserted the review for your fried chicken at Ernie's Eats, you mentioned that you saved some for later. If you want to update your review to reflect the food's tastiness on second consumption, how do you go about that?

2.3.3 *Updating data*

I am going to tell you a secret: you already know how to update data. You've done it before; you did it two subsections ago. In ScyllaDB, inserts and updates are very similar and behave almost identically, with one very nuanced difference around row liveness that we'll discuss later in the book. This combined behavior frequently leads to inserts and updates being combined in the term *upserts*.

In SQL, a successful UPDATE implies that a row previously existed and some number of values in that row were updated. In Scylla, however, the database doesn't check whether the row exists before an update; instead, it writes those values, making the potentially large assumption that you know what you're doing and are updating a row that exists. ScyllaDB wants to write rows as fast as it possibly can; it doesn't want to do a slower read to see if an update is truly an update and not an insert.

To update data, you can run an UPDATE statement. It begins with UPDATE and the table you desire to update. Next, you specify a SET clause: you list the columns you're updating and their values, joined by an equal sign. Finally, you add a WHERE clause, just like a SELECT, telling the database which rows you're updating. The typical performance caveat applies—you want to make sure your updates use the partition key to filter rows. Go ahead and run the statement now:

```
UPDATE initial.food_reviews
  SET review = 'Tasty, saved some for later, reheated well'
  WHERE restaurant = 'Ernie''s Eats'
    AND ordered_at = '2023-05-13 11:30:00'
    AND food = 'Fried chicken';
```

> **A helpful tip!**
> Always write your WHERE clause first, even if you're not working on ScyllaDB. Doing so helps avoid those awkward and scary moments when you forget it and run an update across the entire cluster.

If you read your updated row, you should see the updated value:

```
cqlsh> SELECT * FROM initial.food_reviews
  WHERE restaurant = 'Ernie''s Eats'
    AND ordered_at = '2023-05-13 11:30:00'
    AND food = 'Fried chicken';
```

The chicken reheated well, after all! You see the updated review, but the columns you didn't change remain the same:

```
@ Row 1
-----------+---------------------------------------------
 restaurant | Ernie's Eats
 ordered_at | 2023-05-13 11:30:00.000000+0000
 food       | Fried chicken
 review     | Tasty, saved some for later, reheated well

(1 rows)
```

Having read the data, you have proof that your update applied. An update is an insert—if you happen to not update a column, it will keep the existing column. If the row doesn't exist, your update will insert new values. In a later chapter, we'll dive deeper into the hows and whys, but for now, remember that updates are inserts, and inserts are updates. The following insert statement is equivalent to your update statement. If you run it, you'll get the same results:

```
cqlsh> INSERT INTO initial.food_reviews(
    restaurant,
    ordered_at,
    food,
    review
) VALUES (
    'Ernie''s Eats',
    '2023-05-13 11:30:00',
    'Fried chicken',
    'Tasty, saved some for later, reheated well'
);
```

Sometimes you don't want to update your data—instead, you want it to go away. To accomplish this disappearing act, you can run a DELETE query.

2.3.4   *Deleting data*

Continuing the theme of CQL, a DELETE statement is very similar to its counterpart in SQL. You specify that you want to DELETE FROM, you add a table and a WHERE clause, and upon execution, Scylla deletes the matching rows.

Walking through your town, you discover that Really Good Ramen has closed—it's going to reopen and serve a different kind of cuisine. Because you can no longer go there, you decide to delete its reviews from your database. To remove them, you can run the following query:

```
cqlsh> DELETE FROM initial.food_reviews
  WHERE restaurant = 'Really Good Ramen';
```

Continuing the partition key theme, the DELETE statement works best when you delete using the partition key. Otherwise, Scylla needs to query all partitions to find matching rows.

You've learned how to create, update, read, and delete data from ScyllaDB. In all these examples, you didn't have to consider failures—the database worked. One of ScyllaDB's core benefits, however, is its failure tolerance. Let's see that in action and unleash some chaos on your database cluster!

2.4   Handling failures

You started a three-node cluster to tolerate the failure of a single node when your replication factor is set to 3. If you use quorum consistency in your queries, then with the loss of a single node, your cluster will still be operational for all queries. Therefore, if you stop one node, you should still be able to run quorum queries successfully. Let's verify this experimentally.

2.4.1   Shutting down a node

Step 1 in testing quorum queries is to shut down a node. Luckily, Docker makes killing a container straightforward. By running the docker ps command (named after the Unix ps process status program), you can view all running containers:

```
$ docker ps
```

Like nodetool status, docker ps gives you a lot of high-level information about a container's status. You can see your three nodes—scylla-1, scylla-2, and scylla-3. You're given information about their IDs, uptime, ports, and names:

```
CONTAINER ID    IMAGE               COMMAND              CREATED
  ⇒ STATUS        PORTS
  ⇒ NAMES
1f2fe0375097    scylladb/scylla:5.1   "/docker-entrypoint.…"   24 hours ago
  ⇒ Up 24 hours    22/tcp, 7000-7001/tcp, 9042/tcp, 9160/tcp,
                   ⇒ 9180/tcp, 10000/tcp
  ⇒ scylla-3
9e81feedc38c    scylladb/scylla:5.1   "/docker-entrypoint.…"   24 hours ago
  ⇒ Up 24 hours    22/tcp, 7000-7001/tcp, 9042/tcp, 9160/tcp,
                   ⇒ 9180/tcp, 10000/tcp
  ⇒ scylla-2
```

```
1e76b29391ed    scylladb/scylla:5.1   "/docker-entrypoint.…"   24 hours ago
  ➥ Up 24 hours    22/tcp, 7000-7001/tcp, 9042/tcp, 9160/tcp,
                       ➥ 9180/tcp, 10000/tcp
  ➥ scylla-1
```

To play mad scientist with query consistency, you can shut down `scylla-3` by running `docker stop`:

```
$ docker stop scylla-3
```

The command outputs the name of the stopped container:

```
scylla-3
```

If you run `docker ps` again, it says the container is stopped. `scylla-1` and `scylla-2` are complaining in their logs of being unable to reach `scylla-3`. With this node being down, you can observe the effects on the cluster.

2.4.2 *Experimenting with consistency*

Every query you run has a consistency level that describes how many nodes must respond for the query to be successful. To view what the current consistency level is in `cqlsh`, you can run the `CONSISTENCY` command:

```
cqlsh> CONSISTENCY;
```

Your current consistency level in `cqlsh` is ONE by default. This level indicates that only a single node needs to successfully respond for a query to be successful:

```
Current consistency level is ONE.
```

If you run a read, it will still work because there are two healthy nodes in the cluster:

```
cqlsh> SELECT * FROM initial.food_reviews
  WHERE restaurant = 'Ernie''s Eats';
```

Sure enough, your query is successful:

```
@ Row 1
-----------+-----------------------------------------------
 restaurant | Ernie's Eats
 ordered_at | 2023-05-09 12:00:00.000000+0000
 food       | Grilled cheese
 review     | Outstanding

@ Row 2
-----------+-----------------------------------------------
 restaurant | Ernie's Eats
 ordered_at | 2023-05-13 11:30:00.000000+0000
 food       | Fried chicken
 review     | Tasty, saved some for later, reheated well

 (2 rows)
```

On the other end of the spectrum is the consistency level `ALL`. The consistency levels have descriptive names; as you may surmise, this level requires all nodes to respond. You would expect this level to fail the query because not all nodes are alive. Let's verify this assumption by changing the level to `ALL` and rerunning the query:

```
cqlsh> CONSISTENCY all;                      ◁──┤ The consistency
Consistency level set to ALL.                    │ level is set to ALL.
cqlsh> SELECT * FROM initial.food_reviews
   WHERE restaurant = 'Ernie''s Eats';  ◁──┐    Reruns the select
NoHostAvailable: ...              ◁──┐      │    query, requiring all
                                     │      │    nodes to respond.
              The query fails, reporting
                    NoHostAvailable.
```

It does what you expect! You set the level to `ALL`, and the query doesn't work. It returns a `NoHostAvailable` error because you made `scylla-3` unavailable.

A middle ground for consistency is using a local quorum, which requires a majority of nodes in the same datacenter to respond successfully. Because you have three nodes in your cluster and only stopped one, there should still be a majority of nodes, or a quorum, available to respond to the request. You can see this in action by setting your consistency to `QUORUM` and executing your read again:

```
cqlsh> CONSISTENCY quorum;                ◁──┤ The consistency level
Consistency level set to QUORUM.              │ is set to QUORUM.

cqlsh> SELECT * FROM initial.food_reviews         Reruns the select query,
WHERE restaurant = 'Ernie''s Eats';  ◁──┤ requiring a majority of
                                          │ nodes to respond.
@ Row 1
------------+------------------------------------------
 restaurant | Ernie's Eats
 ordered_at | 2023-05-09 12:00:00.000000+0000
 food       | Grilled cheese
 review     | Outstanding

@ Row 2
------------+------------------------------------------
 restaurant | Ernie's Eats
 ordered_at | 2023-05-13 11:30:00.000000+0000
 food       | Fried chicken
 review     | Tasty, saved some for later, reheated well

(2 rows)   ◁──── The query succeeds.
```

The query worked again; it's still able to return results even with `scylla-3` down. Quorum queries provide stronger consistency than using `ONE`. Imagine a network partition where `scylla-3` is still available but can't communicate with the other nodes: if you were using `ONE`, it could be the only node responding to requests and could have data that is potentially divergent and inconsistent with the rest of the cluster. Although not as strong as `ALL`, quorum queries allow the loss of a node, whereas `ALL` does not. Quorums are a great Goldilocks-esque approach to consistency in ScyllaDB.

Summary

- ScyllaDB only runs in Linux, but you can run it locally using Docker without having to provision a server.
- A Scylla cluster is built one node at a time, using the first node as a seed node that other nodes connect to.
- `nodetool` lets you interact with and analyze the cluster, and supports a variety of commands that you'll use throughout the book.
- `nodetool status` gives an overview of the cluster's status, telling you whether each node is up, what the nodes' states are, and their placement in the cluster.
- When joining a cluster, a node first appears in `nodetool status` as `UJ` (up and joining) and transitions to `UN` (up and normal).
- Data is grouped into rows, which are stored in tables that are grouped by keyspaces. Each row has some number of columns, which label each piece of data. Rows are uniquely identified by a primary key, which also defines how the data is sorted.
- In a table, Scylla groups rows into partitions based on the first portion of the primary key, which serves as the unit of replication across the cluster as each partition is assigned to at least one node in the cluster. This replication is powered by the keyspace's replication settings.
- `cqlsh` is a command-line interface to run queries against the cluster, allowing you to create tables and keyspaces and read and write data.
- Scylla is queried using CQL, a query language intentionally very similar to SQL that uses the familiar `INSERT` and `SELECT` for writes and reads.
- Creating keyspaces and tables is done with the `CREATE KEYSPACE` and `CREATE TABLE` statements.
- In a table, each column has a type that must be specified in your `CREATE TABLE` statement.
- For the best performance, you want a single query to read in a single partition. Each query goes to a coordinator node that reaches out to the nodes that potentially hold that data; if you're not querying by the partition key, that coordinator needs to reach out to each node in the cluster.
- Scylla's `UPDATE` statements are upserts, which update data if there's an existing value and insert data if there isn't.
- You can delete data from Scylla using a `DELETE` statement.

Part 2

Query-first design

The key to a well-performing database in ScyllaDB is a well-designed schema. In part 2, you'll learn how to develop a database schema for ScyllaDB by following a practice called query-first design. In chapter 3, you'll determine what queries fulfill the requirements for a sample application and what tables are being queried. In chapter 4, you'll learn about ScyllaDB's supported data types and use them to fill out the fields in each of your tables. Chapter 5 brings your design together: you'll make some performance tweaks and translate the design into tables in your cluster.

Data modeling
in ScyllaDB

This chapter covers

- Performing query-first design
- How ScyllaDB distributes data across the cluster
- Implementing query-first design to build a
  schema for a sample application

Storing data is the easy part of running a database. ScyllaDB is designed to store data; databases in general are built to make storing and retrieving data easy. The hard part, I often find, is determining what data you need to store and how you store it in the database, doing so in a way that makes it easy to access.

Developing a database schema usually begins with an idea for an application. That application has requirements, and those requirements relate to the database, either directly or indirectly. You, and probably others as well, iterate on those requirements until you have something that most likely needs data to live in a database. You then take the requirements and translate them into a database schema.

In chapter 1, you learned that ScyllaDB is a different database—it distributes data across multiple nodes to provide better scalability and fault tolerance. In chapter 2, you learned that Scylla achieves this distribution by partitioning the data based on a partition key derived from the primary key of a row. This relationship implies that you are responsible for achieving ScyllaDB's benefits: if you design your data to be effectively distributed, that distribution positively affects the database.

When designing a schema, you consider what the application wants to do. You read the requirements and think intently until you have a database schema. Here, you'll be guided through the intense thinking phase of schema design to make a schema that fits ScyllaDB as you expand on the restaurant review database you built in the last chapter.

In this chapter, you'll learn how to perform this data modeling for ScyllaDB. To best use Scylla's design and have a well-performing database, you'll learn an approach called *query-first design* where you'll design your database around the queries it needs to run. Let's dive in!

3.1 Application design before schema design

When designing a database schema, you need to create a schema that is synergistic with your database. If you consider Scylla's goals as a database, it wants to distribute data across the cluster to provide better scalability and fault tolerance. Spreading the data means queries involve multiple nodes, so you want to design your application to make queries that use the partition key, minimizing the number of nodes involved in a request. Your schema needs to fit these constraints:

- It needs to distribute data across the cluster.
- It should also query the minimal number of nodes for your desired consistency level.

There's some tension in these constraints: your schema wants to spread data across the cluster to balance load between the nodes, but you want to minimize the number of nodes required to serve a query. Satisfying these constraints can be a balancing act—do you have smaller partitions that may require more queries to aggregate together, or do you have larger partitions that require fewer queries but spread your data potentially unevenly across the cluster? In figure 3.1, you can see the cost of a query that utilizes the partition key and queries across the minimal number of nodes versus one that doesn't use the partition key, necessitating scanning each node for matching data. Using the partition key in your query allows the coordinator—the node servicing the request—to direct queries to nodes that own that partition, lessening the load on the cluster and returning results faster.

The aforementioned design constraints are each related to queries. You want your data to be spread across the cluster so that your queries distribute the load among multiple nodes. Imagine if all of your data was clustered on a small subset of nodes in your cluster. Some nodes would be working hard, whereas others might not be taking much traffic. If some of those heavily utilized nodes became overwhelmed, you could suffer degraded performance: due to the imbalance, many queries might be unable to complete.

The lines connecting the query
and the nodes show the nodes
required to fulfill the query.

`SELECT * FROM table WHERE partition_key = ?`   `SELECT * FROM table WHERE non_partition_key = ?`

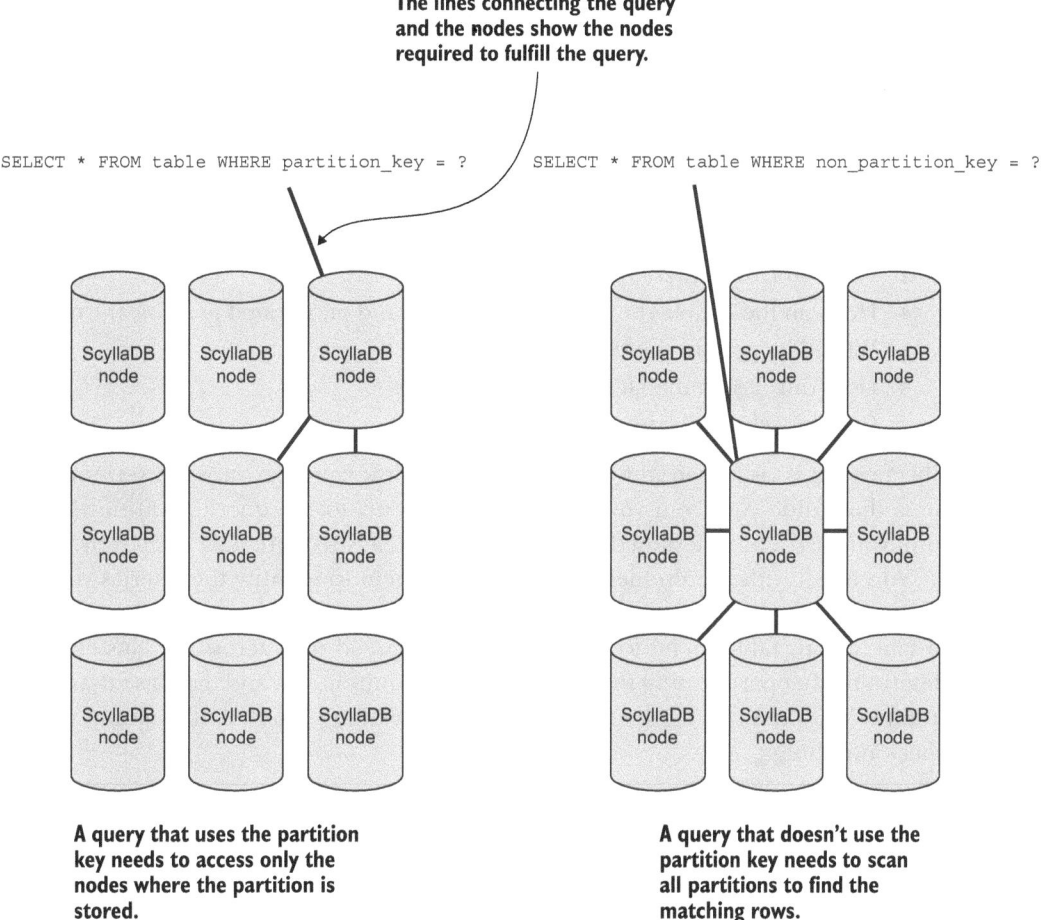

A query that uses the partition
key needs to access only the
nodes where the partition is
stored.

A query that doesn't use the
partition key needs to scan
all partitions to find the
matching rows.

Figure 3.1   Using the partition key minimizes the number of nodes required to serve the request.

However, you also want to minimize the number of nodes hit per query to minimize
the work your query needs to do; a query that uses all nodes in a very large cluster will
be very inefficient. These query-centric constraints necessitate a query-centric
approach to design. How you query Scylla is a key component of its performance, and
because you need to consider the impacts of your queries across multiple dimensions,
it's critical to think carefully about how you query Scylla.

When designing schemas in Scylla, it's best to apply an approach called *query-first
design*, where you focus on the queries your application needs to make and then build
your database schema around that. In Scylla, *you structure your data based on how you
want to query it*—query-first design helps you.

3.1.1 *Your query-first design toolbox*

In query-first design, you take a set of application requirements and ask yourself a series of questions that guide you through translating the requirements into a schema in ScyllaDB. Each of these questions builds on the next, iteratively guiding you through building an effective ScyllaDB schema. These questions include the following:

1   What are the requirements for my application?
2   What queries does my application need to run to meet these requirements?
3   What tables are these queries querying?
4   How can these tables be uniquely identified and partitioned to satisfy the queries?
5   What data goes in these tables?
6   Does this design match the requirements?
7   Can this schema be improved?

This process is visualized in figure 3.2, showing how you ask yourself a series of questions that guide you from your initial requirements to the queries you need to run until you have a fully designed ScyllaDB schema ready to store data effectively.

You begin with requirements and then use them to identify the queries you need to run. These queries are seeking something—those "somethings" need to be stored in tables. Your tables need to be partitioned to spread data across the cluster, so you determine that partitioning to stay within your requirements and database design constraints. You then specify the fields in each table, filling it out. At this point, you can check two things:

- Does the design match the requirements?
- Can it be improved?

This up-front design is important because in ScyllaDB, changing your schema to match new use cases can be a high-friction operation. Although Scylla supports new query patterns via some of its features (which you'll learn about in chapter 7), these come at an additional performance cost; and if they don't fit your needs, they may necessitate manually copying your data into a new table. It's important to think carefully about your design: not only what it needs to be, but also what it could be in the future.

You start by extracting the queries from your requirements and expanding your design until you have a schema that fits both your application and ScyllaDB. To practice query-first design in Scylla, let's take the restaurant review application and turn it into a ScyllaDB schema.

Query-first design involves
determining your application's
queries first and using them to
build a database schema.

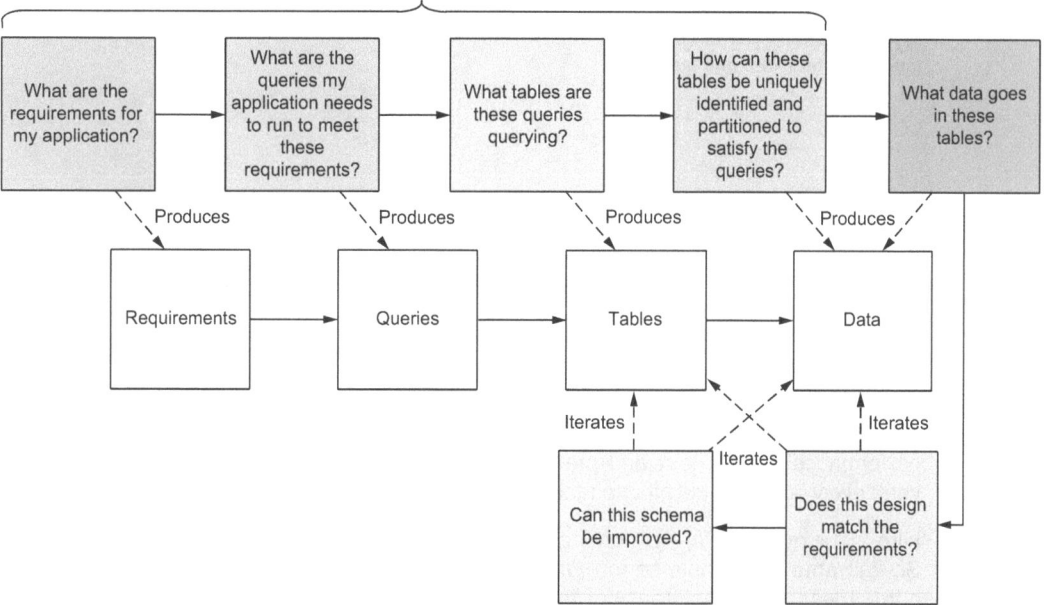

Figure 3.2   Query-first design guides you through taking application requirements and converting them to a ScyllaDB schema.

The tools you don't have

Creating an effective design, like many things with Scylla, requires a different approach than with a relational database. Some tools from PostgreSQL and its friends are unavailable to you: foreign keys, referential integrity, and joins. These limitations, however, do not stop you from creating well-designed and efficient database schemas.

In a relational database, users are free to issue JOIN queries, retrieving data from multiple tables based on common column values. In the food review example from previous chapters, in a relational database, you might further break up your schema to store information about the restaurants in a `restaurant` table. Instead of containing the name of the restaurant, your food reviews might store the ID of the restaurant, which linked to a row in that `restaurant` table. A JOIN query would traverse that link, aggregating data from multiple tables.

(continued)

This JOIN operation is not allowed in ScyllaDB or many other NoSQL databases. If data is distributed via partitions, a hypothetical JOIN query in Scylla could involve extra partitions and nodes, harming the query's performance.

A JOIN query, unsupported in ScyllaDB, enables you to query multiple tables with one query.

```
Restaurant                    Review

ID                            ID
name                          score
location                      restaurant ID
```

```
SELECT review.score, restaurant.name, restaurant.location FROM review JOIN restaurant...
```

JOIN queries are unsupported in ScyllaDB, meaning you need to design your schema so as not to need this pattern.

Scylla wants to have better scalability and fault tolerance, and it wants to ensure that performance is both fast and predictable. Allowing cross-table joins contradicts that goal: every query should hit one table. The JOIN keyword isn't even part of the CQL spec.

Like JOIN queries, foreign keys and referential integrity aren't available to you. As Scylla wants predictable performance, it doesn't run additional queries to validate the correctness and consistency of the database. You can use IDs that refer to data in other tables, but Scylla won't enforce that the IDs are valid.

Before recoiling in horror and swearing to never use a database that doesn't have these properties, remember that ScyllaDB provides a different set of properties as tradeoffs, emphasizing predictable distributed performance, scalability, and fault tolerance. As you encounter techniques and design decisions in this chapter that may initially seem weird, remember this paragraph and these tradeoffs!

3.1.2   *The sample application requirements*

In the last chapter, you took your restaurant reviews and stored them in ScyllaDB. You enjoyed working with the database, and as you went more places, you realized that you could combine your two great loves: restaurant reviews and databases (if these aren't your two great loves, play along with me). You decide to build a website to share your restaurant reviews. Because you already have a ScyllaDB cluster, you choose to use that (this is a very different book if you pick otherwise) as the storage for your website.

The first step to query-first design is *identifying the requirements for your application*, as shown in figure 3.3. After ruminating on your potential website, you identify the features it needs, and, most importantly, you give it a name: Restaurant Reviews. It does what it says! Restaurant Reviews has the following initial requirements:

- Authors post articles to the website.
- Users view articles to read restaurant reviews
- Articles contain a title, an author, a score, a date, a gallery of images, the review text, and the restaurant.
- A review's score is between 1 and 10.
- The home page contains a summary of articles sorted by most recent, showing the title, author name, score, and one image.
- The home page links to articles.
- Authors have a dedicated page containing summaries of their articles.
- Authors have a name, bio, and picture.
- Users can view a list of article summaries sorted by the highest review score.

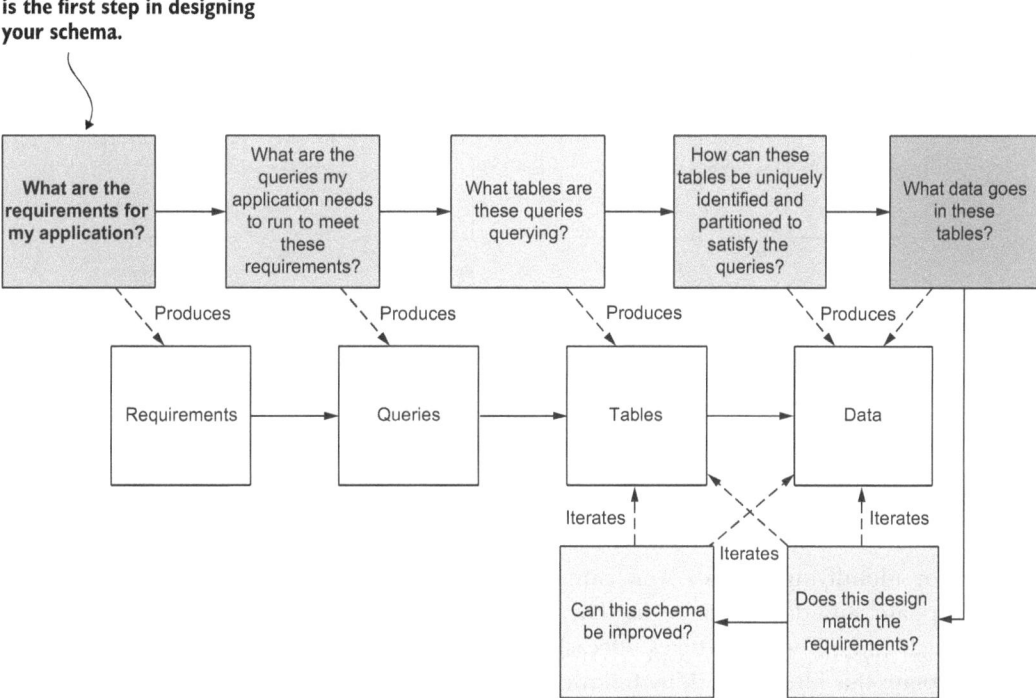

Figure 3.3   You begin query-first design by determining your application's requirements.

You have a hunch that as time goes by, you'll want to add more features to this application and use those features to learn more about ScyllaDB. For now, these features give you a base to practice decomposing requirements and building your schema—let's begin!

3.1.3   *Determining the queries*

Next, you ask, "What are the queries my application needs to run to meet these requirements?" (see figure 3.4). Your queries drive how you design your database schema; therefore, it is critical to understand your queries at the beginning of your design.

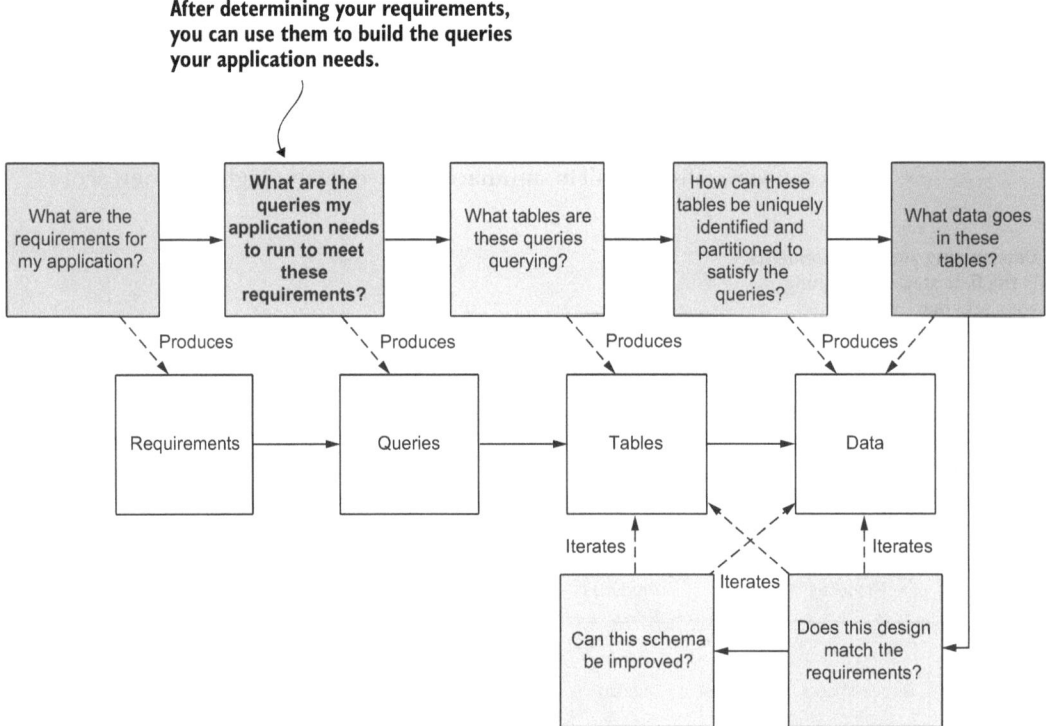

Figure 3.4   Next, you take your requirements and use them to determine your application's queries.

For identifying queries, you can use the familiar *CRUD* operations—create, read, update, and delete—as verbs. These queries will act on nouns in your requirements, such as authors or articles. Occasionally you'll want to filter your queries: you can notate this filtering with by followed by the filter condition. For example, if your app needed to load events on a given date, you might use a `Read Events by Date` query. If you look at your requirements, you'll see several queries you'll need.

> **NOTE**   These aren't the actual queries you'll run; those are written in CQL, as discussed in chapter 2, and look more like `SELECT * FROM your_cool_table WHERE your_awesome_primary_key = 12;`. These are descriptions of what you'll need to query. In later chapters, when you finish your design, you'll turn these into actual CQL queries.

The first requirement is "Authors post articles to the website," which sounds an awful lot like a process that involves inserting an article into a database. Because you insert articles in the database via a query, you need a `Create Article` statement. You may be asking at this point, "What is an article?" Although other requirements discuss these fields, you should skip that concern for the moment. Focus first on what queries you need to run, and later you'll figure out the needed fields.

The second requirement is "Users view articles to read restaurant reviews." Giving users unfettered access to the database is a security no-go, so the app needs to load an article to display to a user. This functionality suggests a `Read Article` query (which is different from the user perusing the article), which you can use to retrieve an article for a user.

The following two requirements refer to the data you need to store and not a novel way to access it:

- Articles contain a title, an author, a score, a date, a gallery of images, the review text, and the restaurant.
- A review's score is between 1 and 10.

Articles need certain fields, and each article is associated with a review score that fits within specified parameters. You can save these requirements for later when you fill out what fields are needed in each table.

The next relevant requirement says "The home page contains a summary of articles sorted by most recent, showing the title, author name, score, and one image." The home page shows article summaries, which you'll need to load by their date, sorted by most recent: `Read Article Summaries by Date`. Article summaries, at first glance, look a lot like articles. Because you're querying different data, and you also need to retrieve summaries by their time, you should consider them different queries.

Querying for an article does the following:

- Loads a title, author, score, date, and gallery of images along with the review text and the restaurant
- Retrieves one specific article

On the other hand, loading the most recent article summaries does this:

- Loads only the title, the author name, the score, and one image
- Loads several summaries, sorted by their publishing date

Perhaps they can run against the same table, but you can see if that's the case further on in the exercise. When in doubt, it's best not to over-consolidate. Be expansive in your designs; if there's duplication, you can reduce it when refining those designs. As you work through implementing a design, you may discover reasons for what seems to be unnecessarily duplicated in one step to be a necessary separation later.

Following these requirements is "The home page links to articles," which makes explicit that the article summaries link to the article. You'll look closer at this one when you determine what fields you need.

The next two requirements are about authors. The website will contain a page for each author—presumably only you at the moment, but you have visions of a media empire. This author page will contain article summaries for each author—meaning you'll need to `Read Article Summaries by Author`. In the last requirement, there's data that each author has. You can study the specifics in a moment, but it means you'll need to read information about the author, so you need a `Read Author` query.

For the last requirement—"Users can view a list of article summaries sorted by the highest review score"—you'll need a way to surface article summaries sorted by their scores. This approach requires `Read Article Summaries by Score`.

> **NOTE** What would make a good partition key for reading articles sorted by score? It's a tricky problem; you'll learn how to attack it shortly.

Having analyzed the requirements, you've determined that your schema needs to support these six queries:

- `Create Article`
- `Read Article`
- `Read Article Summaries by Date`
- `Read Article Summaries by Author`
- `Read Article Summaries by Score`
- `Read Author`

You may notice a problem here: where do article summaries and authors get created? How can you read them if nothing makes them exist? Requirement lists often have implicit requirements—because you need to read article summaries, they have to be created somehow. Go ahead and add `Create Article Summary` and `Create Author` queries to your list. You now have eight queries from the requirements you created, listed in table 3.1.

Table 3.1 Mapping requirements to queries

Requirement	Queries
Authors post articles...	`Create Article`
Users view articles...	`Read Article`
Articles contain a title...	N/A
A review's score is between...	N/A
The home page contains a summary of articles...	`Create Article Summary, Read Article Summaries by Date`
The home page links to articles...	N/A
Authors have a dedicated page...	`Create Author, Read Article Summaries by Author`

Table 3.1 Mapping requirements to queries (continued)

Requirement	Queries
Authors have a name...	`Read Author`
... article summaries ... sorted by the highest review score	`Read Article Summaries by Score`

There's a joke that asks, "How do you draw an owl?" Answer: "You draw a couple of circles, and then you draw the rest of the owl." Query-first design sometimes feels similar. You need to map your queries to a database schema that not only is effective in meeting the application's requirements but also is performant and uses ScyllaDB's benefits and features. Drawing queries out of requirements is often straightforward, whereas designing the schema from those queries requires balancing both application and database concerns. Let's look at some techniques you can apply as you design a database schema.

3.2 Identifying tables

After determining the queries, the next step in query-first design (figure 3.5) is to ask "What tables are these queries querying?" When analyzing the requirements, you identified several queries to implement. You see three primary things you're querying:

- Articles
- Article summaries
- Authors

Because you're planning to query them, you may think these should correspond to tables in your schema. This is usually correct; you need tables to store this data. Before getting too deep into table design, there is a design constraint in ScyllaDB that you need to be aware of: a query can query only one table at a time.

3.2.1 Denormalization

Scylla does not support join operations—you cannot query for rows across multiple tables in a single query. If you want to display the author's name for an article, you need to either store the author's name alongside the article or make multiple queries to the database to retrieve that information.

These approaches may seem unnecessarily duplicative: if the database already has the data, why do you need to store it again? Relational databases strongly encourage the concept of *normalization*, where you store data only once, linking to it via foreign keys whose correctness is verified by the database.

A common example is a database representing a store. Items sold might have their ID, name, and description in a table called `items`, but information about their price might be stored in a `prices` table that contains the item ID and price. A relational database verifies that the item ID in the `prices` table matches an ID in the `items`

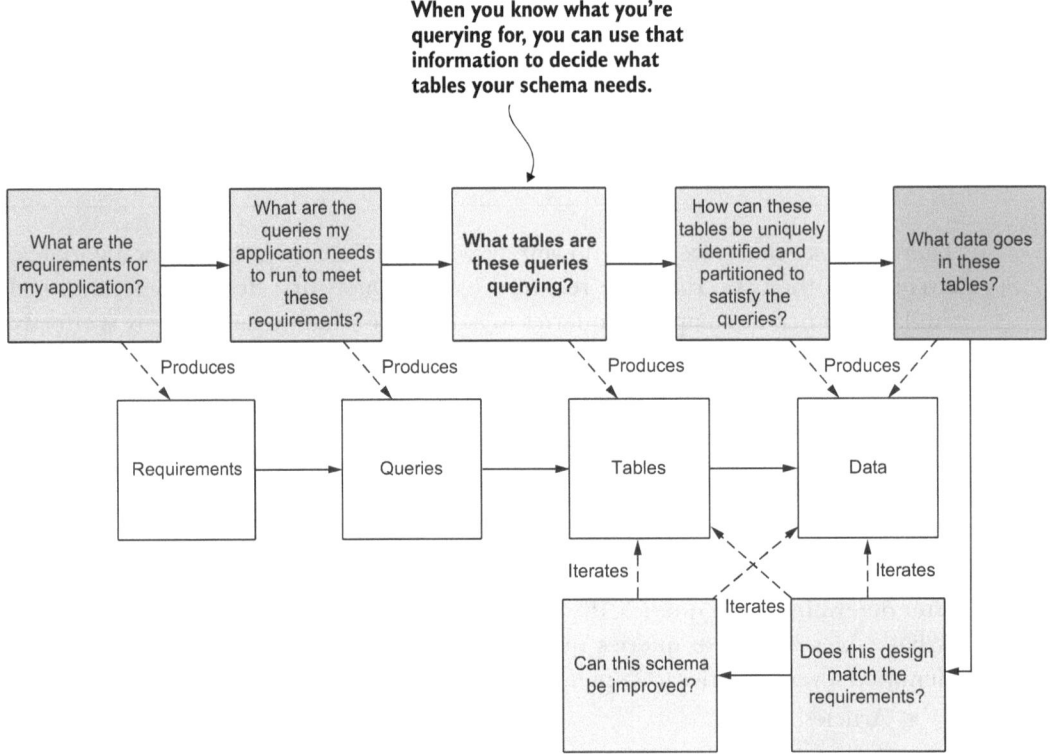

When you know what you're querying for, you can use that information to decide what tables your schema needs.

What are the requirements for my application? → What are the queries my application needs to run to meet these requirements? → **What tables are these queries querying?** → How can these tables be uniquely identified and partitioned to satisfy the queries? → What data goes in these tables?

Requirements → Queries → Tables → Data

Produces / Produces / Produces / Produces

Iterates / Iterates / Iterates

Can this schema be improved? ← Does this design match the requirements?

Figure 3.5   Query-first design takes your queries and extracts what they're querying to determine your tables.

table. It also supports easily retrieving data from multiple tables by following these links during queries, allowing you to aggregate data from multiple tables. It's a core component of relational database design, and if you're familiar with it, it may be challenging not to use that paradigm.

With Scylla, though, how you query your data drives how you store it. Because you need to access data in different ways—you plan to load article summaries in several ways—you'll have to use *denormalization*, storing the same data in multiple places so you can query it in different ways.

If you want to load article summaries based on their author, the article summaries must be partitioned by their author because how data is stored enforces how you query it. If you want to load the highest-scoring article summaries, which, hypothetically, are partitioned by their author, the query must include the partition key—the author. Otherwise, it will check all partitions and have potentially painful performance.

Denormalization is a helpful technique—it preserves the fast writes, scalability, and fault tolerance of ScyllaDB's queries and gives you the flexibility to access your data in a variety of contexts. The downsides are the duplication and the increased effort to maintain it. Instead of inserting a row into one table, you need to also insert it into its denormalized companions to keep that data in sync (figure 3.6). Scylla provides functionality to assist with this process, which we'll cover later.

Denormalizing data unlocks fast retrieval of fields for varying sorts, but at the cost of storing that data multiple times.

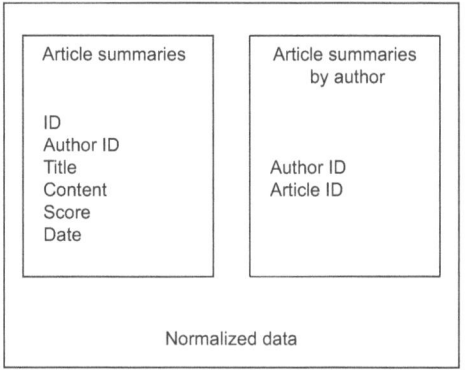

A normalized set of tables minimizes data duplication, by storing data in one place.

When tables are denormalized, values are duplicated across tables.

Figure 3.6   Schema design balances between normalization and denormalization.

Having learned about how Scylla encourages denormalization in your design, you're ready to extend your schema and determine what tables you need.

3.2.2   *Extracting tables*

Keeping denormalization in mind, what tables do you need to satisfy these queries? You've identified the need for several queries:

- `Create Article`
- `Read Article`
- `Create Author`
- `Read Author`
- `Create Article Summary`
- `Read Article Summaries by Date`
- `Read Article Summaries by Author`
- `Read Article Summaries by Score`

The first two queries are about articles. A common theme is going to emerge as you determine your tables: the objects of query verbs (`Create`, `Read`) frequently become tables. Creating an article inserts a row into an `article` table; reading an article reads that row.

Let's examine authors. Just like articles, your queries create an author and read an author. Should you choose the same approach? Yes! You can have an `authors` table that you insert into and read from, giving data about authors.

It's now time to talk about article summaries. At this point, you may be wondering what the difference is between the article and the article summary. If you look closely, the article summary is a subset of the article; it contains a portion of its fields. At the end of your design, this is a great starting point for looking for improvements in your schema.

You want to query article summaries several ways—by date, author, and score. What tables do you need to meet these requirements? If you want to query your data in each of these ways, you need to store your data to support each of these cases. Remember that in Scylla, you should query by the partition key, which means you'll need a table with the appropriate partition key for each way you want to query it. With these varying queries, you'll certainly need to denormalize your data, having multiple tables store article summaries, each partitioned differently to satisfy your query requirements.

Yes, it feels duplicative. You may be thinking, "Do I really have to store the data three times to query it in three different ways?" Potentially, yes (some queries may be able to share partition keys, depending on your use cases), but let's look closer at why.

Remember, ScyllaDB's goal is to provide scalability and fault tolerance through a distributed database. Imagine a hypothetical article summaries table, with rows partitioned by an author ID and a primary key of author ID and an article ID. The article ID uniquely identifies the article, but because your query needs to include the partition key, you include the author ID in the key as well. This table has a replication factor of three, meaning each partition is replicated to three nodes in a cluster. If you want to load the article summaries for a given author, you specify a given author ID, and your query hits only the three nodes where the partition is stored, as in figure 3.7.

But what happens if you want to find the articles with the highest score—10? When querying by the partition key, the author ID won't help you; it only gives you articles written by an author. To find the highest-scoring articles, you need to query against the grain of the partition, scanning each partition individually for high-scoring articles. Loading every partition in the cluster to check for specific rows is a slow operation and does not scale well, leading to user unhappiness.

What about something like an *index*, a traditional database construct that specifies a secondary ordering of rows in a table and provides fast access to those rows? Even if you can magically map directly to those specific rows, they'll still be spread across partitions across all nodes in the cluster, so you'll pay the large performance cost to query that data. This limitation is why ScyllaDB's implementation of indexes uses denormalized data—an index in Scylla stores a duplicate copy of the table with a different partition key. You'll learn more about these concepts in future chapters.

For now, you need to store the denormalized data yourself. To query article summaries by author, you need an `article_summaries_by_author` table. To query them

The lines connecting the query and the nodes show the nodes required to fulfill the query.

The articles are partitioned by author in this example.

```
SELECT * FROM article_summaries WHERE author_id = 3
```

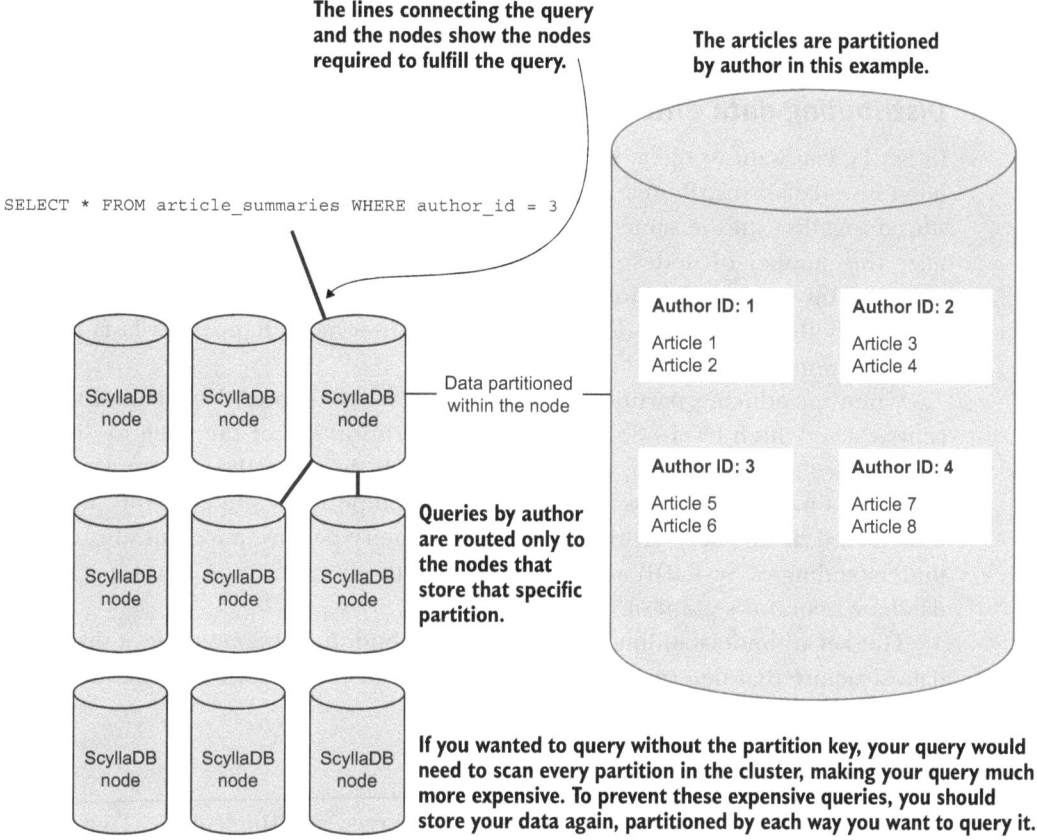

Data partitioned within the node

Author ID: 1

Article 1
Article 2

Author ID: 2

Article 3
Article 4

Author ID: 3

Article 5
Article 6

Author ID: 4

Article 7
Article 8

Queries by author are routed only to the nodes that store that specific partition.

ScyllaDB node

If you wanted to query without the partition key, your query would need to scan every partition in the cluster, making your query much more expensive. To prevent these expensive queries, you should store your data again, partitioned by each way you want to query it.

Figure 3.7   Querying via the partition key is very performant for the cluster, so you should store your data differently for each way you intend to access it.

by date, you need `article_summaries_by_date`; and to query by score, you need `article_summaries_by_score`.

With three article summary tables, how do you create an article summary? You have listed `Create Article Summary` as a query you need to support, but what does it do? You need to insert an article summary into each of those tables. To accomplish that, you need an `INSERT` statement for each table. However, you don't have to make three separate queries; ScyllaDB supports a batching operation, which you'll learn about in chapter 6. For now, you can say that your `Create Article Summary` query needs to insert into each of the article summary tables.

With these table names, you have the beginnings of the schema. Table names alone, however, do not satisfy application requirements. Those tables need to store data, and that begins by defining each table. When determining a table's columns, it is paramount to make the table performant by selecting a good partition key. To learn what this entails, let's look at how Scylla distributes data and how you can use it for fast and efficient queries.

3.3 *Distributing data efficiently on the hash ring*

In Scylla, you want to query by the partition key: the values in the table that determine how data is distributed around the cluster. Data with the same partition key is stored together on the same node, and if you query by the partition key, you minimize the number of nodes involved in the query, helping your request complete quickly. You use the partition key in the WHERE clause; the database can use it to query only the involved nodes. The query is fast—you're happy, Scylla is happy— everyone wins.

When introducing partition keys in the previous chapter, I explained the concept at a very high level—ScyllaDB uses the partition key of the table to distribute data across the cluster. That, although true, is only the tip of the iceberg. Data distribution is a nuanced process involving several components and concepts, but when understood, it not only provides insight into query performance but also gives an understanding of ScyllaDB as a whole from both an application developer's and a database operator's point of view.

The key to understanding Scylla's data distribution is the *hash ring*, a distributed data structure that determines where data lives and what nodes own that data. Let's look at this foundational concept.

3.3.1 *The hash ring*

You begin with one node because every cluster starts with a single node. That first singleton node is responsible at that moment for every row that is written to the database. Writing data to a single-node Scylla cluster is not a great approach, but it helps for illustration purposes. With your one node, no distribution needs to happen; all data can stay local. As you may expect, the fun begins when you start adding nodes. Your original node owns all the data and would like to hand off some of it to the newly joining node. How does the first node hand data to the second node?

Imagine a giant ring. Along the circumference of the ring are points, not dissimilar to seats at a round table. Each point has an integer value associated with it called a *token*. When data is written to the cluster, the partition key is assigned an integer value via a *hashing function*, which maps the partition key to a token on the ring. Rows with the same partition key are assigned to the same spot on the ring, whereas rows with a differing key are almost always guaranteed to be assigned a different spot on the ring. This concept—hashing keys to tokens on a ring—is called a *hash ring* (figure 3.8). ScyllaDB borrowed it from Cassandra, but it's a cornerstone of many distributed systems.

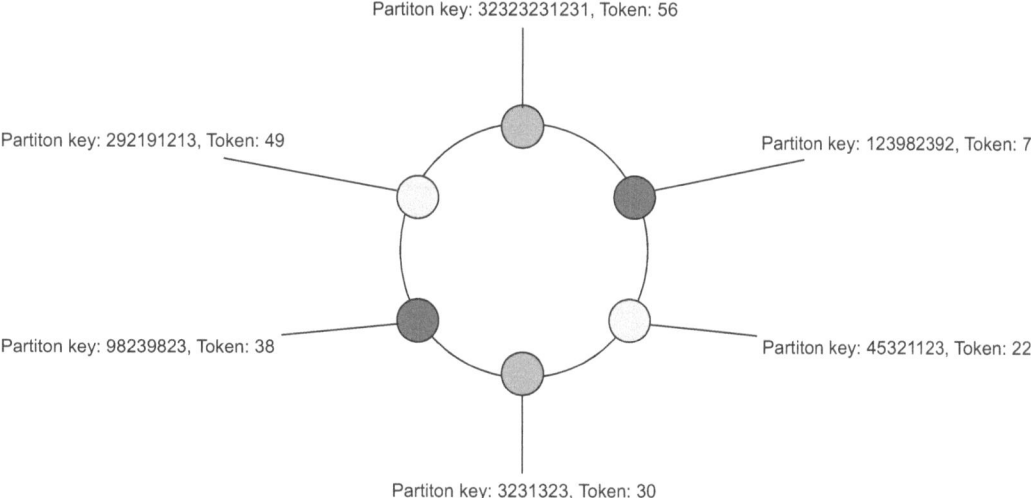

Partiton key: 32323231231, Token: 56

Partiton key: 292191213, Token: 49

Partiton key: 123982392, Token: 7

Partiton key: 98239823, Token: 38

Partiton key: 45321123, Token: 22

Partiton key: 3231323, Token: 30

**Partitions are mapped to a token, which
is mapped to a position on the hash ring.**

Figure 3.8   Partitions are mapped to places on a hash ring.

Each row has a spot on the hash ring, but how does that relate to Scylla distributing data? When a node starts up, it takes up random positions in multiple places on the hash ring, creating virtual nodes on the ring, or *vnodes* (pronounced "vee nodes"), as seen in figures 3.9 and 3.10. By taking up positions on the ring, the node claims responsibility for the data in that slice of the ring until the next node's position. When a new node joins the ring, it takes up data claimed by other nodes, bisecting their slices. Relieved of some of their data burden, the other nodes in the cluster stream data they previously owned to their new owner—the newly joined node.

Vnodes, because they divide the cluster into smaller pieces, provide several benefits. Instead of having each node claim one giant chunk of the hash ring, the data is divided into smaller and easier-to-manage chunks. Because they're smaller, the cluster is more easily able to parallelize streaming data when a node joins the cluster. These small chunks amortize the cost of hash-ring-based operations. Instead of one node having to hand over a large amount of data, harming its latency, Scylla can spread the load across the cluster, performing many small handoffs instead of a single giant data sync.

NOTE This distribution means a hash collision, however unlikely, doesn't cause a problem. The cluster uses the token to determine which node owns that token—a one-way mapping. Even if two partitions have the same token,

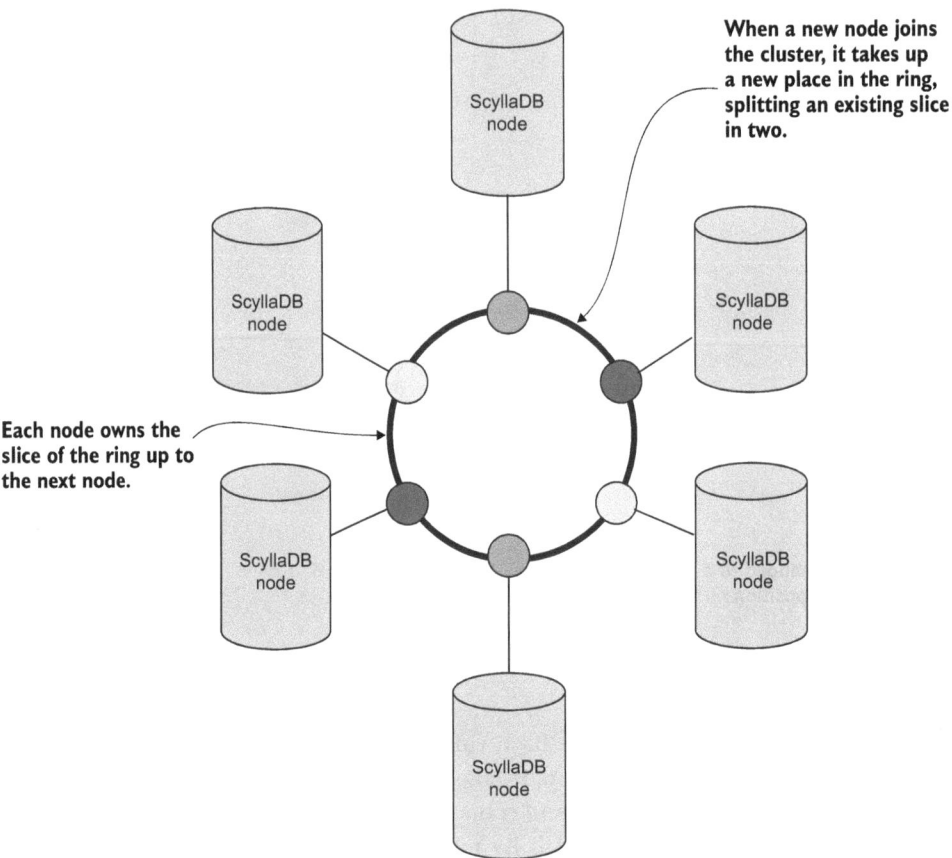

Figure 3.9   **Each node owns a slice of the hash ring.**

the result is that they'll both map to the same node, which is the expected behavior and causes no trouble.

nodetool status flashback

When you ran `nodetool status` in the last chapter, there was a mysterious `Tokens` field in the output:

```
Status=Up/Down
|/ State=Normal/Leaving/Joining/Moving
--   Address    Load    Tokens Owns Host ID                                Rack
UN   scylla-1   572 KB  256     ?    75ddfa00-9624-4137-b926-429dff20e516 rack1
```

That `Tokens` field lists the number of vnodes for a given node, marking the number of places where the node has joined the hash ring.

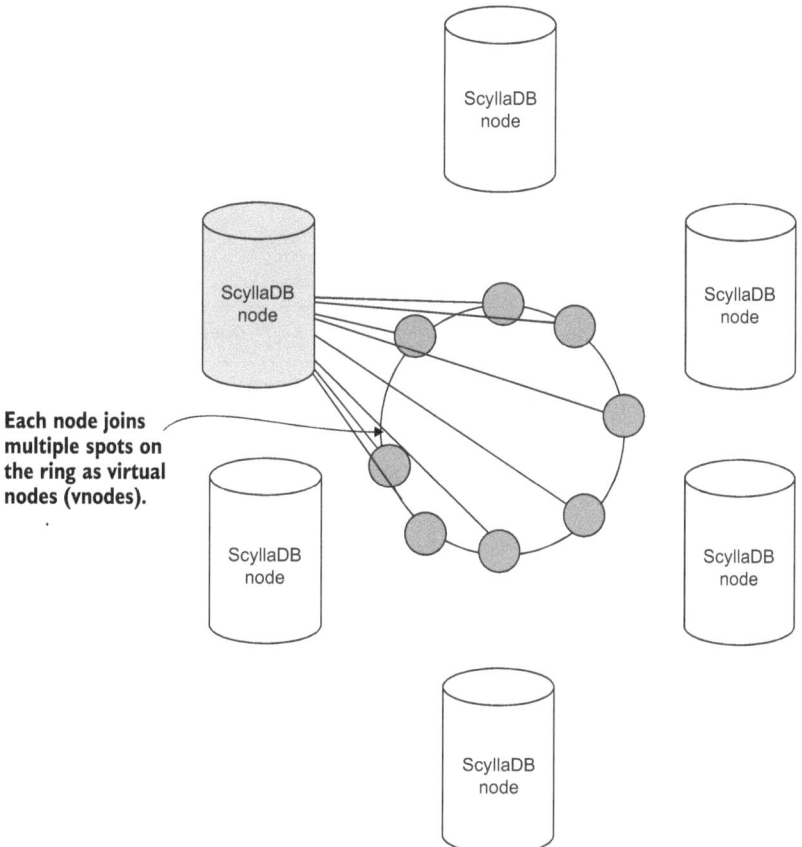

Figure 3.10 **Each node joins the ring in multiple places as vnodes, making the slices of the ring smaller and easier to manage.**

Imagine a hash ring with a token range of 1 to 100. In a hypothetical three-node cluster, each node joins multiple places along the ring. In Scylla, both the token range and the number of vnodes are much larger (see the following note), but the smaller values are helpful here to illustrate. Nodes join multiple random places in the hash ring to get a roughly uniform distribution of data: if everything was clumped together, some nodes would own way more data than others. Distributing data across the cluster follows a similar principle. Scylla performs best when your partitions are small, relatively similar in size, and uniformly distributed across the cluster.

> **NOTE** Scylla uses a `murmur3` hash implementation, meaning the values are hashed to numbers between -9,223,372,036,854,775,808 and 9,223,372,036,854,775,807—the range of a 64-bit signed integer. By default, each node, when joining the cluster, joins with 256 vnodes—owning 256 slices of the hash ring.

Although hashing the partition key helps spread the number of partitions across the cluster, the size of the partitions is driven by your design. Let's return to your application and apply what you've learned about the hash ring to the various tables.

3.3.2 *Making good partitions*

When analyzing the queries your application needs, you identified several tables for your schema (see table 3.2).

Table 3.2   **Mapping tables to queries**

Table	Queries
articles	Create Article, Read Article
authors	Create Author, Read Author
article_summaries_by_author	Create Article Summary, Read Article Summaries by Author
article_summaries_by_date	Create Article Summary, Read Article Summaries by Date
article_summaries_by_score	Create Article Summary, Read Article Summaries by Score

The next step in schema design is to ask "How can these tables be uniquely identified and partitioned to satisfy the queries?" The primary key contains the row's partition key—you learned in chapter 2 that the primary key determines a row's uniqueness. Therefore, before you can determine the partition key, you need to know the primary key.

PRIMARY KEYS

First you should check to see if what you're trying to store contains a property that is popularly used for its uniqueness. Cars, for example, have a VIN (vehicle identification number) that's unique per car. Books (including this one!) have an ISBN (international standard book number) to uniquely identify them. There's no international standard for identifying an article or an author, so you'll need to think a little harder to find the primary and partition keys. ScyllaDB does provide support for generating unique identifiers, but they come with some drawbacks that you'll learn about in the next chapter.

Next, you can ask if any fields can be combined to make a good primary key. What can you use to determine a unique article? The title may be reused, especially if you have unimaginative writers. The content would ideally be unique per article, but that's a very large value for a key. Perhaps you can use a combination of fields—maybe date, author, and title? That probably works, but I find it's helpful to look back at what you're trying to query. When your application runs the Read Article query, it's trying to read only a single article. Whatever is executing that query (probably a web server responding to the contents of a URL) is trying to load that article, so it needs information that can be stored in a URL. Isn't it obnoxious when you paste a link somewhere, and the link feels like it's a billion characters long? To load an article, you don't want to have to keep track of the author ID, title, and date. That's why using an ID as a primary key is often a strong choice.

Providing a unique identifier satisfies the uniqueness requirement of a primary key, and such IDs can potentially encode other information within them, such as time, which can be used for relative ordering. You'll learn more about potential types of IDs in the next chapter when you explore data types.

What uniquely identifies an author? You may think it's an email, but people sometimes change their email addresses. Supplying your own unique identifier works well here, too. Perhaps it's a numeric ID, or maybe it's a username; but as your design stands today, authors need extra information to differentiate them from other authors in your database.

Article summaries, as in the other steps you've been through, are a little more interesting. For the various article summary tables, if you try to use the same primary key as for articles—an ID—you're going to run into trouble. If an ID alone makes an article unique in the `articles` table, presumably it suffices for the index tables. That turns out not to be the case.

An ID can still differentiate uniqueness, but you also want to query by at least the partition key to have a performant query; and if an ID is the partition key, that doesn't satisfy the use cases for querying by author, date, or score. Because the partition key is contained in the primary key, you need to include those fields in your primary key (figure 3.11). For example, for `article_summaries_by_author`, your primary key for the row would become author and your article ID. Similarly, the other two tables would have the date and the article ID for `article_summaries_by_date`, and `article_summaries_by_score` would use the score and the article ID for its primary key.

With your primary keys figured out, you can move forward to determining your partition keys and potentially adjusting your primary keys.

PARTITION KEYS

You learned in the last chapter that the first entry in the primary key serves as the partition key for the row (you'll see later how to build a composite primary key). A good partition key distributes data evenly across the cluster and is used by the queries against that table. It stores a relatively small amount of data (a good rule of thumb is that 100 MB is a large partition, but it depends on the use case). I've listed the tables and their primary key in table 3.3; knowing the primary keys, you can rearrange them to specify your partition keys. What would be a good partition key for each of these tables?

Although a single attribute may uniquely identify an article summary, you may need to include additional fields in your primary key to use them in your partition key.

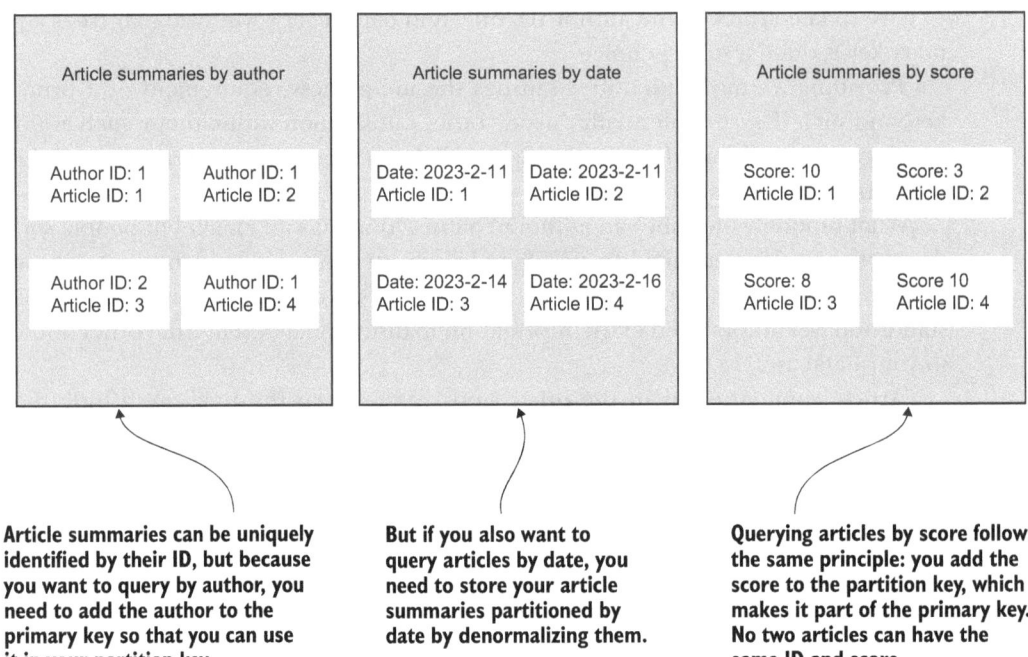

Article summaries can be uniquely identified by their ID, but because you want to query by author, you need to add the author to the primary key so that you can use it in your partition key.

But if you also want to query articles by date, you need to store your article summaries partitioned by date by denormalizing them.

Querying articles by score follows the same principle: you add the score to the partition key, which makes it part of the primary key. No two articles can have the same ID and score.

Figure 3.11   You sometimes need to add fields to an already-unique primary key to use them in a partition key, especially when denormalizing data.

Table 3.3   Each table has a primary key from which the partition key is extracted.

Table	Unordered primary key
articles	id
authors	id
article_summaries_by_author	id, author_id
article_summaries_by_date	id, date
article_summaries_by_score	id, score

For the articles and authors tables, it's very straightforward. There is one column in the primary key; therefore, the partition key is the only column. If only everything was that easy!

WARNING   By only having the ID as the primary key and the partition key, you can look up rows only by their ID. A query in which you want to get multiple rows wouldn't work with this approach because you'd be querying across partitions, bringing in extra nodes and hampering performance. Instead, you want to query by a partition key that contains multiple rows, as you'll do with article summaries.

The article summaries tables, however, present you with a choice. Given a primary key of an ID and an author, for `article_summaries_by_author`, which should be the partition key? If you choose ID, Scylla will distribute the rows for this table around the cluster based on the ID of the article. This distribution would mean that if you wanted to load all articles by their author, the query would have to hit nodes all across the cluster. That behavior is not efficient. If you partitioned your data by the author, a query to find all articles written by a given author would hit only the nodes that stored that partition because you'd be querying within that partition (figure 3.12). You almost always want to query by at least the partition key—it is critical for good performance. Because the use case for this table is to find articles by who wrote them, the author is the choice for the partition key. This distribution makes your primary key `author_id, id` because the partition key is the first entry in the primary key.

`article_summaries_by_date` and `article_summaries_by_score`, in what may be the least surprising statement of the book, present a choice similar to `article_summaries_by_author` with a similar solution. Because you're querying `article_summaries_by_date` by the date of the article, you want the data partitioned by it as well, making the primary key `date, id`, or `score, id` for `article_summaries_by_score`.

> ## Right-sizing partitions
>
> If a partition is too large, data will be unevenly distributed across the cluster. If a partition is too small, range scans that load multiple rows may need several queries to load the desired amount of data. Consider querying for articles by date—if you publish one article a week but your partition key is per day, then querying for the most recent articles will require queries with no results six times out of seven.
>
> Partitioning your data is a balancing exercise. Sometimes it's easy. `author_id` is a natural partition key for articles by author, whereas something like `date` may require finessing to get the best performance in your application. Another problem to consider is one partition taking an outsized amount of traffic—more than the node can handle. In the upcoming chapters, as you refine your design, you'll learn how to adjust your partition key to fit your database just right.

After looking closely at the tables, your primary keys are now ordered correctly to partition the data; see table 3.4.

**The lines connecting the query
and the nodes show the nodes
required to fulfill the query.**

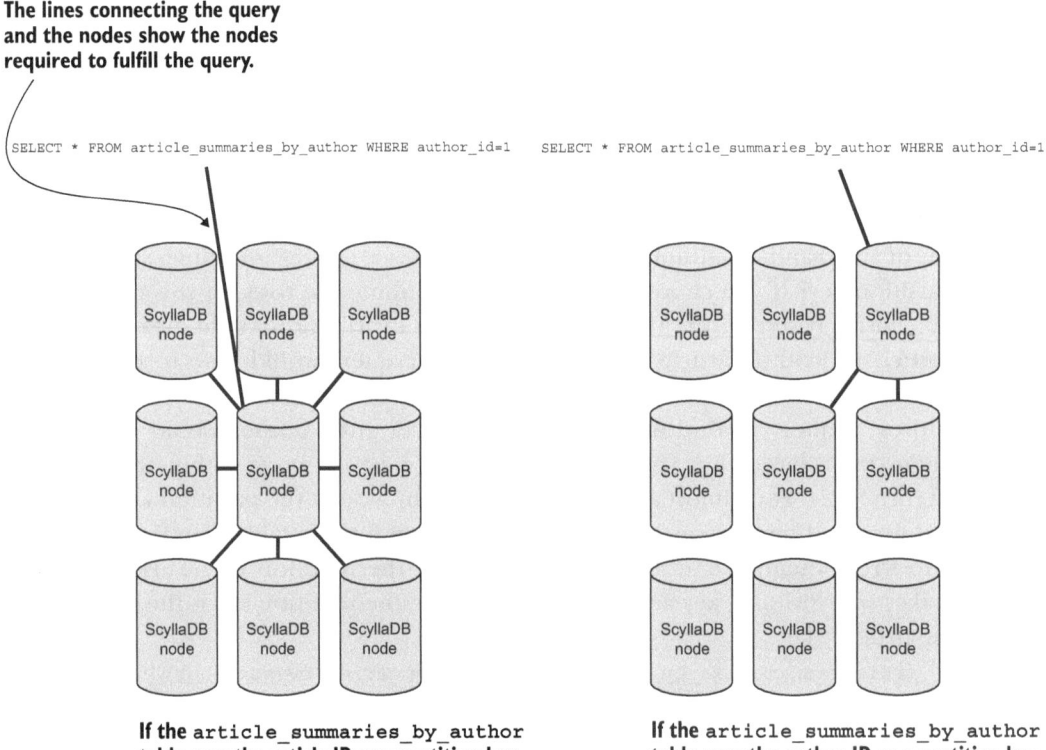

```
SELECT * FROM article_summaries_by_author WHERE author_id=1     SELECT * FROM article_summaries_by_author WHERE author_id=1
```

If the `article_summaries_by_author`
table uses the article ID as a partition key,
your queries need to scan every partition
in the cluster when querying by author ID.

If the `article_summaries_by_author`
table uses the author ID as a partition key,
Scylla is able to route queries directly to
the nodes that own the partitons.

Figure 3.12   The partition key for each table should match the queries you previously determined to achieve the best performance.

Table 3.4   The partition key is the first value listed in the primary key for each table.

Table	Primary key	Partition key
articles	id	id
authors	id	id
article_summaries_by_author	author_id, id	author_id
article_summaries_by_date	date, id	date
article_summaries_by_score	score, id	score

For the article summaries tables, your primary keys are divided into two categories—partition key and not-partition key. The leftover bit has an official name and performs a specific function in your table. Let's take a look at the non-partition keys—*clustering keys*.

CLUSTERING KEYS

A clustering key is the non-partition key part of a table's primary key that defines the ordering of the rows in the table. In the previous chapter, when you looked at your example table, you noticed that Scylla had filled in the table's implicit configuration, ordering the non-partition key columns—the clustering keys—by ascending order:

```
CREATE TABLE initial.food_reviews (        You defined
    restaurant text,                       the table.
    ordered_at timestamp,
    food text,
    review text,
    PRIMARY KEY (restaurant, ordered_at, food)     Scylla filled
) WITH CLUSTERING ORDER BY (ordered_at ASC, food ASC);   in this line.
```

Within the partition, each row is sorted by its time ordered and then by the name of the food, each in an ascending sort (so earlier order times and alphabetically by food). Left to its own devices, ScyllaDB always defaults to the ascending natural order of the clustering keys.

When creating tables, if you have clustering keys, you need to be intentional about specifying their order to make sure you're getting results that match your requirements. Consider `article_summaries_by_author`. The purpose of that table is to retrieve the articles for a given author, but do you want to see their oldest articles first or their newest ones? By default, Scylla is going to sort the table by id ASC, giving you the old articles first. When creating your summary tables, specify their sort orders so you get the newest articles first: id DESC.

You now have tables defined, and with those tables, the primary keys and partition keys are set to specify uniqueness, distribute the data, and order the data within the partition. Your queries, however, are looking for more than just primary keys: authors have names, and articles have titles and content. Not only do you need to store these fields, but you also need to specify the structure of that data. To accomplish this definition, you'll use data types. In the next chapter, you'll learn all about them and continue practicing query-first design.

Summary

- In Scylla, how you query your data drives how you store it. A well-designed database schema distributes data across the cluster and queries the minimal amount of nodes for your desired consistency level.
- Query-first design looks first at the queries your application needs and derives the tables and data from those queries, helping you design a schema that best utilizes ScyllaDB.
- The first step of query-first design takes each requirement and identifies which database query, if any, is needed to support it.
- The nouns your queries act on—in the example, the articles, article summaries, and authors—often become tables in the next step of the design.

- Because Scylla queries only query one table at a time, if you need to load data by different attributes, you must denormalize your data, storing the same data in multiple places to query it in different ways. Without denormalization, a query that didn't use the primary key would need to scan every partition in the cluster.

- Scylla distributes data via a hash ring where nodes sign up to manage slices of the ring. Partitions are assigned to a spot on the ring and therefore a node, based on the hashed value of their partition key.

- Nodes join the ring at multiple spots as virtual nodes or vnodes, which lets the cluster manage many smaller chunks and better balance the load across the cluster.

- Query-first design continues by taking the tables and seeing how they can be uniquely identified to create a primary key and how they can create small and mostly uniform partitions via a partition key.

- Scylla sorts data in a table by the clustering key: the non-partition key portion of the primary key.

Data types in ScyllaDB

This chapter covers
- The basic types ScyllaDB uses to store strings, numbers, dates, IDs, and more
- The collection types Scylla uses to aggregate data
- When to use each of these types to fit your design's needs

In the last chapter, you learned about query-first design, using it to expand your restaurant review database into the beginnings of a database schema for a full-blown restaurant review application. Starting with the requirements, you determined the queries your app needed to run, the tables those queries run against, and the primary keys for those tables. The chapter ended on a cliffhanger: what data goes into those tables, and what are the data types associated with that data? Here, you'll learn the answer to those great mysteries.

In this chapter, you'll focus on the fifth question of query-first design (figure 4.1): what data goes in these tables? To answer this question, you need to know what data types ScyllaDB supports so that you can best represent your data in your schema.

The most basic building blocks of data modeling are the values and the types you give them. In Scylla, every column has a type, and every value in that column

Query-first design involves determining your application's queries first and using them to build a database schema.

Determining your fields and data types is this chapter's focus

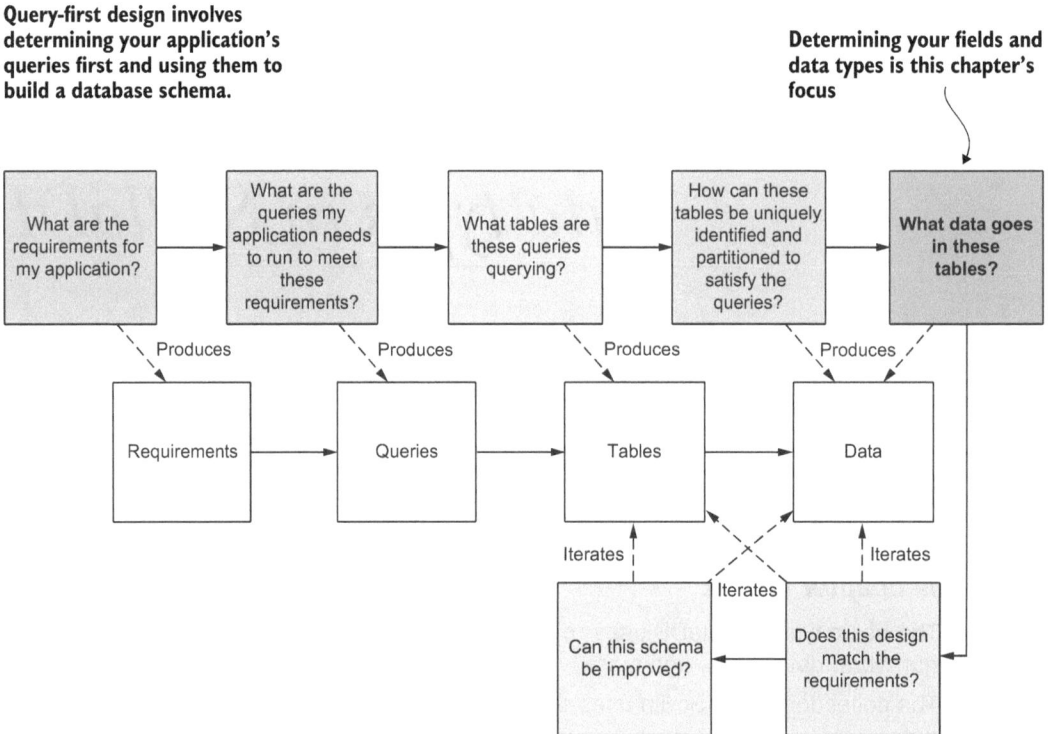

Figure 4.1   **Having designed your tables and queries, it's time to determine the data types and fields you need to store.**

shares that type. Scylla supports a rich variety of types—more than just numbers and text. In this chapter, you'll explore the tools you have to give meaning to your data.

4.1 Preparing yourself

To make your learning hands-on, you're going to build a one-off keyspace for this chapter to try out Scylla's data types. As you learn about the various types, you'll see them in action in your data-type playground. With your new keyspace and tables set up, you can proceed to determine the data types your restaurant application needs. First, though, you need to resurrect the database cluster from chapter 2 and create your new data-type exploration keyspace.

4.1.1 Data-type playground

To begin creating your sandbox, if it's not already running, dust off your Docker Scyl-laDB cluster from chapter 2 and start it back up. Using `docker start`, you can restart any stopped containers:

```
docker start scylla-1
```

Repeat the process for `scylla-2` and `scylla-3` to get your cluster back in action. Note that you can also use `docker-compose up`, using the code repo's included compose.yml file to resurrect your cluster.

To experiment with data types, you're going to begin by creating a new `types` keyspace to hold some test tables. You can set the replication factor to `1`; this is purely a playground for you:

```
cqlsh> CREATE KEYSPACE types WITH replication =
  {'class': 'SimpleStrategy', 'replication_factor': 1};
```

If you tell `cqlsh` to `USE` your new keyspace, you won't have to prefix your table names with their keyspace. I am going to run this `USE` command, and the following examples assume you have as well:

```
cqlsh> USE types;
```

If you look closely, you'll notice that `cqlsh`'s prompt has updated to reflect that you're using the `types` keyspace, as follows:

```
cqlsh:types>
```

Having created the keyspace, you can create a table containing many of the types ScyllaDB supports (listing 4.1). Some aren't included here, but you'll learn about them later in the chapter. You can use this to explore and poke at the various types ScyllaDB offers. Don't worry too much about the meaning of all these types at the moment; they will be covered soon. If you're the kind of person who looks up movie spoilers before watching a movie, I've annotated the code with explanations of each of the different types.

Listing 4.1 **Table to play around with data types**

```
cqlsh:types> CREATE TABLE basic(
    text TEXT,                 ⟵── TEXT is a UTF-8 encoded string.

    ascii ASCII,           ⟵── ASCII is an ASCII-encoded string.

    bigint BIGINT,           ⟵── BIGINT is a 64-bit signed integer.

    blob BLOB,               ⟵── BLOB stores arbitrary bytes.

    boolean BOOLEAN,         ⟵── BOOLEAN is the traditional true or false.

    date DATE,           ⟵── DATE represents a date.

    decimal DECIMAL,         ⟵── DECIMAL represents a floating-point number with
                                 arbitrary precision, enabling accurate calculations.

    double DOUBLE,           ⟵── DOUBLE is a double-precision floating-point number.

    duration DURATION,         ⟵── DURATION is a length of time.
```

```
float FLOAT,          ⟵———  FLOAT is a single-precision floating-point number.

inet INET,           ⟵———  INET represents an IP address in IPv4 or IPv6 format.

int INT,          ⟵———  INT is a signed 32-bit integer.

smallint SMALLINT,       ⟵———  SMALLINT is a signed 16-bit integer.

time TIME,        ⟵———  TIME represents a moment in time without a date.

timestamp TIMESTAMP,       ⟵———  TIMESTAMP combines a date and a time.

timeuuid TIMEUUID,        ⟵———  TIMEUUID is a version 1 UUID.

tinyint TINYINT,        ⟵———  TINYINT is a signed 8-bit integer.

uuid UUID,        ⟵——|  UUID represents any valid UUID but
                         |  is typically a version 4 UUID.

varchar VARCHAR,          ⟵——┐  VARCHAR is a UTF-8 encoded string.

varint VARINT,          ⟵——┐  VARINT is a variable-precision integer.

PRIMARY KEY (text)
);
```

You now have a playground in that table for almost all of ScyllaDB's basic types. One thing you may be worried about, having seen all the columns, is having to populate every column in every insert statement. Luckily for you, every column in Scylla—except the primary key's columns—is nullable. You can skip setting a value, and Scylla won't even insert null: it will skip writing a value altogether for that column. This is nice for learning!

With your data-type playground, you've got something practical to try what you learn as you continue implementing query-first design and determining your columns for the restaurant review application. Let's refresh ourselves on that and get to work learning about data types!

4.1.2 Identifying the fields

In the last chapter, you learned how to apply query-first design to develop a database schema for your restaurant review application. At the end of the chapter, you had designed queries and tables from these requirements, as seen in figure 4.2.

You started with the following requirements:

- Authors post articles to the website.
- Users view articles to read restaurant reviews.
- Articles contain a title, an author, a score, a date, a gallery of images, the review text, and the restaurant.

By following query-first design principles, you took an idea
for a restaurant review application and translated it into
requirements, queries, and the beginnings of your tables.

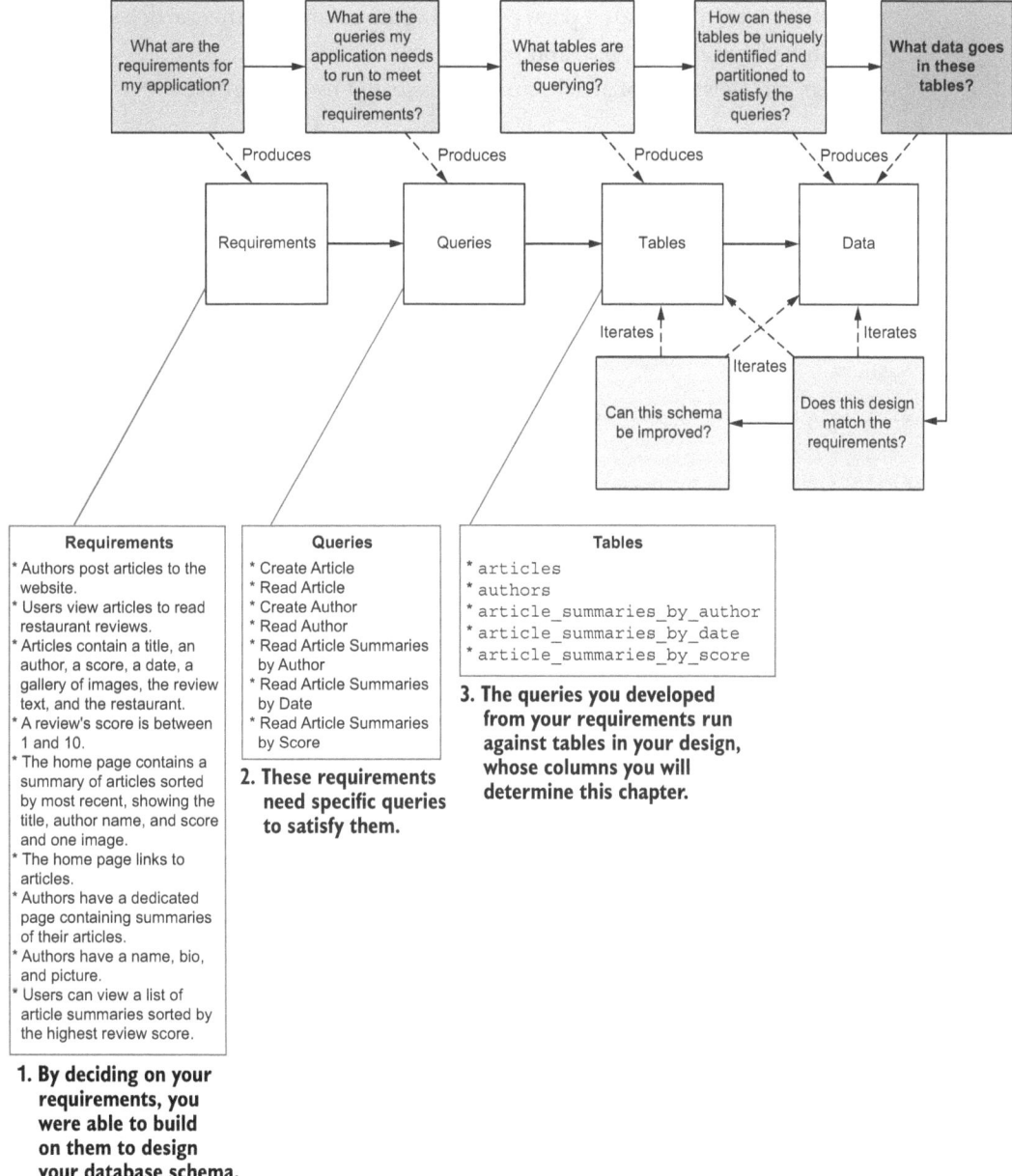

Figure 4.2   In the preceding chapter, you followed query-first design to produce several queries and tables.

- A review's score is between 1 and 10.
- The home page contains a summary of articles sorted by most recent, showing the title, the author name, the score, and one image.
- The home page links to articles.
- Authors have a dedicated page containing summaries of their articles.
- Authors have a name, bio, and picture.
- Users can view a list of article summaries sorted by the highest review score.

Given these requirements, you mapped several queries that your application needs to execute to the tables those queries will run against (table 4.1).

Table 4.1   Mapping tables to queries

Table	Queries
articles	Create Article, Read Article
authors	Create Author, Read Author
article_summaries_by_author	Create Article Summary, Read Article Summaries by Author
article_summaries_by_date	Create Article Summary, Read Article Summaries by Date
article_summaries_by_score	Create Article Summary, Read Article Summaries by Score

In this chapter, your focus is on what data goes in those tables. Not only do you need the fields, but you also need the data type for each column so that you can structure your data appropriately.

Looking at the requirements again, you can get halfway to your goal by listing the fields you need. The third requirement—articles contain a title, an author, a score, a date, a gallery of images, the review text, and the restaurant—is immediately very helpful, listing a variety of fields you need to store. Some of them seem straightforward, like the title and review text, but how do you represent a gallery of images in a ScyllaDB column? Don't despair: you'll learn techniques to do just that later in the chapter.

Article summaries, in their tables sorted by author, date, and score, have similar fields. Your requirements say that users will view summaries showing the title, the author name, the score, and one image. It stands to reason that the data types used for the fields in articles and summaries will be very similar, but what will those types be?

Authors also need fields. The requirements say that an author has a name, bio, and picture. You also have implicit fields that aren't exactly in the requirements but are needed to fulfill them, such as fields for a primary key and a partition key. You need an article ID, an article summary ID, an author ID, as well as the article summary date. Putting it together, you need the fields listed in table 4.2.

Table 4.2   Mapping tables to fields

Table	Fields
`articles`	ID, title, author ID, score, date, image gallery, review text, restaurant
`authors`	ID, name, bio, image
`article_summaries_by_author`	author ID, article ID, title, author name, score, image
`article_summaries_by_date`	date, article ID, title, author name, score, image
`article_summaries_by_score`	score, article ID, title, author name, image`

With these fields, all you need now are the data types. Although you can probably guess some of them—you're not going to store review text as an integer—let's use these to introduce Scylla's data types. First up is how Scylla handles text and numbers.

4.2   The most common types: Text and numbers

Text and numbers are the most commonly used types in many applications. Scylla and CQL's representation of them, however, is nuanced, offering different sizes and variations to fit your needs.

You have several types that you can store as either text or a numeric value: article title, review text, restaurant, review score, author name, author bio, and others. Let's first look at the text types Scylla supports.

4.2.1   Text

As you look to store your text-based fields—author name, author bio, article text, reviewed restaurant name—ScyllaDB provides two string-based types for the discerning data modeler:

- TEXT—A UTF-8 encoded string (VARCHAR is also provided as an alias, as that name for this data type is frequently used in SQL databases)
- ASCII—An ASCII-encoded string

To see the text types in action, you can insert TEXT and ASCII into your basic data-type playground. What's the point of having multiple text types? If each can handle valid text, why does Scylla offer multiple options? The difference between ASCII and UTF-8 is that an ASCII character is limited to 1 of 128 options, whereas a UTF-8 character supports over a million possibilities. To see both types in action, you can insert one of each type into your table.

Note in the following example that each string needs to be wrapped in single quotes:

```
cqlsh:types> INSERT INTO basic(text, ascii)
  VALUES ('utf-8 encoded', 'ascii encoded');
```

If you read back your text, you'll get what you insert: valid text. Each field has the value passed in, which is a good thing for a database to give you:

```
cqlsh:types> SELECT text, ascii FROM basic
  WHERE text = 'utf-8 encoded';

@ Row 1
-------+---------------
 text  | utf-8 encoded
 ascii | ascii encoded

(1 rows)
```

If you insert a non-ASCII string—such as the word résumé—into an ASCII-typed field, you'd expect to see some sort of error, and sure enough, you would:

```
cqlsh:types> INSERT INTO basic(text, ascii)
   VALUES ('résumé', 'résumé');

InvalidRequest: Error from server: code=2200 [Invalid query]
message="marshaling error: Value not compatible with type
org.apache.cassandra.db.marshal.AsciiType: 'résumé'"
```

Types not only provide structure to your schema; they also provide validation. If the database can stop you from making an error with a type, that strengthens the integrity of your data. Many of Scylla's types contain validations to stop you from putting invalid values into the database.

In general, you should stay away from ASCII. Many a software bug has been caused by a system expecting ASCII and getting UTF-8. Unless you have a strong reason to make the type ASCII, prefer using TEXT instead of ASCII. Accordingly, your text-based types—article review, author names, and so on—should all use TEXT. With that decision made, you can see what fields now have types and which ones still need them in table 4.3.

Table 4.3   The types you've elected to use for your fields thus far

Article ID	
Article title	TEXT
Article author ID	
Article score	
Article date	
Article image gallery	
Article review text	TEXT
Article restaurant	TEXT
Author ID	

Table 4.3   The types you've elected to use for your fields thus far *(continued)*

Author name	TEXT
Author bio	TEXT
Author image	

You've sorted out several of the types you need; you use text fields a lot, and TEXT is a great fit. Next, let's look at how ScyllaDB stores numbers and your options for saving review scores.

4.2.2   Numbers

To store the review score, you want to save it as a number. Although it's tempting to think of numbers as not having any differentiating characteristics besides their values, Scylla has several different types for storing numbers, offering different sizes and precisions. There are four integer types in order of increasing size: TINYINT, SMALLINT, INT, and BIGINT (table 4.4). Each of these is a *signed integer*, meaning they can represent either positive or negative numbers.

Table 4.4   The four integer types in CQL

Type	Size	Minimum value	Maximum value
TINYINT	8-bit	-128	127
SMALLINT	16-bit	-32,768	32,767
INT	32-bit	-2,147,483,648	2,147,483,647
BIGINT	64-bit	-9,223,372,036,854,775,808	9,223,372,036,854,775,807

If you insert each of these types into the database, you'll see they behave as you expect:

```
cqlsh:types> INSERT INTO basic(text, tinyint, smallint, int, bigint)
  VALUES ('integers', 6, 10000, 50000, 3000000000);
```

When you read them, you get back your numbers, just as you sent them:

```
cqlsh:types> SELECT text, tinyint, smallint, int, bigint
  FROM basic WHERE text = 'integers';

@ Row 1
----------+------------
 text     | integers
 tinyint  | 6
 smallint | 10000
 int      | 50000
 bigint   | 3000000000

(1 rows)
```

Based on your experience with ASCII, the minimum and maximum values in the preceding table may suggest to you that Scylla validates each integer to verify that it remains within the supported bounds. You're correct; you can see this in action if you try to insert a too-large value into TINYINT, the smallest integer. Trying to write an invalid number triggers a database error:

```
cqlsh:types> INSERT INTO basic(text, tinyint)
  VALUES ('not so tiny int', 5000);

InvalidRequest: Error from server: code=2200 [Invalid query]
➥ message="marshaling error: Value out of range for the type
➥ org.apache.cassandra.db.marshal.ByteType: '5000'"
```

When the value is out of range, Scylla will not let you insert it. Feel free to try this on your own for the other integer types.

Your review score is a value between 1 and 10, but is 7.5 a valid value? Not every number is an integer, so Scylla also supports floating-point numbers via its FLOAT and DOUBLE types. FLOAT is a 32-bit single-precision floating-point number, and DOUBLE is a 64-bit double-precision floating-point number (each with the standard IEEE 754 encoding). Let's see them in action and insert one of each into the database:

```
cqlsh:types> INSERT INTO basic(text, float, double)
  VALUES ('floats', 123.4, 567.8);
```

Continuing a common theme, when you read your floating-point numbers, they are the numbers you inserted:

```
cqlsh:types> SELECT text, float, double FROM basic WHERE text = 'floats';

@ Row 1
--------+--------
 text   | floats
 float  | 123.4
 double | 567.8

(1 rows)
```

Just because a number has a decimal point does not mean it should be stored as a FLOAT or a DOUBLE, however. These numbers have a limited size and sometimes cannot be represented accurately due to their limited precision, leading to rounding errors. You may have seen slightly inaccurate results with floating-point math in other programming languages. To solve this problem, you have two options:

- You can represent your number as an integer and convert it to a floating point later (such as when displaying it to users). A common way to store monetary values is to store them as their base unit (for example, cents for USD) and format the value appropriately in a string when displaying it to a user.

- You can use CQL's DECIMAL type. The DECIMAL type supports any width, meaning it will grow to the necessary size to represent its value precisely.

When storing data as a decimal point value, if accuracy is important—perhaps you're choosing to store monetary values —you can use the DECIMAL type to ensure accuracy.

Another form of accuracy is being able to represent very large values accurately. BIGINT can store numbers up to 9,223,372,036,854,775,807, but what happens if you need to go beyond that? DECIMAL and VARINT can come in handy here; they can each hold values of arbitrarily large sizes. Although this may be a rare case, it's nice to have a type that fits your very, very, very large numeric needs.

When selecting numeric types, it's important to choose those that fit your use case. If you're going to have more than 2 billion of something, don't use an INT for it. At the same time, if a TINYINT works for a column, you should probably avoid using a BIGINT. If you use a number that's too big, you're wasting space in your database. If you use a number that's too small, your queries will eventually fail when that number becomes larger than what its data type can hold. Think carefully about what your number's bounds are now and what they may grow to be in the future.

Despite all these number types, you're looking for only one. What fits best for a review score? Your requirements say that a review score is a number between 1 and 10. Keeping in mind the guidelines from earlier, you want to use a data type that fits what you need. The requirements are ambiguous, though: 7.5 is a valid number between 1 and 10.

You may support 7.5, but you're unlikely to support a review score of 7.54: your rating system isn't nuanced enough to measure to the hundredth of a point. A TINYINT is a good fit here; if you store the review score between 1 and 100, you can convert your scores to the 10-point scale in your application, outside the database, and forgo any of the floating-point complications. With that decision made, you're a little closer to knowing all your data types (table 4.5).

Table 4.5   The types to use for each field, having selected TINYINT for the article score.

Article ID	
Article title	TEXT
Article author ID	
Article score	TINYINT
Article date	
Article image gallery	
Article review text	TEXT
Article restaurant	TEXT
Author ID	

Table 4.5   The types to use for each field, having selected TINYINT for the article score. *(continued)*

Author name	TEXT
Author bio	TEXT
Author image	

Looking at the remaining fields, you see some types that may make sense, such as numbers or text. If you're familiar with autoincrementing integers being used as IDs in primary keys, you may be thinking of using that approach; or you may think you can store the date as text, like `'2023-07-23'`. Hold your horses! ScyllaDB has many other types to fit your needs, including several ways to deal with time. Let's look at how Scylla represents dates and time to figure out what works best for storing article dates.

4.3   Dates and times

Working with time is tricky as a programmer—with time zones, leap seconds, and out-of-sync clocks, there are almost as many pitfalls as there are seconds in a day. To make it easier to work with dates and times, ScyllaDB supports a few time- and date-centric data types (table 4.6) to simplify storing article dates.

When it's time to store a moment in time, ScyllaDB provides four types:

- TIMESTAMP—A date and a UTC-based time
- DATE—A date with no time
- TIME—A time with no date
- DURATION—A length of time not associated with a date

Table 4.6   Table times

Type	Stored as	Acceptable forms
TIMESTAMP	BIGINT representing the number of milliseconds since the Unix epoch (1970-01-01 00:00:00+0000)	1687654894759, '2023-06-24 21:02:00+0000' and other ISO-8601 compliant timestamps
DATE	32-bit unsigned integer representing the number of days since the Unix epoch (1970-01-01), with the epoch in the center of the range (2^31)	'2023-06-24', 641
TIME	64-bit signed integer representing the number of nanoseconds since midnight	'21:07:12.123' with either second, millisecond, microsecond, or nanosecond precision, 76032123000
DURATION	Three integers representing the number of months, the number of days, and the number of nanoseconds	1y4mo3w5d3h6m19s400ms20us141ns or any combination of the units

4.3.1 *Working with dates and times*

To insert the non-DURATION time types into the database, you can insert an ISO-8601-compliant string such as 2023-06-24 for a DATE or 21:07:12.123 for a TIME. You can also insert each as the underlying integer type. This approach is common for timestamps, which are stored across many systems as *epoch seconds* or *epoch milliseconds*, the number of seconds or milliseconds, respectively, since a moment in time called the UNIX epoch (1970-01-01 00:00:00+0000). You can insert one of each to see these types in action:

```
cqlsh:types> INSERT INTO BASIC(text, timestamp, date, time)
  VALUES ('time', '2023-06-25 10:31:00+0000', '2023-06-25', '10:31:00');
```

> **NOTE** When working with timestamps, it's best to specify the time zone via the four-digit time zone specification (+0000, -0500, etc.). If it isn't set, Scylla uses whatever the underlying system is currently configured to use.

When you query your times again, you'll see that cqlsh has expanded them to their highest precision, keeping track of microseconds for TIMESTAMP and nanoseconds for TIME:

```
cqlsh:types> SELECT text, timestamp, date, time FROM basic
  WHERE text = 'time';

@ Row 1
-----------+--------------------------------
 text      | time
 timestamp | 2023-06-25 10:31:00.000000+0000
 date      | 2023-06-25
 time      | 10:31:00.000000000

(1 rows)
```

This behavior remains no matter how you insert the times. If you insert a TIMESTAMP as epoch milliseconds, cqlsh renders it in the more user-friendly string format:

```
cqlsh:types> INSERT INTO basic(text, timestamp)
  VALUES('epoch milliseconds', 1687754894759);
```

No need to copy the value into a converter: cqlsh converts it into the timestamp string:

```
cqlsh:types> SELECT text, timestamp FROM basic
  WHERE text = 'epoch milliseconds';

@ Row 1
-----------+--------------------------------
 text      | epoch milliseconds
 timestamp | 2023-06-25 01:01:34.759000+0000

(1 rows)
```

This conversion is why you should use ScyllaDB's time types and not try to use the underlying integer types directly or roll your own. If you insert a date or a time, ScyllaDB formats it correctly for you when viewing, making it easier to understand visually. It also validates the time, preventing you from inserting an incorrectly formatted value.

> ### Converting times
> Scylla contains a few functions to make converting between time types easier. You'll see these in action throughout the book—in fact, you'll use one of them soon:
>
> - `toDate()` takes a `TIMESTAMP` or a `TIMEUUID` (a type you'll learn about momentarily) and converts it to a `DATE`.
> - `toTimestamp()` takes a `DATE` or a `TIMEUUID` and converts it to a `TIMESTAMP`.
> - `toUnixTimestamp()` can convert a `DATE`, `TIMESTAMP`, or `UUID` to a `BIGINT` representing the Unix epoch time.

4.3.2   *Durations*

Scylla also supports storing a `DURATION`: a length of time. You store a duration via a special syntax that describes lengths of time (table 4.7). For example, `5h6m` corresponds to a duration of five hours and six minutes.

Table 4.7   **Each unit of time has an abbreviation**

Unit	Abbreviation
Year	y
Month	mo
Week	w
Day	d
Hour	h
Minute	m
Second	s
Millisecond	ms
Microsecond	us or μs
Nanosecond	ns

Let's store a duration in the database. It's important to note this data type this isn't a string, despite containing letters and numbers. It must be stored as a constant without quotes:

```
cqlsh:types> INSERT INTO basic(text, duration) VALUES('duration', 13d5h);
```

You stored 13 days and 5 hours. When you read it back, that's exactly what you get:

```
cqlsh:types> SELECT text, duration FROM basic WHERE text = 'duration';

@ Row 1
----------+----------
 text     | duration
 duration | 13d5h

(1 rows)
```

> **NOTE** Durations can't be used in primary keys because they can't be ordered. Is 30 days greater than 1 month? It depends on the month: January has 31 days, but February has 28 (and sometimes one more!). Durations need the extra context of a date to determine an ordering.

When is storing a duration valuable? If you want to store a length of time, a DURATION is potentially a good fit. Imagine that you decide to track how long it takes to receive your food in restaurant reviews to see if fast food establishments are truly fast. You can store a `time_to_receive_food` value as a DURATION. This type lets you specify that duration using clear units: if it takes 5 minutes and 4 seconds, you can store it as `5m4s`. Without a DURATION type, your options either require additional work to compute and convert (suppose you stored it as an integer representing the number of seconds you waited for your food) or lack validation (if you stored that value as a string).

4.3.3 *When to use timestamps, dates, and times*

Given these four time types—TIMESTAMP, DATE, TIME, and DURATION—one of them must work well for storing the article date. Of the date and time types, there's not one you should generally prefer over the other; each has a specific use case, and you should use the one that matches your use case. TIMESTAMP is good when you need to store a specific date and time, whereas DATE and TIME are more specific dates and times, respectively, without the need for the other. Finally, DURATION is useful when you want to store a specific duration of time. With these cases in mind, what works well for your article date?

Because you're storing only a date for the article, DATE is the clear winner. You probably do not care what time of day the article was published, so TIMESTAMP contains unnecessary information. TIME and DURATION do not tell you the date, so they're immediately out of the game. DATE gives the information you need and nothing more; plus, all the others have been ruled out. Having determined that in a shocking upset, DATE is a good match for the article date, you've gotten one step closer to filling out your data-type checklist (table 4.8).

Table 4.8   The types to use for each field, having selected DATE for
the article date

Article ID	
Article title	TEXT
Article author ID	
Article score	TINYINT
Article date	DATE
Article image gallery	
Article review text	TEXT
Article restaurant	TEXT
Author ID	
Author name	TEXT
Author bio	TEXT
Author image	

Several of the remaining fields reference an ID in their names, so let's look at some
support ScyllaDB provides for IDs.

4.4   IDs

A common technique in data modeling is representing an entity with a unique identifier so that you can uniquely identify it; it's in the name! ScyllaDB's most popular ID
scheme is native to the database: universally unique identifiers (UUIDs) (https://
datatracker.ietf.org/doc/html/rfc9562). A UUID can provide both ordering and
uniqueness at the cost of obfuscating its meaning: it's a seemingly random string of
hexadecimal characters. In this section, you'll learn not just about UUIDs but also
about other methods of storing IDs in ScyllaDB. First, let's look at UUIDs and why
they are so useful in Scylla.

4.4.1   UUIDs

A UUID is a 36-character hexadecimal identifier containing 32 hexadecimal characters and 4 hyphens. The characters have a specific order: the UUID starts with a group
of 8, followed by three groups of 4, and ends with a group of 12. Each group is separated by a hyphen.

> **NOTE** Under the hood, Scylla stores UUIDs as 128-bit entries of binary data.

ScyllaDB supports UUIDs in two types: UUID and TIMEUUID. A UUID can be any type of
UUID, but its usage typically corresponds to version 4, where almost the entirety of
the UUID is randomly generated. A TIMEUUID is an implementation of a version 1

UUID, which contains a timestamp component in the identifier. TIMEUUIDs can be sorted temporally, so you can give a row a conflict-free timestamp.

> **NOTE** In this book, UUID refers to the specific data type in ScyllaDB, and UUID refers to the concept as implemented in various other systems. If you'd like to read more about the differences in the various versions of UUIDs (we'll only be using versions 1 and 4), I've found this article to be a helpful read: www.uuidtools.com/uuid-versions-explained.

Why is a conflict-free timestamp important? If a value is conflict-free, that means it doesn't have the same value as other values of that type: it's unique. Primary keys require uniqueness, and if a TIMEUUID is conflict-free, it can serve as the primary key for a row (and by extension, a partition key as well). The fact that it encodes a time-stamp within it is also critical. It allows you to order your data by the timestamp in TIMEUUID, letting you, for example, store article IDs as a TIMEUUID and get the most recent articles only by sorting by their IDs.

What about uniqueness in a UUID? Because they're random, there is a chance of a collision, but it is infinitesimal. A UUID contains 122 bits of randomness—that's a lot! You'd need to generate 2.7 quintillion IDs to even get a 50% chance of a collision. You may be concerned about this, but it's really, really, really, really, really unlikely.

Scylla contains functions to help with both UUID and TIMEUUID. For a UUID, you can call the uuid() function, giving you a random UUID. If you call now(), Scylla gives you a TIMEUUID built from the MAC address of the hardware and the current time. Let's see them in action:

```
cqlsh: types> INSERT INTO basic(text, uuid, timeuuid)
  VALUES ('uuids', uuid(), now());
```

When you load the row, you'll see your generated UUIDs. It is almost certain that everyone who reads this book and follows this example will see a different UUID:

```
cqlsh:types> SELECT text, uuid, timeuuid FROM basic WHERE text = 'uuids';

@ Row 1
----------+--------------------------------------
 text     | uuids
 uuid     | e2672c94-8699-4d78-bc08-fefd07519d90
 timeuuid | 01c23f50-3d66-11ee-8569-f853395f6f49

(1 rows)
```

For TIMEUUID, Scylla also supports extracting the time from the identifier via its toTimestamp function, which you can see in action:

```
cqlsh:types> SELECT text, toTimestamp(timeuuid)
  FROM basic where text = 'uuids';
```

Instead of the big hexadecimal string from the previous example, Scylla has extracted the time and formatted it into something easy to read. Note the column name; it is explicit about telling you that the value is the result of a function:

```
@ Row 1
------------------------------+--------------------------------
 text                         | uuids
 system.totimestamp(timeuuid) | 2023-08-18 01:24:42.053000+0000

(1 rows)
```

If you've worked with a relational database previously, you may be familiar with the database generating integer keys for you. This approach is similar, except instead of an autoincrementing integer key, it's a random and unique TIMEUUID or a so-random-as-to-almost-be-unique UUID.

> **NOTE**   To see why Scylla would struggle with an autoincrementing integer key, stay tuned for the performance challenges with Scylla's counter type.

The downside of letting the database generate the IDs is that your application can't know the generated IDs without reading the row. If you're using that generated value as a primary key, you won't be able to read that single row because you won't know the primary key. Let's examine this problem with pseudo-code.

Imagine that a new author is publishing their first article. As an application developer, let's pretend you have three potentially relevant queries at your disposal, which you trigger via function calls in your language:

- create_author(author...) inserts an author via the query INSERT INTO authors(…) VALUES (uuid(), ….);
- get_author(id...) loads an author by the ID via the query SELECT * FROM authors WHERE id = ?;
- create_article(article, author_id...) inserts an article via the query INSERT into articles(…) VALUES (uuid(), author_id, …)

When an author publishes their first article, you want to generate the author and then add their ID to the article. However, when you create the author, nothing informs you about the author ID. Even worse, to get the author ID, you have to load the author—but you load the author by ID!

```
def add_article_for_new_author(author, article):
    create_author(author)                      ⟵  Creating the author generates
                                                  an ID in the database, but
    article.author_id = ?    ⟵                   you can't see it.
                                 Because you don't know
                                 the author ID, you can't
    create_article(article)      set it on the article.
```

To avoid this problem, applications often choose to generate their IDs outside the database. By doing this generation in your application and not from within the database, you're not limited just to UUIDs but any type that provides uniqueness and ordering. Generating your IDs outside the database solves the unknown-until-read ID problem; you'll already know the ID because you're generating it yourself before inserting it.

UUIDs aren't exclusive to Scylla. Whether it's in a language's standard library or an additional dependency, the various programming languages you'd choose to write your application in can generate a valid version 1 (TIMEUUID) or version 4 (UUID) UUID.

Continuing the preceding example, you can solve the unknown ID problem by generating your IDs before writing the rows. Before each insert, you generate a UUID and attach it to the object you're about to save. You also modify your queries not to generate the IDs, instead saving whatever's passed into the query:

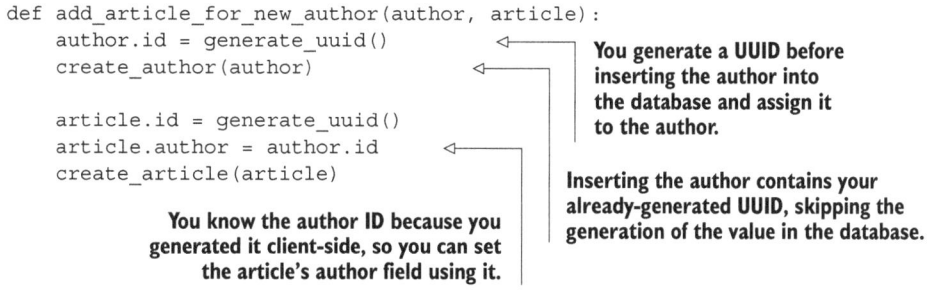

```
def add_article_for_new_author(author, article):
    author.id = generate_uuid()
    create_author(author)

    article.id = generate_uuid()
    article.author = author.id
    create_article(article)
```

You generate a UUID before inserting the author into the database and assign it to the author.

Inserting the author contains your already-generated UUID, skipping the generation of the value in the database.

You know the author ID because you generated it client-side, so you can set the article's author field using it.

Not just UUIDs

Generating your IDs from within your application is a common pattern. As long as you're generating unique (or statistically likely to be unique, in the case of a version 4 UUID) IDs, you're not limited to a UUID for an ID-like data type.

One alternative ID type is Twitter's Snowflake ID, a 64-bit integer that behaves similarly to TIMEUUID. Each ID encodes a timestamp, a worker number for the worker generating the IDs, and a sequence number. Combining these values gives a unique ID, sortable by time, and its generation can be scaled not to make ID generation a bottleneck. Additionally, snowflakes give greater visual clarity: because they're integers, it can be easy to make quick comparisons and say, "This value is older than this other value." The downside is complexity: generating IDs in this manner isn't free, frequently requiring network calls to a dedicated system for ID generation. (For more information about snowflakes, see https://blog.twitter.com/engineering/en_us/a/2010/announcing-snowflake/.)

We'll leave snowflakes here for the remainder of this book, but it's important to remember that an ID can be any data type that provides uniqueness and sortability.

Having learned about Scylla's UUID support, you can now determine which ID types work best for your application. Let's look at the fields you need to uniquely identify and choose the right data type.

4.4.2   *Picking an ID type*

When selecting which fields you needed to store for your restaurant reviews application, you identified three ID fields: article ID, article summary ID, and author ID. Having learned about UUIDs, which ID type will work well for these fields?

In choosing between UUID and TIMEUUID, you're deciding between a type that's predominantly random or a type that's ordered by time, with randomness providing uniqueness. If you recall your requirements, you want to show article summaries by the most recent date. If the ID is orderable by time, you can use that to sort rows by their recency. Using TIMEUUID will accomplish that, as opposed to the jumble from the randomness of UUID.

Should you use TIMEUUID for all your ID fields? I believe it's valuable to have that time encoded into the ID: it allows you to define temporal relationships between your data. As an application grows, being able to say, "This data was created before this other data" is frequently helpful. There are also occasions when a UUID suffices—when you don't need the time, just a quick, random identifier. And at the end of the day, TIMEUUID is only a UUID with extra time encoded in it. You can technically store a version 1 UUID in a UUID type; you just won't have the functions and validations from TIMEUUID. The downside with a TIMEUUID is that there's an upper bound of IDs generated per second: approximately 10 million. If you're generating more than this very high number, you may want to consider a different ID generation scheme.

Having picked TIMEUUID fields, you've almost completed your data-type checklist (table 4.9).

Table 4.9   The types to use for each field, having selected UUID for the various ID fields

Article ID	TIMEUUID
Article title	TEXT
Article author ID	TIMEUUID
Article score	TINYINT
Article date	DATE
Article image gallery	
Article review text	TEXT
Article restaurant	TEXT
Author ID	TIMEUUID
Author name	TEXT
Author bio	TEXT
Author image	

Last in your fields is an image. Storing an image using anything similar to the previous fields sounds very complicated. An image has lots of data associated with it: a file, resolution, caption, and so on. Luckily for you, ScyllaDB provides some higher-level types to simplify aggregating data together. To store images, you can use collection types.

4.5 Collections

Scylla's collection types are very similar to the collections in most programming languages; it offers a LIST, a MAP, and a SET. A LIST is an ordered collection of potentially nonunique values of a specific type. A SET is similar to a list, except it guarantees uniqueness. A MAP is a sorted set of keys and values. Each key is unique, and the map is sorted by key. You can see these differences in figure 4.3.

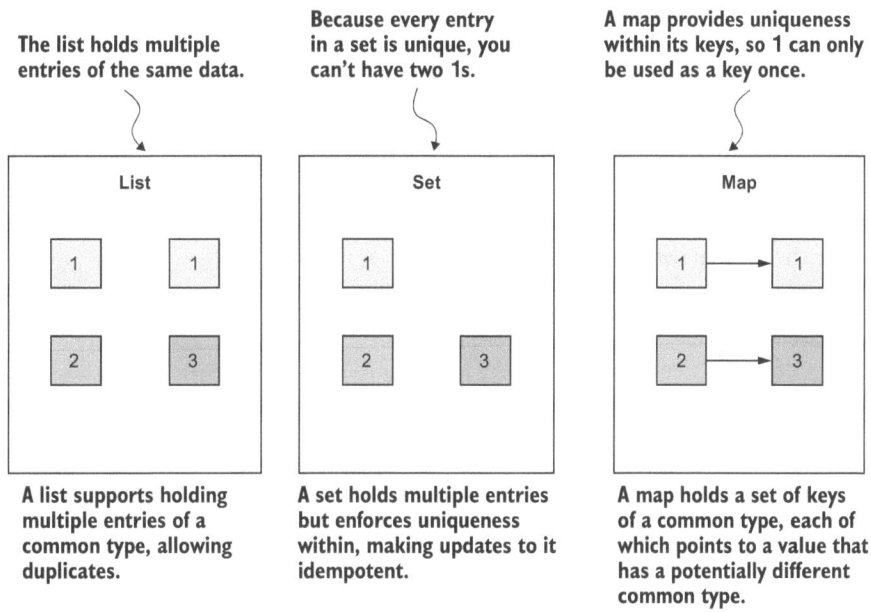

Figure 4.3 Scylla supports storing multiple values in its collection data types: lists, sets, and maps.

Although collections can store multiple items, they're not a replacement for tables. A collection works best for smaller amounts of data. If it will be a lot of data, or it's going to grow to an unknown amount, you're better off breaking it into its own table and giving it its own partition key or clustering keys to allow Scylla to optimize its performance.

Similar to the basic types, you can make a table to play with collections, as seen in listing 4.2. When declaring a collection type, you need to specify the type stored in the collection in angle brackets, like `<TEXT>`. For `LIST` and `SET`, which have only one type, you only need to list one type. For `MAP`, whose keys and values each have a type, you separate the types with commas. I've also named the `SET` column `set_text`—`set` is a reserved word in CQL; you've already used it in `UPDATE` statements.

Listing 4.2   Collection table to experiment with collections

```
cqlsh:types> CREATE TABLE collections(
    text TEXT,
    list LIST<TEXT>,
    set_text SET<TEXT>,
    map MAP<TEXT, TEXT>,
    PRIMARY KEY (text)
);
```

With your `collections` table created, you now have a place to try collection types. Keep your requirements in mind: store a gallery of images for an article.

4.5.1   *Lists*

Lists in CQL behave similarly to lists or vectors in programming languages. You specify a type for the contents of the list, and you can append, remove, access, and replace values at a specific index in the list. Let's begin by inserting an initial list into the table using the typical list bracket syntax:

```
cqlsh:types> INSERT INTO collections(text, list)
  VALUES ('list', ['a', 'b', 'c']);
```

Accessing your list shows you your three text entries: `'a'`, `'b'`, and `'c'`:

```
cqlsh:types> SELECT text, list FROM collections WHERE text = 'list';

@ Row 1
------+-----------------
 text | list
 list | ['a', 'b', 'c']

(1 rows)
```

With this list in the database, you can start to explore Scylla's list operations. You can concatenate two lists together, obtaining one combined list, by using the + operator. The following statement does this combination, adding `'d'` and `'e'` to the stored list:

```
cqlsh:types> UPDATE collections
  SET list = list + ['d', 'e']
  WHERE text = 'list';
```

> **NOTE**   If you had written your update query as …SET list = ['d', 'e'] + list…, it would have prepended `'d'` and `'e'` to the beginning of the list.

If you load the list again, you'll see that `'d'` and `'e'` have been added to the end of the list:

```
cqlsh:types> SELECT text, list FROM collections WHERE text = 'list';

@ Row 1
------+--------------------------
 text | list
 list | ['a', 'b', 'c', 'd', 'e']

(1 rows)
```

You were able to take the current state of the list and update it by taking its contents and appending another list. There's a pitfall here: this operation is not *idempotent*, meaning running it repeatedly will not produce the same state. If you ran this append five times in a row, you'd add five copies of `'d'` and `'e'`, which is potentially not ideal.

If you decide that having `'d'` and `'e'` in your list is no longer desired, you can remove items from the list using the opposite of the way you added them with the - operator. If an item isn't there, Scylla won't error, so feel free to try to delete `'f'` as well:

```
cqlsh:types> UPDATE collections
  SET list = list - ['d', 'e', 'f']
  WHERE text = 'list';
```

If you run your SELECT again, the no-longer-wanted `'d'` and `'e'` are gone:

```
cqlsh:types> SELECT text, list FROM collections WHERE text = 'list';

@ Row 1
------+-----------------
 text | list
 list | ['a', 'b', 'c']

(1 rows)
```

You can also replace values directly at a specific index in the list. If the index is out of bounds, you'll get an error, but if you want to replace the first entry in the list with `'z'`, you can run the following statement:

```
cqlsh:types> UPDATE collections SET list[0] = 'z' WHERE text = 'list';
```

Loading the list again gives you your updated list: `'z'`, `'b'`, and `'c'`:

```
cqlsh:types> SELECT text, list FROM collections WHERE text = 'list';

@ Row 1
------+-----------------
 text | list
 list | ['z', 'b', 'c']

(1 rows)
```

If you decide that 'z' isn't the right value to start your list, you can also delete a value from the list by its index. Go ahead and remove 'z' from the list:

```
cqlsh:types> DELETE list[0] FROM collections WHERE text = 'list';
```

When you load your list again, you're left with only 'b' and 'c':

```
cqlsh:types> SELECT text, list FROM collections WHERE text = 'list';
```

```
@ Row 1
------+------------
 text | list
 list | ['b', 'c']

(1 rows)
```

You can also skip the various accesses on individual portions of a list and replace the entire thing:

```
cqlsh:types> UPDATE collections
   SET list = ['a', 'b', 'c']
   WHERE text = 'list';
```

Loading the list again gives you back the original list: 'a', 'b', and 'c':

```
cqlsh:types> SELECT text, list FROM collections WHERE text = 'list';
```

```
@ Row 1
------+-----------------
 text | list
 list | ['a', 'b', 'c']

(1 rows)
```

It's safer to replace the entire list than to mutate individual elements. The non-idempotent properties of the list operations make it risky to use. If a query times out on the client but still completes in the database, it potentially isn't safe to run again if you're appending data or deleting from the list by index. Additionally, some list operations—such as updating a value at a given index—can trigger a read before the update, slowing down operations. These properties are why it's recommended to use a set, and not a list, whenever possible. Let's look closer at why a set is preferable.

4.5.2   Sets

Sets are very similar to maps, with two differences: each value in a set is unique in the set, and values in the set cannot be accessed directly. These properties prevent the treacherous access patterns from lists—adding is idempotent because you can't add duplicate values; and because you can't delete items by their position, deletes become idempotent as well.

Sets are represented with curly braces. Let's go ahead and insert your first set. Note that the column name is `set_text` because `set` is a reserved word in CQL:

```
cqlsh:types> INSERT INTO collections(text, set_text)
  VALUES ('set', {'a', 'b', 'c'});
```

Accessing your set shows your three text entries, just like your list—`'a'`, `'b'`, and `'c'`:

```
cqlsh:types> SELECT text, set_text FROM collections WHERE text = 'set';

@ Row 1
----------+-----------------
 text     | set
 set_text | {'a', 'b', 'c'}

(1 rows)
```

What happens if you try to reinsert your set but with duplicate values?

```
cqlsh:types> INSERT INTO collections(text, set_text)
  VALUES ('set', {'a', 'b', 'c', 'c'});
```

If you load the set again, the duplicate `'c'` values have been removed without producing an error:

```
cqlsh:types> SELECT text, set_text FROM collections WHERE text = 'set';

@ Row 1
----------+-----------------
 text     | set
 set_text | {'a', 'b', 'c'}

(1 rows)
```

By removing duplicates without surfacing an error to the client, Scylla demonstrates why a set is preferable. Because these operations are idempotent, you can run them again and again, always getting the same result. Not having to worry about the order of operations here or concern yourself with deduplicating makes your application simpler and more resilient.

Just like lists, you can concatenate two sets with the + operator:

```
cqlsh:types> UPDATE collections
  SET set_text = set_text + {'d', 'e'}
  WHERE text = 'set';
```

When you query for the set again, `'d'` and `'e'` have been added:

```
cqlsh:types> SELECT text, set_text FROM collections WHERE text = 'set';

@ Row 1
----------+--------------------------
```

```
 text      | set
 set_text | {'a', 'b', 'c', 'd', 'e'}
```

```
(1 rows)
```

If you run this update five times consecutively, you'll get the same set every time. Idempotency is very cool!

Sets also support removing data via the - operator. As with lists, if the value isn't present, Scylla won't remove it—it can't because it's not there:

```
cqlsh:types> UPDATE collections
  SET set_text = set_text - {'d', 'e', 'f'}
  WHERE text = 'set';
```

After the update, your set is once again 'a', 'b', and 'c':

```
cqlsh:types> SELECT text, set_text FROM collections WHERE text = 'set';
```

```
@ Row 1
----------+-----------------
 text      | set
 set_text | {'a', 'b', 'c'}
```

```
(1 rows)
```

With its smaller interface, guarantees of uniqueness, and lack of footguns, you should prefer using a set over a list whenever possible. Thinking back to your application, you're looking to store a gallery of images. Although it's still unclear how to store an image, a gallery is a grouping of one or more items—which sounds an awful lot like something that can be represented by a set or a list. Because you should use a set over a list, your gallery of images can be represented by a set. The data type in that set, however, is yet to be determined.

The other collection type, map, builds on set's API. A map is a set of key-value pairs—let's look at how to use one.

4.5.3   *Maps*

A map in CQL is very similar to a map or a dictionary in other programming languages. You can think of it as a set of keys: each key in the map is unique, and each key points to a value. Keys all share one common data type, as do values. To create a map, you put the keys and value pairs in curly braces, with each pair delimited by commas and the keys and values separated by a colon:

```
cqlsh:types> INSERT INTO collections(text, map)
  VALUES('map', {'k1': 'v1'});
```

Loading the row shows you your newly created map:

```
cqlsh:types> SELECT text, map FROM collections WHERE text = 'map';

@ Row 1
------+--------------
 text | map
 map  | {'k1': 'v1'}

(1 rows)
```

Just like lists and sets, you can add entries to a map using the + operator:

```
cqlsh:types> UPDATE collections
  SET map = map + {'k2': 'v2', 'k3': 'v3'}
  WHERE text = 'map';
```

Your map now has three entries, k1, k2, and k3:

```
cqlsh:types> SELECT text, map FROM collections WHERE text = 'map';

@ Row 1
------+--------------------------------------
 text | map
 map  | {'k1': 'v1', 'k2': 'v2', 'k3': 'v3'}

(1 rows)
```

You can also remove entries from the map using -. You don't need the full entry; using only the key suffices. When deleting from the map in this manner, you're removing a set of keys from the map:

```
cqlsh:types> UPDATE collections SET map = map - {'k3'} WHERE text = 'map';
```

If you retrieve your map again, it no longer contains the entry for k3:

```
cqlsh:types> SELECT text, map FROM collections WHERE text = 'map';

@ Row 1
------+-------------------------
 text | map
 map  | {'k1': 'v1', 'k2': 'v2'}

(1 rows)
```

You can also perform individual operations directly on entries in the map using the key:

```
cqlsh:types> UPDATE collections
  SET map['k2'] = 'mountain'
  WHERE text = 'map';
```

The value for k2 now says that k2 is a mountain:

```
cqlsh:types> SELECT text, map FROM collections WHERE text = 'map';
```

```
@ Row 1
------+--------------------------------
 text | map
 map  | {'k1': 'v1', 'k2': 'mountain'}
```

```
(1 rows)
```

Just as you can update a value using the key, you can also delete an entry by its key:

```
cqlsh:types> DELETE map['k2'] FROM collections WHERE text = 'map';
```

Reloading the map shows that you're back to your original map, with the entry for k1:

```
cqlsh:types> SELECT text, map FROM collections WHERE text = 'map';
```

```
@ Row 1
------+--------------
 text | map
 map  | {'k1': 'v1'}
```

```
(1 rows)
```

Maps build on the interfaces of the other collections—all three support adding, updating, and deleting data in similar ways. At this point, you may be thinking that a map would be great for storing an image: it supports inserting arbitrary keys and values so that you can store a filename or a resolution in it. However, there is a complication: all values in a map must have the same data type. If the filename is TEXT, you can't store the resolution as an INT in the map. Luckily, you're not out of options. There's another collection type you should know about: user-defined types.

4.5.4   *User-defined types*

A *user-defined type* (UDT) allows a user to define a custom type that behaves similarly to any other type in Scylla; it can be used in a table, in a collection, or even as a primary key. UDTs look a lot like maps—they use similar syntax and map keys to values. UDTs, however, can have different types within them; map values must share a common type. UDTs are valuable when you want to store some data together in a common type, as opposed to breaking it out into separate columns and having to remember to update each and keep them in sync with each other.

To use a UDT, you first need to create it, just as you would a keyspace or table. To create a UDT, imagine a person's contact info: you can email them, call them, DM them on a social network, or maybe even send them a carrier pigeon. Let's create a UDT that models these methods using the CREATE TYPE statement, shown in listing 4.3. It looks similar to CREATE TABLE—you give the type a name, and you specify field names and types.

Listing 4.3 Creating a UDT to represent complex types in a database

```
cqlsh: types> CREATE TYPE contact_info(
    email TEXT,
    phone TEXT,
    social_handle TEXT,
    wake_time TIME,
    sleep_time TIME,
);
```

To view your type, you can run a DESCRIBE TYPE statement. Supply the statement with the name of your type, contact_info, and you'll see your recently created UDT:

```
cqlsh: types> DESCRIBE TYPE contact_info;

CREATE TYPE types.contact_info (
    email TEXT,
    phone TEXT,
    social_handle TEXT,
    wake_time TIME,
    sleep_time TIME,
);
```

To use your type, it must be part of a table, so you need to create one. Similar to your previous explorations, the following CREATE TABLE statement gives you a table to try out the new UDT:

Listing 4.4 Using your UDT as its own type in a new table

```
cqlsh: types> CREATE TABLE udt(
    text text,
    contact_info contact_info,
    PRIMARY KEY (text)
);
```

Inserting a UDT is very similar to using a map literal, except you no longer need to quote your keys. Go ahead and insert a UDT into the table. Our test user looks very generic and gets a good night's sleep:

```
cqlsh: types> INSERT INTO udt(
  text,
  contact_info
) VALUES(
  'user 1',
  {
    email: 'user1@test.com',
    phone: '1-555-555-5555',
    social_handle: '@user1',
    wake_time: '08:00:00',
    sleep_time: '10:00:00'
  }
);
```

If you load the user's contact info, you'll see your newly inserted UDT:

```
cqlsh:types> SELECT * FROM udt WHERE text = 'user 1';

@ Row 1
--------------+----------------------------------------------------------------
 text         | user 1
 contact_info | {email: 'user1@test.com', phone: '1-555-555-5555',
                 ➥ social_handle: '@user1',
                 ➥ wake_time: 08:00:00.000000000,
                 ➥ sleep_time: 10:00:00.000000000}

(1 rows)
```

When inserting a UDT, just like columns in a table, you don't need to set every field. What happens when you skip setting a few? Let's pretend user 2 doesn't have a social handle or scheduled wake and sleep times:

```
cqlsh: types> INSERT INTO udt(text, contact_info)
  VALUES('user 2', {email: 'user2@test.com', phone: '1-555-555-5552'});
```

As with a table, Scylla defaults the unset values to null for you when reading them. No fields in a UDT are required; if you want to enforce that, you need to enforce it in your application:

```
cqlsh:types> SELECT * FROM udt WHERE text = 'user 2';

@ Row 1
--------------+----------------------------------------------------------------
 text         | user 2
 contact_info | {email: 'user2@test.com', phone: '1-555-555-5552',
                 ➥ social_handle: null, wake_time: null,
                 ➥ sleep_time: null}

(1 rows)
```

UDTs are useful tools for storing interrelated data, like an address. The house number on your street doesn't change without your address also changing. You can use UDTs anywhere you can use a type—including in collections and even nested in other UDTs. Let's try using UDTs in a set.

You need to create another table for this test: you can call it udt_set, and you'll use it to store UDTs in a set. Run the following create statement for a surprise.

Listing 4.5 A table with a bug

```
cqlsh:types> CREATE TABLE udt_set (
    text text,
    udts set<contact_info>,
    PRIMARY KEY (text)
);
```

You got an error!

```
InvalidRequest: Error from server: code=2200 [Invalid query]
message="Non-frozen user types or collections are not allowed inside
➡ collections: set<types.contact_info>"
```

What? Non-frozen user types or collections are not allowed in collections? What does that mean? What's a frozen type, and why is the UDT not already frozen? This error doesn't mean you have to use ScyllaDB only in the Arctic Circle; it is a property of collection types that restricts their usage in exchange for certain performance benefits.

4.5.5 *Frozen collections*

A frozen collection can only be modified all at once; piecemeal operations or operations on individual keys are blocked. By freezing a collection, the entire collection is stored together on disk, sharing various metadata. By storing the collection together and allowing only complete replacements when updating, it can be stored more compactly, speeding up reads.

A collection is frozen if the collection type is wrapped in FROZEN<...>. You can see an example of a frozen collection in the next listing.

Listing 4.6   Table of frozen collections that you update by replacing them

```
cqlsh: types> CREATE TABLE frozen_collections (
    text TEXT,
    list FROZEN<LIST<TEXT>>,
    set_text FROZEN<SET<TEXT>>,
    map FROZEN<MAP<TEXT, TEXT>>,
    PRIMARY KEY(text)
);
```

This attribute means the only way you can update a frozen collection is by fully replacing it. The following operations are forbidden on frozen collections:

```
cqlsh: types> UPDATE frozen_collections SET list[0] = 'a' ...
cqlsh: types> UPDATE frozen_collections SET set_text = set_text + 'q' ...
cqlsh: types> UPDATE frozen_collections SET list = list - 'z' ...
cqlsh: types> UPDATE frozen_collections SET map['k2'] = 'new value'...
```

If you're using a collection in a collection, that inner collection must be frozen, which explains the error you saw previously when trying to use your contact_info UDT in a set. Instead of letting you try to update fields in a UDT in a set, Scylla requires you to replace the entire UDT. As you'll see further in later chapters, this behavior simplifies the on-disk storage of the value and reduces the disk space the value requires.

Now that you know about the mysterious error from trying to use the UDT in the other collection without freezing it, you're ready to finish picking your types. Let's look at how you may want to store images for your articles.

4.5.6   *Storing images*

Having learned about collections, you know you have four options:

- A list, which supports storing multiple values together
- A set, which is similar to a list, except it enforces uniqueness
- A map, which supports storing keys of a common type and values of a common type
- A user-defined type, which allows you to store fields of heterogeneous types with specific field names

Which of these best represents an image? A list and a set are ruled out; you need to store something representing an entity, not a list of values. You're down to a map or a UDT. Because you're storing multiple fields that describe a specific entity that may have differing data types for each field, a UDT is the way to go.

> **Exercise**
>
> What fields would you store in an `image` UDT? What data types would those fields need to have?
>
> Although you may be tempted to store an image directly in the database, it's recommended to avoid doing that: images are large files, and the storage cost can be high when you either read or transmit. Instead, applications typically store images in a separate file store like Amazon's S3 or Google Cloud Storage that is designed to serve files. In the database, instead of storing an image, you store metadata about the image: the file's name and location, caption, etc. When building your image UDT, what will you store?

However, you can't stop at just an `image` UDT. You only need to store the image for the article summaries, but the articles themselves contain a gallery of images. To fulfill this requirement, you must store multiple images, which means you also need a data type that stores multiple values. Your choices here are a list or a set. Keeping in mind that you should avoid using a list unless you need duplicate entries, does a set fit your needs?

It does! You shouldn't need duplicate copies of an image, so you're free and clear to use a set of images. However, as you learned previously, if you use a UDT in a collection, that UDT needs to be marked as frozen, making your type `set<frozen<image>>`. Having decided how to store the images, you now know all the data types your schema needs, as seen in table 4.10.

Table 4.10   You've filled out the list of types your application needs.

Article ID	TIMEUUID
Article title	TEXT
Article author ID	TIMEUUID

Table 4.10 You've filled out the list of types your application needs. *(continued)*

Article score	`TINYINT`
Article date	`DATE`
Article image gallery	`SET<FROZEN<image>>`
Article review text	`TEXT`
Article restaurant	`TEXT`
Author ID	`TIMEUUID`
Author name	`TEXT`
Author bio	`TEXT`
Author image	`image`

With your types, you're now ready to complete your query-first design and finish turning your requirements into tables in a database. But before you go ahead, there are a few more types to learn about. Although not used immediately here, they will be helpful in future endeavors.

4.6 A few other types to know

This section is a quick tour of the remaining data types in ScyllaDB. Some of them fit broad use cases, like BLOB, and others are tightly focused, like the INET type, which represents an IP address. First up, it's time to learn about a BLOB.

4.6.1 Blobs

Imagine that you decided to implement a login feature in your application. Users can log in and potentially comment on articles. For them to log in with a username and password, you need some way to verify their credentials. You may think of storing their passwords; but the best practice is to store a hashed version of the password with an additional secret string appended to it called a *salt*, using a cryptographic hash function like Argon2 or scrypt. These hash functions produce a series of bytes, which you can store in your database using Scylla's BLOB data type.

> **WARNING** Implementing a secure application login flow is mostly outside the scope of this book, but please never store passwords as unencrypted text fields in your database. Refer to the Open Web Application Security Project (OWASP) guidelines to guide you toward a secure application.

Scylla supports storing arbitrary bytes in its BLOB type. This type can represent anything—serialized data, arbitrary hexadecimal, encoded values—as long as it's in bytes, you can store it here. You can input a BLOB as a hexadecimal literal using cqlsh:

```
cqlsh:types> INSERT INTO basic(text, blob) VALUES('blob', 0x123ABC456DEF);
```

Reading your inserted row shows your hex-based BLOB:

```
cqlsh:types> SELECT text, blob FROM basic WHERE text = 'blob';

@ Row 1
------+----------------
 text | blob
 blob | 0x123abc456def

(1 rows)
```

Scylla also supports several functions called typeAsBlob to convert a given type to a BLOB. For example, to convert an INT to a BLOB, you can use intAsBlob(). Try inserting the result of that function into the database:

```
cqlsh: types> INSERT INTO basic(text, blob)
  VALUES ('as blob', intAsBlob(12));
```

When you read it out, it prints differently than your original input. You passed in the result of intAsBlob, which is the hexadecimal literal 0xc. Scylla pads the value with leading 0s when you query it, giving you the blob representation of the integer you started with:

```
cqlsh:types> SELECT text, blob FROM basic WHERE text = 'as blob';

@ Row 1
------+------------
 text | as blob
 blob | 0x0000000c

(1 rows)
```

By storing arbitrary bytes, a BLOB can be a powerful tool. Although some types are strongly typed and enforce constraints, bytes, by their flexibility, open up many possibilities. You can serialize objects in your application into bytes and store them, regardless of type, in a generic table, or you can further compress or encrypt a lengthy string. Bytes give you as much flexibility as you're willing to bite off. But just because a BLOB can store anything doesn't mean a BLOB should store everything. As mentioned with images, large binary data shouldn't live in Scylla; put large files in a content delivery network or some other system dedicated to large object storage. Next, you continue the type journey by looking at a much more narrowly-focused data type, INET.

4.6.2 IP addresses

Scylla supports storing IP addresses in the INET type. Like other types, Scylla validates that it is a correctly formatted IPv4 or IPv6 address. To store it in the database, you enter the IP address as a string:

```
cqlsh:types> INSERT INTO basic(text, inet)
  VALUES ('ip address', '127.0.0.1');
```

Reading the value back out provides your inputted address:

```
cqlsh:types> SELECT text, inet FROM basic WHERE text = 'ip address';

@ Row 1
------+------------
 text | ip address
 inet | 127.0.0.1

(1 rows)
```

The last stop on the type train is a type that requires a bit of setup but does one thing and does it well: a counter.

4.6.3 Counters

Back in the early days of the internet, one of the features in vogue on sites across the web was a visit counter. Every time someone visited the page, the counter incremented. Let's pretend you want to add this feature to your application. The COUNTER type in Scylla can help you add this functionality; it's a 64-bit signed integer that supports only two operations: increment and decrement. They require special conditions to work—you have to play by the COUNTER rules.

A COUNTER can't be a part of a primary key, and it must be the only non-primary-key column in the table. Counter updates aren't idempotent, so you can't apply the same increment multiple times and get the same result. You can't INSERT a counter either; you have to update the value using an assignment. To start, you need to create a brand-new dedicated counter table.

> **Listing 4.7 Dedicated table for a counter**

```
cqlsh:types> CREATE TABLE counters(
    text TEXT,
    counter COUNTER,
    PRIMARY KEY (text)
);
```

To set the counter, as mentioned before, you have to run an UPDATE statement, incrementing or decrementing the value. Begin by incrementing the counter by 1:

```
cqlsh:types> UPDATE counters
  SET counter = counter + 1
  WHERE text = 'counter';
```

It does feel weird to run an UPDATE and not an INSERT here, but as you learned in the last chapter, an UPDATE inserts data into a row, updating values where values exist. When you run that initial update, Scylla sees there's no value there, pretends it's 0, and then increments it by the specified amount. Having incremented it by 1, you expect the value of the counter to now be 1:

```
cqlsh:types> SELECT * FROM counters WHERE text = 'counter';

@ Row 1
---------+---------
 text    | counter
 counter | 1

(1 rows)
```

If you decrement the counter by 2, what will the value be?

```
cqlsh:types> UPDATE counters
  SET counter = counter - 2
  WHERE text = 'counter';
cqlsh:types> SELECT * FROM counters WHERE text = 'counter';

@ Row 1
---------+---------
 text    | counter
 counter | -1

(1 rows)
```

If you said -1, you're right! Counters work by taking the existing value and either incrementing it or decrementing it; the result of the operation is dependent on the previous state. This is why a counter update isn't idempotent—you can't directly set a value; you can only change it based on the previous value.

CRDT: Not a computer monitor!

Under the hood, counters are implemented as a conflict-free replicated data type, which, for obvious reasons, is frequently shortened to CRDT. A CRDT, although it may sound like an old cathode-ray tube monitor, is a data type often used in distributed systems to provide scalable updates without requiring heavy coordination. The conflict-free portion of the name hints at how it works: updates can happen at any time without coordination, and it can automatically resolve conflicts.

The seemingly weird restrictions on a counter—it must be the only non-primary-key column—are related to its implementation as a CRDT. Although a counter appears to be a number, it's actually stored as several data types to achieve its conflict-free goals. Scylla has a blog post from when it first released counters that goes deep into the implementation; you can read it at www.scylladb.com/2017/04/04/counters/.

Because counters involve looking at the current state and modifying it—a read-modify-write pattern—there is an increased performance cost when using them. As you'll see in the next chapter, Scylla is designed for writes to be as fast as possible, saving the heavy performance lifting for read-time. Because counters need to read the current data locally to update the counter's state, a counter update is a more complicated operation than the standard ScyllaDB write. It needs to lock the counter locally, query the counter's current state, and update it before it can replicate data to other nodes. These performance costs amplify another challenge with counters: they don't guarantee an exact count. In systems under load, updates can be missed or retried, causing the counter's value to drift from its expected correct state. These drawbacks are something to be mindful of when considering using counters. Even with these flaws, sometimes this pattern is what you need: an incrementing counter that's reliant on the previous state of the value.

You now have all the types of ScyllaDB at your fingertips. Some will be immediately useful; you'll use them in the upcoming chapters when you create your tables and learn further about reads and writes in Scylla. Others can stay in your mind for a rainy day, and you can dust them off when you need them to solve a problem. Next up, it's time to finish implementing query-first design and turn these designs into actual statements for your Scylla cluster.

Summary

- Query-first design continues by assigning fields and types to your tables from the requirements.
- Scylla's TEXT type is the best option for storing strings in the database, as it can represent any character in the UTF-8 encoding.
- Scylla contains support for both integers and floating point numbers through a variety of numeric types such as TINYINT, BIGINT, and DOUBLE. You should use the data type whose bounds fit your use case.
- When storing dates or times, use TIMESTAMP if you need the date and time or DATE or TIME if you only need the date or time, respectively. DURATION is also useful for storing a length of time.
- When creating a unique identifier, ScyllaDB has native support for a UUID, but you may have to generate it in your application to avoid being unaware of the actual value on creation.
- A TIMEUUID is sorted temporally, allowing for a conflict-free timestamp.
- A UUID-based type is a strong choice for a unique identifier, but you may need to generate it in your application to avoid your application being unaware of the actual value on creation.
- Scylla's SET type is the best collection type to use when storing multiple values together as it provides idempotent operations.
- Scylla supports a LIST, but it should be used with caution as operations against a list—appending to it—are not idempotent and may result in duplicate entries in the list.
- A MAP is used to associate keys with values of a common data type, providing per-key uniqueness in the map.

- When you need to represent a complex type, you can use a user-defined type instead of a map to have values with differing data types.
- Freezing a collection by wrapping it in the FROZEN type can improve performance and is a requirement for a UDT or a collection to be used in a collection

Tables in ScyllaDB

This chapter covers

- Completing query-first design by reviewing your work
- Replicating your keyspaces appropriately
- Creating tables for the restaurant review application

For a book with the word *Action* in its title, you may think you're doing a lot of design work and not spending much time exercising the database. A good design, however, is the cornerstone of a well-functioning ScyllaDB cluster. How you query the data drives how you store it, so changes in how you query it can be very expensive. You may need to completely rearchitect your data!

This chapter focuses on finishing your design. You'll look at the work you've done thus far: validating that the design meets the requirements and taking an overall look at your design to see if there's anything worth changing or improving from a design or performance pitfall perspective (and you'll learn some tips for things to watch out for). With that design, you'll translate your work to actual keyspaces and tables, getting ready to begin filling it with data. Before you can query, you have to complete your query-first design.

5.1   Completing your query-first design

In the previous chapter, while learning about data types, you answered the fifth question in query-first design: what data goes in the tables? Taking your restaurant review application, you selected data types for each field in your database. At this point, you may think you're ready to settle down, play your favorite coding playlist, and turn that design into CQL statements. Before that moment, however, you need to tackle the last two questions in query-first design, which are all about refining and verifying your design:

- Does this schema match the requirements?
- Can this schema be improved?

Let's refresh our knowledge of the design thus far.

5.1.1   Reviewing restaurant reviews

Over the previous couple of chapters, you've developed your design for the restaurant review application. You've identified several queries you need to run and turned them into full-fledged tables: `authors`, `articles`, `article_summaries_by_author`, `article_summaries_by_date`, and `article_summaries_by_score`. Each of these tables contains several fields and a primary key to uniquely identify each row and a partition key built from the primary key to spread data around the cluster. Figure 5.1 shows how you've progressed your design, as well as all the items you've produced.

Seeing it all together shows the magnitude of what you've designed thus far. But your query-first design isn't finished yet. You've produced what appears to be a complete design, but it's important to loop back to the first question and verify that you built a design that meets the requirements. Additionally, when looking at the whole picture, you may see things you want to change or little inefficiencies that can be cleaned up. To solve these problems, you can ask yourself the final two questions and complete your design.

5.1.2   The final two questions

The final two questions of query-first design are interrelated (figure 5.2):

- Does this design match the requirements?
- Can this schema be improved?

They each encourage you to reconsider your design, verify that it accomplishes the goals, and make sure there are no obvious areas that need improvement.

These questions are also self-referencing:

- If you improve something, you should also check that your changes don't cause your design to no longer meet the requirements.
- If you change something to meet the requirements, you should also check that those changes don't require improvement in your schema.

By following query-first design principles, you took an idea
for a restaurant review application and translated it into
requirements, queries, and the beginnings of your tables.

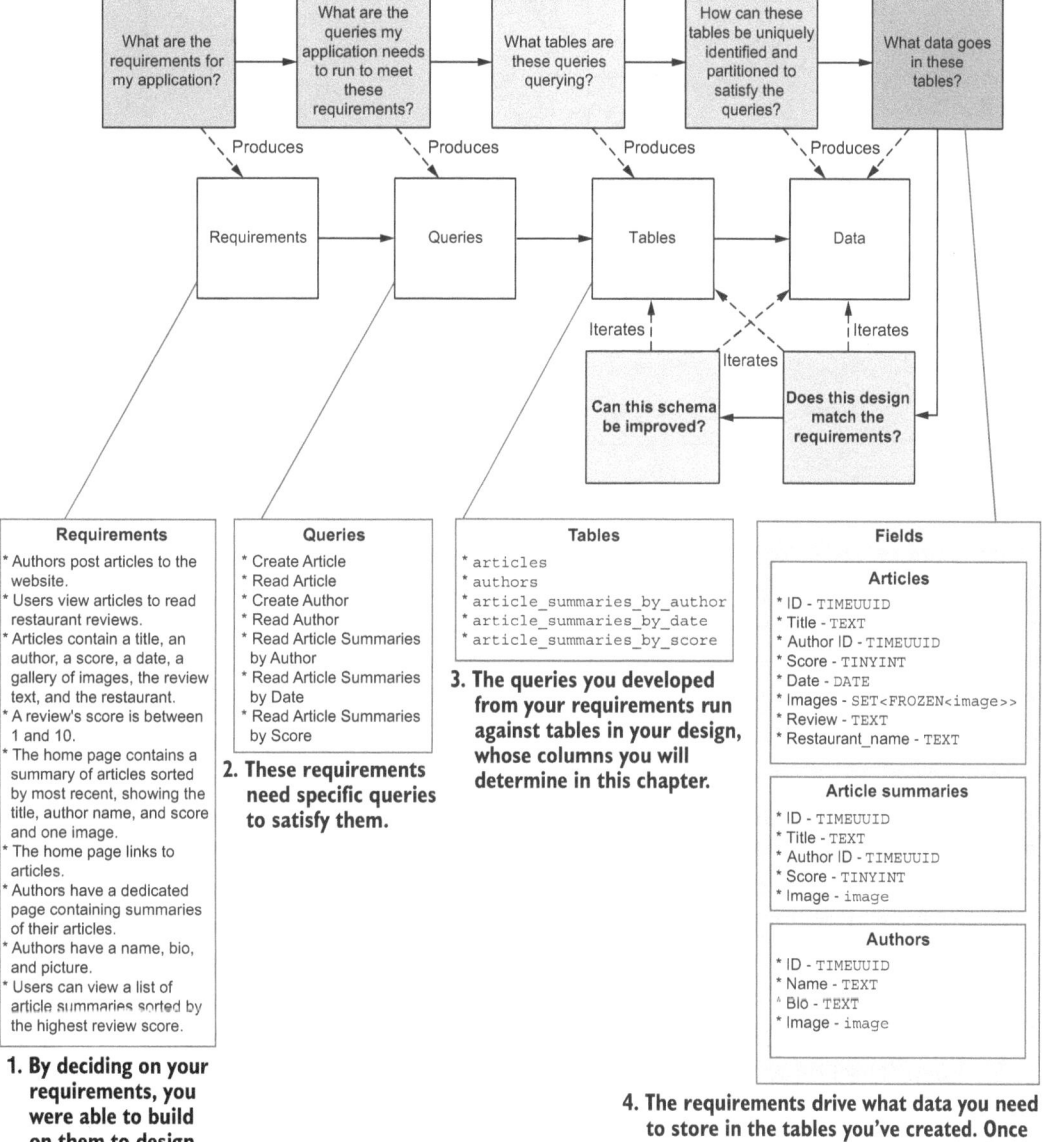

Figure 5.1 In the preceding chapter, you followed query-first design to determine the data in your tables.

Query-first design involves determining your application's queries first and using them to build a database schema.

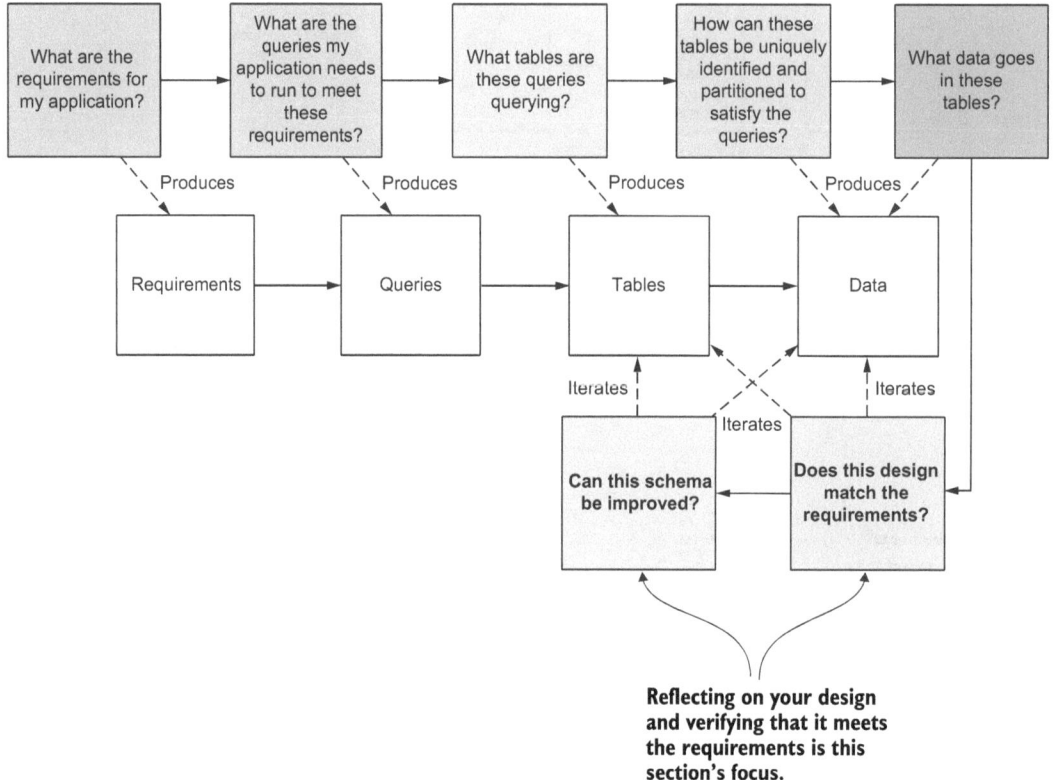

Figure 5.2   You'll focus on making sure your design meets the requirements and checking to see if there's anything to improve, taking advantage of looking at the entire design.

Of the two questions, query-first design begins with checking that the design matches the requirements. Although you may think this should be the final question, you ask it here to encourage a look at your overall design; consider the requirements, the queries, the tables, and the fields together instead of only as the output of the previous step. This holistic view gives you a different viewpoint of your design, helping you spot areas for improvement that you may have previously missed. Taking everything into account, ask yourself whether this design matches the requirements.

As you recall, in chapter 3, you determined that the requirements were the following:

- Authors post articles to the website.
- Users view articles to read restaurant reviews.

- Articles contain a title, an author's name and image, a score, a date, a gallery of images, the review text, and the restaurant.
- A review's score is between 1 and 10.
- The home page contains a summary of articles sorted by most recent, showing the title, author name, score, and one image.
- The home page links to articles.
- Authors have a dedicated page containing summaries of their articles.
- Authors have a name, bio, and picture.
- Users can view a list of article summaries sorted by the highest review score.

If you look at the requirements one by one, you'll see that your design satisfies them. Authors posting articles is fulfilled by your `Create Article` query, saving the article in a database. Users can read articles via the `Read Article` query, which can uniquely select one article by its ID.

Your next requirement defines the structure of an article; you store each of these fields in your `articles` table. The review score bounds are satisfied by using a `TINYINT` as the data type for the field. The home page contains a summary of articles, and it defines the fields an article summary needs: title, author name, score, and an image. These article summary fields are a subset of the article fields, so is this duplication a potential area of improvement? Let's look at their common fields, as seen in table 5.1.

Table 5.1 Article summaries have the same values for some fields, but other fields have subtle differences.

Articles	Article summaries
Title	Title
Author ID	Author name
Score	Score
Gallery of images	One image

Title and score are the same between articles and their summaries, but they differ in how they store and present authors and images. You want articles to show some author-related information, so you store the author's ID. This means that to display information about an author for an article, you'll need to load the author from the database in your application. This extra call isn't too painful; there's only one article on the page, so you're making the call only once to load the article.

What about article summaries? Could you reuse the `articles` table and select only a subset of data for loading summaries by date? Authors make it tricky (my editor is surely nodding in agreement at this statement). You want a summary to display only the author's name, whereas you want the article to show the name and image. If you reused the `articles` table for your article summaries, you would have to make additional calls to load each article's author—one database call per article! If using the `articles` table with its author ID, loading 10 article summaries could mean up to 11 total database calls (classically known as the $N + 1$ problem). If you store article summaries in their own table, you can denormalize articles and authors as well—storing only the author's name and not the ID. That's what your design currently does, so no change is necessary, but you've verified that this denormalized approach is what you want.

Having confirmed that you need a separate article summaries table, let's double-check that the query works for the requirements. You should always pay special attention to your read queries during this step: is your schema designed in such a way that it's performant and also meets the application requirements? When you load article summaries on the home page, you want to query the most recent articles, which is why you're using article date as a partition key.

How does this query load the article summaries? Because you're querying by the partition key—article date—you're able to select articles only one day at a time. You'll need to load the August 23 articles, then the August 22 articles, and so on until you've found the desired number of articles. If a lot of articles are written each day, that's not so bad; you can read all you need in one go. However, if you have only one article per partition, you'll potentially need many queries to select enough articles to load the home page. That sounds inefficient! What if there are no articles for a week? You may be making more queries than you have articles to load. Figure 5.3 shows these disadvantages; small partitions can require more queries when you're loading data across partitions.

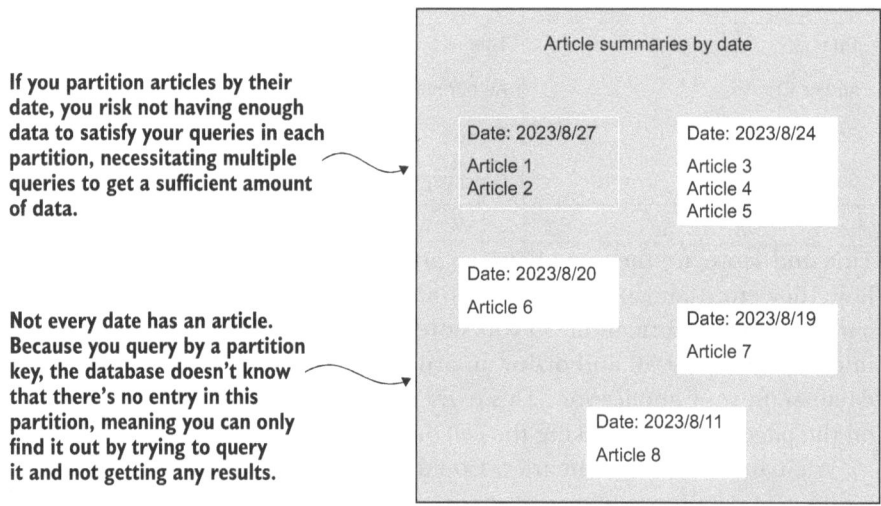

Figure 5.3 Overly partitioned data makes your database less efficient.

This inefficiency may feel like an existential crisis: "I made this table that looked like it would meet my needs, but now it's too inefficient!" No need to tear everything up and start over; you can solve this dilemma by applying a technique that allows you to group your partition keys to fine-tune partition sizes—*bucketing*. Let's take a look!

5.1.3   Bucketing

Sometimes your partition keys are too good at partitioning; they overly divide the data across the cluster, requiring too many queries to load the necessary data. You identified this problem with `article_summaries_by_date`: because you're using a DATE field as the partition key, either your review authors need to be prodigious writers and eaters, or retrieving articles for the home page will take several queries (figure 5.4).

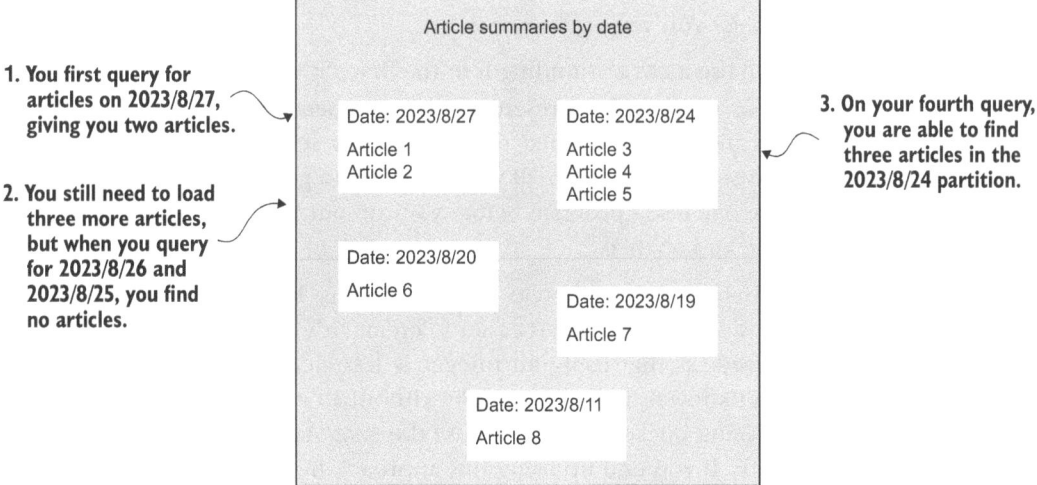

Figure 5.4   Querying across partitions has to work not only with partitions with small amounts of data but also with partitions without any data.

To protect against overly partitioned data, you can bucket your data, aggregating similar values in a partition key into a single group or *bucket*. The goal of using a bucketed value as a partition key is to fine-tune the balance between the number of queries to read the data and the size of your partitions. If your partition key is too narrow, you'll have to make many queries to load 10 articles.

Imagine, at one extreme, that you partitioned your articles by a timestamp; to find 10 articles, you would have to query millisecond by millisecond. With that partitioning scheme, if you published one article a day, it would take up to 86 million queries to find just that day's article. On the other hand, if you were to cram every row into one

partition, you'd lessen your fault tolerance and concentrate traffic and load on specific nodes in the database because the entire table would be stored together.

Today you're using a DATE as your partition key, which has the precision of a day.
To effectively bucket your data, you need a larger timeframe where you're very likely
to have at least 10 articles. Ten articles a week may be a high bar to meet. How about
10 articles a month? That means you'll need to publish a review every three days at a
minimum. Luckily, this is a book about data modeling and not about writing. We can
assume that you and your crack team of restaurant-reviewing authors can easily meet
that goal, and move on with refining the schema.

> **NOTE** Just because you're bucketing your data doesn't mean every query will
> get the 10 articles you're looking for. If you group your data into months,
> when your bucket rolls over and a new month begins, you'll start with no arti-
> cles in that bucket. Although it probably will fill up over time, your applica-
> tion may need to query multiple buckets to retrieve enough articles.

Having elected to bucket your article summaries by date, what data type should you
use for your buckets? You've got some options:

- You can still use a DATE, rounding it to the first day of the month.
- You can use an integer representing the number of months since launching
  your application—0 is the first month, 1 is the second month, and so on. A
  TINYINT gives you more than 20 years of room to grow, and a SMALLINT means
  it'll be someone else's problem before you run out of months, barring advances
  in medicine and science.

A SMALLINT is a 16-bit integer, whereas a DATE is 32 bits. From a storage size perspective, a SMALLINT uses less space and is easier to create; it's the number 12 versus 2023-
08-16. The downside is that using an integer is less clear; someone looking at the
bucket value won't know its meaning initially without an explanation. Because it's just
me and you discussing bucketing, you can use the SMALLINT; it uses less space, and it's
easier to work with. If you end up using this approach in an application, you can use
DATE if you value that initial clarity, or you may choose to translate the bucket to a date
in your application.

Bucketing is a powerful technique. By right-sizing your partitions, you balance
the time spent querying data with the database's fault tolerance. It's not just for too
narrow partitions: you can use it to break up large partitions into smaller chunks.
Imagine a popular social network's "Like" functionality: someone posts something,
and other users can choose to like it. A post among your friends probably has a small
number of likes, whereas a post by a celebrity could have millions. An implementation of likes may choose to bucket its data. You can parallelize traversing the buckets
to count the number of likes, and it lessens the impact if a partition is unavailable
due to a node outage.

With bucketing, you've solved a pitfall and improved your application's design by
decreasing the number of queries to your database. But your goal wasn't to make one

improvement and then be done. Let's look at the remainder of the requirements and be sure your design meets them and that there are no further improvements to make to the schema.

5.1.4   Finishing the design

I've reproduced the requirements you haven't verified from the preceding section here, along with your updated design (figure 5.5):

- The home page links to articles.
- Authors have a dedicated page containing summaries of their articles.
- Authors have a name, bio, and picture.
- Users can view a list of article summaries sorted by the highest review score.

The next requirement to double-check is that the home page links to articles. What this means for your design is that something in the article summary can load the article. Because your article summaries contain the article ID, you can use that ID to load an article.

Following that requirement are two about authors:

- An author has a dedicated page for summaries of articles.
- Authors have a name, bio, and picture.

By having a table that partitions article summaries by author ID, you're able to retrieve articles for a given author. In the last section, you learned about bucketing, and you applied it to your `article_summaries_by_date` table so you can load articles for multiple dates at once. Do you need to use the same technique here?

When querying for article summaries by author, you can load only one author's worth of articles at a time. Luckily for you, that's exactly what your requirements specify. Author ID is a great example of a natural partition key that matches your desired query patterns. Authors having a name, picture, and bio is straightforward. Your `authors` table can hold each of these, and your application can load them by the author ID when needed.

The last requirement is that users can view a list of article summaries sorted by the highest review score. To fulfill this requirement, you designed a table that partitioned article summaries by score. Your requirement is to show the article summaries sorted by their scores, which means you'll need to query articles across multiple partitions again. You may be thinking about bucketing your scores, but because they're represented as `TINYINT`, they're practically bucketed already. Even if you had scores to a tenth of a point, there are only 100 possible buckets.

> **NOTE**   Especially when you begin, many of your partitions may be empty. Because you query by individual score (10, 9, 8, and so on), that can lead to queries without results. One common pattern you may choose to follow to reduce load on the database and return responses faster to the user is to maintain an *empty bucket cache* in your application, which stores the buckets that contain no results. We'll discuss this approach later in the book.

By following query-first design principles, you took an idea
for a restaurant review application and translated it into
requirements, queries, and the beginnings of your tables.

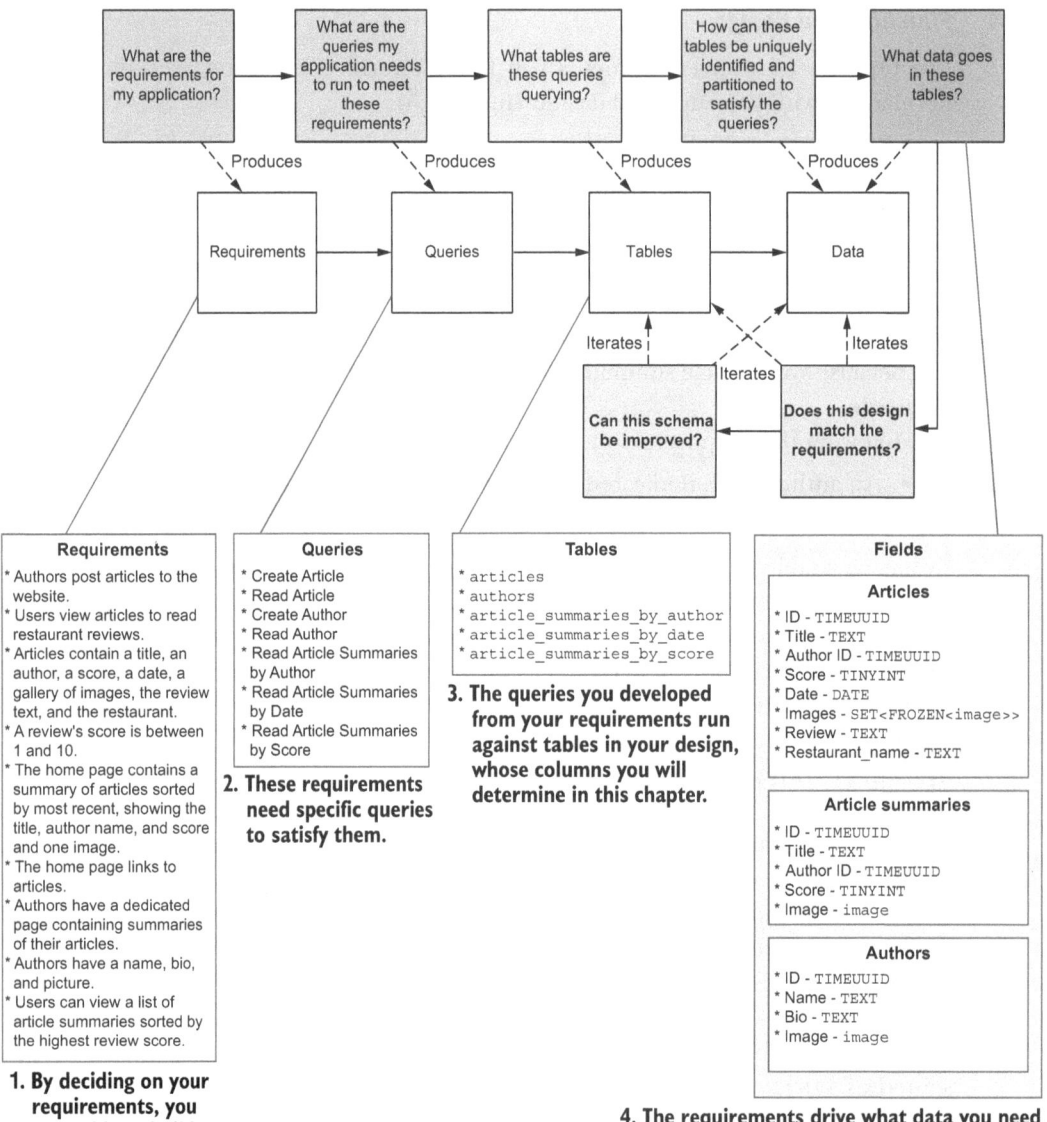

1. By deciding on your
   requirements, you
   were able to build
   on them to design
   your database schema.

2. These requirements
   need specific queries
   to satisfy them.

3. The queries you developed
   from your requirements run
   against tables in your design,
   whose columns you will
   determine in this chapter.

4. The requirements drive what data you need
   to store in the tables you've created. Once
   you have your fields and data types, it's
   time to make sure your design meets the
   requirements and that there are no
   obvious areas of improvement.

Figure 5.5   You've improved your query first design, adding a date bucket to article summaries.

Having reached the end of the requirements, you've completed your query-first design. Starting with requirements, you turned them into queries and then into tables and the fields in them. You verified that the design met the requirements, and you checked for improvements and made them. You now have a design for your restaurant review application. Let's turn it into real tables in a database.

5.2 Keyspace configuration

As you learned in chapter 2, tables live in a keyspace, which controls how the database replicates the data in it across the cluster. In this section, you'll create the keyspace for your restaurant review schema and learn about how to configure the keyspace's replication settings. Before you can do that, you need to make sure the Scylla cluster running in Docker that you built in chapter 2 is up and running. By running `docker start`, you can restart your stopped containers:

```
docker start scylla-1
```

Repeat the process for `scylla-2` and `scylla-3` to get your cluster back in action.

To house your restaurant review tables, you need a reviews keyspace. Remember, to create a keyspace, you need a `CREATE KEYSPACE` statement with two things: a keyspace name and the replication configuration. The keyspace name is straightforward; you want something that has meaning for your application. You can call it `reviews`.

The replication configuration is more complicated. Previously, you've been using `SimpleStrategy`—a simplistic strategy that minimally fulfills the requirements. However, there are better options for you to use; the simplicity of `SimpleStrategy` makes it a poor fit for production systems. First, let's look at how `SimpleStrategy` works and examine its pitfalls.

5.2.1 SimpleStrategy

`SimpleStrategy` is an aptly named strategy: it describes its basic functionality and hints at more robust options. When a keyspace uses this strategy, the operator supplies how many nodes it wants the data to be replicated to, called the *replication factor*, and Scylla replicates each partition in that keyspace to that desired number of nodes. This replication occurs through the hash ring; the partition is assigned to a given node via its placement on the ring and then replicated to successive nodes on the ring until the threshold is met, as shown in figure 5.6.

Why is `SimpleStrategy` not preferred? After all, it successfully replicates the data across the cluster, giving you the desired level of fault tolerance. Recall from chapter 2 that you can organize your clusters into datacenters and racks. Similar to physical datacenters, a datacenter in Scylla is a grouping of nodes, potentially split into multiple racks. The other replication strategy takes datacenters and racks into consideration, replicating data separately between datacenters. If you're more familiar with

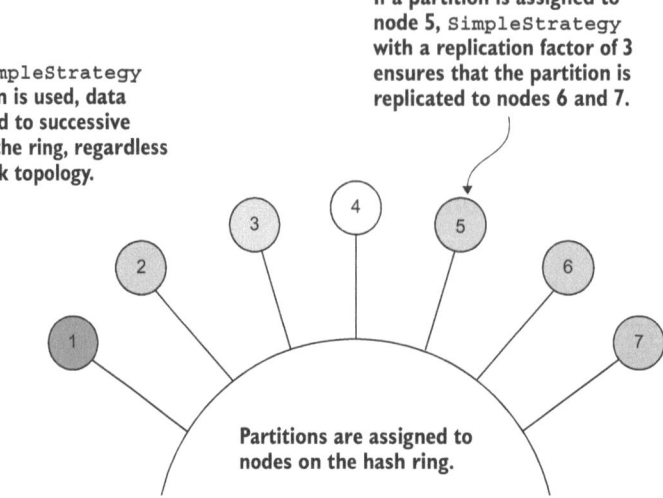

If a partition is assigned to node 5, `SimpleStrategy` with a replication factor of 3 ensures that the partition is replicated to nodes 6 and 7.

When `SimpleStrategy` replication is used, data is assigned to successive nodes in the ring, regardless of network topology.

Partitions are assigned to nodes on the hash ring.

Figure 5.6 `SimpleStrategy` **provides a straightforward replication solution, but its simplicity can lead to pitfalls.**

cloud providers, you can imagine a region in Amazon Web Services or Google Cloud Platform corresponding to a datacenter and an availability zone corresponding to a rack.

Why would you need multiple datacenters? Here are a couple of potential use cases:

- You want to run time- and compute-intensive background data-processing jobs without affecting user traffic, so you set up a secondary datacenter.
- You're setting up an additional datacenter in another region for increased fault tolerance.

In these scenarios, `SimpleStrategy` can't take multiple datacenters into account. It sees only nodes on the ring and accordingly replicates data to the next one, regardless of its datacenter. To have replication cooperate with these new topologies, you need to use the more complex but production-friendly replication strategy `NetworkTopology-Strategy`.

5.2.2   *NetworkTopologyStrategy*

`NetworkTopologyStrategy` is a superior replication strategy because it takes into account the network topology—the placement of nodes into datacenters and racks. It operates under the following algorithm:

- Each datacenter has a specified replication factor.
- Each partition is assigned a spot on the ring and to a node in each datacenter that owns that partition on the ring.

- For each datacenter, that partition is replicated to the next node that is in the same datacenter and has a different rack.
- If every node in each rack has already been used as a replica for that partition, the partition is replicated to the next node in the same datacenter.
- This replication is repeated until each datacenter's replication factor is satisfied.

In short, when this replication strategy is used, Scylla will replicate the data to the number of nodes specified in the replication factor in each datacenter specified, replicating it across racks. Imagine that you have a six-node datacenter, `datacenter1`, with nodes in racks `rack1`, `rack2`, and `rack3`. You have a second datacenter, `datacenter2`, with a similar topology. Each datacenter has a replication factor of 3 for a given keyspace. This setup may seem odd, but it's powerful both for demonstration purposes and in real life. With this setup, your cluster can tolerate the loss of an entire rack; you can lose two nodes (if they're the right two nodes) and continue serving traffic with no interruptions if you're using quorum-based consistency. We'll discuss this setup again in greater detail later in the book.

> **NOTE** If you have multiple datacenters with the correct query consistency levels, you can also tolerate the loss of an entire datacenter. You'll learn more about these consistency options in chapter 8 and how to configure your datacenters and racks (and why you might choose to have multiple datacenters) in chapter 9.

If you replicate a keyspace only to `datacenter1`, it will only consider nodes in that datacenter when selecting replicas, additionally spreading data across racks. If you replicate it to multiple datacenters, it will apply this replication algorithm separately for each datacenter; replication with this strategy is datacenter-independent. You can see this process in action in figure 5.7.

> **NOTE** You may be wondering what this replication strategy means when your queries are using quorum consistency. You'll learn more about Scylla's consistency later, but `LOCAL_QUORUM`, the consistency level you experimented with in chapter 2, requires only a quorum, a majority of nodes, to respond locally. *Local* is defined as the datacenter you're currently connected to, so a local quorum means a majority of replicas in that datacenter have to respond for the query to succeed.

Why should you prefer `NetworkTopologyStrategy`? Because it's aware of the cluster's topology, it can distribute data more effectively to give you better fault tolerance. Even if you're using only one datacenter and one rack, it future-proofs your keyspace if or when you choose to expand the number of datacenters or racks. If you're using `SimpleStrategy`, data will be randomly dispersed when you add datacenters or racks, creating potential imbalances in traffic and increasing the effect of node downtime. In short, always use `NetworkTopologyStrategy`.

Imagine a partition only replicated to DC 1 using `NetworkTopologyStrategy` **with a replication factor of 3.**

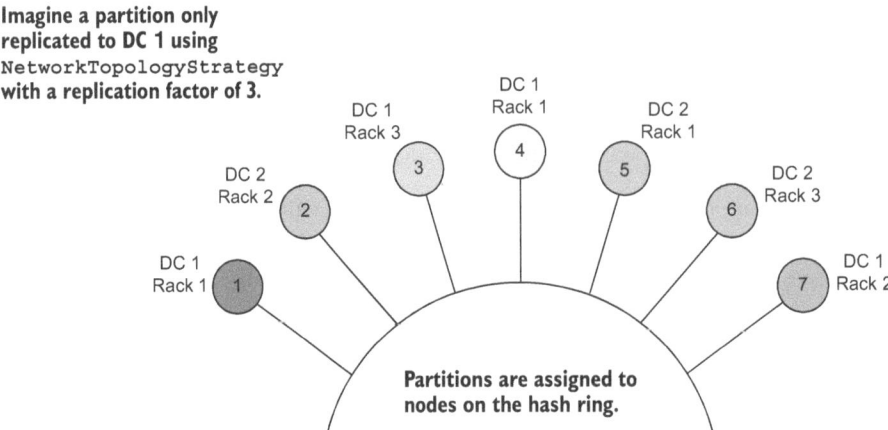

Partitions are assigned to nodes on the hash ring.

1. The partition is assigned to node 1, which is **DC 1** and rack 1. The partition will be replicated to nodes in differing racks within the same datacenter.

2. Node 2 is ineligible to be a replica, as it is located in **DC 2**.

3. Node 3 is in **DC 1** and in a different rack, so it's selected as a replica.

4. Node 4 is in **DC 1**, but it's in an already used rack. This node can only become a replica if no other nodes satisfy the constraints.

5. Node 5 is ineligible to be a replica, as it is located in **DC 2**.

6. Node 6 is ineligible to be a replica, as it is located in **DC 2**.

7. Node 7 is in **DC 1** and in an unused rack (rack 2), making it the third replica and satisfying the replication strategy.

Figure 5.7 `NetworkTopologyStrategy` **brings an awareness of ScyllaDB's cluster topology to replication.**

Having learned about the benefits of `NetworkTopologyStrategy`, you're almost ready to put your keyspace together. You need to gather the datacenter name, which you can determine for now via your old friend, `nodetool status`:

```
(scylla-1) $ nodetool status --resolve-ip
```

The very first line of the output contains the datacenter name—`datacenter1`:

```
Datacenter: datacenter1         ◁──┐  The datacenter
=======================            │  name
Status=Up/Down
|/ State=Normal/Leaving/Joining/Moving
--  Address    Load    Tokens Owns Host ID                               Rack
UN  scylla-2   944 KB  256    ?    2b38db3b-1b00-41f8-a3d5-1e66afc31db8  rack1
UN  scylla-1   572 KB  256    ?    75ddfa00-9624-4137-b926-429dff20e516  rack1
UN  scylla-3   1.11 MB 256    ?    2b769a73-1119-4981-ba82-5a5b92af61b9  rack1
```

You also need to pick your replication factor to determine how many nodes each partition will be replicated to. This value can be different per datacenter, but because you have only one datacenter, you need to choose only one value. In general, 3 is a good value; it allows the loss of one node and still maintains a quorum but also lessens the number of nodes required to complete a query, reducing the traffic in the cluster. You can combine these to create your keyspace.

Connect to your cluster via `cqlsh`:

```
$ docker exec -it scylla-1 cqlsh
```

You can now execute your CREATE KEYSPACE statement. You've named it `reviews`, and it's using the `NetworkTopologyStrategy`, assigning a replication factor of 3 to your datacenter, `datacenter1`.

> **Listing 5.1 Creating your keyspace**

```
cqlsh> CREATE KEYSPACE reviews WITH replication = {
    'class': 'NetworkTopologyStrategy', 'datacenter1': '3'};
```

With that, you've got your keyspace. We'll be working in this keyspace for several chapters, filling it out and using it as an avenue to learn all sorts of things about Scylla—from how Scylla handles deleting data to how the database can help you denormalize your data. To begin, you'll need to create your tables. Let's take your design and turn it into actual tables in your new keyspace.

5.3 Creating your application's tables

The culmination of your design is taking it and translating it to tables in a database. You need to create five tables from your design (figure 5.8):

- `articles`
- `article_summaries_by_author`
- `article_summaries_by_date`
- `article_summaries_by_score`
- `authors`

In this section, you'll create these tables, unlocking the schema that you'll use to learn the ins and outs of how Scylla's reads and writes work. This section isn't groundbreaking; you've already done all the hard work—you're only combining it into CREATE TABLE statements. First, tell `cqlsh` that you're going to use the new `reviews` keyspace for all of the following statements:

```
cqlsh> USE reviews;
```

The prompt should reflect your selection:

```
cqlsh:reviews>
```

By following query-first design principles, you took an idea
for a restaurant review application and translated it into
requirements, queries, and the beginnings of your tables.

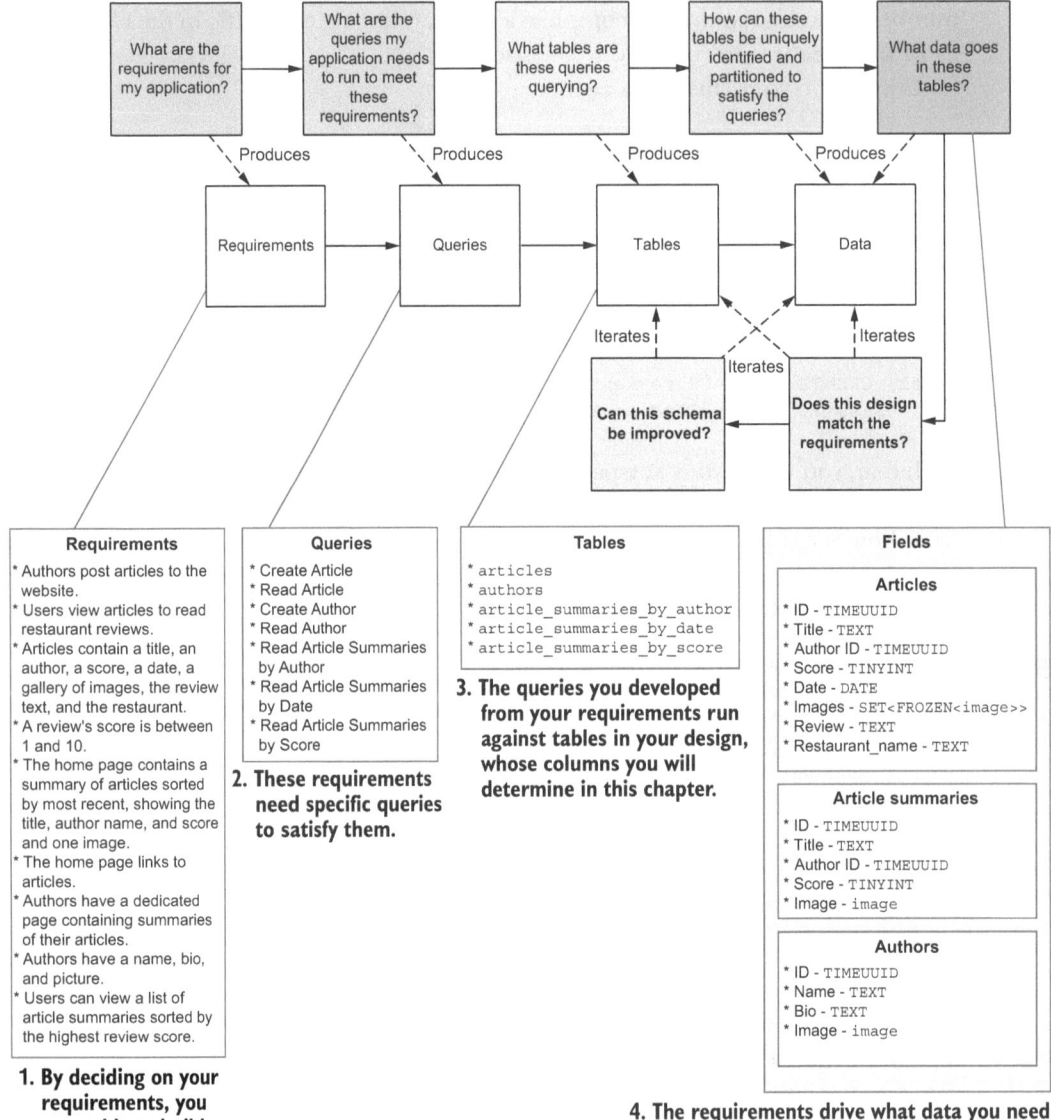

Requirements

* Authors post articles to the website.
* Users view articles to read restaurant reviews.
* Articles contain a title, an author, a score, a date, a gallery of images, the review text, and the restaurant.
* A review's score is between 1 and 10.
* The home page contains a summary of articles sorted by most recent, showing the title, author name, and score and one image.
* The home page links to articles.
* Authors have a dedicated page containing summaries of their articles.
* Authors have a name, bio, and picture.
* Users can view a list of article summaries sorted by the highest review score.

1. By deciding on your requirements, you were able to build on them to design your database schema.

Queries

* Create Article
* Read Article
* Create Author
* Read Author
* Read Article Summaries by Author
* Read Article Summaries by Date
* Read Article Summaries by Score

2. These requirements need specific queries to satisfy them.

Tables

```
* articles
* authors
* article_summaries_by_author
* article_summaries_by_date
* article_summaries_by_score
```

3. The queries you developed from your requirements run against tables in your design, whose columns you will determine in this chapter.

Fields

Articles

* ID - `TIMEUUID`
* Title - `TEXT`
* Author ID - `TIMEUUID`
* Score - `TINYINT`
* Date - `DATE`
* Images - `SET<FROZEN<image>>`
* Review - `TEXT`
* Restaurant_name - `TEXT`

Article summaries

* ID - `TIMEUUID`
* Title - `TEXT`
* Author ID - `TIMEUUID`
* Score - `TINYINT`
* Image - `image`

Authors

* ID - `TIMEUUID`
* Name - `TEXT`
* Bio - `TEXT`
* Image - `image`

4. The requirements drive what data you need to store in the tables you've created. Once you have your fields and data types, it's time to make sure your design meets the requirements and that there are no obvious areas of improvement.

Figure 5.8   It's time to translate this design into ScyllaDB tables.

You can begin with articles because four of your five tables have something to do with them. Besides, the entire point of your application is to serve articles to readers—it feels appropriate to begin there.

5.3.1 Articles

Your `articles` table holds restaurant reviews that are read by the users of your application. When going through your design, you determined that articles contain several fields and data types (table 5.2).

Table 5.2 Your design helped determine the fields and data types an article needs in the databases, but you're not ready to create your table—you need to create the image user-defined type.

Field name	Data type
ID	TIMEUUID
Title	TEXT
Author ID	TIMEUUID
Score	TINYINT
Date	DATE
Image gallery	SET<FROZEN<image>>
Review Text	TEXT
Restaurant	TEXT

However, you need to do one thing before you can create the `articles` table—there's a missing type! You need to create the user-defined type (UDT) used for images. In the previous chapter, I gave you an exercise: what fields does an image need? You need at least a path to where the image is stored and a caption. You can use these fields to create your image UDT (listing 5.2), or you can add your own.

> **Listing 5.2 Creating a UDT to store all the fields in an image in one value**

```
cqlsh: reviews> CREATE TYPE reviews.image(
    path TEXT,
    caption TEXT,
);
```

With the UDT created, you're ready to create your `articles` table. From your design, it needs the following:

- An article ID stored as a TIMEUUID, giving you both uniqueness and a temporal sort
- A title stored as TEXT
- An author ID stored as a TIMEUUID

- A score stored as a `TINYINT`
- The date stored as a `DATE`
- A gallery of images stored as a `SET<FROZEN<image>>`
- The review text stored as `TEXT`
- The restaurant name stored as `TEXT`
- The article ID as the primary key

Putting these together in a `CREATE TABLE` statement gives you your `articles` table, as shown in the following listing. Go ahead and run that statement.

Listing 5.3   Building the `articles` table from your design

```
cqlsh: reviews> CREATE TABLE reviews.articles(
    id TIMEUUID,
    title TEXT,
    author_id TIMEUUID,
    score TINYINT,
    date DATE,
    images SET<FROZEN<image>>,
    review TEXT,
    restaurant_name TEXT,
    PRIMARY KEY (id)
);
```

Having run that statement, you now have a table for your application's articles. Your stomach may be grumbling in anticipation of the food you'll sample to fill the table with reviews, but for now you have to create the other tables. Onward to article summaries.

5.3.2 Article summaries

The three article summary tables each store miniaturized versions of articles to entice users to read the full article:

- `article_summaries_by_author` enables users to view the article summaries for a given author.
- `article_summaries_by_date` powers your home page, showing the most recent articles.
- `article_summaries_by_score` lets users see the best restaurants according to the reviews.

These tables are denormalized—you're storing different copies of the data, designed to be queried in different ways to support different use cases. Accordingly, each table will contain much of the same data. Each table shares the following:

- The article ID stored as a `TIMEUUID`
- The article title stored as `TEXT`
- The author name stored as `TEXT`

- The score stored as a TINYINT
- One image, stored using your image UDT

These tables differ in their primary keys: specifically, in the partition key portion of them. Because you're storing the data in different ways, each table has a distinct primary key:

- article_summaries_by_author uses an author ID and an article ID.
- article_summaries_by_date uses a bucketed date, stored as a SMALLINT, and an article ID.
- article_summaries_by_score uses the score and an article ID.

Because each table also contains a clustering key, you'll want to specify the order here. This addition is especially important because, as you determined in chapter 3, the ordering you want is different from Scylla's default. You want each table to have the most recent articles first, so you need to specify the clustering order of the table—id DESC.

With these fields, you're equipped to create each of the article summary tables. First, create article_summaries_by_author, as shown in listing 5.4. Remember, you specify the partition key by listing it first in the primary key, making your primary key (author_id, id). The WITH CLUSTERING ORDER BY clause specifies the desired sort order for your clustering keys.

Listing 5.4 article_summaries_by_author stores summaries by author

```
cqlsh: reviews> CREATE TABLE article_summaries_by_author(
    author_id TIMEUUID,
    id TIMEUUID,
    title TEXT,
    author_name TEXT,
    score TINYINT,
    image image,
    PRIMARY KEY (author_id, id)
) WITH CLUSTERING ORDER BY (id DESC);
```

You can also create the other two article summary tables by applying the following statement, which, as you may have surmised, looks very similar to article_summaries_by_author.

Listing 5.5 article_summaries_by_date: stores summaries by bucketed date

```
cqlsh: reviews> CREATE TABLE article_summaries_by_date(
    date_bucket SMALLINT,
    id TIMEUUID,
    title TEXT,
    author_name TEXT,
    score TINYINT,
    image image,
    PRIMARY KEY (date_bucket, id)
) WITH CLUSTERING ORDER BY (id DESC);
```

Finally, create `article_summaries_by_score`.

```
cqlsh: reviews> CREATE TABLE article_summaries_by_score(
    score TINYINT,
    id TIMEUUID,
    title TEXT,
    author_name TEXT,
    image image,
    PRIMARY KEY (score, id)
) WITH CLUSTERING ORDER BY (id DESC);
```

Once you've finished running the `CREATE TABLE` statements, you have all three of your article summary tables. Next up is your last table—`authors`.

5.3.3 *Authors*

The `authors` table is your smallest table and your last hurdle before your design has been completely translated into tables in a ScyllaDB cluster. Authors have four fields—an ID, a name, a bio, and a picture. The ID, as you've done throughout the schema, is a `TIMEUUID`. The name and bio are stored as `TEXT`, and the picture is stored as your good friend the `image` UDT, as seen in the next listing.

```
cqlsh: reviews> CREATE TABLE reviews.authors(
    id TIMEUUID,
    name TEXT,
    bio TEXT,
    image image,
    PRIMARY KEY (id)
);
```

Having applied that, your design is now wholly in the cluster. You can view it by describing your `reviews` keyspace:

```
cqlsh:reviews> DESCRIBE reviews;
```

Sure enough, all your work is there; you can view it on the book's website or in the Git repo if you're curious. You see the keyspace with its `NetworkTopologyStrategy` for replication and your `image` UDT. Each of your tables is also there, along with the myriad default configuration options ScyllaDB provides. In the coming chapters, you'll learn more about these options, what they affect, and what they mean.

You've come a long way. What were loose requirements two chapters ago are now actual tables, defined in a database and ready to store data on disk. The next chapter focuses on writing data to ScyllaDB. We'll move beyond `INSERT` statements and look at write performance, and tools and techniques you can use in your application.

Summary

- The last part of query-first design encourages you to look at your entire design by verifying that it meets the requirements and seeing if there are improvements to be made from this new perspective.
- When partitions are too small or too large, you can size them just right by subdividing them into buckets, such as by date, to balance the number of queries required to scan the partition with the amount of data required to satisfy your use cases.
- When creating keyspaces, you should avoid using `SimpleStrategy` for replication, instead preferring `NetworkTopologyStrategy`, as it's able to consider the cluster's topology when replicating data, spreading data across racks in a datacenter.
- When you have multiple datacenters, `NetworkTopologyStrategy` supports setting a replication factor per datacenter.
- A complete query-first design is straightforward to translate into tables in your database, as you've already determined all the tables, fields, and data types needed.
- When creating tables, if you don't want to use the default ascending sorts based on your primary key, you can override the sort via the `CLUSTERING ORDER BY` clause in your `CREATE TABLE` statement.

Part 3

Querying the database

Databases exist to read and write data, and in this part of the book, you'll dive into how reads and writes work in ScyllaDB. Chapter 6 focuses on writes; you'll learn how inserts, updates, and deletes work under the hood. In chapter 7, you'll do the same for reads, and study why read queries are the most performance-critical operations in Scylla.

Writing data to ScyllaDB

6

This chapter covers

- Inserting, updating, and deleting data
- Executing multiple concurrent queries via batch query
- Deleting data automatically via time to live
- Updating data conditionally with lightweight transactions

If you want to learn about writes to ScyllaDB, this chapter is the place: you'll learn how Scylla handles mutating data—creating it, updating it, and deleting it. Writes may have seemed a straightforward operation when first introduced in chapter 2, but that's the beauty of Scylla's implementation: it provides a less-complicated interface and hides the complexity of the operation while still exposing some neat features to fit specialized use cases. Let's first look at inserting and updating data.

6.1 Inserting and updating data

In chapter 2, you learned how to insert and update data in ScyllaDB. It's a skill you've been using; you had your first basic reviews and your data-type playgrounds. You've got the basics, but in this section, we'll look deeper into how inserts and updates work, the small differences between them, and some ScyllaDB features that interact with writes and how Scylla stores data.

> **Starting your cluster**
>
> If your Docker-based Scylla cluster isn't up and running, start the three nodes by running the `docker start` command:
>
> ```
> docker start scylla-1
> ```
>
> Repeat this command for `scylla-2` and `scylla-3` to restore your cluster.

In the previous chapter, you created your database schema by adding a new `reviews` keyspace and filling it with tables. With your cluster up and running, you can run `cqlsh` on a given node:

```
$ docker exec -it scylla-1 cqlsh
```

With `cqlsh` started, you can USE your `reviews` keyspace, in which you'll remain for the rest of the chapter (and the next one as well):

```
cqlsh> USE reviews;
```

Having ensured that your local cluster is set up, you're ready to put some data into it. Let's first refresh on inserts and updates in Scylla.

6.1.1   Writing data

Chapter 2 showed you how inserts and updates work in ScyllaDB—they're two very similar operations that allow you to write data into a database. To look closer at inserts and updates, you can utilize the `authors` table.

If you're anything like me, you're an expert at forgetting the specific fields in your tables. To refresh your memory, you can tell Scylla to describe the table for you via the aptly named DESCRIBE command. When supplied with only a table, DESCRIBE shows you the unabridged CREATE TABLE statement with all settings made explicit:

```
cqlsh:reviews> DESCRIBE authors;

CREATE TABLE reviews.authors (
    id timeuuid PRIMARY KEY,
    bio text,
    image image,
    name text
)...
```

Because you're only concerned with what data you need to insert a row, I've shortened the following output. You'll need to insert at least the primary key—required to store the row—to successfully add an author to the database.

You can begin by inserting your first author—Alice Author. Perhaps Alice has been tardy in sending her bio and image over to you, so you have only her name to start with. You actually don't need values for every column to insert a row; you can skip some columns in your INSERT statement. Because you have only the author name for now, you can generate an ID via the now() function and proceed with an INSERT statement that uses only the ID and name columns. You can also generate a UUID externally and pass it directly to your query, which I've chosen to do here to make it easier to copy/paste and follow:

```
cqlsh:reviews> INSERT INTO authors(id, name)
    VALUES (eff9bd01-4a73-11ee-8863-c02b3f99d2b2, 'Alice Author');
```

Unused columns aren't listed.

The order of values matches the order of listed columns.

> **NOTE** For the remainder of this chapter, I'll be using pregenerated TIMEUUIDs, also known as *version 1 UUIDs*, to avoid not knowing the ID when I create the row and having to requery the database. I have obtained my UUIDs from the Online UUID Generator at www.uuidgenerator.net.

After inserting the row, you can query the entire table and see your newly added author.

```
cqlsh:reviews> SELECT * FROM authors;

@ Row 1
-------+----------------------------------------
 id    | eff9bd01-4a73-11ee-8863-c02b3f99d2b2
 bio   | null
 image | null
 name  | Alice Author

(1 rows)
```

The missing values

When you skip inserting a value for a column, ScyllaDB doesn't set it to null, despite what reading it in cqlsh may lead you to believe. Instead, it does nothing! It inserts no value, creating no data on disk. This behavior is why Scylla is called a wide-column database: a single write can choose whether to include any of the non-primary key individual columns, changing the "wideness" of the row. On the other hand, if you explicitly insert a null value, Scylla stores that null on disk, taking up a very small amount of space. Not inserting null into your database is a performance win, as Scylla won't have to consider it when performing queries. In a SELECT, however, Scylla interprets these missing values as null.

With that primary key, not only can you read the individual row, but you can also update it. Let's imagine that Alice has sent her bio to you, so you're free to update it in the system. Recall that when crafting an UPDATE statement, you need to specify the table, the fields being updated, and—in a WHERE clause—the primary key of the row to update. You can see the UPDATE statement to add Alice's bio as follows:

```
                                    Table           Columns being updated.
                                    name.
cqlsh:reviews> UPDATE authors    ◄────┘
   SET bio = 'Alice loves writing about food.'  ◄──────  Primary key of the row as
   WHERE id = eff9bd01-4a73-11ee-8863-c02b3f99d2b2;  ◄──  copied from the SELECT.
```

The UPDATE statement uniquely identifies a row and updates Alice's bio. If you read just the row because you know the ID, you'll see the updated bio:

```
cqlsh:reviews> SELECT *
    FROM authors
    WHERE id = eff9bd01-4a73-11ee-8863-c02b3f99d2b2;

@ Row 1
-------+------------------------------------
 id    | eff9bd01-4a73-11ee-8863-c02b3f99d2b2
 bio   | Alice loves writing about food
 image | null
 name  | Alice Author

(1 rows)
```

Alice's bio now correctly reflects that she loves writing about food. What a coincidence! Your application is going to feature her writing about food. As you learned in chapter 2, inserts and updates are almost identical (you'll know the difference soon); you could have updated Alice's bio as well with the following statement:

```
cqlsh:reviews> INSERT INTO authors(id, bio)
    VALUES (
        eff9bd01-4a73-11ee-8863-c02b3f99d2b2,
        'Alice loves writing about food.'
    );
```

You may be familiar with more complex write statements in SQL, such as inserting the results of a SELECT query. Just as Scylla doesn't support relational joins, it also doesn't support the entirety of SQL's query operations and concepts. Scylla favors simplicity in its user interface in exchange for potentially greater operational complexity. We'll examine these tradeoffs by discussing how Scylla handles concurrent writes.

6.1.2   Concurrent operations

There comes a time in every system when you're not the only user accessing it. One day, you'll release your restaurant review application, and multiple users will be making queries against it. Perhaps two people will try to edit an article at the same time. In a distributed system with eventual consistency, it's possible to have a potential conflict—how does the database choose what is the correct value?

Imagine two editors updating an author simultaneously, changing the bio. Editor 1, Edith, uses a request with QUORUM consistency, requiring a majority of the nodes to respond successfully. Editor 2, Emily, writes to the row just milliseconds after Edith, but with ONE consistency, and it's only acknowledged by that single node (figure 6.1). You have two nodes with Edith's update, but one node contains Emily's later update. What value does the database converge to?

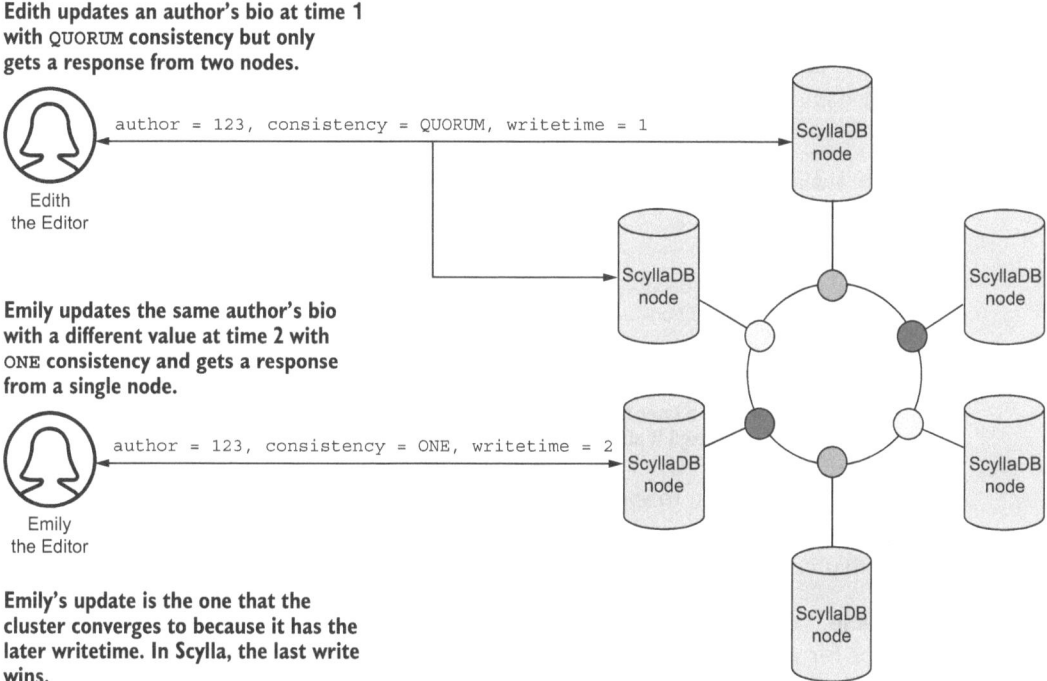

Edith updates an author's bio at time 1 with QUORUM consistency but only gets a response from two nodes.

`author = 123, consistency = QUORUM, writetime = 1`

Edith
the Editor

Emily updates the same author's bio with a different value at time 2 with ONE consistency and gets a response from a single node.

`author = 123, consistency = ONE, writetime = 2`

Emily
the Editor

Emily's update is the one that the cluster converges to because it has the later writetime. In Scylla, the last write wins.

Figure 6.1   In Scylla, the write timestamp of a query takes precedence over the number of replicas a node is stored on.

ScyllaDB chooses a simple approach for conflict resolution: *last write wins.* Every update is assigned a microsecond-precision timestamp (by default based on the coordinator's time; but as you'll see soon, this default can be overridden by a query), and the database converges to the value with the latest timestamp, making the winning write the most recent one. In the Great Edith versus Emily Editing Conflict, Emily wins. Because her update happened after Edith's, Scylla sees that it has a higher timestamp and eventually replicates that value to all replicas, making it the final updated value.

This approach isn't necessarily a bad one; at minimum, it's straightforward for both the database and its users to understand. However, Emily and Edith have demonstrated its drawback—the potential for lost writes. Scylla can't take into account any extra context, such as perhaps Edith sending everyone a message that she was updating the author's bio, but Emily didn't see the update, so she updated it herself. The database is limited to the information at hand—write timestamps. Beyond Scylla's write timestamps, you can help prevent lost updates by using other Scylla concepts like conditional updates, which you'll learn more about soon, or further client-side coordination techniques, such as distributed locking.

For every non-primary-key value, Scylla assigns a timestamp to that *cell*, the value for a given column and row. You can see this behavior in action via a SELECT query; Scylla supports viewing these timestamps via the WRITETIME function. If you check these write times for your friend Alice Author, you'll see that the bio has a later time than her name, because you updated the bio later:

```
cqlsh:reviews> SELECT id, WRITETIME(name), WRITETIME(bio)
    FROM authors
    WHERE id = eff9bd01-4a73-11ee-8863-c02b3f99d2b2;


@ Row 1
----------------+----------------------------------------
 id             | eff9bd01-4a73-11ee-8863-c02b3f99d2b2
 writetime(name) | 1693757230282977          ◁──── The name has an
 writetime(bio)  | 1693758687592177    ◁────         earlier timestamp.
```

The bio has a later timestamp because you updated it after inserting the name.

ScyllaDB also allows you to specify the timestamp by adding a USING TIMESTAMP clause to your writes. If you try to update Alice's bio with a timestamp older than the current one for that cell, your update won't be saved.

> **WARNING** You should use the default timestamp generated for your query, except for a specific case you'll learn about in chapter 12 when we discuss data migrations.

We use a very old timestamp to make its age as clear as possible.

```
cqlsh:reviews> UPDATE authors
    USING TIMESTAMP 1          ◁──
    SET bio = 'This bio is obsolete'    ◁──
    WHERE id = eff9bd01-4a73-11ee-8863-c02b3f99d2b2;
```

Your update of the bio won't be saved to the database, as it's older than the current cell.

What about inserts?

The syntax for doing the same operation with an INSERT query is very similar:

```
cqlsh:reviews> INSERT INTO authors(id, bio)
    VALUES (
        eff9bd01-4a73-11ee-8863-c02b3f99d2b2,
        'This bio is obsolete')
    USING TIMESTAMP 1;
```

If you read Alice's row, you won't see the obsolete bio field:

```
cqlsh:reviews> SELECT *
    FROM authors
    WHERE id = eff9bd01-4a73-11ee-8863-c02b3f99d2b2;

@ Row 1
-------+---------------------------------------
 id    | eff9bd01-4a73-11ee-8863-c02b3f99d2b2
 bio   | Alice loves writing about food
 image | null
 name  | Alice Author

(1 rows)
```

Scylla assigns these timestamps per write; you can't assign different timestamps to different cells as part of the same query. This behavior is how Scylla provides atomicity per partition key per query. The entire update has an associated timestamp, as shown in figure 6.2. While updates are applied, the timestamps are resolved when the data is read. From your read queries' point of view, if the update's timestamp is higher than a

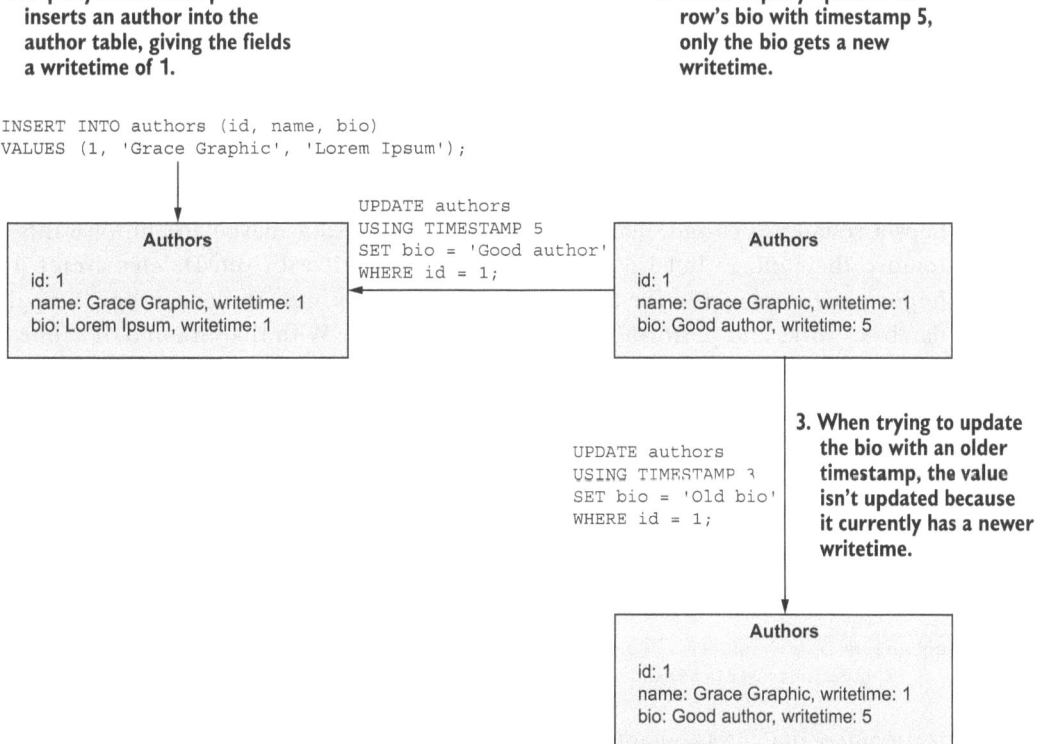

Figure 6.2 **The query's timestamp must be newer than a cell's write timestamp to update the value.**

previous write, all cells it mutates are updated. If the update's timestamp is lower, then no cells are updated. This behavior is worth accentuating—in inserts, updates, and deletes, operations in a partition key are atomic. All provided values are either set, or they aren't.

If you like to think about edge cases, you may be wondering, what about ties? What happens if two updates have the same timestamp? In this scenario, Scylla falls back on the lexicographic ordering of the values—the higher value wins.

Is last-write-wins the only option?

Last write wins, although simple, isn't perfect. As evidenced earlier in the editing example, it's possible to have overwritten updates; two readers can read a value and update it in divergent ways. Although Scylla is clear about how it resolves that situation, it doesn't mean you want to get into that behavior in the first place. To help you avoid this scenario, Scylla provides support for conditional updates of a row, which you'll learn about later in the chapter.

Now that you've written data, you may find yourself wanting to remove some of it. You did deletions in chapter 2, but there's surprising complexity under the hood in Scylla. Let's look at deletions and learn how they can have a big impact on your cluster's performance.

6.2   Deleting data

To delete data, you learned about executing a `DELETE` query, which deletes rows from your database. You may choose to delete data for any number of reasons: perhaps a restaurant closed, making the review obsolete, or maybe an author wants to remove their image but isn't sure what to replace it with yet. Deletes aren't just important functionality for Scylla; they're a window into understanding how the database works and performs, for better or for worse. With that in mind, it's time to delete some data.

6.2.1   Executing deletes

Of course, before you can delete data, you need to first have data to delete. You may be thinking of removing your friend Alice Author, but that seems harsh; instead, you can make an incomplete article to delete. Don't worry about creating summaries for it; you can proceed with only an ID and a title for now:

```
cqlsh:reviews> INSERT INTO articles(id, title)
    VALUES(c0bc0491-50ee-11ee-99e3-5d999e6ddbc5, 'Coming Soon!');
```

If you query the articles, you'll see the article with its primary key:

```
cqlsh:reviews> SELECT * FROM articles;

@ Row 1
----------------+----------------------------------------
 id             | c0bc0491-50ee-11ee-99e3-5d999e6ddbc5
 author_id      | null
 date           | null
 images         | null
 restaurant_name| null
 review         | null
 score          | null
 title          | Coming Soon!

(1 rows)
```

Alas, this article isn't long for this world; it's time to delete it. As you recall, a DELETE statement lists the table, along with a WHERE clause to specify the rows to delete. You want to delete from articles because that's where the soon-to-be-gone row lives. When deleting, be as exact as possible so you don't accidentally delete more than you intend. Like many things in Scylla, it's best to specify at least the partition key, if not the full primary key. You can go ahead and use the primary key. For me, that's the ID c0bc0491-50ee-11ee-99e3-5d999e6ddbc5. Because your delete query contains the primary key, Scylla can delete that row directly, avoiding scanning multiple partitions. Run the following DELETE query to delete your recently created article:

Table you're deleting from.

```
cqlsh:reviews> DELETE FROM articles
        WHERE id = c0bc0491-50ee-11ee-99e3-5d999e6ddbc5;
```

WHERE clause specifying the data to delete.

Once you've deleted the row, it no longer appears in your SELECT queries, which you can see in the following query output:

```
cqlsh:reviews> SELECT * FROM articles
        WHERE id = c0bc0491-50ee-11ee-99e3-5d999e6ddbc5;

 id | author_id | date | images | restaurant_name | review | score | title
----+-----------+------+--------+-----------------+--------+-------+-------

(0 rows)
```

One neat feature of deletes is that you can use a DELETE query to delete specific cells in a row. Go ahead and re-create the mostly empty article from before (you can reuse the ID):

```
cqlsh:reviews> INSERT INTO articles(id, title)
        VALUES(c0bc0491-50ee-11ee-99e3-5d999e6ddbc5, 'Coming Soon!');
```

If you load the article again, you'll see that it's returned because you re-created it:

```
cqlsh:reviews> SELECT * FROM articles
    WHERE id = c0bc0491-50ee-11ee-99e3-5d999e6ddbc5;

@ Row 1
----------------+-------------------------------------
 id             | c0bc0491-50ee-11ee-99e3-5d999e6ddbc5
 author_id      | null
 date           | null
 images         | null
 restaurant_name | null
 review         | null
 score          | null
 title          | Coming Soon!

(1 rows)
```

You can delete individual cells by adding their column names to your DELETE query between the DELETE and the FROM clause where you specify the table name. Because you have only one column set in your row, you can clear it out by adding title to your query. You can see this behavior in action by running the following statement:

```
cqlsh:reviews> DELETE title FROM articles
    WHERE id = c0bc0491-50ee-11ee-99e3-5d999e6ddbc5;
```

If you query the article again, it has even less data than before because you deleted its title:

```
cqlsh:reviews> SELECT * FROM articles
    WHERE id = c0bc0491-50ee-11ee-99e3-5d999e6ddbc5;

@ Row 1
----------------+-------------------------------------
 id             | c0bc0491-50ee-11ee-99e3-5d999e6ddbc5
 author_id      | null
 date           | null
 images         | null
 restaurant_name | null
 review         | null
 score          | null
 title          | null

(1 rows)
```

When you delete data, you may think it goes off to The Great Disk in The Sky, free to run around with all the other bits. Although this idea eventually becomes true, deletes are a nuanced process in ScyllaDB. Under the hood, Scylla uses a special marker data type called a *tombstone* to indicate that a deletion has occurred. Let's take a closer look at how tombstones and deletions work.

6.2.2   *Tombstones*

ScyllaDB is an *eventually consistent* database. Eventually, every update to the database is replicated to all nodes. Keeping this principle in mind, imagine the following scenario in a three-node cluster:

1   A query deletes a row, but it's received by only two of the three nodes.
2   Two nodes delete the row, but one node does not.

If Scylla immediately deleted the data from disk, you would have two nodes without the row and one node with a row. If you—the person considering this hypothetical— choose to ignore that a query deleted the row, you may notice that the database is in an ambiguous state, as shown in figure 6.3:

- Did one node miss a deletion, leaving that single node without any data?
- Did two nodes miss an insert from a query with a consistency of ONE, leaving two nodes without that data?

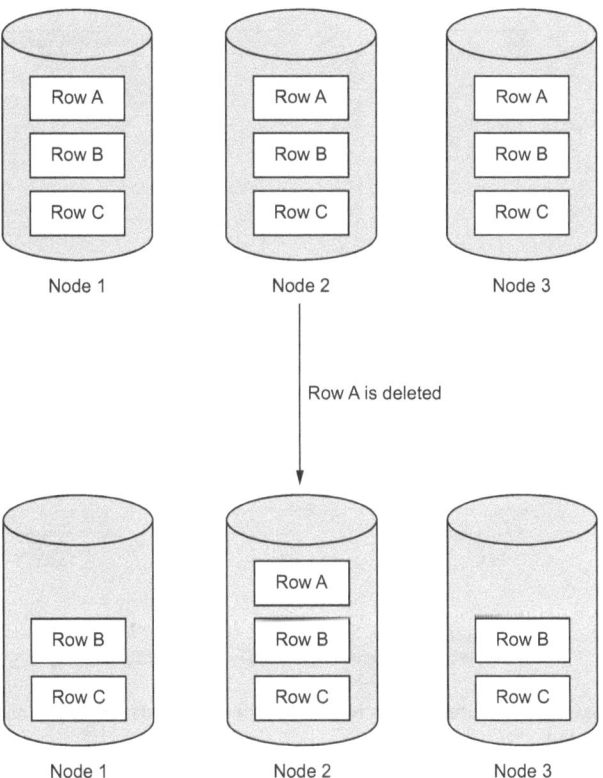

When a row is present on only one node, it's impossible to tell without context whether:
- Node 2 missed a deletion
- Nodes 1 and 3 missed an insert

Figure 6.3   The database needs context to determine how to reconcile missing data between nodes.

Without any information to associate with the row to signify that a deletion has occurred, it's unclear why the database is in that state and how it should proceed toward consistency. Does it need to replicate the deletion to the single node, or does it need to potentially replicate that row's data to the other two nodes? To solve this dilemma, ScyllaDB uses a special type of value called a tombstone, which, deep in the row's representation on disk, marks a value as deleted. The presence of this value indicates to Scylla that the value has been deleted so that it can differentiate between a missing value and a deleted value. Figure 6.4 shows how this ambiguity is resolved.

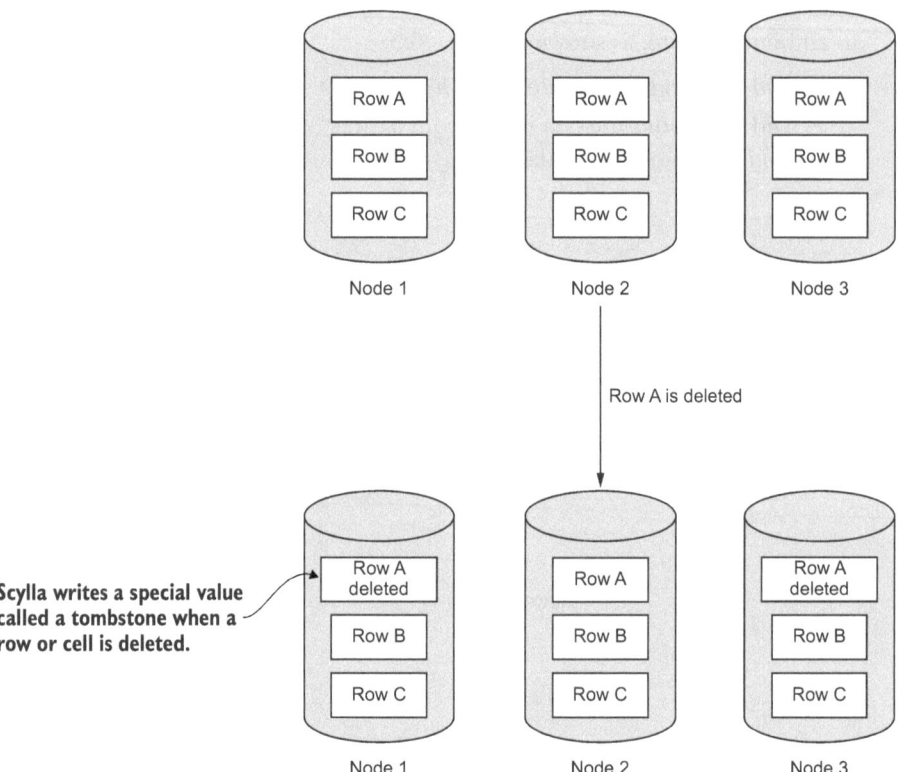

With tombstones, Scylla is able to tell that Node 2 missed the deletion and can replicate the tombstone over to it.

Figure 6.4   By writing a tombstone on deletes, Scylla is able to reconcile a missed delete and ensure that deleted data is deleted.

Technically, when you delete data, the data isn't removed from disk. Scylla adds *more* data: it's writing a tombstone. Whether you're deleting a single value, a row, or an entire partition, a deletion writes a tombstone to represent that the data has been deleted. Because it marks deleted data, the tombstone needs to stick around long enough for Scylla to reach consistency for that row. When can that tombstone be deleted, or are you cursed to carry it around forever? To answer that question, we need to consider the lifecycle of on-disk data in Scylla.

When a write request comes into the database, its data is stored in two places:

- In memory in a data structure called the *memtable*
- On disk in an append-only file called the *commit log*

Storing data in memory in the memtable makes the data quickly accessible and allows the database to buffer writes to disk, grouping writes together to save a little compute on the overhead of writing data. Writing data to the commit log gives it persistence; if the node crashes, you'd lose the data if it was only stored in memory. As data comes into Scylla, the memtable grows. When the memtable reaches a configured size (you'll learn about Scylla's various configuration options and the all-powerful scylla.yaml file in a later chapter), Scylla flushes it to disk, storing it in immutable files called *SSTables*—sorted strings tables. Because these SSTables are immutable, they aren't modified; if you want to make changes, Scylla has to create a new SSTable. This process is illustrated in figure 6.5.

> **NOTE** You'll look closer at SSTables in chapter 8, but for now, it's important to know that they're immutable files on disk that hold data.

When a query that updates a row comes into the cluster, Scylla writes the updated value to the memtable and persists it to the commit log. When that memtable hits the configured threshold, it's flushed to disk, creating SSTables. A deletion follows the same flow: Scylla writes a tombstone to the memtable and persists it to the commit log. That tombstone is flushed to disk when the memtable reaches the configured size. This behavior is why writes are faster than reads in Scylla: they need to append to only a single file on disk, not checking constraints or requiring cross-file coordination. Reads, however, need to reconcile the memtable and any SSTables that may hold the partition to retrieve the data and return the correct and latest values. As your database grows, tables that are frequently written to may need to read many SSTables to correctly serve a read query, slowing down performance. To remediate this slowdown, Scylla provides functionality to help speed up queries.

You may have noticed that at no point in this process has Scylla deleted the data on disk. Each insert, update, or delete is storing data in memory, appending data to the commit log, and persisting it to new SSTables. Is data ever truly deleted in Scylla, or is it stuck forever in your database, ever-growing and causing heartache? Scylla eventually deletes data through a process called *compaction* that combines SSTables into new, more compact ones.

Compaction is a critical part of Scylla's performance and one you'll come back to throughout the book. How frequently it runs, as well as how frequently it doesn't run, can have a large effect on your cluster. Before you can dive deep into compaction strategies and configuration, you need to learn two things: what it is and how it works.

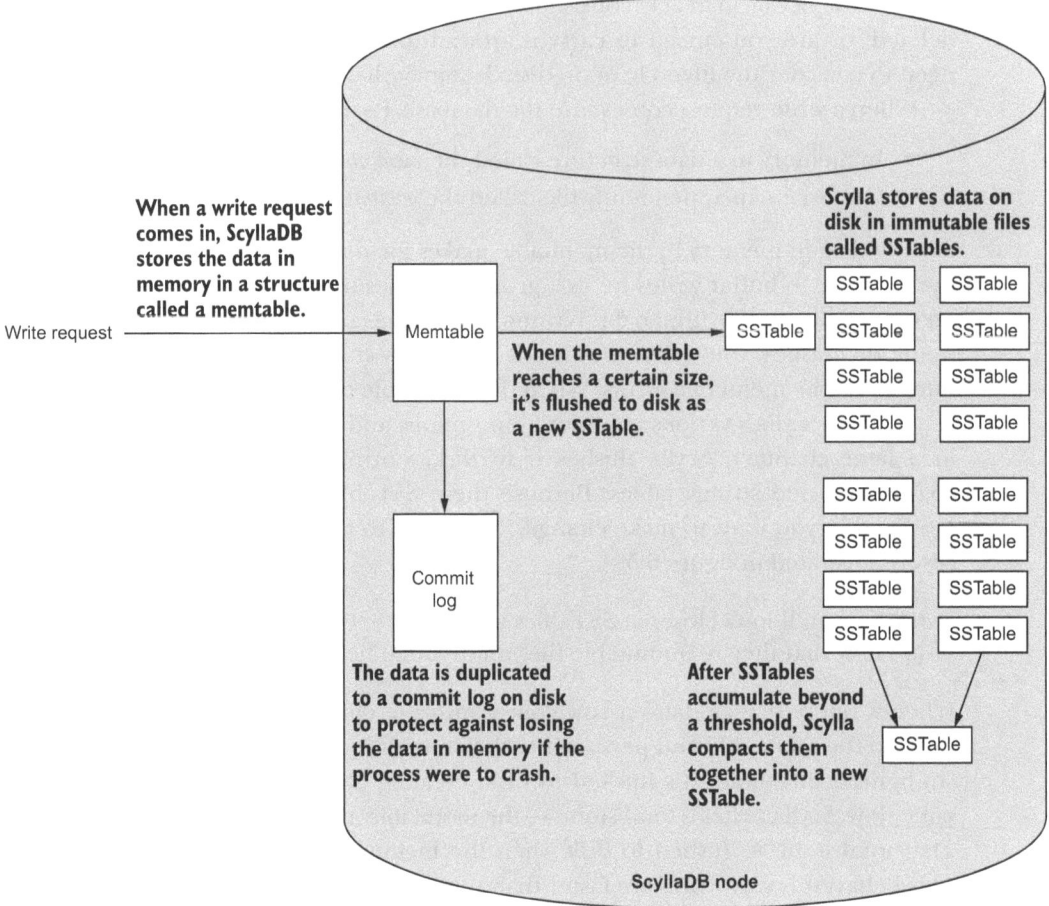

Figure 6.5   A write request is initially stored in memory but is flushed to disk to be stored in an immutable file called an SSTable.

6.2.3   *Compaction*

ScyllaDB accrues data from applications writing rows to the database, and its on-disk storage model also leads it to retain some unused data. When you update or delete a row, the old value remains stored on disk—unqueryable but replaced by a new value if there's an update or a tombstone in the case of a deletion. Left unchecked, disk usage would grow continuously—hence, compaction.

Scylla has two choices to run compaction:

- Automatically, referred to as a *minor compaction*, where Scylla triggers compaction against some number of SSTables based on configuration.
- User-prompted, referred to as a *major compaction*, where the user, via `nodetool`, tells Scylla to compact every SSTable. Users can further specify a keyspace or

table to compact to limit the amount of data compacted. You'll see this approach in action when you learn about cluster maintenance tasks in later chapters.

What happens during these compactions? A compaction involves two or more SSTables; Scylla checks each of them to see if they share any common data. If multiple copies of a value exist, one of those values must be newer than the others. Scylla can take the newest copy and merge it into a new SSTable, *compacting away* the old one, as seen in figure 6.6.

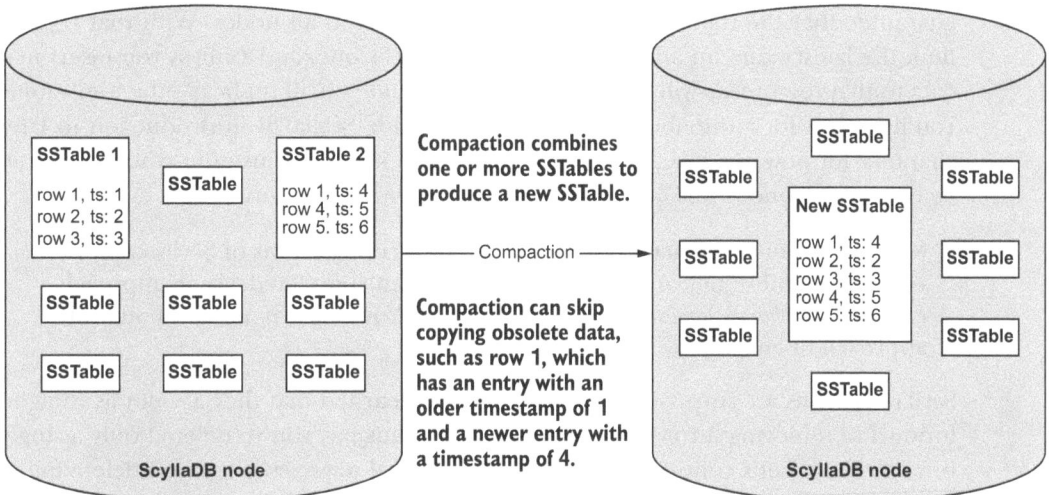

Figure 6.6 Compaction combines multiple SSTables into a newer SSTable, skipping obsolete rows and eligible-for-deletion tombstones.

Tombstones, however, are a special case. To compact away a tombstone, you have to wait for a configured time to elapse, called `gc_grace_seconds`, an abbreviation for *garbage-collection grace seconds*. `gc_grace_seconds` is the amount of time a tombstone has to live for before it can be garbage-collected and removed from the database. Removing a tombstone is a balancing act that includes the following:

- Removing the tombstone too soon risks deleting the tombstone before all nodes know about it, placing the database in the hypothetical scenario where one node still hasn't deleted the data but without the tombstone to guard against the problem.
- Persisting the tombstone leaves unnecessary data in the database. If you've deleted data after a certain point, not compacting the tombstone takes up space.

`gc_grace_seconds` is designed to consider these two cases; you specify a "Goldilocks" value that's not too quick (to avoid removing tombstones before other nodes know about them) and not too slow (to avoid the unnecessary accumulation of data). Scylla defaults this value to 10 days.

This table-level configuration is important; if your database hasn't achieved consistency for a deleted row in the `gc_grace_seconds` period, you run the risk of resurrecting deleted data. Although this risk sounds initially terrifying, it's straightforward to mitigate. You'll learn more about how to lessen this risk in later chapters, but as a preview, Scylla supports an operation to synchronize data among replicas and drive the cluster toward consistency: a *repair*. If you fully repair your cluster within the `gc_grace_seconds` window, there is no risk of data resurrection because you can then guarantee that the tombstones have been replicated to all nodes. With that replication, the latest value on all nodes will be that tombstone, and (unless you insert new data to that row) reads will see the correct latest value on all replicas—the tombstone. You'll learn a lot more about repairs and operating ScyllaDB in production in later chapters; for now, the takeaway is that repairs help keep the cluster in sync and should be run at least once every `gc_grace_seconds`, as shown in figure 6.7.

> **NOTE**   To avoid this race against time, more recent versions of Scylla support removing tombstones only after a repair has been completed, via an approach called *repair-based tombstone garbage collection*. You'll learn more about this approach in chapter 8.

Scylla deletions are surprisingly complex; you've learned that they are not as straightforward as removing a row from a file on disk. Thus far, you've deleted only a single row at a time. Let's continue and look at the several ways Scylla lets you delete multiple rows.

6.2.4   *Deleting multiple rows*

Scylla provides several options for deleting more than one row at a time. Some are precise, such as deleting via a partition key, but others are a bit more drastic—like dropping the entire table. First up is deleting by the partition key, which enables you to delete an entire partition at once.

When you delete data by its partition key, that's a very formal way to say "delete an associated group of data." Because you're grouping data into partitions as part of your query-first design, you'll have use cases where you want to delete a partition. Imagine that a rapscallion of an author, Connor Controversial, has published a review proclaiming that tacos aren't delicious. You would rightly question his reviews and might elect to remove all of them from the database. Instead of deleting each article individually from `article_summaries_by_author`, you can delete all of his articles at once by supplying the partition key. Let's see this in action.

BY PARTITION KEY

Technically, you've already done partition-key deletes: for single-column primary keys, that single column is both the entire primary key and the partition key. When you deleted an article from the `articles` table, you deleted it by its partition key, which

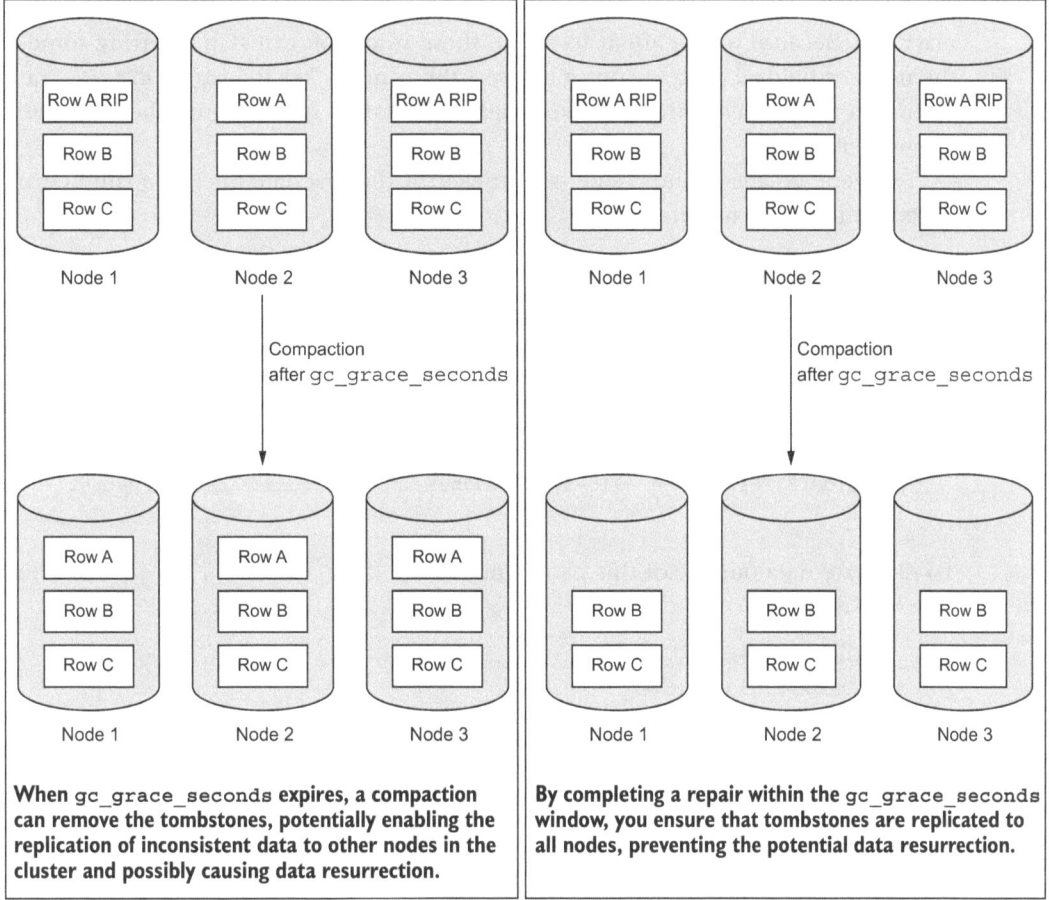

Not repairing before gc_grace_seconds expires | Repairing before gc_grace_seconds expires

When `gc_grace_seconds` **expires, a compaction can remove the tombstones, potentially enabling the replication of inconsistent data to other nodes in the cluster and possibly causing data resurrection.**

By completing a repair within the `gc_grace_seconds` **window, you ensure that tombstones are replicated to all nodes, preventing the potential data resurrection.**

Figure 6.7 Repairing your data is important to ensure that tombstones are replicated to all nodes.

also happened to be its primary key. For tables with multiple columns in a primary key, just like a read query, you can specify only the partition key, and Scylla scopes your query to that partition. Let's try this in practice.

You need to create some data before you can delete it. This time, you can use `article_summaries_by_date`. Recall from your design that you need the following fields:

- A `date_bucket` to partition articles by date in a SMALLINT
- An `id` for the article
- An author's name
- An image stored as the `image` UDT
- A score
- An article title

The date_bucket is the partition key, and together with the id, it makes up the primary key. Because you're about to delete these rows, you can skip inserting some of the non-key fields. I suggest you only insert the primary key fields (date_bucket and id) and a title, which will give you enough information to distinguish between them when querying.

To begin, go ahead and create two articles for the first date bucket, 0 (numbering starts from 0; we're not monsters):

```
cqlsh:reviews> INSERT INTO article_summaries_by_date (
    date_bucket, id, title
) VALUES (
    0, c251fe11-5434-11ee-9919-5d9a9e6ddbc5, 'The first time was good'
);
cqlsh:reviews> INSERT INTO article_summaries_by_date (
    date_bucket, id, title
) VALUES (
    0, c51def51-5434-11ee-9919-5d9a9e6ddbc5, 'The second time was better'
);
```

To illustrate data outside of this partition, insert a third article but put it in the next date bucket:

```
cqlsh:reviews> INSERT INTO article_summaries_by_date (
    date_bucket, id, title
) VALUES (
    1, 29ee3161-5435-11ee-9919-5d9a9e6ddbc5, 'The third time was mediocre'
);
```

What a beguiling restaurant; you went three times in two months! If you read all output rows in article_summaries_by_date, you see the three summaries you've inserted:

```
cqlsh:reviews> SELECT * FROM article_summaries_by_date;

@ Row 1
-------------+--------------------------------------
 date_bucket | 0
 id          | c251fe11-5434-11ee-9919-5d9a9e6ddbc5
 author_name | null
 image       | null
 score       | null
 title       | The first time was good

@ Row 2
-------------+--------------------------------------
 date_bucket | 0
 id          | c51def51-5434-11ee-9919-5d9a9e6ddbc5
 author_name | null
 image       | null
 score       | null
 title       | The second time was better
```

```
@ Row 3
-------------+------------------------------------
date_bucket | 1
id          | 29ee3161-5435-11ee-9919-5d9a9e6ddbc5
author_name | null
image       | null
score       | null
title       | The third time was mediocre

(3 rows)
```

You've come here to bury rows, not to create them. To delete all rows in a partition, you need to specify only the partition key in the WHERE clause of your DELETE query. Executing the following query deletes the rows in that first date-bucket partition:

```
cqlsh:reviews> DELETE FROM article_summaries_by_date WHERE date_bucket = 0;
```

If you read the table again, you no longer see the rows. You're left with only the article in the 1 date bucket:

```
cqlsh:reviews> SELECT * FROM article_summaries_by_date;

@ Row 1
-------------+------------------------------------
date_bucket | 1
id          | 29ee3161-5435-11ee-9919-5d9a9e6ddbc5
author_name | null
image       | null
score       | null
title       | The third time was mediocre

(1 rows)
```

Deleting an entire partition is powerful and straightforward: you specify the partition key, and the rows are gone. Sometimes, though, you need a middle ground between deleting the entire partition and deleting only a single row. One technique for selective deletions in a partition is to extend your WHERE clause with the IN relation, which lets you select specific rows in a partition.

THE IN CROWD

ScyllaDB allows you to delete multiple rows by adding the IN relation to your query. IN applies to a specific column in your query; you list values for that column, and Scylla matches values *in* that list for deletion—hence the name IN. You can use this approach on only two specific kinds of columns, as follows:

- The last column in the partition key
- The last column in the primary key

To see it in action, you need to re-create the previous rows:

```
cqlsh:reviews> INSERT INTO article_summaries_by_date (
    date_bucket, id, title
) VALUES (
    0,
    c251fe11-5434-11ee-9919-5d9a9e6ddbc5,
    'The first time was good'
);
cqlsh:reviews> INSERT INTO article_summaries_by_date (
    date_bucket, id, title
) VALUES (
    0,
    c251fe51-5434-11ee-9919-5d9a9e6ddbc5,
    'The second time was better'
);
```

Having created the rows, you can see the power of IN in action by using it to delete them. First, take the two IDs:

- c251fe11-5434-11ee-9919-5d9a9e6ddbc5
- c251fe51-5434-11ee-9919-5d9a9e6ddbc5

They are different values, I promise! The timestamp portion is the first part of the UUID.

With these IDs, you can begin with the standard DELETE query and specify the partition key again—the date bucket 0. IN can be applied only to the last column of the partition key or the last column of the primary key. Use it to delete the two IDs in the preceding bullets, which works because id is the last column in the primary key. In your WHERE clause, include the column, the IN relation, and then a list containing the values you want to match. With that query, you can selectively delete multiple rows:

```
cqlsh:reviews> DELETE FROM article_summaries_by_date
    WHERE date_bucket = 0
    AND id IN (
        c251fe11-5434-11ee-9919-5d9a9e6ddbc5,
        c251fe51-5434-11ee-9919-5d9a9e6ddbc5
    );
```

If you read your article summaries output again, you see that you've deleted two articles by using the power of IN:

```
cqlsh:reviews> SELECT * FROM article_summaries_by_date;

@ Row 1
-------------+-------------------------------------
 date_bucket | 1
 id          | 29ee3161-5435-11ee-9919-5d9a9e6ddbc5
 author_name | null
 image       | null
 score       | null
 title       | The third time was mediocre

(1 rows)
```

The IN relation lets you specify rows to delete and delete multiple rows at once, but because it's deleting explicit rows, you have to enumerate the exact rows you want to delete. That's not always the desired behavior. Although you can delete by the partition key, Scylla supports yet more ways to delete multiple rows at a time. One approach is to delete a range of data by replacing the equality operators in your query with greater-than or less-than operators. Let's examine how you can perform range deletions.

RANGE DELETES

When specifying fields in your WHERE clause, you've previously used the equality operator, =. That operator tells Scylla to look for rows where this column's value is equivalent to the supplied value. But, as in many other languages, CQL supports other comparison-based operators, as shown in table 6.1.

Table 6.1   Scylla supports the typical comparison operators.

Operator	Meaning	Valid example
=	Equal to	1 = 1
>	Greater than	2 > 1
<	Less than	28 < 34
>=	Greater than or equal to	247 >= 12
<=	Less than or equal to	43 <= 66

To see this in action, you can once again re-create the oft-deleted summaries that you've created and deleted in this section:

```
cqlsh:reviews> INSERT INTO article_summaries_by_date (
    date_bucket, id, title
) VALUES (
    0,
    c251fe11-5434-11ee-9919-5d9a9e6ddbc5,
    'The first time was good'
);
cqlsh:reviews> INSERT INTO article_summaries_by_date (
    date_bucket, id, title
) VALUES (
    0,
    c251fe51-5434-11ee-9919-5d9a9e6ddbc5,
    'The second time was better'
);
```

How can you do a range deletion here, keeping in mind that you want to specify at least the partition key? Can you do a range deletion using only the partition key? This would potentially query multiple partitions—a Scylla anti-pattern. date_bucket is such an easy field to access because it's a SMALLINT—it's worth a try. Imagine that you want to delete everything before the 1 date bucket. By using the < operator, you can guarantee that nobody sneakily puts an article summary in a -10 date bucket or something. You can run the query, but it will error:

```
cqlsh:reviews> DELETE FROM article_summaries_by_date WHERE date_bucket < 1;
InvalidRequest: Error from server: code=2200 [Invalid query]
➥ message="Only EQ and IN relation are supported on the
➥ partition key (unless you use the token() function or allow
➥ filtering)"
```

Your error message tells you that you can use only EQ (=) or IN on a partition key. If you think about it, this limitation makes sense. At query time, Scylla can map a partition to a node via the partition key's token, but it can't know all possible partitions. Because a range deletion wants to delete everything in the specified range, it would need to check every partition to see if it's in that range. To do an actual range deletion, you're going to have to use another value instead of the partition key.

article_summaries_by_date has another column in its primary key: the ID. Range deletions work best with non-partition key values in the primary key because Scylla sorts data by order in the primary key, making range deletions efficient: it can tell when a value is in range or isn't.

You chose TIMEUUID as the type for your IDs in your application because it supports ordering values by time, but when you look at an actual value—c251fe11-5434-11ee-9919-5d9a9e6ddbc5—the time it represents doesn't seem immediately apparent. Although Scylla supports range queries on the UUID, figuring out what the underlying time is and then manually constructing a valid UUID is both tedious and unnecessary. ScyllaDB provides the following two functions to turn a timestamp into a TIMEUUID:

- minTimeUuid() takes a timestamp and converts it to the minimum UUID value for that time.
- maxTimeUuid() takes a timestamp and converts it to the maximum UUID value for that time.

> **WARNING** These aren't guaranteed to be unique UUID values. You should use only the output of these functions in a WHERE clause. *Do not use them to insert data!*

Using these functions makes it straightforward to perform a range query on a TIMEUUID field. Let's imagine that you want to delete every article with a date bucket of 0 before September 17, 2023. By using the minTimeUuid function, you can construct a range-deletion query to delete exactly those rows you want to remove. You pass it the timestamp of 2023-09-17 00:00:00, and that function converts your timestamp to a TIMEUUID. Your WHERE clause can look for rows with an ID less than what you've specified, and if you also use the date_bucket to further narrow it to a single partition, you'll accomplish your desired deletion goal. Go ahead and run that query:

```
cqlsh:reviews> DELETE FROM article_summaries_by_date
    WHERE date_bucket = 0 AND id < minTimeUuid('2023-09-17 00:00:00');
```

If you load the table yet again, you'll see the query did its job and your articles are once again deleted:

```
cqlsh:reviews> SELECT date_bucket, toTimestamp(id), title
    FROM article_summaries_by_date;

@ Row 1
-----------------------+---------------------------------
 date_bucket           | 1
 system.totimestamp(id) | 2023-09-16 02:03:00.854000+0000
 title                 | The third time was mediocre

(1 rows)
```

Range deletions are a neat tool; by adding multiple conditions via AND, you can set a bounded range and further constrain your deletions. If you wanted to only delete articles between September 14 and September 17, you could adjust the preceding query to reflect your new conditions:

```
cqlsh:reviews> DELETE FROM article_summaries_by_date
    WHERE date_bucket = 0
      AND id < minTimeUuid('2023-09-17 00:00:00')
      AND id > maxTimeUuid('2023-09-14 00:00:00');
```

The last deletion mechanism to learn about is much less precise, although equally effective. With a simple command, Scylla lets you clear all data in a table. It's time to learn about the two commands that do this, which you should be very careful with: TRUNCATE and DROP.

TRUNCATING AND DROPPING

You'll sometimes want to delete an entire table. Perhaps the table is obsolete, or you were testing something locally and now you're finished. To delete all data in a table, Scylla provides the following two options:

- TRUNCATE deletes every row in the table at once.
- DROP TABLE deletes every row in the table at once, along with the table itself.

These can be scary commands to run; if you absolutely have to run them in a production system, you should always triple-check that you're doing exactly what you intend to do. Test in a testing environment first and make sure nothing is accessing what you intend to remove! It's best to avoid setting a new personal record for Biggest Incident Caused. Luckily, this is a test database we're playing with, so you can feel free to TRUN-CATE to your heart's desire.

Let's clear the test data you've created thus far in article_summaries_by_date. To truncate a table, you need only the table's name. The following query clears all data in article_summaries_by_date:

```
cqlsh: reviews> TRUNCATE article_summaries_by_date;
```

If you read the table, there are no rows!

```
cqlsh:reviews> SELECT * FROM article_summaries_by_date;

 date_bucket | id | author_name | image | score | title
-------------+----+-------------+-------+-------+-------

(0 rows)
```

Truncating clears the data in the table. Dropping the table is very similar, but it also deletes the underlying table. You won't be able to insert or update it anymore without re-creating it. You can also drop a keyspace via DROP KEYSPACE, but similarly, you'll need to re-create its structure before you can use it again. You'll get a chance in a moment to run DROP TABLE after you create a temporary table to test another Scylla feature.

With that, you've learned how you can delete data on demand. You know that deletes are secretly an insert of the special tombstone data type and that you can use CQL to achieve your desired deletion. There's one last deletion feature: Scylla supports automatically deleting data after a specified period via its *time-to-live* functionality.

6.3 *Time to live*

When you're writing data, you typically want the value you're writing to stick around, at least until you update it again. But sometimes that's not the case. Instead of requiring you to manually delete it every time, Scylla supports automatically deleting data after a certain period has elapsed—a feature called time to live (TTL).

6.3.1 *Expiring temporary data*

Scylla's TTL functionality is supported at both the table and query levels. When set, you specify a number of seconds so that when they elapse, Scylla automatically marks the data as deleted. It is important to understand that this is a deletion: reading an elapsed TTL'd value returns a null, not the previous value of the row.

Because of its time-based deletion, a TTL is used for ephemeral data in an application. Imagine partnering with restaurants to show a one-week-only coupon on each review. Instead of manually cleaning up the coupon when it expires, you can store it with a TTL, and it will automatically be deleted when the coupon expires. If you don't need a time-based cleanup of your data, then a TTL is an unnecessary option.

You can see a TTL in action by using it in a query. First, insert an author:

```
cqlsh:reviews> INSERT INTO authors(id, name)
    VALUES(
        6e556331-556d-11ee-9919-5d9a9e6ddbc5,
        'Victoria Vanishing'
    );
```

To see the TTL in action, you can update Victoria Vanishing's bio field with a TTL in your update statement. The query looks similar to the usual update, but it adds a USING TTL clause. You need to specify how long you want the value to live; 120 seconds is a good value for demonstration purposes. Too much longer, and you'll get tired of waiting to see it disappear!

```
cqlsh:reviews> UPDATE authors                          ┐ 120-second TTL
    USING TTL 120                          ⭠┘
    SET bio = 'This bio will soon disappear'  ⭠       ┐ Deleted when the
    WHERE id = 6e556331-556d-11ee-9919-5d9a9e6ddbc5;   ┘ TTL expires
```

If you read the row in the next two minutes, you can see both the temporary bio and, via the `ttl` function, how many seconds are remaining on the TTL:

```
cqlsh:reviews> SELECT id, name, bio, ttl(bio)
    FROM authors
    WHERE id = 6e556331-556d-11ee-9919-5d9a9e6ddbc5;

@ Row 1
----------+------------------------------------
 id       | 6e556331-556d-11ee-9919-5d9a9e6ddbc5     ┐ To be deleted
 name     | Victoria Vanishing                       │ when the TTL
 bio      | This bio will soon disappear   ⭠         │ expires
 ttl(bio) | 53                          ⭠            ┐ How long the TTL
                                                      ┘ has remaining
(1 rows)
```

While you wait for the TTL to expire, here are some helpful things to do:

- Take a deep breath
- Unclench your jaw
- Drink some water
- Light stretching

Database health is important, but your health is even more important! The TTL has presumably expired at this point, so go ahead and read the row again:

```
cqlsh:reviews> SELECT id, name, bio, ttl(bio)
    FROM authors
    WHERE id = 6e556331-556d-11ee-9919-5d9a9e6ddbc5;

@ Row 1
----------+------------------------------------        ┐ Still exists
 id       | 6e556331-556d-11ee-9919-5d9a9e6ddbc5       │ because it didn't
 name     | Victoria Vanishing          ⭠             ┘ have a TTL
 bio      | null             ⭠          ┐ Deleted because
 ttl(bio) | null          ⭠             ┘ the TTL expired

(1 rows)                               ┐ No value because
                                       ┘ the TTL expired
```

The bio is now null, as is the TTL: 120 seconds elapsed, and Scylla deleted the value. This functionality isn't limited to updates but can also be used in insert queries. Inserting data with a TTL is, like updates, similar to inserting data without a TTL, but it exposes the differences between inserts and updates in Scylla. Let's look at this difference and insert data with a TTL.

6.3.2 *The difference between inserts and updates*

A fun thing about Scylla is that every table has a secret column: the *row marker*. Despite the intro, it's not very mysterious; it's used to hold the write timestamp and TTL data about the row. This row marker is the big difference between inserts and updates:

- An insert inserts the row marker.
- An update doesn't touch the row marker.

To better understand this, first insert a row with a TTL. Just like an update, it's similar to a normal INSERT query but with a USING TTL clause. You can reinsert Victoria's author row, but this time with a TTL. But if you attach a TTL to an insert statement, that TTL applies to the entire row because it sets the row marker with a TTL. When the TTL expires, the entire row is gone:

```
cqlsh:reviews> INSERT INTO authors(id, name, bio)
    VALUES(
        6e556331-556d-11ee-9919-5d9a9e6ddbc5,
        'Victoria Vanishing',
        'This bio will soon disappear'
    )
    USING TTL 60;
```

If you run your SELECT statement from before with the ttl function, you see time ticking down on your bio:

```
cqlsh:reviews> SELECT id, name, bio, ttl(bio)
    FROM authors
    WHERE id = 6e556331-556d-11ee-9919-5d9a9e6ddbc5;

@ Row 1
----------+--------------------------------------
 id       | 6e556331-556d-11ee-9919-5d9a9e6ddbc5
 name     | Victoria Vanishing
 bio      | This bio will soon disappear
 ttl(bio) | 53

(1 rows)
```

When the TTL has elapsed, if you try reading Victoria's row again, it has vanished:

```
cqlsh:reviews> SELECT id, name, bio, ttl(bio)
    FROM authors
    WHERE id = 6e556331-556d-11ee-9919-5d9a9e6ddbc5;

 id | name | bio | ttl(bio)
----+------+-----+----------

(0 rows)
```

The entire row's deletion highlights the difference between inserts and updates. Updates can't delete the entire row because they can't touch the row marker. If you updated every field with a TTL, the row would remain after the TTL expired.

Having seen Scylla's query support for TTLs, it may feel redundant. If you want a table to always expire data after a certain period, it seems repetitive to set a TTL on every query. Fortunately, Scylla supports setting TTLs at a table level, which you can see in action in the next section.

6.3.3   *Table TTLs*

TTL is a supported table configuration option; you set the config, and Scylla automatically applies a TTL to every insert or update. To set this value, you need to add a WITH default_time_to_live clause to your CREATE TABLE statement. You can see this in action with another example table; create a ttl_temp table with a short TTL:

```
cqlsh:reviews> CREATE TABLE ttl_temp(
    number INT,
    words TEXT,
    PRIMARY KEY (number))
WITH default_time_to_live = 120;
```

Having created the table, go ahead and insert a row, but don't set the TTL explicitly:

```
cql:reviews> INSERT INTO ttl_temp(number, words) VALUES(1, 'temp');
```

If you read the row, checking the TTL with the ttl function, you see in the output that the TTL is set and your row is soon to be deleted:

```
cql:reviews> SELECT number, words, ttl(words)
    FROM ttl_temp
    WHERE number = 1;

@ Row 1
------------+------
 number     | 1
 words      | temp
 ttl(words) | 28

(1 rows)
```

Sure enough, after the TTL has elapsed, the row is gone:

```
cqlsh:reviews> SELECT number, words, ttl(words)
    FROM ttl_temp
    WHERE number = 1;

 number | words | ttl(words)
--------+-------+------------

(0 rows)
```

> **Cleanup time**
>
> Earlier in the chapter, you learned about the `DROP` command, but you didn't have any great candidates to use it on—you're going to keep using every table you have. But after learning about TTLs, you're done with your `ttl_table`, making it an excellent candidate to try the `DROP` command. Use it to remove the `ttl_temp` table:
>
> ```
> cqlsh:reviews> DROP TABLE ttl_temp;
> ```

With TTLs, you've learned how you can use Scylla to automatically delete temporary data. Next, you'll see how Scylla can keep saving you time and effort and do multiple queries at the same time via *batching*.

6.4   *Batching data*

Your reviews application has several tables you'd like to keep in sync: `articles`, `article_summaries_by_author`, `article_summaries_by_date`, and `article_summaries_by_score`. When adding an article, you need to add it to each of these four tables. But you want to insert it into all four or none; if an article appears in only some of the tables, that mismatch can cause data-inconsistency errors for your application. Imagine if an article summary didn't have an underlying article; users might be unhappy if they clicked a link to nowhere. This dilemma is a classic database problem: how do you ensure that these linked writes complete together or fail together? Scylla's answer is a `BATCH` statement.

6.4.1   *Executing a batch*

In a `BATCH` statement, you can group multiple `INSERT`, `UPDATE`, and `DELETE` queries, and Scylla ensures that all are completed or none are applied. To test a batch, you can insert an article and its summaries. Set the fields from table 6.2.

Table 6.2   Write the following fields to each of the article and summaries tables in a single batch query.

Field	Value
ID	`a843bb3c-558b-11ee-8c99-0242ac120002`
Author	`eff9bd01-4a73-11ee-8863-c02b3f99d2b2` (Alice Author)
Title	`'Great Food at Gr8 Food'.`
Score	9
Date	2023-09-10
Review	`'It was great!'`

To begin your batch, your statement starts with `BEGIN BATCH`. You then list each query you want in your batch, ending each query with a semicolon. Last, you close your batch with `APPLY BATCH;`. Putting the pieces together gives you the following query:

```
cqlsh:reviews> BEGIN BATCH                     ⟵─┤ Your BATCH query begins
    INSERT INTO articles(                           with BEGIN BATCH.
            id, title, author_id, restaurant_name, score, date, review
        ) VALUES(
            a843bb3c-558b-11ee-8c99-0242ac120002,
            'Great Food at Gr8 Food',
            eff9bd01-4a73-11ee-8863-c02b3f99d2b2,
            'Gr8 Food',
            9,                                       The BATCH query contains other
            '2023-09-10',                            write queries that succeed
            'It was great!'                          together or fail together.
        );                                     ⟵─┘
    INSERT INTO article_summaries_by_date(
            date_bucket, id, author_name, score, title
        ) VALUES(
            0,
            a843bb3c-558b-11ee-8c99-0242ac120002,
            'Alice Author',
            9,
            'Great Food at Gr8 Food'
        );
    INSERT INTO article_summaries_by_author(
            author_id, id, author_name, score, title
        ) VALUES(
            eff9bd01-4a73-11ee-8863-c02b3f99d2b2,
            a843bb3c-558b-11ee-8c99-0242ac120002,
            'Alice Author',
            9,
            'Great Food at Gr8 Food'
        );
    INSERT INTO article_summaries_by_score(
            score, id, author_name, title
        ) VALUES(
            9,
            a843bb3c-558b-11ee-8c99-0242ac120002,
            'Alice Author',
            'Great Food at Gr8 Food'
        );
APPLY BATCH;                     ⟵─┤ The BATCH is closed
                                     via APPLY BATCH;.
```

If you query the `articles` table, you see your inserted article:

```
cqlsh:reviews> SELECT * FROM articles
    WHERE id = a843bb3c-558b-11ee-8c99-0242ac120002;

@ Row 1
----------------+------------------------------------
 id             | a843bb3c-558b-11ee-8c99-0242ac120002
 author_id      | eff9bd01-4a73-11ee-8863-c02b3f99d2b2
 date           | 2023-09-10
 images         | null
```

```
restaurant_name | Gr8 Food
review          | It was great!
score           | 9
title           | Great Food at Gr8 Food
```

(1 rows)

If you query `article_summaries_by_date`, your summary is also there:

```
cqlsh:reviews> SELECT * FROM article_summaries_by_date
    WHERE date_bucket = 0 AND id = a843bb3c-558b-11ee-8c99-0242ac120002;
```

```
@ Row 1
-------------+-------------------------------------
 date_bucket | 0
 id          | a843bb3c-558b-11ee-8c99-0242ac120002
 author_name | Alice Author
 image       | null
 score       | 9
 title       | Great Food at Gr8 Food
```

(1 rows)

If you query the two other article summary tables, you see that the BATCH query made
sure the article summaries were also saved in these tables:

```
cqlsh:reviews> SELECT * FROM article_summaries_by_author
    WHERE author_id = eff9bd01-4a73-11ee-8863-c02b3f99d2b2
    AND id = a843bb3c-558b-11ee-8c99-0242ac120002;
```

```
@ Row 1
-------------+-------------------------------------
 author_id   | eff9bd01-4a73-11ee-8863-c02b3f99d2b2
 id          | a843bb3c-558b-11ee-8c99-0242ac120002
 author_name | Alice Author
 image       | null
 score       | 9
 title       | Great Food at Gr8 Food
```

(1 rows)

```
cqlsh:reviews> SELECT * FROM article_summaries_by_score
    WHERE score = 9
    AND id = a843bb3c-558b-11ee-8c99-0242ac120002;
```

```
@ Row 1
-------------+-------------------------------------
 score       | 9
 id          | a843bb3c-558b-11ee-8c99-0242ac120002
 author_name | Alice Author
 image       | null
 title       | Great Food at Gr8 Food
```

(1 rows)

Batch queries simplify your operations by letting you group queries together without having to worry about manually implementing atomic updates to your database. Running a batch can come at a cost, however. Let's examine the cost of batches and Scylla's options to mitigate it.

6.4.2 Logged vs. unlogged batches

When you executed the batch query in the previous section, you inserted rows into several partitions:

- `articles` is partitioned by the article ID.
- `article_summaries_by_date` is partitioned by the date bucket.
- `article_summaries_by_author` is partitioned by the author ID.
- `article_summaries_by_score` is partitioned by the score.

Because these are four distinct partition keys, they each get their own token and can map to different nodes in the hash ring. Given three replicas for your keyspace in a large enough cluster, your batch statement could potentially involve up to 12 nodes, putting extra stress on the cluster.

The batches you've executed thus far are powered by a specific Scylla internal component:

- Scylla maintains a *batch log* on a single node to ensure that updates across multiple partitions succeed, coordinating the updates to achieve the batch's guarantees. Because of this need for coordination, these batched operations are called *logged batches.*
- You can elect to skip this batch log by running an *unlogged batch*, but that means batch operations that span multiple partitions may partially fail on some partitions but succeed on others.
- To explicitly run an unlogged batch, replace your `BEGIN BATCH` statement with `BEGIN UNLOGGED BATCH`.

Unlogged batches are most useful in one scenario: updates sharing a single partition key. Scylla can perform atomic batch updates in a single partition automatically without the batch log. In fact, as an optimization, Scylla automatically turns logged batches into unlogged batches under the hood when a `BATCH` statement uses a single partition. Accordingly, the type of batch is mostly a hidden detail: Scylla selects the appropriate batch based on your query. Although there is an additional performance cost to using logged batches, they're the table stakes for getting atomic multipartition inserts.

That use case—atomic multipartition inserts—is the only time you should use a multipartition batch. If you don't need a multipartition update to be applied all at once, you're paying an extra performance cost for no reason. If you're updating multiple partitions, that batch coordinator node is communicating and managing several nodes, putting additional load on that node and the cluster as a whole. If you don't need atomicity, you can send your requests in parallel from your application instead.

It may feel like you've learned every way you can update data in ScyllaDB, but there's one more technique: you haven't updated a row based on that row's current state. Continuing the theme of Scylla offering ways to provide better coordination at an additional compute cost, Scylla supports conditional updates of data via *lightweight transactions*, which let you change a row if a supplied condition evaluates to true.

6.5   *Lightweight transactions*

In your Scylla query toolbox, taking action based on the current state of a row is tricky at this point. If you want to conditionally update, you have to read the row, make a decision in your application, and potentially write it back to the database. If you want to avoid overwriting a value, you need to find some way to lock that data in your application or get comfortable with Scylla dictating that the last write wins.

To mitigate these design challenges, Scylla offers support for conditional updates of rows via lightweight transactions (LWTs). In a LWT statement, Scylla allows you to supply a condition, and the statement updates a row only if the condition evaluates to true.

To see these benefits in action, imagine the following scenarios:

- User A reads an author's bio in preparation for updating it.
- User B deletes that author, removing the row from the database.
- User A updates the author's bio, which inserts a new row with only the ID and the bio.

Without some sort of coordination, users A and B unintentionally cooperate to insert into the database a logically corrupted author row with no name. LWTs can help prevent this; if user A's update query can check whether the row exists, it can avoid the awkwardly empty row. To see how, let's examine LWTs in action.

6.5.1   *The power of IF*

The key to LWTs is the word `IF`. If you see an `IF`, think LWT. To use an LWT, a query needs to include an `IF` clause, which triggers an LWT on execution. That `IF` clause can contain one of three clauses:

- `EXISTS` verifies that the row exists.
- `NOT EXISTS` does the opposite and verifies that the row doesn't exist.
- You can use the contents of a `WHERE` clause, but without the `WHERE`: one or more conditions that must match for the transaction to be applied.

To see an LWT, begin by loading your old friend Alice Author in the `authors` table in preparation for updating her bio to announce that she's expanded her writing coverage to include drinks:

```
cqlsh:reviews> SELECT * FROM authors
WHERE id = eff9bd01-4a73-11ee-8863-c02b3f99d2b2;

@ Row 1
-------+------------------------------------
 id    | eff9bd01-4a73-11ee-8863-c02b3f99d2b2
```

```
bio   | Alice loves writing about food
image | null
name  | Alice Author
```

(1 rows)

You can use an LWT to update her bio, avoiding the update-after-delete race condition. Granted, you're the only person updating her bio right now, but this is a book about learning ScyllaDB, so a little suspension of belief is necessary to study some of the features. Let's say you want to update only the bio if the name field is set to Alice Author. Adding an IF clause to your UPDATE statement tells Scylla to use an LWT to verify that the name is truly Alice Author before changing the row. Run the following query, and Scylla will do the work behind the scenes to make this update:

```
cqlsh:reviews> UPDATE authors
    SET bio = 'Alice loves writing about food and drink'
    WHERE id = eff9bd01-4a73-11ee-8863-c02b3f99d2b2
    IF name = 'Alice Author';

@ Row 1
-----------+--------------
 [applied] | True
 name      | Alice Author
```

Whoa! You got back extra data: Scylla returned the fields used in the condition, along with an [applied] value telling you that the LWT successfully updated the row. If it was unable to update, presumably you'd see [applied] set to False. You can verify this assertion by changing the IF clause to another author's name, like Bob Bookwriter:

```
cqlsh:reviews> UPDATE authors
    SET bio = 'Alice loves writing about food and drink'
    WHERE id = eff9bd01-4a73-11ee-8863-c02b3f99d2b2
    IF name = 'Bob Bookwriter';

@ Row 1
-----------+--------------
 [applied] | False
 name      | Alice Author
```

And as you expected, [applied] is set to False, because Alice's name isn't Bob Bookwriter. Scylla returns the row's name value to show you why it failed the condition and therefore why the LWT was not applied.

If you want to avoid the update-after-delete race condition by checking the row's existence, you can use the IF EXISTS clause, which verifies that the row is present in the database. Replacing name = … with an EXISTS accomplishes this goal. Run this query to see how the output differs based on the calculation because it checks the entire row as opposed to checking only a value within a condition:

```
cqlsh:reviews> UPDATE authors
    SET bio = 'Alice loves writing about food and drink'
    WHERE id = eff9bd01-4a73-11ee-8863-c02b3f99d2b2
    IF EXISTS;

@ Row 1
-----------+-----------------------------------------
 [applied] | True
 id        | eff9bd01-4a73-11ee-8863-c02b3f99d2b2
 bio       | Alice loves writing about food and drink
 image     | null
 name      | Alice Author
```

When checking whether a row exists, Scylla returns every value in the row. This behavior suggests that Scylla is reading the entire row when using IF EXISTS, which makes sense. If it needs to check a conditional expression, it needs to read data to validate that. This read comes at a performance cost, however. In the next section, you'll learn how lightweight transactions aren't exactly lightweight.

6.5.2   *Not lightweight*

ScyllaDB is a database designed for eventual consistency. When a replica misses a write, the cluster has mechanisms to repair this mismatch. In the case of conflicting writes, Scylla settles on last-write-wins for its conflict-resolution strategy. LWTs, however, go against the grain of this approach. An LWT wants to have a consistent view of the data so that it can accurately verify its condition and update the row. If a transaction isn't isolated, meaning no other requests interfere with it, it could be possible for an LWT's condition to become untrue between checking the condition and updating the row. This problem—making sure multiple nodes agree on a given value to have a consistent view of data—is referred to as *distributed consensus*. To solve these problems, Scylla needs an additional coordination mechanism.

To solve this challenge, Scylla reaches for an algorithm designed for distributed consensus: *Paxos*. Paxos defines ways for nodes to achieve distributed consensus for a given value stored between them.

> **NOTE**   Going into detail on Paxos is beyond this book (the "Paxos Made Simple" paper is 11 pages long). If you want to read more about it, you can check out Scylla's usage of Paxos at https://mng.bz/9oAj and the paper "Paxos Made Simple" at https://lamport.azurewebsites.net/pubs/paxos-simple.pdf.

For our purposes, the important thing is that Scylla's implementation of Paxos requires three round-trips between nodes to coordinate the LWT—three requests back-to-back-to-back. Additionally, Scylla locks updates to the rows you're attempting to update, so any concurrent requests are blocked while the cluster goes through this coordination to serve the request.

This cost increases if used in a BATCH request. Because you can run any query in a batch, using an IF clause triggers a *conditional batch*, where the batch succeeds only if all conditions in every statement in the batch evaluate to true. If that doesn't occur, the conditional batch fails. You may choose to do this if you want to update multiple rows based on their state concurrently, but keep a close eye on performance (which you'll learn more about in later chapters). Performing this operation could harm throughput and increase resource usage on the cluster.

> **NOTE** One thing coming to future versions of Scylla is greater usage of the Raft algorithm—a different distributed consensus algorithm designed to be more understandable than Paxos. It's currently the engine behind how Scylla reconciles schema updates, and in the future, it will replace Paxos for LWTs. You'll learn more about Raft in chapter 8.

LWTs are a useful technique. They give you behaviors similar to a relational database, but their cost means you should watch performance closely. When needed, however, they can be helpful. With that, you've learned about all of the write-time tools at your disposal in Scylla. In the next chapter, you'll focus on the more expensive operation: reading data from this distributed database.

Summary

- The DESCRIBE command can be applied to a table to list the table's fields and settings.
- If you skip updating a column in a WRITE statement, Scylla writes no data to the database as opposed to writing a null value.
- Every write to Scylla gets a write timestamp that is used to reconcile concurrent operations via the last-write-wins algorithm. The new value overwrites the older one.
- To view a column's write timestamp, you can apply the WRITETIME function to that column. You can also override this timestamp on a write with a USING TIMESTAMP clause.
- Because the absence of data may indicate either a deleted value or a value never written, Scylla writes a special data type called a tombstone when deleting data to indicate that the value has been deleted.
- Scylla writes data to an in-memory data structure called a memtable and replicates it to a commit log for persistence. When the memtable fills up, Scylla flushes it to an immutable SSTable file.
- As the database accrues SSTables, it combines them into a new SSTable through a process called compaction.
- Tombstones can't be compacted away until the gc_grace_seconds period has elapsed. It's important to run a repair to sync tombstones within this period, or your cluster risks data resurrection.
- Deletion queries can combine the partition key with an IN clause or range deletions to selectively delete multiple rows.

- The `minTimeUuid` and `maxTimeUuid` functions let you convert a timestamp into its representative `TIMEUUID`.
- Truncating a table deletes every row in the table, whereas dropping the table truncates and removes the underlying table.
- Time to live allows you to automatically delete rows after a specified period and can be applied on a query or set as a default option on your table.
- A batch query groups multiple queries together and ensures that each of them executes successfully or that none of them are applied. You can skip this safety by running an unlogged batch, which allows for partial failures.
- Lightweight transactions enable you to conditionally update a row based on that row's current state, but as they're a more expensive operation than a normal write, they should be used with caution.

Reading data from ScyllaDB

This chapter covers

- Limiting, grouping, sorting, and paginating queries
- Understanding read performance
- Using ScyllaDB to denormalize your data via materialized views and indexes

When you store data in a database, you're saving it there to read later. In the previous chapter, you learned about saving data to—and deleting it from—ScyllaDB. Accordingly, in this chapter, it's time to learn about reads. You've done some basic SELECT queries already, but here, you'll learn more about the various clauses you can add to those queries to get exactly the data you're looking for. You'll also look into read performance so that you can understand your queries' behavior and avoid burdening your cluster with a deluge of slow queries. Finally, you'll learn about how ScyllaDB can aid you in denormalizing your data models, offering tradeoffs between query speed and data storage to reduce your maintenance efforts.

In preparation for this chapter, I've included a dataset containing some sample rows in the book's code repo, which is available at www.manning.com/books/scylladb-in-action and https://github.com/scylladb-in-action/code. The ch07 folder contains a file: 1_dataset.cql. Copying its contents into your `cqlsh` session in one of the Scylla Docker containers will insert several rows into each of the tables, giving you rows to query against that you don't have to type and insert yourself. Once you've got that set up, it's time to begin reading about reading.

7.1 Selecting

Reading data from the database is something you've already done throughout the book. It's very hard to teach inserts into a database without at least dipping our toes into reads; you have to demonstrate that the data was successfully inserted into the database! In this section, you'll learn deeper techniques beyond the straightforward `SELECT` statement to meet your read needs. Let's begin by recalling what you've learned about `SELECT` queries.

7.1.1 The basics

After inserting data in the previous chapter, you frequently read it back using a `SELECT` query. You specified the specific columns you wanted to read (or a wildcard if you wanted every column), the table name in a `FROM` clause, and a `WHERE` clause containing at least the partition key. Scylla found the rows that matched your `WHERE` clause and returned them to you. Go ahead and reread your old friend Alice Author's row:

```
cqlsh:reviews> SELECT *          ⟵——| Columns to select.
    FROM authors                              ⟵——| Table to read from.
    WHERE id = eff9bd01-4a73-11ee-8863-c02b3f99d2b2;   ⟵—— Columns to
                                                          match to find
                                                          results.
@ Row 1
-------+------------------------------------
 id    | eff9bd01-4a73-11ee-8863-c02b3f99d2b2
 bio   | Alice loves writing about food
 image | null
 name  | Alice Author

(1 rows)
```

Recall that you don't need to select every column by default; you can also specify a subset of columns to be retrieved by your query. If you only wanted Alice's bio, you could write a query that retrieves only the bio. This approach is useful when you only need partial data from a row; it saves the cost of transmitting that extraneous data to the client if it's not going to be used. You can see the filtered columns in the following query:

```
cqlsh:reviews> SELECT bio      ⟵——| Only the bio
    FROM authors                      | is selected.
    WHERE id = eff9bd01-4a73-11ee-8863-c02b3f99d2b2;

@ Row 1
-------+------------------------------------
 bio   | Alice loves writing about food

(1 rows)
```

When writing a read query, you almost always want to query no more than a single partition of data. Multipartition queries add extra load to each node in the cluster, harming the cluster's overall performance. Similarly, Scylla enforces restrictions on queries in a partition. You observed in chapter 2 that attempting to filter data by a column that's not part of the primary key is disallowed by default and requires the addition of an `ALLOW FILTERING` clause to succeed.

Additionally, if you have multiple primary keys, Scylla only allows queries that use consecutive columns, starting with the partition key. Imagine a table with a four-column primary key: `a, b, c, d`. Table 7.1 illustrates valid queries against that table.

Table 7.1 Valid queries for a table with a four-column primary key.

Query	Valid?	Explanation
...WHERE a = ?	Valid	Uses the leftmost column
...WHERE a = ? AND b = ?	Valid	Uses consecutive columns, starting with the leftmost
...WHERE b = ?	Invalid	Doesn't use the leftmost column (the partition key)
...WHERE a = ? AND b = ? AND c = ?	Valid	Uses consecutive columns, starting with the leftmost
...WHERE a = ? AND c = ?	Invalid	Doesn't use consecutive columns
...WHERE a = ? AND b = ? AND c = ? ⇒ AND d = ?	Valid	Uses consecutive columns, starting with the leftmost

Running one of these queries without following the consecutive leftmost rule gives you a large error message:

```
InvalidRequest: Error from server: code=2200 [Invalid query]
⇒ message="PRIMARY KEY column "c" cannot be
⇒ restricted as preceding column "b" is not restricted"
```

Because your query doesn't restrict the value of `b`, it can't restrict the value of `c`. You've broken the consecutive leftmost rule, and Scylla won't let your query continue because Scylla stores your data on disk based on the ordering of your clustering keys—the non-partition portion of the primary key. Although the partition key tells it which node it lives on, the clustering keys determine the relative ordering of data. Breaking that ordering by not following consecutive leftmost makes it less efficient to read data, so Scylla stops you from performing those queries.

With this functionality as a baseline, you can expand your querying toolkit to perform more complicated operations. Next, let's look at how ScyllaDB provides functionality to limit the results it returns.

7.1.2   Limiting results

On the home page, your applications wants to retrieve the most recent article summaries. Although the summaries are partitioned by their date, as time goes by, you'll have more and more articles to display. If you only want to show 10 articles, what do you do when your query loads more? Your application could load all the summaries possible and only display what it wanted to, but it's inefficient to send that amount of data over the wire. To solve this dilemma, Scylla supports a LIMIT clause, allowing you to limit the number of rows returned by a query.

> **WARNING**   The LIMIT clause doesn't limit the number of rows scanned, only the number of results returned.

In your LIMIT clause, you specify that number and place it after your WHERE clause. To see it in action, you can query the larger article_summaries_by_date partition from earlier, limiting it to two results:

```
cqlsh:reviews> SELECT id, title
    FROM article_summaries_by_date
    WHERE date_bucket = 0
    LIMIT 2;                       ←———  Your query is limited
                                         to two results.
@ Row 1
-------+-------------------------------------
 id    | 7fcf4e82-704d-11ee-b962-0242ac120002
 title | So Many Flavors at 9000 wings

@ Row 2
-------+-------------------------------------
 id    | 9f545786-704b-11ee-b962-0242ac120002
 title | Life-changing Potatoes

(2 rows)        ←———  Only two results
                      are returned.
```

Even though more rows match your query's WHERE clause, LIMIT did its job and limited the number of rows in the response. As its name implies, if your query returns fewer rows than the limit, that's fine; it's under the limit. You can observe this behavior by querying with the same limit against a smaller partition—try querying article_summaries_by_date again but with a very large number as a limit:

```
cqlsh:reviews> SELECT id, title
    FROM article_summaries_by_date
    WHERE date_bucket = 0
    LIMIT 100;

@ Row 1
-------+-------------------------------------
 id    | 7fcf4e82-704d-11ee-b962-0242ac120002
 title | So Many Flavors at 9000 wings
```

```
@ Row 2
-------+----------------------------------------
 id    | 9f545786-704b-11ee-b962-0242ac120002
 title | Life-changing Potatoes

@ Row 3
-------+----------------------------------------
 id    | b71e77f8-704a-11ee-b962-0242ac120002
 title | Lack of Variety at Pepperoni Pizza Only

@ Row 4
-------+----------------------------------------
 id    | 78fb3d92-7047-11ee-b962-0242ac120002
 title | Good Tacos at Main Street Tacos

@ Row 5
-------+----------------------------------------
 id    | 1e24e04c-7044-11ee-b962-0242ac120002
 title | Ernie's Eats Exceeds Expectations

(5 rows)
```

As expected, your query retrieves fewer rows than the limit because there are not enough rows to be limited.

Per-partition limits

Each `LIMIT`'d query you've run up to this point has limited results in a single partition because Scylla performs best when you're querying against a single partition, as querying multiple partitions gets expensive quickly. Occasionally, however, you may want to query all partitions, such as when you know the dataset is very small or you're looking to perform a cluster-wide query in an ad hoc fashion.

To support finer-grained limits in those scenarios, Scylla supports a per-partition limit clause via `PER PARTITION LIMIT`. It functions similarly to the `LIMIT` clause, except its limit is applied to each partition, not against the entire result set. Of course, if you query only a single partition, they're effectively the same.

By limiting the number of rows returned, you can return an amount of data large enough to be meaningful but small enough to be useful to users. Let's examine how you can return results after the first limited group by applying pagination to the database. What happens, however, when the user wants to keep querying, finding results after the initial grouping? Let's examine how you can use `LIMIT` to achieve this goal.

7.1.3 Paginating queries

The best practice in production applications is to provide an upper bound to the number of results a query can return. Instead of passing hundreds of summaries to a user, you can load 10, and if they want more, they can request the next 10, an approach called *pagination*—similar to reading pages from a book. When you purchased *ScyllaDB in Action*, it didn't come in one gigantic page (even PDFs have pages), but rather as a few hundred pages stitched together (potentially digitally). When you read all the words on a page, you turn to the next page, getting another set of words to read; this process is how pagination works.

Pagination isn't an explicit ScyllaDB feature; it's a common data-querying technique that utilizes ScyllaDB's concepts to make it work with your cluster. A paginated query has two key components:

- A LIMIT clause to specify your page size
- A WHERE clause that matches rows based on the previous page's state

Internal pagination

Under the hood, Scylla also performs pagination internally. If you write a very large query that returns thousands of rows, the driver will limit the number of rows via a lower-level protocol, returning a paging state data structure with the query. You can then pass this token on to the next query, getting you the next page of results.

NOTE   If you're familiar with relational databases, you may remember performing pagination using both LIMIT and an OFFSET clause, which tells your query to skip a specified number of records. ScyllaDB doesn't support OFFSET; because Scylla is querying multiple SSTables and then aggregating the results, it would need to fully execute the query and then throw away the results to accurately compute an OFFSET query—an expensive operation!

Recall that in chapter 5, when you created your article summary tables, you specified an ordering for the table: descending by id. Because the id is a TIMEUUID, your earlier LIMIT query gives you the two most recent article summaries. Let's run that query again:

```
cqlsh:reviews> SELECT id, title
    FROM article_summaries_by_date
    WHERE date_bucket = 0
    LIMIT 2;

@ Row 1
-------+-------------------------------------
 id    | 7fcf4e82-704d-11ee-b962-0242ac120002
 title | So Many Flavors at 9000 wings

@ Row 2
-------+-------------------------------------
 id    | 9f545786-704b-11ee-b962-0242ac120002
 title | Life-changing Potatoes

(2 rows)
```

When querying for the second page of results, you are looking for two rows that have IDs less than the last row on your page—because your table is sorted by id, descending. Thinking back about the key components of a paginated query, you need the following:

- A LIMIT of 2
- id < 9f545786-704b-11ee-b962-0242ac120002, meaning the articles are older than the last row of your previous query

Combining these, you get a query that gets the second page. Execute that now, and you see two older articles:

```
cqlsh:reviews> SELECT id, title
    FROM article_summaries_by_date
    WHERE date_bucket = 0
      AND id < 9f545786-704b-11ee-b962-0242ac120002
    LIMIT 2;

@ Row 1
-------+----------------------------------------
 id    | b71e77f8-704a-11ee-b962-0242ac120002
 title | Lack of Variety at Pepperoni Pizza Only

@ Row 2
-------+----------------------------------------
 id    | 78fb3d92-7047-11ee-b962-0242ac120002
 title | Good Tacos at Main Street Tacos

(2 rows)
```

If you want the page after this one, take the ID of the last result and swap it into your query, giving you the next (and final for now) page:

```
cqlsh:reviews> SELECT id, title
    FROM article_summaries_by_date
    WHERE date_bucket = 0
      AND id < 78fb3d92-7047-11ee-b962-0242ac120002
    LIMIT 2;

@ Row 1
-------+-----------------------------------
 id    | 1e24e04c-7044-11ee-b962-0242ac120002
 title | Ernie's Eats Exceeds Expectations

(1 rows)
```

Executing paginated queries is similar to a loop in your favorite programming language; your application needs to eventually stop the loop. When you get results that are less than the desired page size, that's your stopping point. User interfaces are often paginated, and you can help facilitate this pattern by loading one page only when the user requests it.

Pagination is a querying technique that uses the ordering in a partition to accomplish its goals. Let's look further at how you can use ordering in your queries via an ORDER BY clause.

7.1.4 Ordering results

Back in chapter 5, when defining your article summary tables, you created them with a specific ordering, sorting the tables by their article IDs. That sorting is reflected in your queries: in the last section, your paginated article queries had the most recent articles first. This behavior is enforced by the ordering provided to the clustering keys for your table—the non-partition primary keys. For the article summaries tables, you provided the id as a clustering key and told Scylla to sort it in descending order.

A table's sort, however, isn't something you set when creating the table and are stuck with forever; ScyllaDB supports changing it at query time, with some restrictions you'll soon encounter. To sort your queries by a different order, you can use an ORDER BY clause, listing the clustering key columns you'd like to sort by and the direction to sort them in: ascending (ASC) or descending (DESC) by their natural order. The clause goes after your WHERE clause; you can see it in action by sorting your queries by id ASC in your original LIMIT query to retrieve the oldest articles in the partition:

```
cqlsh:reviews> SELECT id, title
    FROM article_summaries_by_date
    WHERE date_bucket = 0
    ORDER BY id ASC           ← Orders by ascending
    LIMIT 2;                     id—oldest first.
                              Results contain the older
@ Row 1            ←          article summaries.
-------+------------------------------------
 id    | 1e24e04c-7044-11ee-b962-0242ac120002
 title | Ernie''s Eats Exceeds Expectations

@ Row 2
-------+------------------------------------
 id    | 78fb3d92-7047-11ee-b962-0242ac120002
 title | Good Tacos at Main Street Tacos

(2 rows)
```

The article summaries returned by your query are different; these are the two oldest ones. This query, because of how it sorts the results, is often referred to as a *reverse query*, because it reverses one of the defined sort orders of your keys. A small performance cost is associated with this operation; if you're doing a reverse query more frequently than the normal one, it's an indication that you may want to migrate the data to a different sort if you're having performance troubles (you'll learn more about large data migrations in chapter 12).

I hinted at the restriction with ORDER BY previously: you're limited to only the clustering key columns of your table. If you try to sort a query by a nonclustering key column, you'll get a big error, which you can see for yourself by trying to sort your article summaries by score:

```
cqlsh:reviews> SELECT id, title
    FROM article_summaries_by_date
    WHERE date_bucket = 0
    ORDER BY score ASC
    LIMIT 2;

InvalidRequest: Error from server: code=2200 [Invalid query]
➥ message="Order by is currently only supported on the
➥ clustered columns of the PRIMARY KEY, got score"
```

As seen in the preceding example, ScyllaDB restricts you to the clustering key columns of your primary key. The partition key isn't a valid sorting key, either; Scylla wants you to only query a single partition at a time. Sorts using the clustering keys are straightforward for Scylla to perform: the data is already sorted on disk and only potentially needs to be reversed. Other sorts, if allowed, would require Scylla to perform an additional sort in memory, increasing load on the node and cluster as it can't rely on the existing on-disk orderings.

Next up in your querying journey is a special function that counts the number of rows returned by a query: COUNT.

7.1.5 *Counting*

Imagine that the restaurant reviews business is booming, and a potential investor asks you how many articles you've published this month. Assuming you don't remember off the top of your head, your choices at this point are as follows:

- Run a query against article_summaries_by_date and count the number of results.
- Load your homepage and start counting.
- Pick a random number that sounds impressive yet plausible.

The second option is the same as the first one but with a shinier user interface. Lying is frowned on, and when talking about your business, it can potentially be considered fraud. The first option is the one to choose, but you don't have to count every row yourself; ScyllaDB can do that with its COUNT function.

With COUNT in your SELECT clause, Scylla tells you the number of rows that match the WHERE clause. Instead of giving you a list of rows, it gives you the number of rows found. When paginating through article_summaries_by_date earlier, you found five summaries. If you count the number of rows in that partition using COUNT, you should arrive at the same quantity. If you replace your wildcard with a COUNT(*), you'll count the number of rows in the specified partition: the date bucket 0. Run the following query to execute this count:

```
cqlsh:reviews> SELECT COUNT(*)
    FROM article_summaries_by_date
    WHERE date_bucket = 0;
```

And as expected, Scylla tells you there are five results:

```
@ Row 1
-------+---
 count | 5

(1 rows)
```

The usual querying rules apply: you want to query by at least the partition key, and you can't filter your query by non-primary key values. Although you *can* use COUNT against an entire table, doing so is not recommended. Think about how Scylla queries data. A full-table COUNT will need to query every partition—an expensive operation that scales with the number of records to check. Scylla will let you run the query, but it will be slower than a per-partition count. Running locally, there's a brief but noticeable pause before results return. You can see this in action by counting your authors:

```
cqlsh:reviews> SELECT COUNT(*) FROM authors;

@ Row 1
-------+---
 count | 2

(1 rows)
```

Built-in aggregate functions

COUNT is a special type of function in Scylla called an *aggregate function*, which operates on multiple rows in a SELECT statement. Other aggregate functions include the following:

- MIN(column) gives you the minimum value in a column in your result set.
- MAX(column) gives you the maximum value in a column in your result set.
- SUM(column) adds up all values for a given column in your result set.
- AVG(column) provides the average of all values for a given column in your result set.

Scylla also supports defining your own aggregate functions: user-defined functions. Supporting either Lua or WebAssembly, you can create a FUNCTION and use it in an AGGREGATE, unlocking the ability to run it on groups of rows in your results.

Counting is useful not only for knowing how many results you have but also for presenting data to a user. If you're building pagination on an author's page for their articles, it's valuable to know the total number of articles so the user knows how many pages to expect. Counting can also be used to check the presence of a row. Perhaps you only want to validate that the author exists—you don't care about retrieving specific fields when a user loads an article. A COUNT query against the authors table for a given ID accomplishes that goal. Counting is a flexible tool and one that can be very useful in your application. Continuing our tour of Scylla's querying tools, let's look at how you can apply COUNT and other aggregate functions more selectively to further tune your results via grouping.

7.1.6 Grouping rows in your queries

As an aggregate function, COUNT works on multiple rows. So far, you've only used it to answer straightforward questions, like how many articles are in a data bucket. Not all questions are simple, though; you may wonder what the distribution of scores is for a given author. Maybe you're suspicious that they tend to give higher (or lower) scores than other reviewers. If you've looked closely at the dataset I gave you at the beginning of the chapter, you may have noticed a second author: Alice Author has a friend now—Reginald Reviewer (id 33a753de-704c-11ee-b962-0242ac120002). Let's examine Reginald's reviews.

Load Reginald's reviews using the article_summaries_by_author table, and you'll see two reviews—both high-scoring:

```
cqlsh:reviews> SELECT *
    FROM article_summaries_by_author
    WHERE author_id = 33a753de-704c-11ee-b962-0242ac120002;

@ Row 1
------------+---------------------------------------------
 author_id   | 33a753de-704c-11ee-b962-0242ac120002
 id          | 7fcf4e82-704d-11ee-b962-0242ac120002
 author_name | Reginald Reviewer
 image       | {path: 'wings.jpg', caption: 'They claim...'}
 score       | 90
 title       | So Many Flavors at 9000 wings

@ Row 2
------------+---------------------------------------------
 author_id   | 33a753de-704c-11ee-b962-0242ac120002
 id          | 9f545786-704b-11ee-b962-0242ac120002
 author_name | Reginald Reviewer
 image       | {path: 'potatoes.jpg', caption: 'Mash ''em up!'}
 score       | 100
 title       | Life-changing Potatoes

(2 rows)
```

Checking Reginald's review scores is straightforward at the moment; there are two reviews, so it's easy to find the scores. But what happens as time goes by and Reginald writes more and more reviews? In preparation for this question, I've included a new table in the dataset: article_scores_by_author. If you use your old friend DESCRIBE, you can learn more about the table, which is partitioned by author_id and contains score and id as the primary key:

```
CREATE TABLE reviews.article_scores_by_author (
    author_id timeuuid,
    score tinyint,
```

```
    id timeuuid,
    PRIMARY KEY (author_id, score, id)
) WITH CLUSTERING ORDER BY (score DESC, id DESC)
    AND ...
```

To query Reginald's scores, you need to query the new table by his author ID. Executing this query shows you the scores for the two articles he's written thus far:

```
cqlsh:reviews> SELECT *
    FROM article_scores_by_author
    WHERE author_id = 33a753de-704c-11ee-b962-0242ac120002;

@ Row 1
-----------+-------------------------------------
 author_id | 33a753de-704c-11ee-b962-0242ac120002
 score     | 100
 id        | 9f545786-704b-11ee-b962-0242ac120002

@ Row 2
-----------+-------------------------------------
 author_id | 33a753de-704c-11ee-b962-0242ac120002
 score     | 90
 id        | 7fcf4e82-704d-11ee-b962-0242ac120002

(2 rows)
```

Even if you only queried for scores, thus far you can't get a histogram of scores to determine their frequency. Instead of copying these out to a spreadsheet app, Scylla supports grouping data via the appropriately named GROUP BY clause: it takes a column and groups together rows that have the same value for that column, as shown in figure 7.1.

After organizing the rows, its return value is either

- The result of an aggregation function applied to the group
- The first value of the group

Of these two choices, you'll almost always use an aggregation function—such as COUNT—with your GROUP BY clause. You can use GROUP BY to get the count of scores for each article by grouping articles by score and selecting a count:

```
cqlsh:reviews> SELECT score, COUNT(*)         ⟵  Each group
    FROM article_scores_by_author                 is counted.     The query
    WHERE author_id = 33a753de-704c-11ee-b962-0242ac120002  ⟵  filters by
    GROUP BY score;              ⟵                             author ID.
                                    Rows are grouped
                                    by score.
```

For Reginald's reviews, each score becomes a group because of the GROUP BY score in your query. There's a group of 90 and a group of 100, each with only one member, as there are only two rows in the table for Reginald. The aggregation function is then applied to each member of the group. Because there's only one member in each

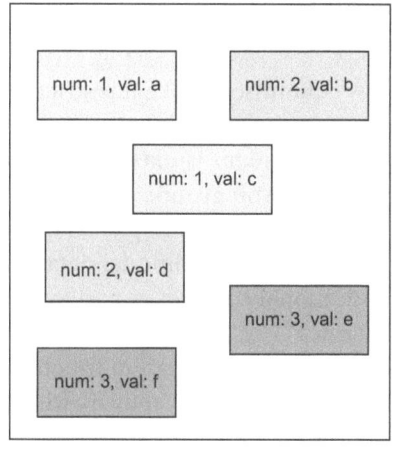 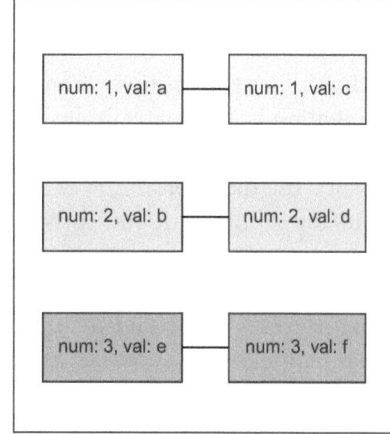

Ungrouped query	Query grouped by num
A GROUP BY clause within a query groups rows together by a common value, enabling you to apply aggregate functions on each group.	Grouping here allows you to determine how many rows there are for each value of num.

Figure 7.1 Adding GROUP BY to your read queries groups rows together by a specified value, unlocking the ability to apply aggregate functions to each of these groups.

group, the count is also straightforward. Put together, you're given the number of reviews for each score:

```
@ Row 1
-------+-----
 score | 100
 count | 1

@ Row 2
-------+-----
 score | 90
 count | 1

(2 rows)
```

Grouping fields and applying aggregation functions gives you a more granular view of your data by allowing you to select a partition and aggregate it together based on the clustering keys. However, you are limited to using the clustering keys; you cannot use other columns that aren't in the primary key for grouping. If you try to group by the score in `article_summaries_by_author`, you'll get an error message:

```
cqlsh:reviews> SELECT score, count(*)
    FROM article_summaries_by_author
    WHERE author_id = 33a753de-704c-11ee-b962-0242ac120002
    GROUP BY score;
```

```
InvalidRequest: Error from server: code=2200 [Invalid query]
⇥ message="Group by non-primary-key column score"
```

Scylla doesn't let you group by non-primary key columns, just like it restricts ordering. This limitation is, like many things with Scylla, to prevent additional resource usage in the cluster. Deep in the system's internals, when a query is executed, an ORDER BY clause sorts the data before the GROUP BY groups it. If you grouped the query in a way that's incompatible with the sort—such as grouping by a non-primary key—Scylla would have to either resort the retrieved data or maintain additional data in memory to satisfy the query. Instead of taking on this additional complexity and overhead, the database prevents you from executing these queries.

What happens with GROUP BY when you don't use an aggregation function? I mentioned earlier that you had two options for what your query returns when using a GROUP BY clause. You've seen the first one—the result of an aggregation function. The second option is the value in the first row for a column selected in your query in that group. If you think about the contents of the results of a CQL query, it wants to map keys (such as a column or function name) to single result values, creating rows. However, if you're grouping rows into a single row, it needs that single value to return.

Applying this principle to the article_scores_by_author table, what would you expect to see if you queried for score and ID for a given author, grouped by score? You'd expect to get back the values for the first row in each group. Because you're querying for IDs, you'd expect to get the grouped score and the ID of the first article in the group:

```
cqlsh:reviews> SELECT score, id
    FROM article_scores_by_author
    WHERE author_id = 33a753de-704c-11ee-b962-0242ac120002
    GROUP BY score;

@ Row 1
-------+---------------------------------------
 score | 100
 id    | 9f545786-704b-11ee-b962-0242ac120002

@ Row 2
-------+---------------------------------------
 score | 90
 id    | 7fcf4e82-704d-11ee-b962-0242ac120002

(2 rows)
```

Looking at your query, that is indeed the case. It can be much less intuitive when you have more than one row per group, but every time, in the absence of an aggregation function, the result will be pulled from the first row of the group.

For the majority of cases, you'll use GROUP BY with an aggregation function. When you add GROUP BY to your query, you're doing so because you want to consider rows a specific grouping and extract some information—such as counting them or getting the average value of all rows. Selecting a specific column without an aggregation function is typically done on a more ad hoc basis, such as seeing what a "typical" value is like for a column in that group. My experience suggests that 99 times out of 100, you'll be using an aggregation function.

And with that, you're an expert at SELECT queries. You can limit, paginate, sort, apply aggregation functions, and group rows together. Even if you have a query that utilizes all the techniques you know and perfectly fits your use case, your users will be sad if it returns slowly or, even worse, times out or errors out! In the next section, you'll learn how reads perform in Scylla and how you can help your queries return speedily.

7.2 Read performance

Reads are the likeliest operation in ScyllaDB to be slow and cause you and your systems problems. This challenge is intentional; it relates to the core of Scylla's design. Back in chapter 6, you learned about what happens in Scylla when you write data. Let's take another look at that diagram (figure 7.2) to compare it to a similar visualization of a

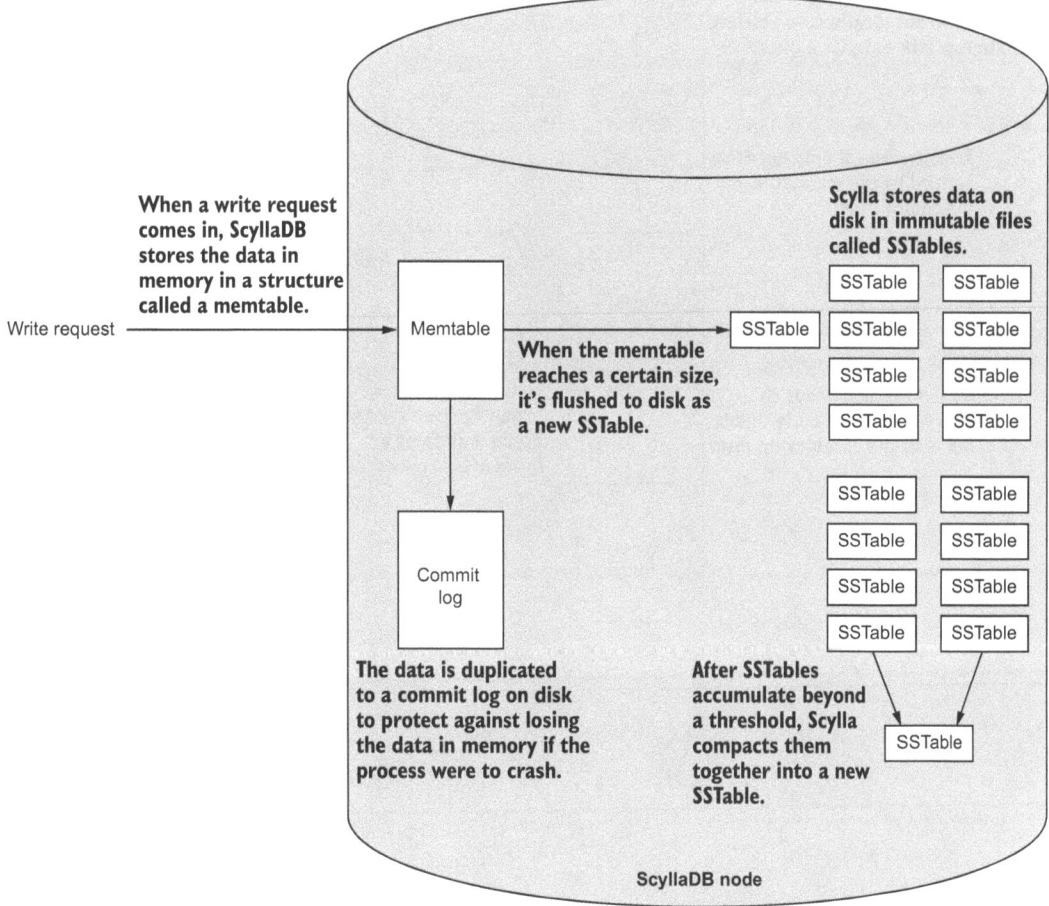

Figure 7.2   A write query starts out being written to memory and appended to a commit log but is eventually flushed to disk.

read query. When a write query is sent to the database, it's added to the in-memory memtable and appended to a commit log on disk for persistence. Later, that memtable gets flushed to disk, but from a client's point of view, the write is complete once it's been added to the memtable and commit log—two quick insertions, and you're done.

The tradeoff here is that reads are often slower than writes. Because Scylla doesn't overwrite previous versions of data on inserts, it needs to potentially read multiple versions of data on disk to find the most recent one. The data can be spread across multiple SSTables, and Scylla may need to read multiple of them to satisfy the query. Because of these design decisions, reads tend to be the more heavyweight operation in Scylla; they're almost always the bottlenecked operation, as shown in figure 7.3.

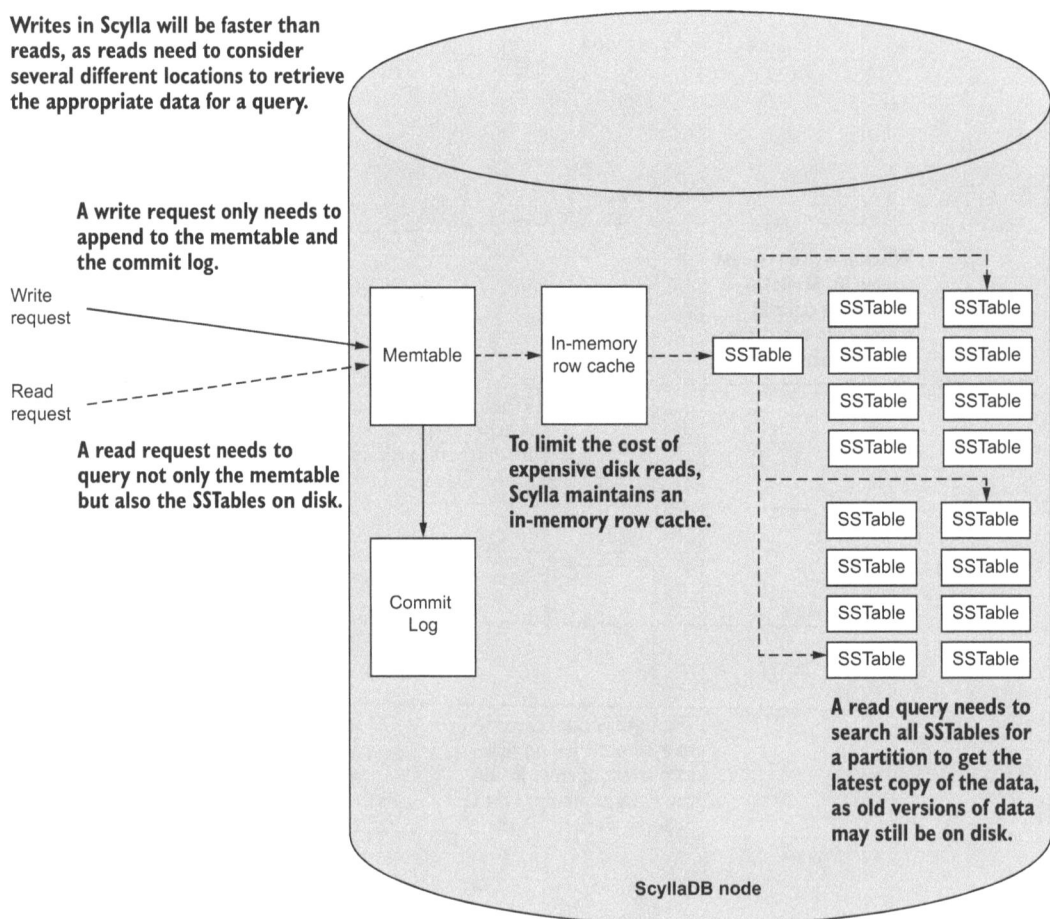

Figure 7.3   Reads are a more complicated operation than writes in ScyllaDB, so they tend to be the slower operation.

Just because reads are slower, however, doesn't mean they need to be slow. In this section, you'll learn how both you and Scylla can combine your powers to make the database serve fast, efficient reads.

7.2.1   What does a read do?

To serve a SELECT query, Scylla needs to select all rows that match the query's WHERE clause. If there's no WHERE clause, the query selects all rows—simple but bad for performance. With a WHERE clause, you specify the partition key and—if they exist on the table you're reading—one or more clustering keys, following the consecutive leftmost rule you learned about earlier in the chapter.

With these columns specified in your WHERE clause, Scylla takes your query and begins scanning the memtable and the on-disk SSTables for rows matching your query. In each SSTable, the row's partition key and clustering keys are specified in dedicated fields. Because you're querying with a partition key and Scylla enforces the consecutive leftmost rule for clustering keys, Scylla quickly identifies the relevant rows and sees if they match, because—as you may have guessed—SSTables also store their clustering keys in the consecutive leftmost order as defined in the table.

Because writes are append-only operations, a query may find different versions of a row on disk. The row may have been updated or even deleted. In your database, you'll have many rows spread across many SSTables on many nodes. Each time your query finds a row, it needs to ensure that the most recent copy of that row is returned to the client. Although ideally every query runs as fast as you've always dreamed, sometimes that's not the case. Let's look at how you can avoid slow queries.

7.2.2   Avoiding slow queries

The most important action you can take to help your database's performance is to query only one partition key at a time. Have I mentioned this in previous chapters? Yes! Will I mention it again? Almost certainly! It's important: by querying a single partition at a time, you minimize the number of nodes required to serve a request, lessening the load on the database.

This pattern is enforced from way back when you first designed your schema. The entire point of query-first design is to design your schema based on how you want to query it, and how you want to query it is by partition key so you're querying only one partition at a time. This behavior is table stakes for performance; it's low-hanging fruit, and if you're not doing it, reducing the number of partitions per query will provide immediate performance gains. Sometimes, however, it's not enough.

You can query a single partition and still have a slow query. I got paged for one during my last on-call shift! Before looking at possible solutions, it's important to understand what we're looking at—what makes a query slow?

WHAT MAKES A QUERY SLOW?

Query speed is a function of several things—including disk speeds and network bandwidth—but I find it's best to focus on three factors:

- The size of a row
- The number of rows in a partition
- The resources available on the node to execute the query

When a query is slow, to speed it up, you can try adjusting these parameters to boost its performance. Imagine that each of your reviews is a gigabyte in the database. It's a far-fetched scenario, but a larger row takes more time to read than a smaller row. Although Scylla does compress data on disk, the size of the rows you're trying to read has a big influence on your query's speed.

And even if you're querying in a single partition, that partition itself can also be large. If you're reading an entire very large partition, your query is necessarily going to be slower than a query against your small dataset's `article_summaries_by_date` partitions.

Finally, to execute the query, the database's underlying server needs available resources: CPU time, disk I/O, and memory. If the server is constrained on any of these, the query's performance will also be constrained. As your cluster handles more and more concurrent queries, they will each consume resources, and at a certain point, performance will degrade. Later in the book, you'll learn how to monitor Scylla for these performance problems and mitigate them.

Recall from chapter 6 that a row doesn't map to a single entity on disk; it can be stored across multiple SSTables based on each time you update a row. Each update generates additional data in your database. Let's look closer at how that can have an outsized effect on performance.

THE EFFECT OF UPDATES

Imagine that you want to know the last time someone read an article, and you decide to add a `TIMESTAMP` column to your `articles` table called `last_read_at`. Every time your application loads the article, you fire a quick request to the database to update `last_read_at` to `now()` for that article. Writes in Scylla are fast, and you're updating only a single column, so it seems an innocent enough operation.

Thinking back to the lifecycle of data after it's written, the following things happen:

- Your update is stored in a memtable in memory.
- The memtable is flushed to disk and stored in an SSTable.
- These SSTables are eventually compacted together.

This operation happens each time you update `last_read_at`. Although ideally, compactions would condense all of these updates down to one entry in one SSTable, practically, the process is not that efficient. Frequent updates generate data that gets spread across SSTables, making it hard to completely clean up. You'll look more at the nuances of compaction in the next chapter, but for now, know that it considers a limited number of SSTables together when executing, so it can't effectively condense every update into its minimal representation.

These frequent updates increase the size of your partitions. The row becomes larger because your query needs to scan multiple SSTables to read each of the updates to determine the correct value for the row. Because the row becomes larger, you're taking additional time to read the row, increasing the CPU time and the disk bandwidth consumed. Reading a table that has frequently updated rows can often cause a cascading effect on your queries' performance, harming your database and its upstream clients.

Just because it can harm performance, however, doesn't mean it will. I advocate a reactive approach: there's no hard-and-fast rule that says if your queries reach a certain threshold, you'll run into slow queries. Performance problems are a function of your data and the cluster's design—every situation is different. We've all heard the Donald Knuth quote—premature optimization is the root of all evil. *Design your database schema to encourage single-partition queries by following query-first design, and you'll avoid 80% of all performance problems.* Someday, though, you'll run into a slow query.

> ### How Scylla helps you with speedy reads
> Speeding up queries isn't solely your responsibility. Internally, Scylla maintains a *row cache* in memory to speed up disk reads. Because disk I/O is the slowest low-level operation Scylla performs, it maintains a read-through cache to cache results from disk reads. You'll learn more about this speed-up (and others, like Scylla's Bloom filters) in the next chapter as we dive into ScyllaDB's architecture.

To see an example of a query that can make your database struggle, let's look at a query that looks like it may fit a use case but can cause big problems.

7.2.3 Allowing filtering

Way back in chapter 2, you attempted to filter a query by a column that wasn't in your primary key, and you got a scary warning. Let's reproduce that now by selecting Alice Author's row by her name, which isn't part of the primary key:

```
cqlsh> SELECT * FROM reviews.authors WHERE name = 'Alice Author';

@ Row 1
-------+----------------------------------------
 id    | eff9bd01-4a73-11ee-8863-c02b3f99d2b2
 bio   | Alice loves writing about food
 image | null
 name  | Alice Author

(1 rows)

Cannot execute this query as it might involve data filtering and thus may have
unpredictable performance. If you want to execute this query despite the
performance unpredictability, use ALLOW FILTERING
```

At the end of the query, you get the error message telling you that you should use ALLOW FILTERING to run this query. This type of query is a *filtered query*, which filters data in a nonstandard way. This message seems totally innocuous, but this query is actually a performance trap. A filtered query selects all rows that match the supplied partition and clustering keys (if any are present in the WHERE clause) and then performs server-side filtering against the remaining columns. If you're specifying the partition key and following the consecutive leftmost rule with primary keys, you'll get the usual single-partition performance. If you're not following those best practices, you're in for an adventure—not the good kind. Even if you use a LIMIT in your query, Scylla is unable to control the size of the initial query. If you don't include the partition key, you're going to scan every row in the database! Scanning every row is, as you may have guessed, not great for database performance.

ALLOW FILTERING can be a tempting solution. Sometimes you'll want to add a new query to your database that isn't supported by your existing schema, such as querying for authors by name. Although you may think that slapping an ALLOW FILTERING on a new query is the way to go, it's almost always something to test first because the query can be slow to run. If it's too slow for your needs, you don't have to completely rearchitect your schema to avoid this pitfall; ScyllaDB contains support for adding new queries via its denormalization options: materialized views and indexes. Let's look at how you can use these special table types to make your life simpler.

7.3   *Materialized views*

When you worked through your query-first design earlier in the book, you identified in your requirements that you needed to query article summaries in a few different ways: by author, by date, and by score. Because you need to store your data by how you query it in ScyllaDB, you denormalized your article summaries, storing them in three tables. Keeping them in sync is your responsibility; batch writes help by giving you an all-or-nothing insertion for writing the summaries together, but you're still responsible for making sure your queries go to the right places.

To assist your denormalization, Scylla provides functionality that enables you to query existing tables without the standard partition key and clustering keys, but it requires some initial setup. First is a *materialized view*, which constructs what is effectively a new table based on a few pieces of information:

- A base table to construct the view from
- A new primary key that you want to query by, containing your new partition key and the remaining primary key fields of the base table
- A SELECT query to select the rows and columns to be included in the view

By combining these things, Scylla can select rows from the base table into a new special materialized view table. Because it has a different primary key than the base table, you can query it efficiently, as shown in figure 7.4.

To see it in action, you can create a materialized view using one of your denormalized article summary tables. Let's use it as a lens to view how a materialized view works.

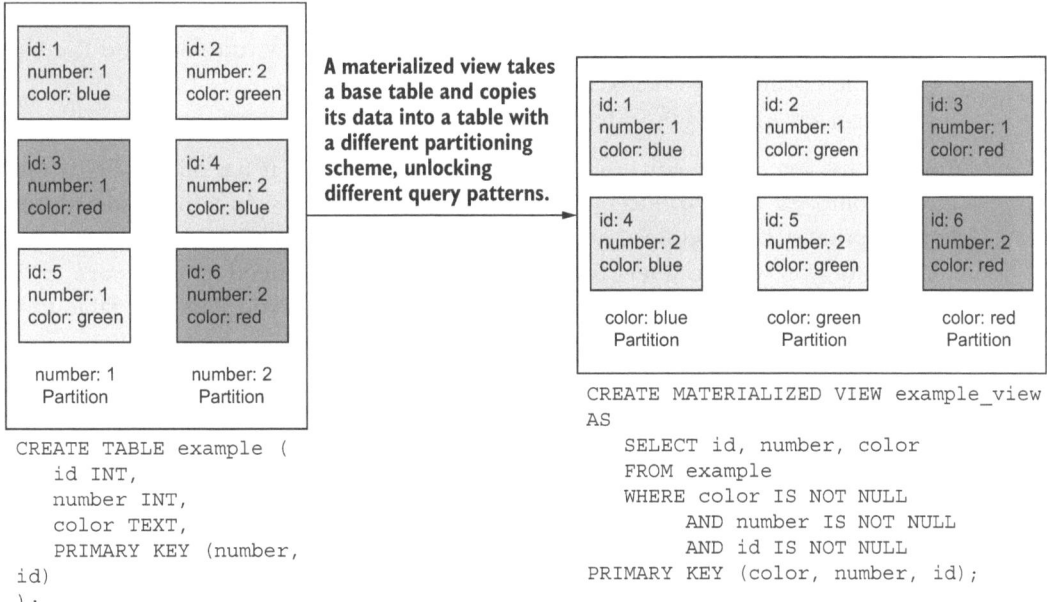

A materialized view takes a base table and copies its data into a table with a different partitioning scheme, unlocking different query patterns.

```
CREATE TABLE example (
    id INT,
    number INT,
    color TEXT,
    PRIMARY KEY (number,
id)
);
```

```
CREATE MATERIALIZED VIEW example_view
AS
    SELECT id, number, color
    FROM example
    WHERE color IS NOT NULL
        AND number IS NOT NULL
        AND id IS NOT NULL
PRIMARY KEY (color, number, id);
```

Figure 7.4   A materialized view copies data into a new table with a different partition key, trading additional disk usage for flexibility in the queries your schema offers.

7.3.1   Constructing a view

You have three article summary tables today, with almost all the same fields between them. I've reproduced each in table 7.2.

Table 7.2   Your article summaries tables denormalize your data to enable querying it in different ways.

article_summaries_ by_author	article_summaries_ by_date	article_summaries_ by_score
author_id TIMEUUID	date_bucket SMALLINT	score TINYINT
id TIMEUUID	id TIMEUUID	id TIMEUUID
title TEXT	title TEXT	title TEXT
author_name TEXT	author_name TEXT	author_name TEXT
image image	image image	image image
score TINYINT	score TINYINT	

To see the materialized view in the wild, you can reimplement article_summaries_ by_score to use one. You'll need three things:

- A base table
- A new primary key consisting of the new partition key you need and the base table's primary key fields
- A SELECT query against that base table to select rows

You can use article_summaries_by_date as your base, as it has all the fields (and more) you need to reproduce article_summaries_by_score in a materialized view. For the primary key, you need at least the base table's primary key: date_bucket and id. Because you want to query this table by score, you also need to add score to the view's primary key. Just like article_summaries_by_score, you want this table to be partitioned by score, making the primary key score, date_bucket_id.

> **WARNING** One of the restrictions with materialized views is that you're limited to adding one non-primary key column from the base table to the view's primary key. For example, you can't add score and author_name.

To select your rows, you only need the fields you'll store in your view, so you can dispense with the base table's date_bucket. You need to select the following:

- score
- id
- title
- author_name
- image

> **NOTE** If you want every column, your SELECT query can use a *.

The FROM clause in your SELECT query will be your base table: article_summaries_by_date. Finally, to complete your SELECT query, you need a WHERE clause, which adds rules in the materialized view creation flow. Fields in the view's new primary key must be included in the WHERE clause and restricted by at least IS NOT NULL. Because non-primary key fields can be null in the base table, this restriction is required even for columns that are in both the base table's primary key and the view's primary key. Accordingly, your WHERE clause needs to include the following:

- score is NOT NULL
- date_bucket IS NOT NULL, because it's in the primary key
- id IS NOT NULL, because it's in the primary key

Further filtering the view

If you want to further filter this SELECT clause, you can, as long as you're restricting it by columns in the view's primary key. If you only want articles with passing scores, you can replace score is NOT NULL with score >= 60.

Combining these, you can produce a CREATE MATERIALIZED VIEW statement, which only needs the name to complete it. Call it `article_summaries_by_score_view`. With that finishing touch, you can run your statement, which produces a view.

Listing 7.1   `article_summaries_by_score` materialized view

```
                                    Indicates that you're
                                    creating a materialized view.
                                                              Name of the view.
cqlsh:reviews> CREATE MATERIALIZED VIEW      ◄
   article_summaries_by_score_view           ◄              SELECT query with
   AS                                                       the desired columns.
       SELECT score, id, title, author_name, image    ◄
       FROM article_summaries_by_date               ◄        Base table.
       WHERE score IS NOT NULL         ◄
         AND date_bucket IS NOT NULL          WHERE clause to
         AND id IS NOT NULL                   match the rows.
   PRIMARY KEY(score, date_bucket, id);      ◄      View's primary key.
```

When you create the view, Scylla executes the WHERE clause, selecting the rows and copying them into the new view table.

> **TIP** For larger tables, you can monitor the progress of a materialized view's build via `nodetool viewbuildstatus`.

Because there are only five rows in the base table, the view builds almost instantly. As you add more rows, the view's initial build time scales with the number of rows in the base table. With a built view, you're ready to see the fruit of your labors. Let's query the materialized view!

7.3.2   *Easier denormalization*

To query your materialized view, you query the view directly, just as you would any other table. Go ahead and get a row from the table via a SELECT query with LIMIT 1:

```
cqlsh:reviews> SELECT * FROM article_summaries_by_score_view LIMIT 1;

@ Row 1
-------------+-------------------------------------------------------------
 score       | 100
 date_bucket | 0
 id          | 1e24e04c-7044-11ee-b962-0242ac120002
 author_name | Alice Author
 image       | {path: 'ernie.jpg', caption: 'Ernie, the eponymous...'}
 title       | Ernie''s Eats Exceeds Expectations

(1 rows)
```

As you can see, the articles from the base table were copied over to the view when it was built, triggered by your CREATE MATERIALIZED VIEW statement. Going forward, any additional articles added will be automatically asynchronously replicated to the view. You can see this in action by inserting a quick example article:

```
cqlsh:reviews> INSERT INTO article_summaries_by_date(
        date_bucket, id, score, title, author_name
    ) VALUES (
        1,
        093f0d72-7bf4-11ee-b962-0242ac120002,
        97,
        'Example Article Is Replicated',
        'Alice Author'
    );
```

When you insert this article into the base table, Scylla asynchronously inserts the row into the materialized view's table. This happens almost instantaneously unless your cluster is overloaded, which you can detect via the monitoring tooling you'll learn about in chapter 11. If you query the table again, you see that the article summary has been replicated to the materialized view:

```
cqlsh:reviews> SELECT * FROM article_summaries_by_score_view WHERE score = 97;

@ Row 1
-------------+--------------------------------------
 score       | 97
 date_bucket | 1
 id          | 093f0d72-7bf4-11ee-b962-0242ac120002
 author_name | Alice Author
 image       | null
 title       | Example Article Is Replicated

(1 rows)
```

> **WARNING** If you update a materialized view's partition key, ScyllaDB will acquire a lock to perform this operation. Because it's the partition key, it can't be easily set to a new value. That updated partition key can cause the data to be stored on different nodes, so Scylla can't simply update the row; it must insert a new value and delete the old one. To avoid a data race and losing concurrent updates, Scylla acquires a lock when performing this operation. Locking for this behavior isn't necessarily a problem; in fact, it prevents problems by avoiding data loss. Nevertheless, it does increase the cost of using the view, so update a view's partition key value with caution.

Materialized views make it easier to denormalize your data. Although query-first design guides you through building a database schema based on how you query it, new use cases can evolve in unexpected ways. Creating a materialized view allows

Scylla to shoulder the burden of denormalizing your data, avoiding complicated data migrations (which you'll learn more about in chapter 12) or requiring you to manually maintain a view-like table via batch writes from chapter 6.

Materialized views aren't the only denormalization tool Scylla provides; it provides further non-primary key lookups via *indexes*, which map those non-primary key columns to specific rows in your partition, just as the index at the back of a book maps words to their usage on specific pages. Let's examine how they work and how they may be useful to you.

7.3.3   Indexes

An index is a common database concept that is used heavily in relational databases. You create an index—a data structure—on a given set of columns, and databases can efficiently query for rows when using those columns. A common question I've heard when working with others on data modeling with Scylla and needing to add a new query pattern to a table is "Can't I just add an index or something?" Although Scylla does support indexes, they're less of a magic performance fix than they may be in other databases.

An index is very similar to a materialized view; under the hood, it *is* a materialized view. The difference between an index and a materialized view is that with an index, instead of querying the view, you still query the base table, and Scylla recognizes that you're attempting to query by an index and utilizes the index.

Let's pretend that you want to search authors by their names, something not available to you because `authors` uses only `id` as a primary key. To efficiently execute this query, you can create an index on the author's name, which will allow you to query by name. You create an index via a `CREATE INDEX` statement that takes a table name via an `ON` clause. This `ON` clause also includes the list of columns to be indexed. Running the statement in the following listing creates this index for you.

> **Listing 7.2   Indexing authors by author name**

```
cqlsh:reviews> CREATE INDEX authors_by_name ON authors(name);
```

Under the hood, this statement creates the index, which creates a materialized view. When you query by the index—using only `name`—Scylla uses this materialized view to look up the primary keys of rows that match your query. It then takes these primary keys and queries the base table automatically for the rows that match your indexed query, as shown in figure 7.5.

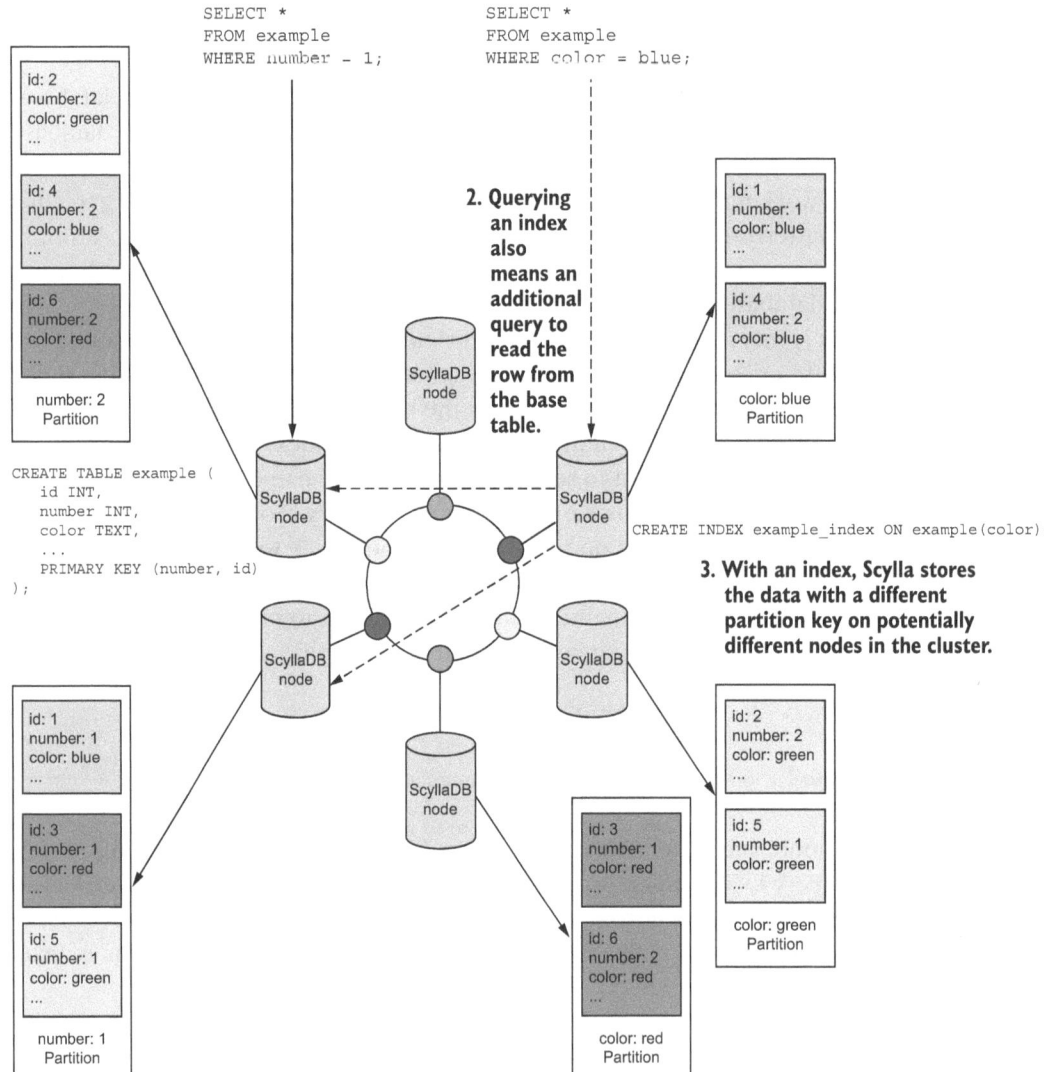

Figure 7.5   An index provides a mapping for specific indexed columns to rows in the base table, allowing you to seemingly query the base table but use the index to read rows without using the base table's partition key.

If you DESCRIBE your keyspace, you see in the output your index and its underlying materialized view:

```
cqlsh:reviews> DESCRIBE reviews;
...
CREATE TABLE reviews.authors (
    id timeuuid PRIMARY KEY,
    bio text,
    image image,
    name text
) ...
CREATE INDEX authors_by_name ON reviews.authors (name);

CREATE MATERIALIZED VIEW reviews.authors_by_name_index AS
    SELECT name, idx_token, id
    FROM reviews.authors
    WHERE name IS NOT NULL
    PRIMARY KEY (name, idx_token, id)
    WITH CLUSTERING ORDER BY (idx_token ASC, id ASC)
...
```

The underlying materialized view maps the indexed column—name—to the specific author rows based on their token—to indicate which nodes own the partition—and the primary key.

If you query for authors by name, as you did earlier when executing a filtered query, you see that you no longer receive the scary ABOUT FILTERING warning:

```
cqlsh> SELECT * FROM reviews.authors WHERE name = 'Alice Author';

@ Row 1
-------+----------------------------------------
 id    | eff9bd01-4a73-11ee-8863-c02b3f99d2b2
 bio   | Alice loves writing about food
 image | null
 name  | Alice Author

(1 rows)ti
```

> ### Pattern matching in queries
>
> Because you're querying your authors via a text-based field—thanks to the index—you can try out pattern matching in your queries via the LIKE operator. This operator takes a text pattern and matches columns whose value matches the pattern. Your pattern can utilize three special characters:
>
> - % matches a substring.
> - _ matches a single character.
> - \ escapes the next character, enabling you to match against a % by including \% in your pattern.

(continued)

To find all authors named Alice, you can use the `LIKE` operator to match against author rows whose `name` is Alice. The catch is that because you're doing a range scan on a partition key—by finding rows that match your pattern—you need to use `ALLOW FILTERING`:

```
cqlsh> SELECT * FROM reviews.authors
WHERE name LIKE 'Alice%' ALLOW FILTERING;    ◁──  The LIKE operator
                                                  matches name fields
                                                  beginning with Alice.
@ Row 1
-------+-----------------------------------------
  id    | eff9bd01-4a73-11ee-8863-c02b3f99d2b2
  bio   | Alice loves writing about food
  image | null
  name  | Alice Author

(1 rows)          ◁──  The query returns
                       authors named Alice.
```

Because you're using an index, you're no longer doing an inefficient full scan. However, you're not safe from performance challenges just yet. Even though you're not doing a full scan, that doesn't mean you're doing the most efficient query; indexes come with performance tradeoffs. Although they potentially use less data than a materialized view because you don't have to replicate the entire table, looking up a row requires two sets of queries: the initial read to the index and then reading the matched rows found in the index from the base table. It's this second set of queries where you can get your cluster in trouble. Because an index is a way to quickly look up data across partitions, a query that looks across many partitions using the index can read lots of data across your entire cluster, adding additional load to every node in the cluster. This approach contrasts with a materialized view, which, by duplicating the data, allows the new view table to be partitioned to match your queries and, critically, be served by only a subset of nodes according to your keyspace's configured replication factor. Figure 7.6 illustrates the difference between these two structures.

Scylla supports two types of indexes. Up to this point, you've used a *global secondary index*, where your index is partitioned differently than the base table. Because it has a different partition key, the indexed data has a different distribution in the cluster. In a global secondary index, Scylla maintains a mapping from the specified index columns to rows in the indexed table to efficiently query via the indexed columns.

To combat these challenges, Scylla also supports a second index type: *a local secondary index*, which indexes data with the same partition key as the base table. Because global secondary indexes don't use the underlying table's partition key, you may have correctly guessed that a local one does. By using the base table's partition key as the local index's partition key, Scylla can store the index on the same nodes as the base table.

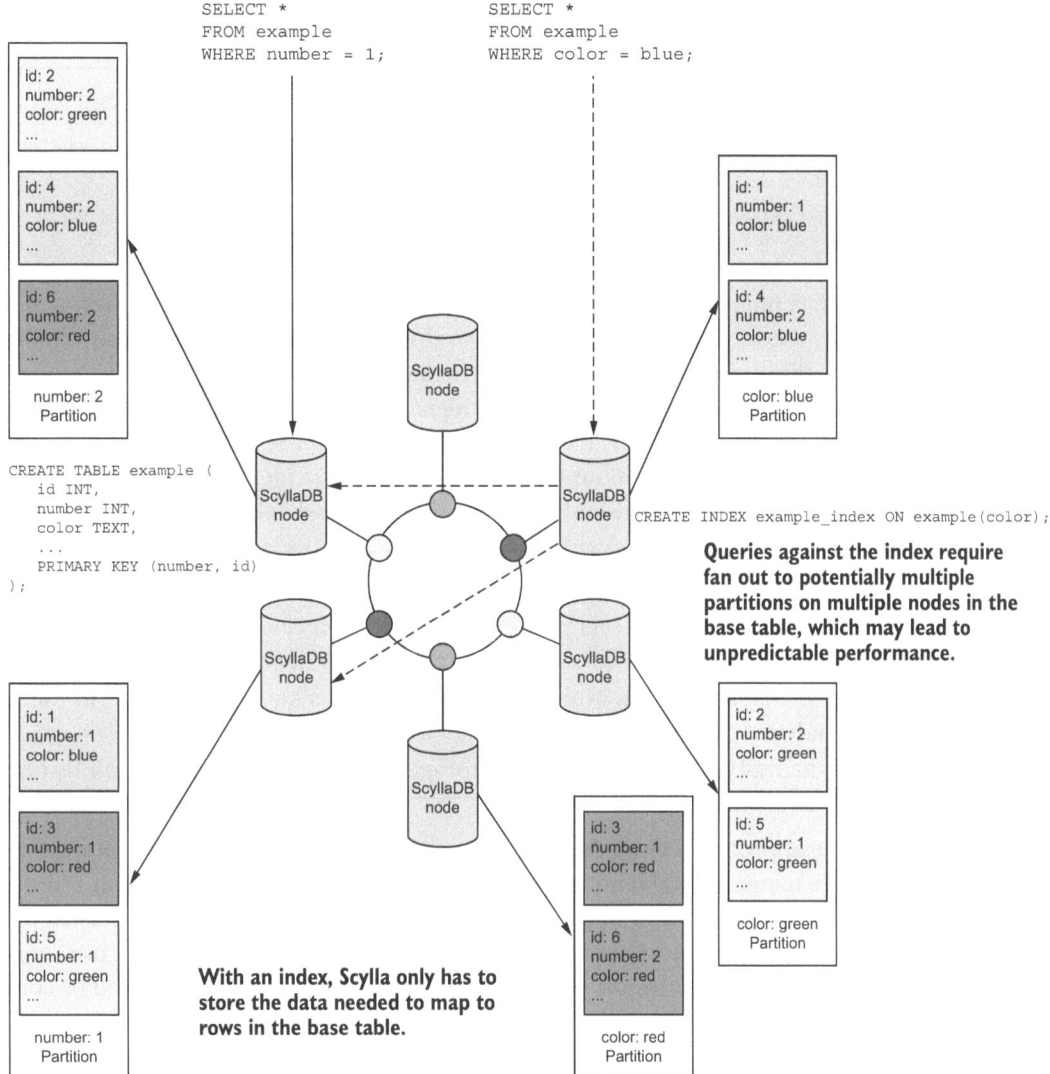

```
SELECT *
FROM example
WHERE number = 1;
```

```
SELECT *
FROM example
WHERE color = blue;
```

```
CREATE TABLE example (
    id INT,
    number INT,
    color TEXT,
    ...
    PRIMARY KEY (number, id)
);
```

```
CREATE INDEX example_index ON example(color);
```

Queries against the index require fan out to potentially multiple partitions on multiple nodes in the base table, which may lead to unpredictable performance.

With an index, Scylla only has to store the data needed to map to rows in the base table.

Figure 7.6   A materialized view and an index make different tradeoffs between storage cost and query compute cost.

Creating a local index is very similar to creating a global one. There are no special keywords in your CREATE INDEX statement; Scylla creates a local index when your index is partitioned by the base table's partition key, as indicated by including your base table's partition key, wrapped in an additional set of parentheses, as the first value in your index. Table 7.3 shows how Scylla differentiates between the two indexes when creating an index.

Table 7.3   ScyllaDB creates a local secondary index when you create an index that shares the same partition key as its base table.

Index	Index type	Why?
`CREATE INDEX ON authors(name)`	Global	`authors` is partitioned by `id`, which isn't part of the index.
`CREATE INDEX ON authors((id), name)`	Local	`authors` is partitioned by `id`, which is included in the index.

Local secondary indexes get to skip a global index's query fanout because, as they share a partition key, the matched rows should be local to that node. Because of this locality, unlike materialized views and global indexes, Scylla updates local indexes synchronously, so updates are reflected immediately in the index. The downside to this approach is that if updating the index fails for any reason, the client receives an error from the database.

With that, you've learned about four tools ScyllaDB provides to aid in denormalization. Each of them is broadly useful, but they all have drawbacks:

- Materialized views can perform reads without any additional steps, but they add complexity to your writes and effectively double the storage used by a table.
- Global secondary indexes let you query the base table and store less data, but they can introduce expensive query fanout to all nodes in the cluster for large queries.
- Local secondary indexes avoid their global cousin's query fanout, but to use it, your indexed queries must also use the base table's partition key.
- `ALLOW FILTERING` requires no extra storage or queries but can perform terribly if not used with caution.

Each of these approaches also adds complexity to your writes, as any write requires an update of the materialized view powering it. At the end of the day, though, it's better than scanning every partition in your database to hunt for a row. In my experience, a materialized view is the most useful of these; it's generic enough to fit most use cases, and I've found that if the clusters you're working with tend to be more limited by compute power than by storage, the additional data cost of a materialized view is less than the effect the other approaches have on a cluster.

In this chapter, you've gone beyond the `SELECT *`: you've learned about Scylla's various querying features, you understand how read queries perform, and you're familiar with how Scylla can help you with denormalization via materialized views and indexes. In the next chapter, you'll dive deep into the internals of ScyllaDB, building on what you know to learn how it works under the hood so that you can reason about performance as an operator.

Summary

- Read queries perform most efficiently when querying only a single partition of data.
- Through a `LIMIT` clause, Scylla supports limiting the number of results, which can be used with a `WHERE` clause to paginate results, lessening the load on your database.

- ScyllaDB supports grouping rows in queries via the GROUP BY clause, which allows you to execute aggregate functions like COUNT and MAX against your results.
- Reads are typically slower operations than writes because they have to scan both the memtable and on-disk SSTables to find the latest versions of the rows that match your query.
- Query speed depends on the size of a row, the number of rows in a partition, and resources available on the node to execute the query.
- To help speed up reads, Scylla maintains a row cache in memory.
- Querying outside of a primary key via ALLOW FILTERING may seem like an easy solution when you want to filter on a non-primary key field, but use this approach very carefully: it can be a performance trap that can lead to scanning many rows across many partitions.
- Materialized views support easier denormalization by synchronously replicating data to the view, which has a different primary key, when you add to the base table, eliminating the need to keep denormalized tables in sync manually.
- An index is a specialized materialized view that maps keys in the view to rows in the base table.
- Because a global secondary index contains a different partition key than the base table, meaning it stores its keys on different nodes, a query against a global secondary index can negatively affect your cluster if it fans out queries across many different partitions.
- Local secondary indexes mitigate their global sibling's weakness by sharing the same partition key as the base table, preventing cluster-wide query fanout.
- Although indexes help avoid a full scan of tables, they still pose potential performance challenges because looking up a row requires two sets of queries: the initial read to the index and then reading the matched rows from the base table.

Part 4

Operating the database

The final part of the book focuses on operating ScyllaDB in production. You'll begin by getting a solid grounding in ScyllaDB's design and its goals in chapter 8—understanding the database is key to operating it. In chapter 9, you'll apply this knowledge to configure a production cluster and perform safe operations against it. Chapter 10 walks you through building a REST API on top of Scylla API, demonstrating how applications use ScyllaDB via a driver. In chapter 11, you'll see how to monitor ScyllaDB—detecting problems and learning how to resolve them. The book closes in chapter 12 by examining how to move data in bulk both into and out of your cluster.

ScyllaDB's architecture

This chapter covers
- Scylla's architectural goals
- The distributed systems that Scylla utilizes to provide speed and fault tolerance
- Scylla's on-disk architecture
- The interplay between these components when performing cluster operations

Thus far, the topics in this book have been very hands-on. You've built a cluster, designed a schema, and made queries against the database. This chapter takes a step back and fills in the context around Scylla's behavior by examining its architecture. You'll be able to answer questions like these:

- How does a read find the data it needs?
- What consistency options do you have, and which one should you use?
- How does Scylla compact data?

In my experiences with running and operating Scylla, having a firm understanding of the database's architecture is tremendously valuable in helping to reason about the database's performance. I've tried to distill my biggest lessons learned throughout the chapter, but I have no doubt that the day after this book goes to the printer,

I'll learn something new about Scylla. It's through understanding the database's architecture that you can make a mental model of how it behaves and performs and how you can refine it when you learn something new.

You'll follow the database from a top-down perspective, starting with the distributed systems concepts that Scylla utilizes and following them down to the details of how it stores data on disk. Finally, you'll see how both the high-level abstractions and the low-level implementations collaborate to perform critical cluster maintenance operations. Let's begin by revisiting Scylla's design goals, which you learned about way back in chapter 1.

8.1 Scylla's design goals

I find that when looking at a system's architecture and design, it's important to consider its goals. Knowing what a system hopes to achieve provides background and color for why it does what it does. That's why I want to revisit Scylla's high-level goals as a database from chapter 1, recontextualizing its intentions after you've learned more about its capabilities.

A popular way to classify distributed systems—of which Scylla is very much one—is their positioning in the CAP theorem. Recall that the CAP theorem says that in the event of a network partition where some nodes are unable to communicate with others, a distributed system must choose two of the following three properties: consistency, availability, or partition tolerance (figure 8.1).

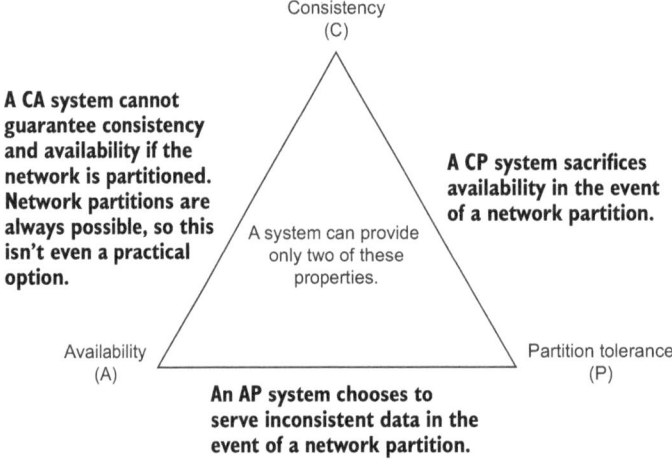

Figure 8.1   The CAP theorem says a system can only provide two of three properties: consistency, availability, and partition tolerance. ScyllaDB is classified as an AP system.

Partition tolerance is a given, so a system chooses to sacrifice either availability or consistency. As you've learned about Scylla's tunable consistency throughout the book, it has reinforced Scylla's general positioning as an AP or availability/partition-tolerant database. Scylla's goal is to preserve availability. This focus on availability provides fault tolerance to the database. Allowing developers to choose weaker consistency levels to tolerate the loss of nodes preserves availability in the cluster when possible.

Scalability is an additional important principle for Scylla, empowered by its approach to availability and fault tolerance. In any single-node database, if that single node is offline, so is your database. Therefore, a database that strives for availability must have multiple nodes. If you have multiple nodes, you shouldn't make scaling up your database arduous, complicated, and something that can only be done under the light of the full moon in a leap year. Adding nodes to meet capacity should be a straightforward, well-supported, first-class process.

A corollary to the decision to favor availability over consistency is that the database ends up biased toward speed over consistency. When a query becomes slow enough, the database is effectively unavailable. Although that's a very, very subjective transition between states, a system that favors availability makes decisions to encourage availability. If Scylla wants queries to be as fast as possible, it trades away some consistency and validation at query time. Part of this validation is allowing any non-primary key column to be nullable. Any row in a table—or column family, as Cassandra originally called them—can be arbitrarily wide, leading to Scylla's description as a wide-column database.

Despite focusing on availability, Scylla still has the responsibility of being eventually consistent. A database that doesn't save data or has wildly divergent views of its state isn't useful. Therefore, the database converges toward correctness. To achieve this eventual consistency, however, it must do it while respecting Scylla's availability, scalability, and fault tolerance.

These design goals weren't decided in isolation; they were almost completely inherited from Cassandra. Scylla's original goal was to be a more performant API-compatible rewrite of Cassandra; the focus on availability, scalability, fault tolerance, and speed are derived from Cassandra. Scylla looks to take these properties and improve on them. When Scylla diverges from Cassandra, it does so to further improve on one of these properties. For example, further sharding the dataset beyond the hash ring improves the database's fault tolerance and speed: one overloaded shard limits the effect only to that shard. Cassandra, meanwhile, only shards the dataset via the hash ring.

As you learn more about Scylla's architecture, keep these goals in mind:

- Scylla generally wants to prioritize availability over consistency via scalability, fault tolerance, and speed, but it also gives you the tools to tune this balance yourself.
- Scylla is a wide-column database where the only truly required values from a storage perspective are the primary key values.
- Scylla's architecture is inherited from Cassandra, and it diverges when it wants to further emphasize one of its other goals.

With this review out of the way, you're ready to dive into the distributed systems that make up ScyllaDB. Let's take a look.

8.2   *Distributed systems in Scylla*

Distributed systems are a very deep subject in computer science. Building a distributed database brings many of its subfields together: consensus, consistency, gossip, failure detection, etc. In this section, you'll learn more about each of these concepts and how Scylla implements them to tackle a specific challenge. First up, a concept that you've already learned a good deal about, and the one that's probably the most critical for understanding Scylla's behavior: the hash ring.

8.2.1   *Revisiting the hash ring*

Chapter 3 covered how Scylla utilizes a hash ring to distribute data across the cluster. The ring represents the range of possible tokens generated from a hash function. A node joins the ring at multiple places as a virtual node (vnode), signing up to manage the tokens for each joined slice of the ring (figure 8.2).

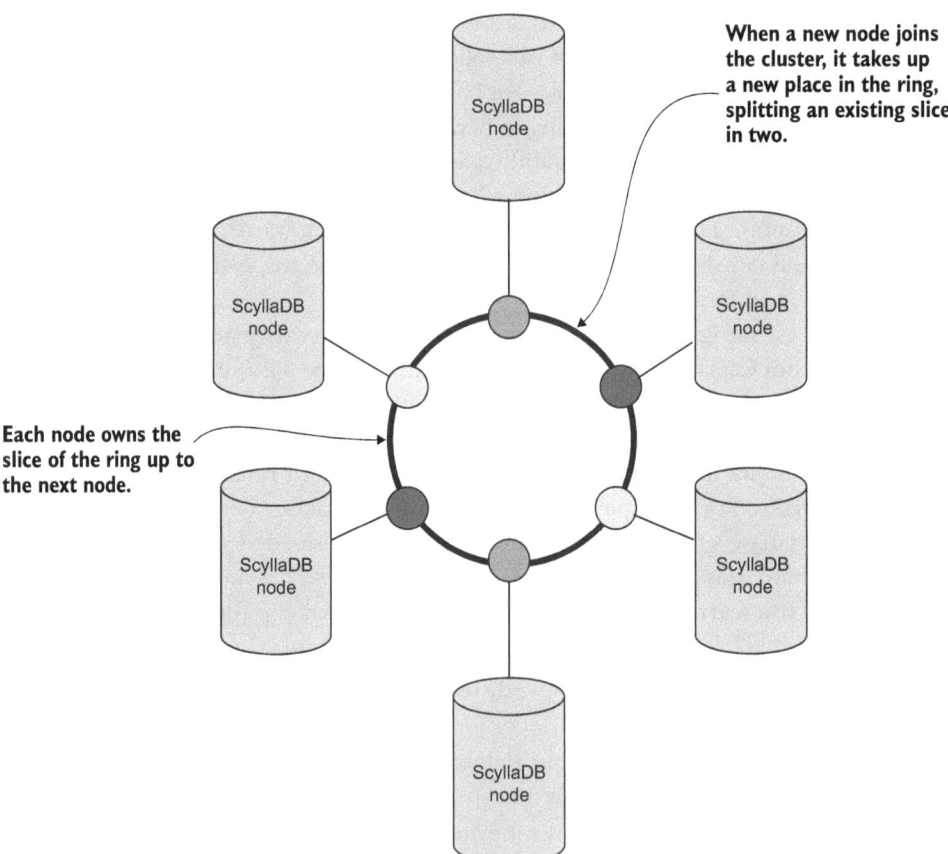

Figure 8.2   When a node joins the hash ring, it signs up to manage slices of data along the ring.

When data is read or inserted, the query determines the applicable token by hashing the partition key and forwarding the request to the node that owns the token. Scylla provides a window into a partition's token via the TOKEN function:

```
cqlsh> SELECT TOKEN(id), id FROM reviews.authors;

@ Row 1
-----------------+-------------------------------------
 system.token(id) | -9052038385137236336
 id               | 33a753de-704c-11ee-b962-0242ac120002

@ Row 2
-----------------+-------------------------------------
 system.token(id) | 6676340635825406971
 id               | eff9bd01-4a73-11ee-8863-c02b3f99d2b2

(2 rows)
```

By using this TOKEN function, you can see where a value shows up on the hash ring.

The hash ring helps Scylla provide availability and scalability. Data is easily replicated by assigning it to the next node (on a different rack, if possible) that doesn't already have a copy on the ring, repeating until the replication factor is satisfied. It facilitates adding additional nodes by its design: new nodes join the ring and take over a portion of slices from other nodes in the cluster.

The hash ring, in combination with your keyspace's replication factor, spreads data among nodes. To determine which of them need to respond for a successful query, Scylla offers a variety of consistency options; let's look at them and which ones are typically best to use.

8.2.2 Consistency

When looking at Scylla's database goals, tunable consistency is the magic that empowers all of them. As you learned earlier in the book, each query has a consistency level it executes with, suggesting the number of nodes required to successfully respond to the request for the query to succeed. A query with ALL consistency needs every replica node to respond, whereas a query with ONE consistency needs a single replica node. Scylla contains many consistency-level options, as shown in table 8.1.

Table 8.1 Scylla supports many consistency-level choices for your queries to balance consistency and availability.

Consistency level	Required nodes to respond
ANY	Any node in the cluster can respond, even if it's not a replica
ONE	A single replica
LOCAL_ONE	A single replica in the same datacenter

Table 8.1 Scylla supports many consistency-level choices for your queries to balance consistency and availability. *(continued)*

Consistency level	Required nodes to respond
TWO	Two replicas
THREE	Three replicas
QUORUM	A majority of replicas
LOCAL_QUORUM	A majority of replicas in the same datacenter
EACH_QUORUM	A majority of replicas in every datacenter
SERIAL (used to get the latest data via Paxos)	A majority of replicas
LOCAL_SERIAL	A majority of replicas in the same datacenter
ALL	Every replica in the cluster

These consistency levels enable you to tune your cluster's consistency and availability balance at a per-query level. Using ONE consistency on a query is great for availability; you only need a single replica to respond for a query to succeed. However, it also makes it much easier to read inconsistent data by reading from a replica that hasn't seen a previous write (figure 8.3).

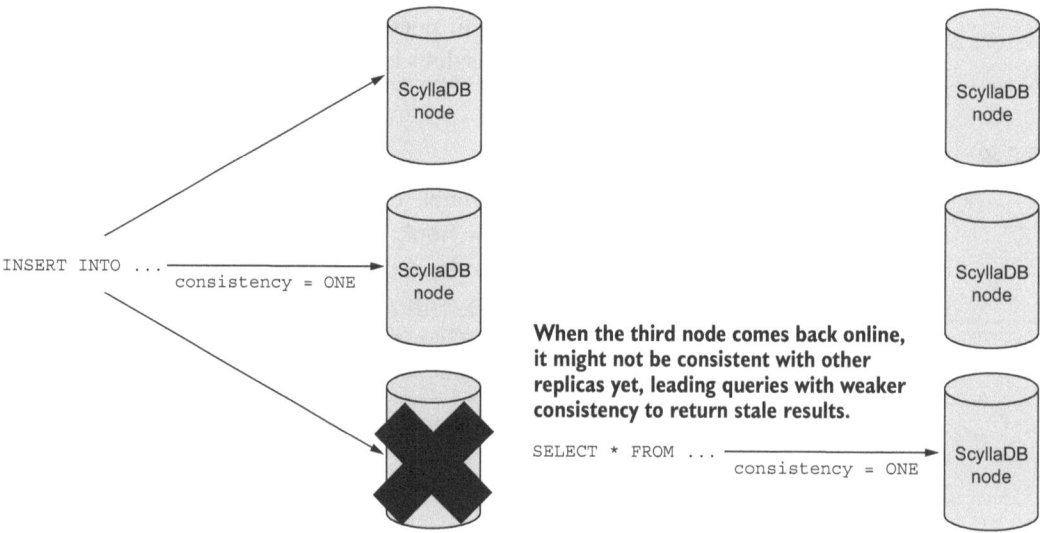

Figure 8.3 Using weaker consistency levels makes it easy to read stale data in your cluster.

On the opposite end of the spectrum is the ALL consistency level, requiring every replica to respond. As you may surmise, it's great for consistency but less ideal for availability; if any replicas are down, your query will fail.

Of course, you don't have to choose between these extremes. Table 8.1 shared a variety of options, and I want to look a little closer at the new entries. First is the ANY option: it's even more permissive than ONE, allowing a nonreplica node to respond if all replicas are down. You may be wondering how that works—where does the non-replica node write the data? ANY consistency uses a procedure called *hinted handoff* that I'll cover more later in the chapter. To give you a preview, the coordinator saves writes to unavailable nodes locally and sends them over when the node recovers.

The other new consistency level is SERIAL consistency (figure 8.4). With this consistency level, you can guarantee that a read query is reading the latest data. To fulfill this promise, Scylla uses Paxos to determine the most recent value. This consistency level offers a degree of consistency referred to as *linearizability*: each read appears to take place in order, and that ordering mirrors the real-life ordering of reads.

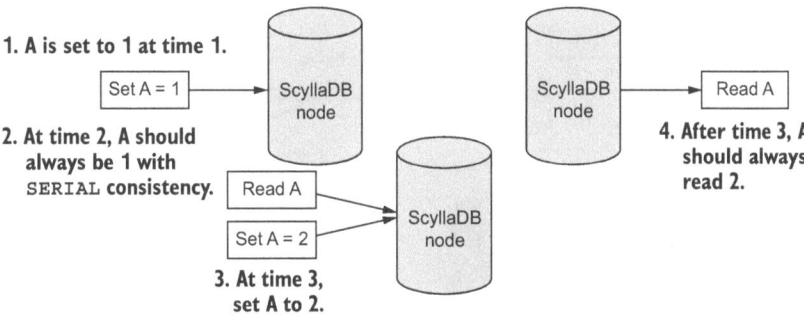

SERIAL consistency enforces a stronger consistency (linearizability)
where each read mirrors the real-life ordering of events.

Figure 8.4 Using SERIAL consistency enforces an ordering on reads to make sure it's reading the latest and correct value.

Linearizability via SERIAL consistency sounds powerful, and it is. But it's also expensive. As you've seen with LWTs, Paxos can be expensive to execute. In practice, you can get SERIAL consistency's benefits without doing an LWT-based read. How? Always using QUORUM consistency gives you the best of both worlds.

> **NOTE** You'll learn more shortly about Paxos's costs and how Scylla tries to mitigate them when seeing how Scylla solves distributed consensus in the cluster.

If you use QUORUM consistency on writes, a majority of replicas will have that updated value. If you also use QUORUM consistency on reads, because a majority of replicas have the most recent value, your queries will read the most recent value. Because a quorum is powered by a majority of nodes having consensus for a given value, *it's important to set your replication factor to be an odd number*. If you have an even number of replicas, your

QUORUM consistency may be unable to reach a quorum because equal numbers of nodes may disagree about data.

During QUORUM consistency (or with consistency level) reads, if any conflicts are discovered—one node may have a stale value—Scylla reconciles this mismatch via a special type of repair you'll learn more about later in the chapter. Figure 8.5 illustrates these benefits.

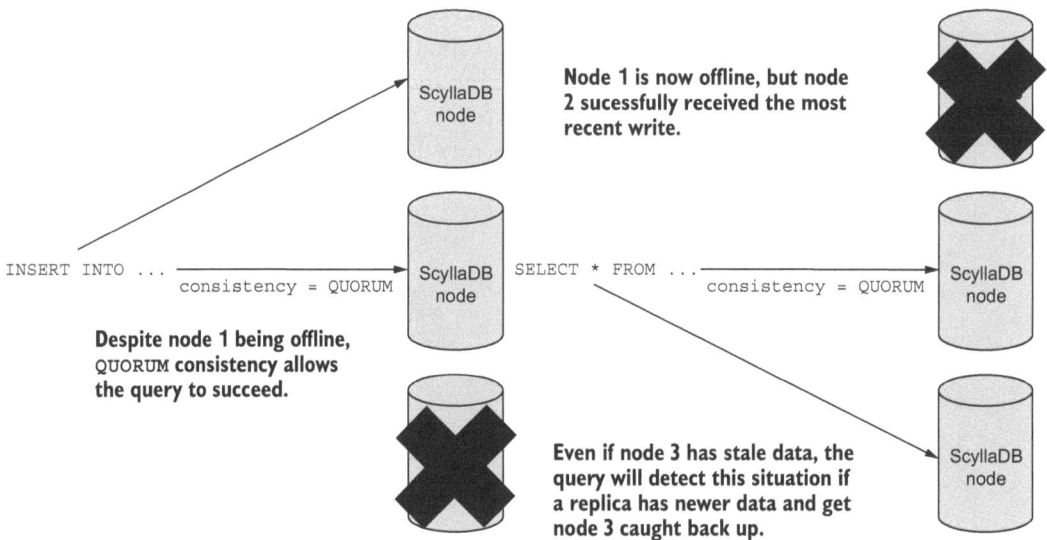

If you read and write data with QUORUM consistency, you can guarantee that as long as you have a quroum of nodes, at least one node has the most recent update.

Figure 8.5   Using QUORUM consistency for both reads and writes prevents your queries from accessing stale data.

Consistency looks complicated: you've got lots of options, and it may feel overwhelming and scary to try to pick the right one. Here's what I suggest: almost all the time, I prefer QUORUM consistency for both reads and writes. It allows you to tolerate the loss of at least one node (assuming a replication factor of 3) and gives you read-your-writes consistency. That's exactly what it sounds like: your reads will read just written data. Read-your-writes is the behavior people using a database expect, removing many edge cases. ONE is also a useful option for reads when you want to reduce load in your cluster and you're sure your application is okay with tolerating potentially stale reads.

However, as the consistency level table told you, you have a few options for QUORUM consistency. The number of consistency levels is increased by some levels having special variants: LOCAL and EACH. ONE has a LOCAL_ONE variant, QUORUM has LOCAL_QUORUM and EACH_QUORUM variants, and SERIAL has the LOCAL_SERIAL variant. When Scylla uses LOCAL_ and EACH_ in a level, they refer to how they behave in multiple datacenters:

- A LOCAL_ consistency level only requires nodes in a configured datacenter (set in your application) to reply.
- An EACH_ consistency level requires nodes in every datacenter to meet the consistency level's obligations.

Figure 8.6 illustrates this behavior.

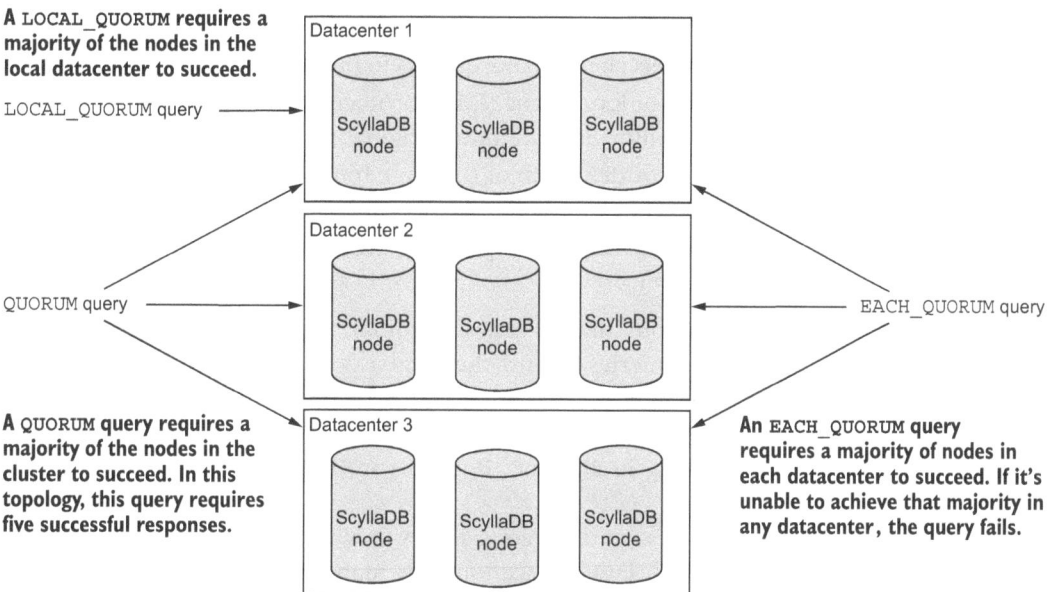

A LOCAL_QUORUM requires a majority of the nodes in the local datacenter to succeed.

LOCAL_QUORUM query ⟶

A QUORUM query requires a majority of the nodes in the cluster to succeed. In this topology, this query requires five successful responses.

QUORUM query ⟶

EACH_QUORUM query

An EACH_QUORUM query requires a majority of nodes in each datacenter to succeed. If it's unable to achieve that majority in any datacenter, the query fails.

Datacenter 1 — ScyllaDB node, ScyllaDB node, ScyllaDB node

Datacenter 2 — ScyllaDB node, ScyllaDB node, ScyllaDB node

Datacenter 3 — ScyllaDB node, ScyllaDB node, ScyllaDB node

Figure 8.6 In a multidatacenter topology, the various quorum options behave differently.

When may you choose to use these options? Like all consistency-level choices, the right answer depends on your desired balance of consistency and availability. If you have a single datacenter, these variations behave identically. Proceed as follows for QUORUM and its variations:

- Use LOCAL_QUORUM when you want to emphasize consistency (while allowing some unavailability) in a single datacenter.
- Use EACH_QUORUM when you want all datacenters to have the same consistency.

For example, you may choose to use LOCAL_QUORUM when you have a second datacenter to run analytics queries and workloads against. Because your primary datacenter hosts user-facing traffic, you want to make sure it's always up to date, but you're okay with relying on eventual consistency for data in the second datacenter.

On the other hand, EACH_QUORUM is for when you want to ensure that multiple datacenters are in sync. If you have multiple datacenters that can each serve user traffic, you can use EACH_QUORUM to ensure that writes are reflected in all datacenters immediately.

These consistency levels are communicated to the database via a query request, which leads the coordinator node to communicate the data it needs to the other replica nodes. Next, let's look at how this communication happens and how Scylla facilitates it via multiple communication protocols.

8.2.3 Communication protocols

Scylla's nodes predominantly use four communication protocols to talk among themselves and allow clients to talk to the cluster:

- The CQL protocol lets clients make queries to the database.
- The Java Management Extensions (JMX) protocol is inherited from Cassandra, preserving compatibility with Cassandra-originating tools like `nodetool`.
- The API protocol provides much of the same functionality as the JMX protocol but is accessible via HTTP requests.
- The remote procedure call (RPC) protocol defines how Scylla's nodes communicate with each other.

The CQL protocol is the one that feels most familiar; you've been using it throughout the book to execute queries against the database. Scylla preserves compatibility with Cassandra's version of it and extends it with features such as shard awareness so that clients can direct queries directly to the owned shard for the request. You'll see how to enable this routing in chapter 10 when you build an application that connects to ScyllaDB.

The JMX protocol, as its name suggests, is very much a Java construct. JMX defines an API for interacting with Java applications; it's highly specific to Java and its runtime. Scylla isn't written in Java, so why are we concerned about this protocol? Blame `nodetool`. Cassandra uses JMX to have its tooling interact with the database. Because Scylla wants to be compatible with Cassandra tooling—you should be able to drop in any Cassandra tool and have it work with Scylla—Scylla maintains this JMX interface.

This compatibility is preserved by Scylla running a special adapter component: Scylla JMX. This piece listens for JMX requests and translates them to a format that Scylla—a non-Java application—can understand and handle. For example, when `nodetool` gets the status of a cluster, it makes a request through Scylla JMX. Scylla JMX then converts it to the next protocol you'll learn about: Scylla's REST API.

The API provides an interface for administrative commands, such as querying a node's status or preparing to turn off a node. It's your standard REST API: you make HTTP requests to it, and Scylla returns data to you and potentially performs some action. You won't interact with the REST API very often unless you're building management tooling on top of Scylla. In that case, I've found it easier to work with than executing `nodetool` via a subprocess, as it provides a friendlier interface to parse response data—JSON.

> **TIP** If you want to see what routes the API supports, you can point your browser to a Scylla node, connecting on port 10000 and at /ui. Note that your

current Scylla cluster doesn't have this port forwarded, so you'll need to stop and start the container again with the port forwarded if you're interested. Also, a warning: if you try this on a production cluster, the requests the UI makes will occur for real, so you can make some dangerous changes if you're not careful.

Finally, there is the RPC API, which is how nodes communicate among themselves. RPC traffic makes up the majority of traffic in your clusters because every request from every other protocol triggers several RPC requests. Think about what happens when you read data from the cluster. One node services the request, and it needs to gather the data from the replica nodes. How does it tell the other nodes that someone is attempting to read a given row? The RPC framework! This traffic isn't only triggered by user requests. Internally, the cluster keeps up a steady stream of traffic. All of it occurs over RPC— exchanging information, replicating data, health checking, and more.

> **Enabling additional protocols**
>
> Scylla supports additional protocols that are disabled by default. An alternative to using the CQL protocol is to use Scylla's Alternator protocol, designed for compatibility with Amazon's DynamoDB. DynamoDB is a key-value store database offered by Amazon Web Services. Just as CQL works for Cassandra, Scylla's Alternator protocol allows you to use a DynamoDB client directly with ScyllaDB.
>
> I'm not going into detail about DynamoDB in this book, but it's important to note that this API is provided on top of Scylla's concepts and constructs. Although it may look like a key-value store because of the API, under the hood it uses partition keys, compacts data, and runs repairs. Additionally, Dynamo offers some transactional guarantees—read-modify-write—that Scylla can only support via LWTs, potentially harming performance. If you're building a new application for Scylla, it's best to stick with CQL.

NOTE   By default, each of these protocols is unencrypted. Don't worry; encryption is supported!

When Scylla nodes communicate with each other over RPC, one of the primary tasks they're accomplishing is exchanging state. Nodes need to inform each other about how the cluster is performing and exchange relevant info. Just like information is disseminated from the metaphorical office water cooler, Scylla exchanges information via gossip.

8.2.4   Gossip

Gossip can be dangerous for communities but good for distributed systems. It refers not to the latest rumors in a workplace but to a classification of communication protocols. In a *gossip protocol*, one node communicates state to a selected number of other nodes, which update their state to match the original node's if they're passed more recent information.

ScyllaDB nodes exchange information via its gossip protocol. Every second, each node in the cluster picks between one and three nodes to gossip with. It then gives them the latest news in the cluster: how fresh the info is, the state of the nodes, the current schema, version, etc. Each node sends its state to the randomized recipients; when the recipients get the message, they update their local state if the received data is newer. When the next second ticks, each of the recipients gossips this new state to a new set of randomly selected nodes (figure 8.7). State propagates through the cluster via this mechanism: node A tells node B, and then node B tells nodes C and D. Meanwhile, node A tells nodes E and F.

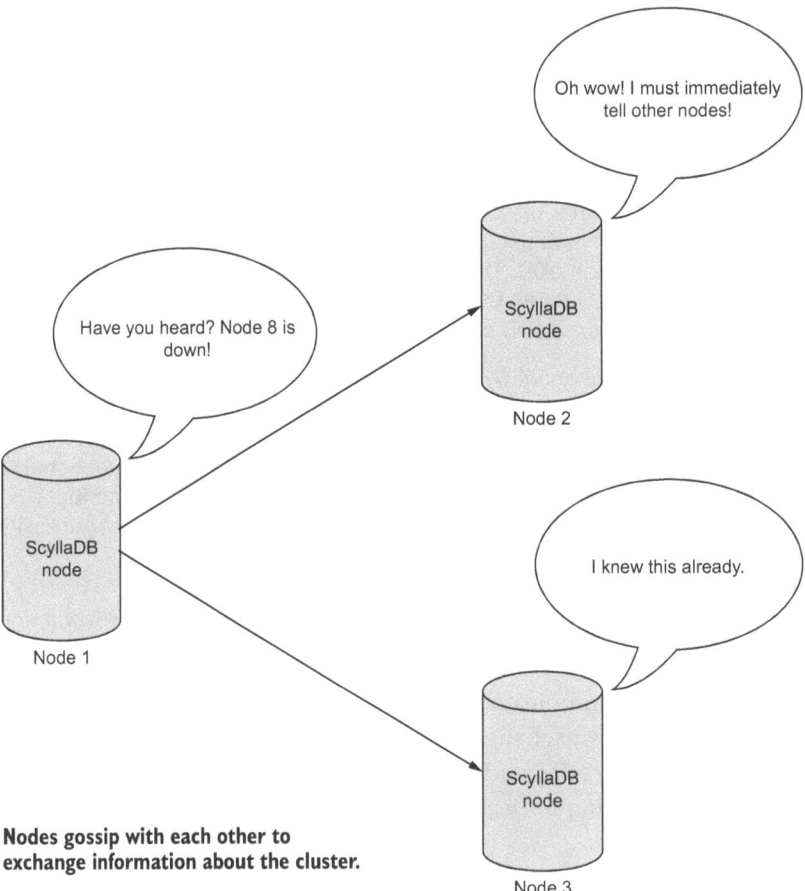

Figure 8.7 Scylla nodes exchange information via its gossip protocol, where nodes randomly pick other nodes and exchange state.

Under the hood, gossip is a three-step process. It borrows terminology from TCP's three-way handshake: SYN, ACK, and ACK2, as shown in figure 8.8.

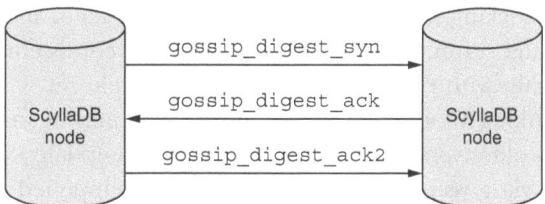

1. The `gossip_digest_syn`
   message tells another
   node about the sender's
   application state versions.

2. The `gossip_digest_ack`
   message tells the original
   sender that the receiver
   already knows these states,
   that the receiver has newer
   versions than the sender, or
   that it needs the original sender
   to send it newer versions.

3. The `gossip_digest_ack2`
   message sends any new
   states to the original
   receiver, after it
   requested them in the
   `gossip_digest_ack`
   message.

Figure 8.8   Nodes gossiping exchange up to three messages to share application state among each other.

When a gossip request kicks off, the sender sends a `gossip_digest_syn` message to its randomly selected recipients. This message contains the sender's generation—a value that increments each time a node starts—and a version number for each node's application state, as seen by the sender. This *application state* contains the values communicated through gossip: datacenter and rack placement, schema information, node status, feature flags, RPC addresses, and more.

> **TIP**   You can view the application states on a given node by running `nodetool gossipinfo`.

The recipient nodes receive this `gossip_digest_syn` message and parse it, comparing the application state versions in the message to the node's local copies. Like any numeric comparison, there are three possibilities:

- The receiving node is up to date with the sender.
- The receiving node has a newer version than the sender.
- The receiving node has an older version than the sender.

The first state is easy: if the receiver is up to date, there's nothing to do. If the receiving node has a newer version of an application state, it sends the full newer version for each state directly to the sender in a single `gossip_digest_ack` message. If the receiving node has an older version than the sender, it asks the sender to send the full application state over via that same `gossip_digest_ack` message.

Now the original sender needs to parse the `gossip_digest_ack` message. If it has received a new application state, it updates that node's state locally. If it needs to send an updated state to the `ack` message's sender, the node sends that update state via a third message type: `gossip_digest_ack2`.

Gossip has also traditionally powered failure detection in Scylla. Every node pings every other node every second with a *heartbeat message* to check if the node is still alive.

If it's not, the checking node updates its application state, and information is shared via the gossip algorithm. This approach, although comprehensive, is inefficient: it scales quadratically with the number of nodes in the cluster.

If you're thinking about edge cases in gossip, you may be wondering about concurrent updates. In older versions of Scylla, each schema update was propagated throughout the cluster via gossip. If two schema updates happened at the same time, you might see errors warning of an inconsistent schema. If these inconsistent schemas were additionally incompatible, you might even see errors running queries. To avoid developers having to consider this problem, Scylla's long-term goal is to stop sharing application state via its gossip protocol.

As of Scylla 5.2, schema updates have moved to a strongly consistent system based on the *Raft protocol*—a distributed consensus algorithm. With each release, Scylla moves functionality out of gossip and into Raft. In the next section, you'll learn more about how Scylla handles distributed consensus and why using Raft solves the concurrency problems that gossip encounters.

8.2.5   *Consensus*

When we discussed Scylla's design goals, you saw that Scylla chooses to diverge from Cassandra when it can better emphasize one of its other goals. Eventually consistent schema updates, if conflicting, may be permanently inconsistent. By moving operations out of gossip and into an algorithm that provides greater consistency, Scylla can provide an ordering of events, stopping you from encountering conflicting schema updates or cluster topology changes.

Chapter 6 showed lightweight transactions and how Scylla uses the complex Paxos algorithm to solve distributed consensus: the challenge of getting multiple nodes to agree on a given value. It solves the problem of making sure the IF condition in an LWT is consistent in the cluster, but it comes with a performance tax. In addition to the LWT locking the row as discussed in chapter 6, it needs to make three round-trip requests to complete the query. These requests are by design in Paxos; they correspond to the steps of the algorithm.

You might have thought Scylla would also use Paxos to provide stronger consistency when replicating the internal cluster state between nodes, but this decision is a further point of divergence. Scylla eschews Paxos, with its triple round trips and associated complexity, in favor of a different, simpler distributed consensus algorithm: Raft.

Raft is a leader-driven protocol: one node is elected as the leader and given special responsibilities by a majority of the nodes in the cluster, just as Scylla's quorum consistency requires a majority of nodes in the cluster to acknowledge a query. However, the use of a leader contrasts with Scylla's leaderless approach. Any node can service any request in Scylla; but in Raft, the leader is responsible for handling all client requests, coordinating between nodes, and ensuring that all nodes agree on a given value. Because of the leader's extra workload, if the leader goes offline, there is a period of downtime while a new leader is being elected. Raft-based systems sacrifice availability to preserve consistency in the event of a network partition, classifying them as CP systems under the CAP theorem.

This positioning contrasts with Scylla's overall classification as an AP—available and partition-tolerant—system. Just because Scylla uses Raft for some internal systems doesn't mean it eschews availability during network partitions; it only means those internal systems emphasize consistency. Concurrent schema changes can cause chaos in a cluster, so instead of worrying about how to reconcile changes by preserving availability, Scylla chooses to make sure these changes have a consistent view of the cluster state to proceed safely.

Raft works by managing a *replicated log*: a series of entries replicated to each node in the system. Each of these entries contains a mutation of the system's state. You can think of it as similar to the commit log: an append-only data structure containing entries for each write request.

If you consider the problem Scylla's trying to solve—avoiding concurrent updates to cluster state by establishing an ordering for schema changes—you can see how Raft helps solve this problem. Because every request goes to the leader and the leader stores each change in an append-only log, one request must be entered into the log before the other. You avoid the scenario where node A begins one schema change while node B is concurrently handling a second conflicting change.

On writes, Raft performs two operations on the replicated log: *append* and *commit*. An entry is first appended to the log, saving its spot. Once a majority of nodes have appended the entry to the log, it's committed—locked in and persisted forever. To see why this distinction is valuable, let's look at a streamlined example of how Raft handles adding a new entry, as shown in figure 8.9.

When a write comes in, the leader begins by appending the write to its local copy of the log. It then tells the other nodes in the system that it has a new value that those nodes need to append to their logs. In its request to the other nodes, the leader includes the index of its last committed entry in the log. The replica nodes append the new entry, and if they have any uncommitted entries, they commit through the index of the leader's last committed entry, as determined by the request. Once a majority of nodes in the cluster have appended the entry, the leader commits the entry into its local log and returns a successful response to the client. Subsequent communication from the leader as it performs regular traffic or appends other entries informs the replicas to commit that entry.

Raft concentrates on understandability; you can learn about it at a high level with a few paragraphs and some pictures. In the algorithm are several subtopics: distributed consensus, failure detection, and leader election. If you're curious to learn more, Raft has a website with links to the paper describing the algorithm (it's such an interesting read!) and providing a visualization and lists of talks and implementations: https://raft.github.io.

Raft is Scylla's present and its future. As mentioned previously, schema updates moved to use Raft in 5.2. In the 6.0 release, Scylla is moving all cluster metadata to go

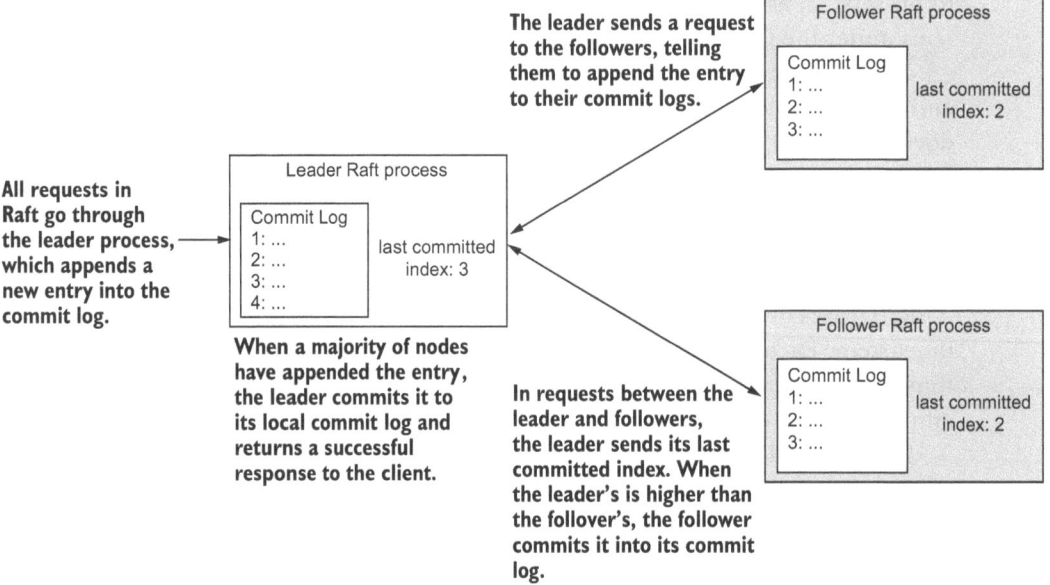

Figure 8.9   Raft's leader appends entries to its log, committing them when a majority of nodes have also acknowledged the append operation.

through Raft. This change unlocks further benefits, which you'll see in the next section when looking at Scylla's on-node design and architecture.

8.3   On-node architecture

Scylla uses distributed systems to shard data, communicate, and exchange state on its nodes. Complexity doesn't stop once a request reaches a node; inside the node is a rich array of systems to ensure that a given node stores and accesses data efficiently and safely. In this section, you'll learn more about how Scylla divides and stores data on the node. Let's begin with a query's first stops on the node: the memtable, the commit log, and the row cache.

8.3.1   The memtable and the commit log

As we saw in chapter 6, when data is written to a node, it first goes to two places:

- The memtable
- The commit log

The memtable allows Scylla to buffer writes to disk and provides immediate access to recently written data. Because this data hasn't been persisted to disk yet in an SSTable (more on SSTables soon), Scylla needs to store it somewhere to prevent data loss on process death. This protection is achieved by writing data to the append-only commit log, which is replayed into the memtable on startup. Figure 8.10 shows the lifecycle of written data, starting in the memtable and commit log and eventually on disk as an SSTable.

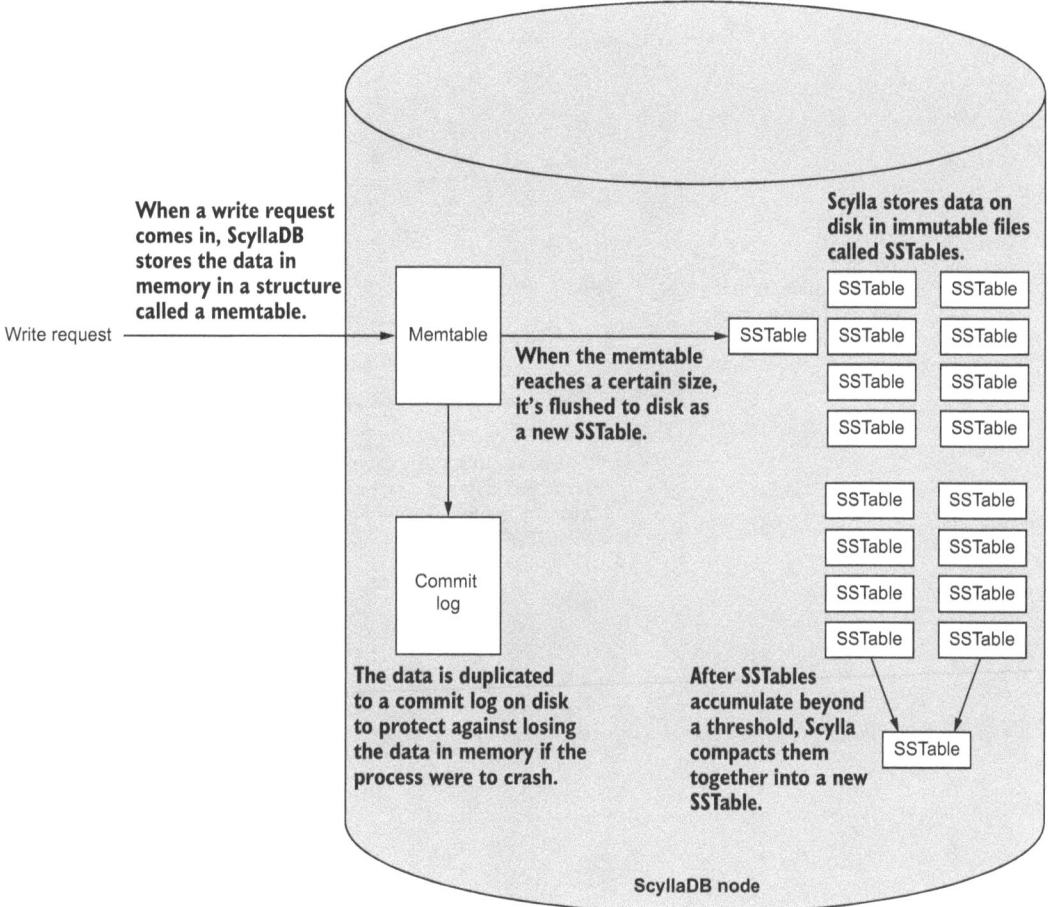

Figure 8.10 When data is written to the node, it first goes to the memtable and the commit log before eventually being flushed to disk into an SSTable.

These approaches, like most of Scylla's components, are inherited from Cassandra and accentuate Scylla's speed and fault tolerance. Writes don't need to insert themselves into an appropriate place on disk; they only need to append to the shard's commit-log file (which lives in /var/lib/scylla/commitlog/). The commit log exists to aid fault tolerance; restarts would be disastrous for data durability without it.

When the memtable and commit logs reach a certain size, Scylla flushes them to disk, creating brand-new SSTables. If data is written and updated later, it can be spread across many of these SSTables. To facilitate speedier reads, Scylla maintains a *read-through* row cache (figure 8.11). Every row your queries read is entered into the cache.

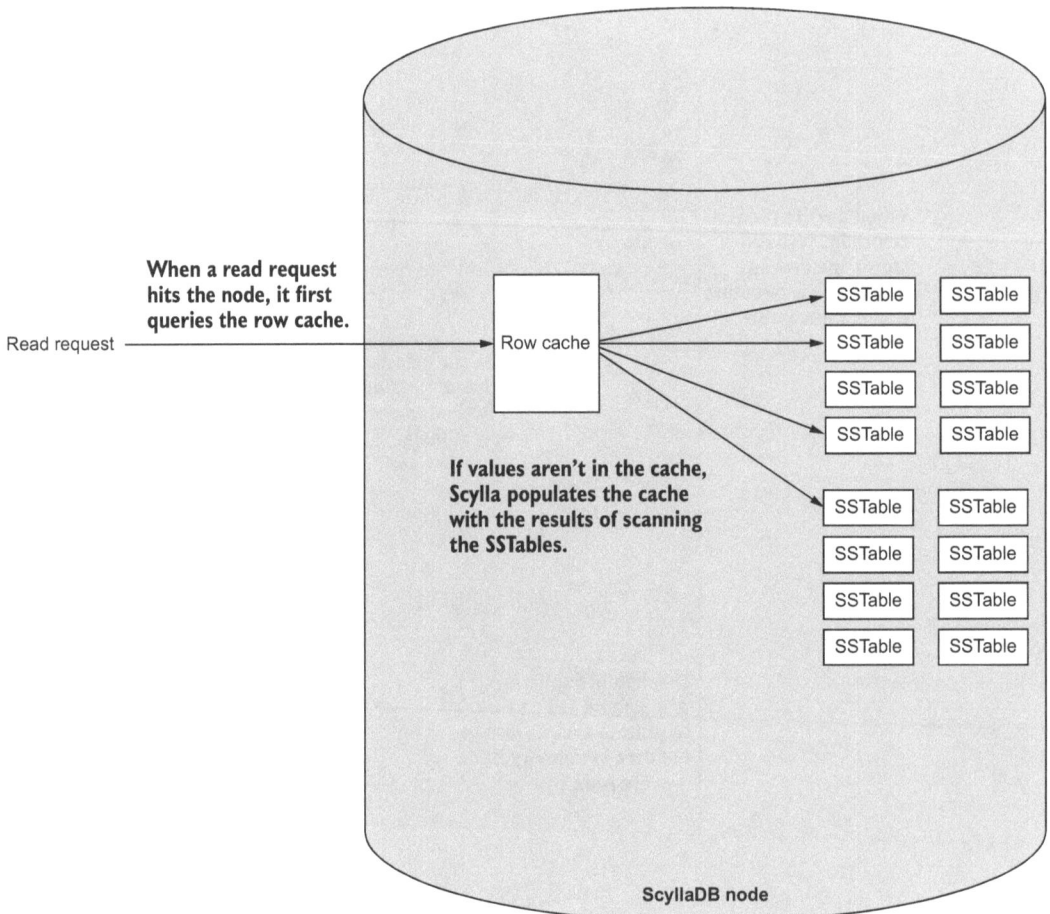

Figure 8.11 Scylla's row cache stores rows obtained by reading SSTables in response to a query.

Each of these components reduces the performance cost of reading and writing data. The memtable approach requires minimal disk I/O, buffering writes to the SSTables by only doing them once the memtable is full. The row cache stores previously read rows, meaning your most frequently run queries often hit the cache.

As an operator and a student, it's helpful to think of these as large monolithic components; but Scylla further subdivides the memtable, commit log, and row cache to provide yet more sharding and distribution within a node. Let's open the curtain and examine Scylla's shard-per-core architecture and how it provides even more fault tolerance in a node.

8.3.2   Shards

Sharding a dataset provides many benefits: it distributes load and provides fault tolerance, mitigating the effect of an outage of a given slice. As you know, Scylla shards its dataset across nodes via the hash ring, distributing data in a configured number of replicas. However, on each node, Scylla performs further sharding, spreading the datasets across *shards*: slices of data that correspond to a CPU core. *Shards* sounds like a generic term; after all, the hash ring shards data, so why not refer to the slices of a hash ring as a shard? In Scylla, it has a specific meaning: the portion of an on-node partitioning applied to a given CPU core or hyperthread.

Scylla's shards are miniature pieces of a node; each shard has a dedicated CPU core and memory (figure 8.12). Although some components can still be shared—disks,

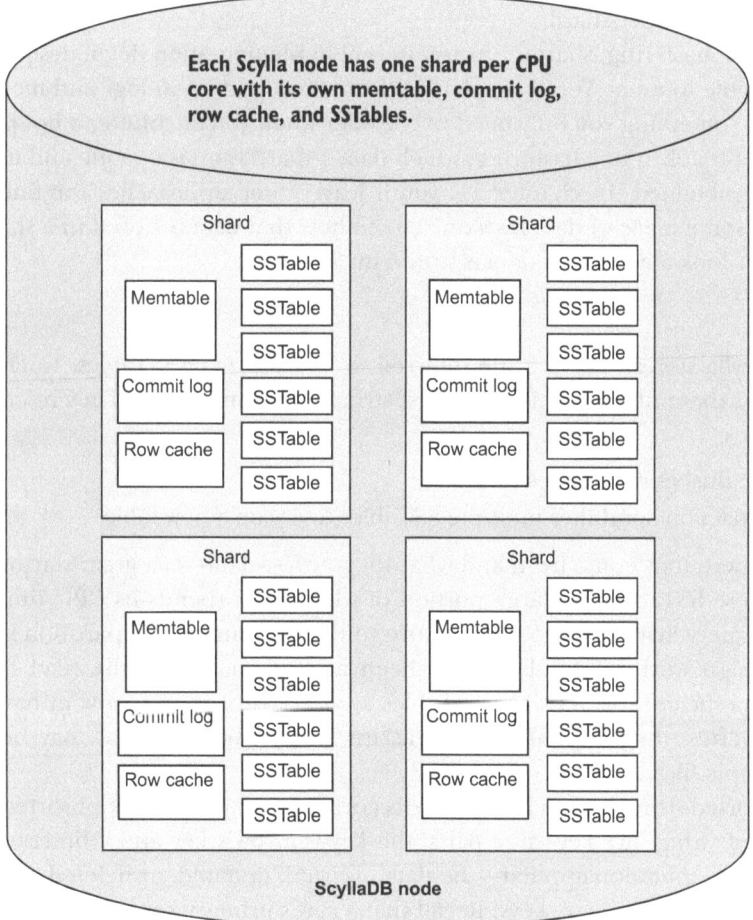

Figure 8.12   Scylla further distributes the dataset by sharding it per CPU core in each node.

network bandwidth—this sharding further helps mitigate failures. If one shard gets much more traffic than others and becomes degraded—a situation called a *hot parti-tion* that you'll learn more about in chapter 11—the node can help confine that degra-dation to only the affected shard, although that slow shard can also slow down cross-shard operations it's involved in.

Sharding is powered by a framework ScyllaDB has developed: Seastar. It allows for asynchronous I/O by pinning work to a specific CPU core and using a *shared-nothing architecture* where each piece has all the components necessary to accomplish its work. Each core gets a dedicated internal task scheduler, TCP/IP stack, and storage APIs. Scylla uses this architecture: each shard is a stand-alone piece, communicating with each other via shared memory queues. Each shard even has its own row cache, mem-table, and commit log. Later in the chapter, you'll learn more about the cluster opera-tions Scylla executes. Each of these happens on a node, but on that node, each operation happens per shard.

Unlike the hash ring, sharding is an internal implementation detail designed to be mostly invisible to users. You'll see shard information pop up in logs and metrics, but it's typically something you only need to consider when you encounter a hot partition. And unlike the token in a hash ring, which data a shard is on is opaque and not some-thing easily obtained. In chapter 11, you'll learn some approaches for finding out what shard some piece of data lives on. To see how that data is stored in a shard, let's take a closer look at what that data is stored in: SSTables.

8.3.3   SSTables

On disk, Scylla stores data in a file referred to by its format: SSTables. In chapter 6, you saw that these files, containing sorted strings, are immutable. They're created in two scenarios:

- Scylla flushes memtables to disk.
- Compaction combines multiple SSTables to create a new table.

Knowing where they come from and what they store—data—is a great starting point. Reading these SSTables is a large portion of what Scylla spends its CPU time doing. From your query-first design to making sure you're querying by the partition key, most of your design work in this book has been around making Scylla read from the SSTables as efficiently as possible. SSTables aren't passive participants in having per-formant queries; they facilitate speedy access to reading data that may be spread across multiple files.

As its "sorted-string" name implies, at its core, an SSTable is a list of sorted strings. These sorted strings are key-value pairs; the key is a row's key and a timestamp, and the value is the mutation applied—the data inserted, updated, or deleted. How is the data sorted? By your primary keys! Recall that a row's primary key is made up of a par-tition key and potentially some clustering key columns. The SSTables are sorted in the order defined in your CREATE TABLE statement.

Checking out an SSTable

To look at an SSTable's contents, you first need to flush it to disk via `nodetool flush`:

```
(scylla-1) $ nodetool flush
```

You can dump the SSTable's contents via the `scylla sstable` tool in your container. You'll need the name of the SSTable. These files live in /var/lib/scylla/data. Each keyspace has a directory, and each table has a directory inside it. The table's directory name has a schema version associated with it, so your version will be different than mine. A similar challenge awaits with the SSTable name. I've included the output of loading an SSTable for an author. If you run this command for yourself, be sure you're running it from the directory containing the SSTable:

```
(scylla-1) $ scylla sstable dump-data \
  $(pwd)/long-example-version-big-Data.db \
  --keyspace reviews --table authors
{
  "sstables": {
    "me-3gdx_1m6x_5i9cg297kgbxs0iicb-big-Data.db": [
      {
        "key": {                                        The partition's
          "token": "6676340635825406971",              token
          "raw": "0010eff9bd014a7311ee8863c02b3f99d2b2",
          "value": "eff9bd01-4a73-11ee-8863-c02b3f99d2b2"
        },                                              The partition key
        "clustering_elements": [
          {
            "type": "clustering-row",
            "key": {
              "raw": "",
              "value": ""
            },
            "marker": {
              "timestamp": 1708894607216077
            },
            "columns": {
              "bio": {                  ◄───── The author's bio
                "is_live": true,
                "type": "regular",
                "timestamp": 1708894607216077,
                "value": "Alice loves writing about food"
              },
              "name": {                 ◄───── Alice's name field
                "is_live": true,
                "type": "regular",
                "timestamp": 1708894607216077,
                "value": "Alice Author"
              } } } ] } ] } }           ◄─────  Forgive my JSON formatting
                                                crimes. It's better than a ton
                                                of empty whitespace.
```

When either the memtable flushes or the number of SSTables reaches a certain threshold, a new SSTable is created from the memtable or via combining new SSTables through compaction, a process you'll learn much more about later in the chapter. Because these are the ways an SSTable is created, all the values needed to correctly read a row can be spread across multiple files.

Imagine writing an author to the database and, a year later, updating their bio. Each of these writes first goes to the memtable and is eventually persisted to disk. Because of the elapsed time between these writes, it's likely this data—your original entry and the updated bio—is stored in separate SSTables.

How can Scylla efficiently read the data it needs in that scenario? It's not going to read every line of every SSTable to make sure it can find the entries it needs; that would be massively inefficient. To narrow down the searchable dataset, Scylla takes advantage of a previous design decision: SSTables are per shard.

To further narrow the list of SSTables to search, Scylla uses *Bloom filters*—a probabilistic data structure designed to tell you if a file doesn't contain a specific value. Bloom filters work by holding an array of bits. For each key stored in the SSTable, Scylla applies multiple hash functions, storing the results from these hash functions in the associated place in a bit array.

To see it in action, imagine that you have a Bloom filter with 10 bits (in practice, this value is significantly larger—often megabytes worth of data in Scylla). When creating the SSTable, Scylla applies a few hash functions for a given key. Let's say the key gets hashed to 2, 4, and 6. The Bloom filter sets those bits in its array, repeating this process for all keys. You can see why a large Bloom filter is required. When reading data, you apply the same hash functions to your partition key. If the resulting bits aren't set in the Bloom filter, the data isn't in the SSTable, as shown in figure 8.13.

The Bloom filter sets bits for the result of each hash function it applies against a given key.

Store key 1   Hashes to 2, 4, 6

Applying the hash functions against a given key and checking to see if those bits are set in the filter allows you to check whether the key is potentially in the set.

Figure 8.13   The Bloom filter allows a query to quickly check whether an SSTable contains a given key.

Like many hash-related data structures, there is the possibility of a collision. In this toy Bloom filter, it's easy to imagine how it might fill up after adding several keys. In a fully set Bloom filter, every membership check would say that the file contained the value, even if it wasn't there—not ideal! This behavior is referred to as a *false positive*: the Bloom filter is giving an incorrect positive answer. Increasing the size of the filter helps minimize these chances: more slots, fewer chances of collision. Nevertheless, false positives can and will happen. What the Bloom filter guarantees is the absence of *false negatives*: if it tells you a value isn't there, it's definitely not present. If the bit isn't set for each of the hash functions applied to a key, the value isn't tracked in the data structure, and readers can assume it doesn't exist.

> **NOTE** You can view Bloom filter performance in your database via `nodetool tablestats`, which I'll cover in chapter 9, or via the monitoring tooling you'll learn about in chapter 11.

The effects of a false positive are mitigated by the second enhancement to SSTable reading: indexes. Scylla maintains an index that points to the position in the SSTable file for every key in the table, allowing the reader to immediately go to the relevant place in the file instead of scanning it from the beginning. A false positive only means an additional check of the index.

To further improve performance, Scylla takes the indexing concept even further and maintains an index of the index—an index summary. This index summary holds samples of the keys in memory, telling the reader where it can go in the index to find the data it's looking for. The nested indexing approach stops there; Scylla doesn't maintain indexes of indexes of indexes for SSTables.

How obsolete data affects performance

Recall from chapter 6 that when a query updates or deletes data, it doesn't immediately remove previous versions of the data on disk; those values are cleaned up later through compaction. Frequently updated or continuously re-created data can balloon the size of your SSTables if compaction doesn't clean up behind you. Compaction may not even be able to do so yet if the data is a tombstone that is not eligible for garbage collection. Although the indexes on the SSTables avoid reading other unrelated large partitions, if a query is trying to read a partition with lots of obsolete data, it can consume a disproportionate share of the shard's compute, slowing down queries across the shard. Reading large amounts of data across many SSTables is a recipe for a slow query.

This overall data structure is referred to as a *log-structured merge-tree* (LSM tree). This data structure is designed to support efficiently accessing frequently written data by first storing it in memory—Scylla's memtable—and persisting it to disk in batches—flushing to an SSTable. The LSM tree empowers Scylla's focus on availability and speed. Writes should be as fast as possible; writing them first to memory (and the commit log) fulfills that goal. Buffering writes to disk lets all inserts, updates, and deletes skip disk access, moving the cost to read-time, as a read query potentially has to read multiple SSTable files to return the correct data.

Next, let's look at how Scylla is working to provide another sharding mechanism in the cluster to speed up cluster operations: tablets.

8.3.4   Tablets: The future

One day in the future, you'll need to expand a Scylla cluster, adding nodes. Thus far, you've learned that Scylla distributes data via hashing the partition key and assigning it a place on a token ring, along with further sharding the data per CPU core in the node. When you add a new node, each node in the cluster streams data to the newly joining member that's claimed its multiple spots on the ring. For your production clusters, this process can take hours. If you're having to do this in a crisis (maybe your app is suddenly much more popular), it can be a stressful time as you monitor the new node's progress.

Even trickier is that you're limited to having only a single node join at a time. These cluster topology change operations need to be executed serially—and even worse, you're the one responsible for that orchestration. You have to manually add the first node and then manually add the second, repeating until you're done expanding. Although the approach is inherited from Cassandra, these pain points are clear areas for improvement.

Scylla is working to move away from vnode-based replication and embrace a new replication paradigm: *tablets*. A tablet is a further abstraction in a shard: a memtable and a collection of SSTables. Each shard can contain multiple tablets, and each node still has a shard per core (figure 8.14). By themselves, tablets don't solve the bootstrapping and orchestration problems, but with the addition of further concepts, they can realize large improvements in the cluster.

> **WARNING**   Tablets are Scylla's future, but they're not the present. Experimental support for them is enabled in version 5.4, and more features and improvements will be added in future versions.

Tablets are empowered by a tablet load balancer: a centralized component that uses Raft to control and synchronize the placement of tablets in the cluster. The tablet becomes the unit of operation for many cluster operations; adding a node migrates tablets from other nodes in the cluster to the new node. With this approach, a node is online and has joined the cluster (`UN` in `nodetool status`) immediately. The tablet load balancer sees that it's very underloaded compared to the rest of the

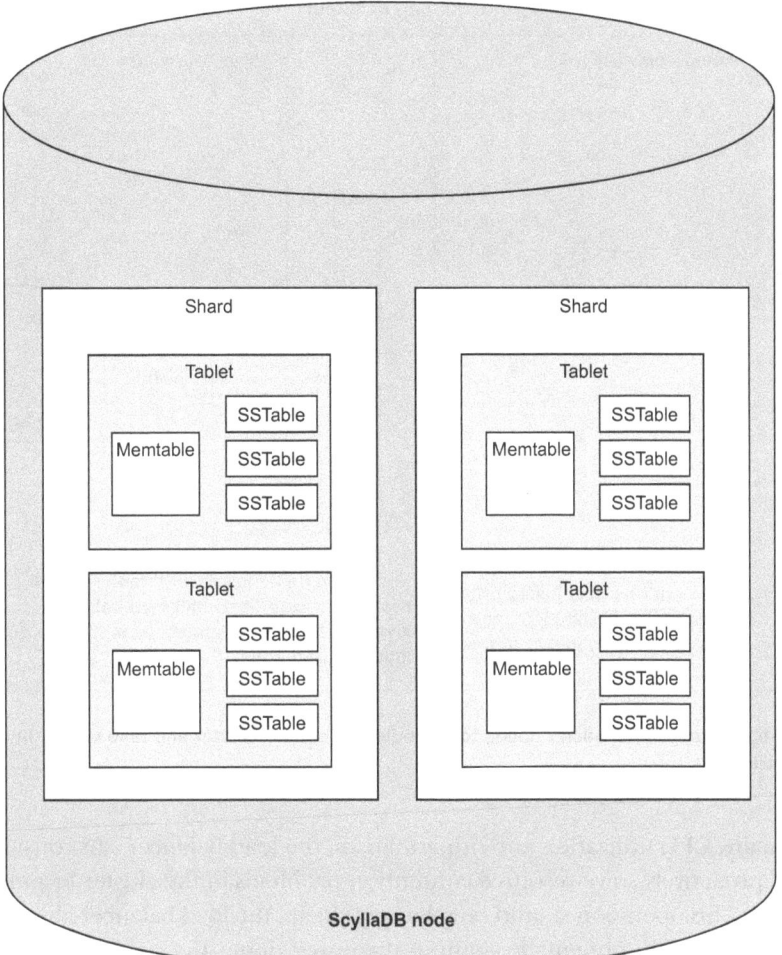

Scylla shards the data even further by breaking up the shards into
tablets, switching from vnode-based replication to a tablet-centric
approach that moves tablets around the cluster to best fit the
cluster's performance and topology.

Figure 8.14 Scylla unlocks faster and simpler topology changes by further sharding
the data on the node into tablets.

cluster and begins migrating tablets. Figure 8.15 illustrates this approach. If you're
expanding a very stressed Scylla cluster, the new node can start picking up the slack
immediately.

If the load balancer can assign tablets to underloaded nodes, it stands to reason
that it can also migrate tablets away from overloaded nodes. Whether it's disk pressure

New node joining a cluster

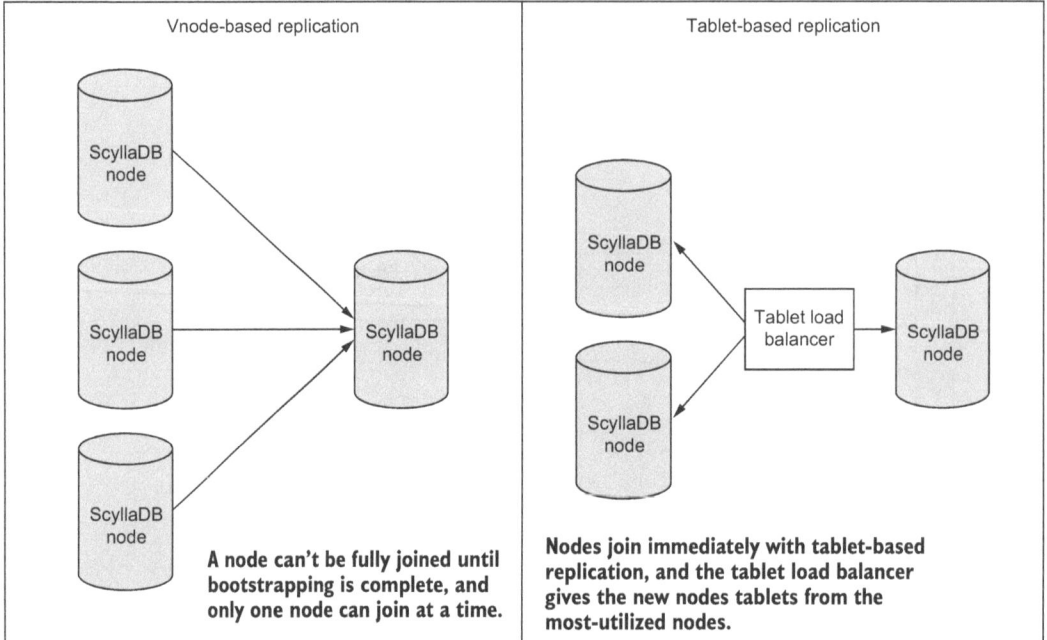

Figure 8.15   Tablet-based replication allows nodes to immediately join the cluster and take traffic, in contrast with vnode-based replication.

or, eventually, CPU utilization and other metrics, the load balancer can consider these cases and proactively solve resource contention problems in the cluster by moving tablets around. This operation should be relatively cheap: the load balancer also endeavors to keep tablets small, potentially splitting them—or doing the opposite and merging them when necessary.

And with tablets, you're caught up on Scylla's on-disk architecture. From memtables to SSTables, Scylla balances speed and fault tolerance. In the next section, you'll look at Scylla's core cluster-wide operations and how you can tune and utilize them to help your cluster run its best.

8.4   *Cluster operations*

While your application queries Scylla—or even when it isn't—Scylla is continuously running background operations to maintain the cluster's health. In this section, you'll learn more about these core cluster operations. Compactions reduce redundant data in your SSTables; if there's less data to read, reads will be faster. Repairs, as you learned a little about in chapter 6, reconcile data among the nodes, and hinted handoff sends missed writes to downed nodes once they recover. These operations keep your cluster in optimal working condition, and although you can interact with them directly, they often remain background operations. First, let's look at how Scylla compacts data in SSTables.

8.4.1 Compaction

In your application, imagine an author who frequently updates their bio. They first insert the bio, which eventually is flushed to disk and stored in an SSTable. They then update their bio, which perhaps ends up in a different SSTable. They do this update several more times, and suddenly 10 copies of their bio are strewn across many SSTables. Every time the database loads the author, they need to read each of these bios from across the SSTables and get the most recent one.

Although it sounds inefficient, it's probably fine for a single row. Spread that across every entry in the database, and you've got a recipe for infinite growth—good for companies, not ideal for databases—and slowing your queries over time. To combat this problem, Scylla compacts away obsolete data via compaction, as we discussed in chapter 6.

Compactions are triggered based on their *compaction strategy*: a property defined for each table. Scylla supports three strategies:

- Size-tiered compaction strategy (STCS)
- Leveled compaction strategy (LCS)
- Time-window compaction strategy (TWCS)

NOTE Enterprise users of ScyllaDB have access to a fourth option: the incremental compaction strategy (ICS). ICS is designed to be an improved version of STCS.

COMPACTION STRATEGIES

In STCS, SSTables are grouped into buckets based on their size—hence the name *size-tiered*. When a bucket reaches a configured capacity, Scylla compacts every SSTable in that bucket together, which creates a new, bigger SSTable that ends up in a different tier (figure 8.16). Compaction is fun because that new SSTable can also trigger further compaction—perhaps its creation fills the next bucket.

STCS is the default choice for tables. It's straightforward to understand and results in fewer SSTables (albeit larger ones). It does have drawbacks; hence the need for other strategies. Continuous modification of rows still spreads data across SSTables, and it can't be compacted away until the tier fills up and triggers compaction. If you have obsolete data in your highest tier, removing this data can take a while. Additionally, STCS can require a lot of disk space to execute. When it creates a new SSTable, it needs to allocate temporary disk space before filling that table. In the worst-case scenario, you may need half of the disk to be free to preemptively allocate enough disk space for the new bigger SSTable.

LCS, as its name suggests, is all about levels. Instead of STCS's size-tiered SSTables, SSTables in LCS have a small fixed-size: 160 MB, although you can change it when setting the strategy on your table. These tables are grouped into levels, and each level has an exponentially increasing number of SSTables. Importantly, in a level, a key can be in only one SSTable, as the SSTables in a level are divided into non-overlapping ranges.

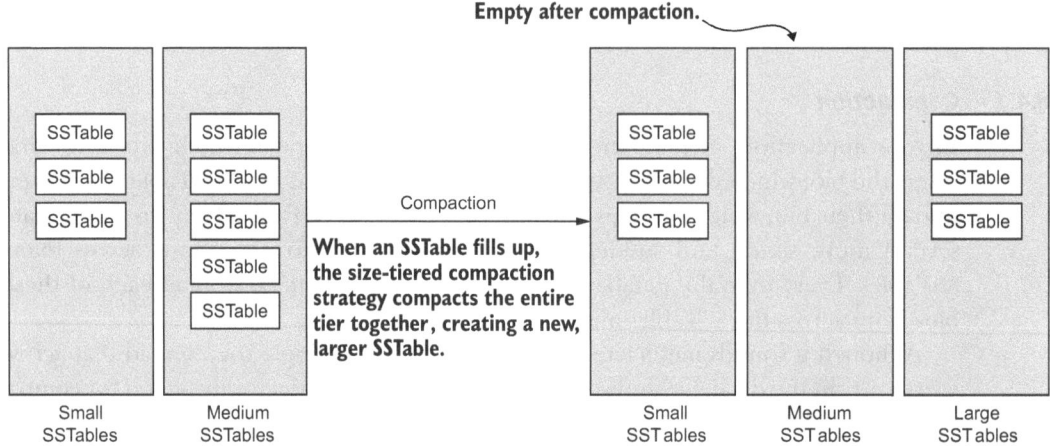

Figure 8.16   STCS compacts SSTables together when its tier runs out of room for additional SSTables.

In LCS, when a level fills up, Scylla starts a compaction with the filled level, compacting it together with the tables containing its key ranges in the higher level (figure 8.17).

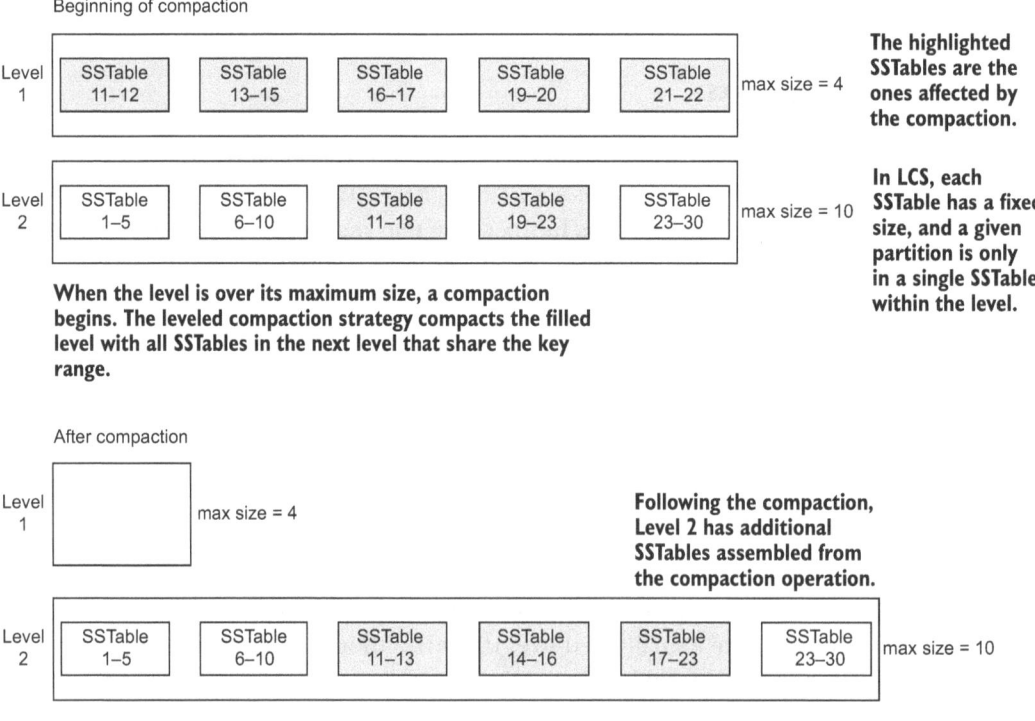

Figure 8.17   LCS divides fixed-sized SSTables into levels. In a level, a partition key can be in only one SSTable.

Just like STCS, this compaction, once complete, can trigger further compactions in higher levels.

LCS reduces the number of SSTables read in comparison to STCS; a given key can only be in a single table per level, so at worst, a query only needs to read the SSTables in each level. The disk space required for compactions is also reduced: because SSTables have a fixed size with this strategy, the most disk space needed will be 10× the configured SSTable size—by default, 1.6 GB.

With these benefits, you may be curious why this option isn't the default. LCS needs to maintain its disjoint SSTable invariant: a given key can only be in one SSTable per level. A compaction may require the rewrite of an entire level—a relatively expensive operation that consumes more disk bandwidth than STCS typically does. This problem is called *write amplification*: the amount of data written to the database relative to its original size. In practice, LCS sees about 10× amplification compared to STCS's 4×. Although STCS may use more disk space in compactions, LCS is more bandwidth-intensive.

When choosing between these two compaction strategies, default to STCS. If you're concerned about disk usage or running into space problems when compacting, you may consider using LCS, although it will use additional disk bandwidth compared to STCS.

The third compaction strategy, TWCS, is designed for use with *time-series data*: data that is associated with a specific point in time and is deleted after a period has elapsed. This compaction strategy is designed to sort data by time and enable compacting and dropping data by time windows. Within a window, Scylla applies STCS. Once a time window ends, Scylla compacts together all data points in that window into a single SSTable, which is never compacted with another window's table (figure 8.18). You should generally use TWCS with time-series data or data that has a known stable time to live.

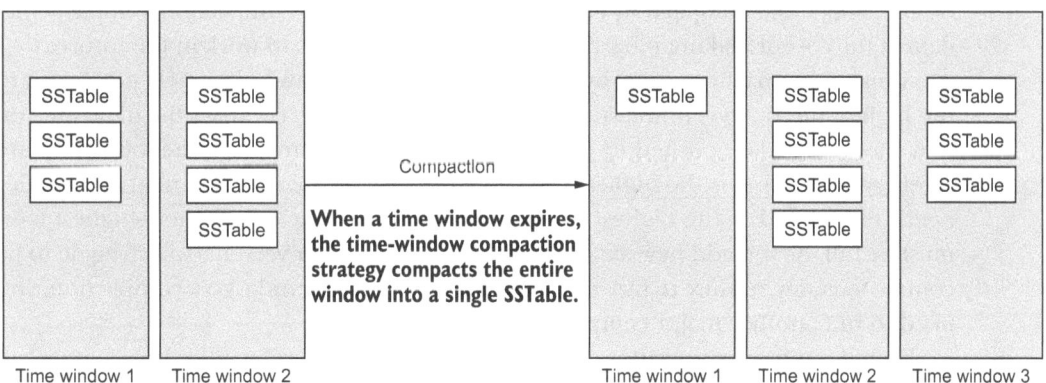

Figure 8.18 **TWCS is only used with time series data, dividing the data into windows and compacting it together when the window expires.**

You know when to use these strategies (default to STCS; use LCS if you have space concerns or TWCS if you have time-series data), but how you set them is somewhat of an unknown. Let's clear up this mystery and look at how you can set and configure compaction strategies.

SETTING A COMPACTION STRATEGY

The compaction strategy is a table-level property. You can see it being set by describing one of your tables; compaction is a map containing a `class` and additional parameters depending on the strategy:

```
CREATE TABLE ...
    WITH compaction = {'class': 'SizeTieredCompactionStrategy'}
    ...
```

To use LCS, set `compaction` to `{'class': 'LeveledCompactionStrategy'}`; TWCS is set similarly. You can also alter a table's compaction strategy via an `ALTER TABLE` statement:

```
ALTER TABLE reviews.authors
    WITH compaction = {'class': 'LeveledCompactionStrategy'};
```

These compaction strategies trigger regular compactions when criteria are met; in chapter 6, we saw that these compactions are called *minor compactions* and happen automatically over time. Let's examine the other kind—major compactions—and see why they should be used with caution.

MAJOR COMPACTIONS

You can intervene directly in the compaction process by executing a major compaction via `nodetool compact`. Although compactions do run by default, you may choose to trigger a compaction directly on a specific table or even a specific token range. You may be looking to improve latency from reading a partition with lots of tombstones or obsolete data that compaction hasn't cleaned up. A major compaction compacts that data at the cost of making it harder for minor compactions to work in the future.

A major compaction works by taking the desired data and ultimately pushing it to the highest tier or level of the strategy. This does effectively compact the data, but you now have older data pushed to the highest level of your strategy—the levels that are rarely compacted. For the highest tier in STCS to be compacted, the next-highest tier needs to be full. For the highest level in LCS to be compacted, the next-highest level must be full. As you add new data to the cluster, these older versions will struggle to be compacted away, as they're rarely compacted. For them to undergo a compaction, you need to run another major compaction frequently.

Even if a minor compaction runs against the highest level, you're not guaranteed to compact old data away. For a compaction to remove data, the data it shadows must be part of the compaction. A compaction can't just remove data because it's been around for a while; it needs to know there's a newer version that makes the older copy obsolete. So even if data at the highest level undergoes compaction, if the data shadowing it isn't part of that compaction, that data won't be removed. Figure 8.19 demonstrates this dilemma.

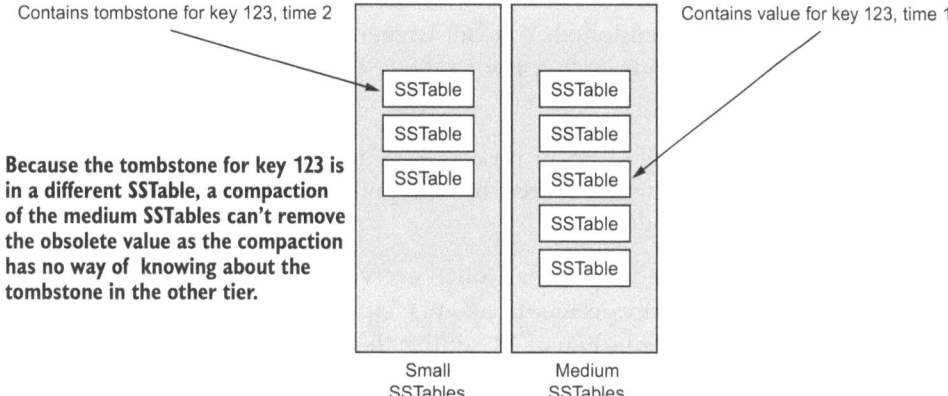

Figure 8.19 For a compaction to remove data, a newer version of that data must also be included in the compaction.

> **NOTE** Tombstones are an exception; they're eligible for removal once the `gc_grace_seconds` period has expired.

Major compactions compact your data, but they have significant drawbacks going forward. To mitigate them, you may eventually need to replace the node, let the cluster rebuild it, and start building your SSTables from scratch. It's best to let compactions run in the background, intervening manually only when you're looking to solve a specific problem that compaction hasn't solved yet. Repairs are similar; let's look at the ways Scylla works to synchronize its data.

8.4.2 Repairs

If one node in your cluster goes offline, it misses any write that passes the query's consistency requirements and is successfully written elsewhere in the cluster. The lack of consistency introduces—to borrow a physics term—*entropy* into the database, a state of disorder where the replicas disagree on the correct value for a given key. This isn't bad; Scylla's tunable consistency is designed to mitigate such a scenario. To recover from it, however, Scylla executes several *anti-entropy mechanisms*, which are more popularly known as *repairs*.

In chapter 6, we saw that repairs synchronize data in the cluster. Tombstones make repairs critical to run; by default, tombstones are eligible for compaction once the `gc_grace_seconds` period has expired. If a tombstone is compacted away before it's replicated to all nodes, your cluster runs the risk of data resurrection of those deleted rows.

Scylla has three methods to perform repairs. The first is simply called a repair; it runs on a single node and can be optionally filtered by keyspace, table, and token range. When a node repairs itself, it calculates a checksum for each row and compares it with the other replicas' copies of it, streaming the updated data to the repairing node if there's a mismatch. This is the operation you think of when running repairs are mentioned. You can trigger it via `nodetool repair` or via a standalone Scylla operation orchestrator called Scylla Manager, which you'll learn more about in chapter 11.

> **NOTE**   This row-level repair process is so useful that Scylla uses it to execute many of its other procedures: bootstrapping, decommissioning, rebuilding, and replacing nodes.

Running this procedure at least once every `gc_grace_seconds` is critical for your cluster's data integrity. As mentioned in chapter 7, newer versions of Scylla allow you to skip this time requirement by setting the `tombstone_gc` configuration on your table to `repair`:

```
ALTER TABLE ... WITH tombstone_gc = {'mode':'repair'};
```

When this configuration option is set, Scylla makes tombstones eligible for compaction once repairs have been completed against that row. Instead of trying to complete repairs in a certain time and then potentially waiting even more time for `gc_grace_seconds` to elapse, Scylla can automatically compact the tombstones away without the time crunch. Just because you can set this configuration parameter doesn't mean you can skip running repairs; they're important for driving your cluster toward consistency.

Data isn't just repaired when you run repairs; Scylla also triggers repairs on reads via another anti-entropy mechanism: read repairs. When a coordinator node receives the responses for a read, it has all the data it needs to detect inconsistencies in the data because each replica has sent a copy of the data. If it notices an inconsistency and hasn't satisfied the desired consistency level yet, it performs a repair synchronously, updating the replica. If the desired consistency has already been reached, it does this process in the background.

Scylla can also do this read repair probabilistically, driven by the `read_repair_chance` configuration option on a table. If your request is a lucky one, the coordinator will query all replicas in the cluster—even if they're not needed to achieve the desired consistency level—and trigger this repair process.

Repairs make Scylla's eventual consistency eventual. Scylla has one more anti-entropy mechanism to help synchronize the cluster's data in the event of downtime, but this process behaves differently than repairs. Let's look at the final cluster operation in this chapter: hinted handoff.

8.4.3   *Hinted handoff*

When a node goes offline, it misses written data. Although regular and read repairs help reconcile data, they happen over time: read repairs require the row to be read, whereas regular repairs typically wait on a scheduler to kick them off. Because this missed data was recently written, it would be pretty cool if each coordinator node saved a copy locally and sent it to the offline node when it came back online. That's exactly what a *hinted handoff* is: Scylla saves writes locally and replays them to offline nodes.

When a coordinator detects that a replica is offline or the replica doesn't respond within the server-side write timeout, it writes a *hint* locally—a copy of that write request. When the coordinator detects that the node is back, it replays each of these requests, handing them off to the new node—hence, *hinted handoff* (figure 8.20).

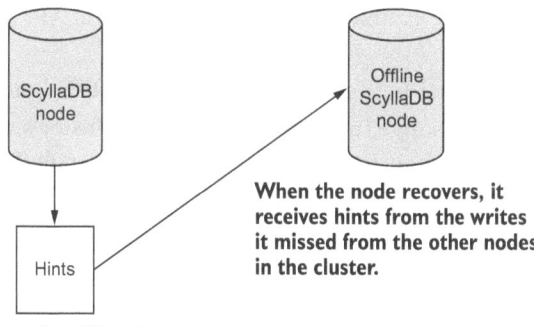

When the node recovers, it receives hints from the writes it missed from the other nodes in the cluster.

When a node is offline, the coordinator for a write query writes a hint (a copy of the data) locally.

Figure 8.20   In a hinted handoff, nodes send missed writes to offline nodes once they recover.

> **NOTE**   Earlier in the chapter, I mentioned that ANY consistency uses hinted handoffs, but you didn't know what those were yet. If a write with ANY consistency can't contact replicas, it saves a hint locally and performs hinted handoff when the replicas return.

A hinted handoff isn't an unlimited process; after a node has been down for a certain period –max_hint_window_in_ms—nodes will stop generating hints. But regular repairs and read repairs can help the node reconcile missed writes.

Compactions, repairs, and hinted handoffs all help Scylla read consistent data efficiently, interacting with the database's architecture to compact and replicate the SSTables on disk. These operations are a preview of what a running Scylla cluster in production looks like. In the next chapter, you'll learn how to configure and operate a production cluster, correctly and safely operating it to preserve the architecture's goals of speed, availability, and scalability.

Summary

- Scylla's architectural goals accentuate availability over consistency via scalability, fault tolerance, and speed.
- Scylla's architecture is inherited from Cassandra, and it diverges when it wants to accentuate one of its other goals.
- The TOKEN function can tell you a key's position on the hash ring.
- Using QUORUM consistency for both reads and writes gives you read-your-writes consistency and should be your default consistency option.
- In a multidatacenter topology, prefer LOCAL_QUORUM to emphasize consistency in a single datacenter or EACH_QUORUM when you want each datacenter to have the same consistency.
- Scylla supports several communication protocols in its operations. CQL lets clients make queries to the database, whereas JMX and the API allow tooling like nodetool to function.
- Scylla nodes communicate between themselves via an RPC framework.
- Nodes in the cluster exchange information about the cluster's state via its gossip protocol, synchronizing their latest view of each node's state via exchanging up to three messages.
- Newer versions of Scylla move the sharing of the cluster metadata out of gossip and through the Raft protocol, a distributed consensus algorithm, to provide a strong ordering for events like schema and topology changes.
- Raft manages an append-only replicated log, where a leader process instructs followers to append entries, committing them when a majority of nodes have acknowledged the append.
- In-memory components speed up requests to Scylla by buffering writes to disk in a memtable (backed by a commit log) and caching rows in the row cache.
- Scylla further distributes data in the node by sharding the dataset per CPU core, giving each shard its own memtable, commit log, cache, and SSTables.
- The SSTable is an immutable list of sorted strings created when the memtable flushes to disk or when compaction combines multiple SSTables.
- To efficiently read SSTables, Scylla maintains a Bloom filter per SSTable to check membership, along with indexes to quickly access values in the file.
- To allow for faster cluster operations, future versions of Scylla will replace its vnode-based replication with tablets, a further iteration of the intra-node sharding scheme.
- The size-tiered compaction strategy (STCS), the default compaction option, groups SSTables into size-based tiers and triggers a compaction when a tier hits the configured number of SSTables.
- The leveled compaction strategy (LCS) enforces that a partition can be in only one SSTable per level and triggers a compaction when the level fills up.

- The time-window compaction strategy (TWCS) groups SSTables by a time window, compacting them together once the window has elapsed.
- Major compactions compact data to the highest tier but may make compaction less effective going forward. Use with caution!
- Minor compactions happen as needed based on the configured compaction strategy.
- Scylla works toward eventual consistency via its anti-entropy mechanisms: repair, read repairs, and hinted handoffs.
- Repairs allow Scylla nodes to synchronize their data by checksumming rows and reconciling mismatches.
- If a coordinator node notices a mismatch during a read, it performs a read repair.
- Hinted handoff allows offline nodes to catch up to missed requests by replaying copies of writes from other nodes on recovery.

Running ScyllaDB
in production

This chapter covers

- Configuring your ScyllaDB cluster
- Sizing a production-ready database
- Performing operations safely in production

Up to this point, you've been looking at ScyllaDB from the perspective of a user, examining how the database reads and writes data to fulfill an application's requirements. In the previous chapter, you followed a top-down view of Scylla's architecture, beginning at the high-level constructs, such as gossip and the hash ring, continuing down to how ScyllaDB stores data on-disk, and learned how these components interact to perform important cluster operations like repairs.

With that knowledge, you're ready to become an Experienced and Knowledgeable ScyllaDB Operator and run a ScyllaDB cluster in production. In this chapter, you'll learn the tools and techniques you need to operate ScyllaDB, beginning with configuring the database and continuing onward to performing increasingly complex cluster operations safely without affecting applications connecting to and using the database. Let's first look at how you can build a production-level ScyllaDB cluster.

9.1 Building a production cluster

Up to this point, you've been running a three-node ScyllaDB cluster in Docker containers. However, when your database is running in the wild, you won't be running it on a single machine; you'll be running each node on a dedicated server either in the cloud or on-premises. In this section, you'll focus on building a production-ready cluster; but first, what does *production-ready* mean?

A production-ready cluster

- Contains multiple nodes
- Has sufficient resources to effectively handle the traffic it's receiving
- Has strict requirements about uptime and operation safety
- Demands durability and retaining data

In this chapter, you won't be spinning up servers in AWS (it's expensive, and learning AWS is a book by itself), so you'll have to use your imagination in some cases.

Building a production cluster begins with its configuration—the all-powerful scylla.yaml file. With this file, you have tons of configuration options open to you. Let's look at this file and the important settings it contains to build your best cluster.

9.1.1 The config file

Each Scylla node is configured by a YAML configuration file that lives in /etc/scylla/scylla.yaml. On startup, the Scylla process reads this file, and its parameters drive the database's behavior in several areas. If you print it to the terminal in your Docker container, you'll see that it's a very large file with an almost overwhelming number of options:

```
$ docker exec -it scylla-1 cat /etc/scylla/scylla.yaml
```

The file does a good job of explaining what each option means, but you don't need to set all of them. Changing `enable_optimized_reversed_reads` to `false` sounds like a non-optimal thing to do. In this section, you'll learn how to configure Scylla via this file.

> **NOTE** ScyllaDB also supports setting many of these configurations via the command line; it's how the Docker container works! Recall that in chapter 2, you passed `seeds` to your containers as a command-line argument when building your Docker-based cluster. You'll read more about seeds shortly.

Although you won't be mutating this file in this chapter, in your production environments, it's best to keep the scylla.yaml file in source control, updating it with some sort of configuration-management tool—Ansible, Salt, Chef, Puppet, etc. Using one of these tools is important: the config options should be identical between nodes—excluding arguments such as the node's IP address—and divergence can lead to trouble for your cluster.

The first option in the file is `cluster_name`. It's not just a descriptive name; the cluster name also protects the cluster from pollution. Imagine that you had one cluster for restaurant reviews and another cluster for book reviews (it's a side project). What would happen if a node from the first cluster joined the other? Scylla has protections to stop this mishap, but if it did happen, it probably wouldn't be ideal. Chief among these protections is the cluster name. On startup, when a node joins the cluster, it asks, "Hey, is this the cluster I'm trying to join?" If it isn't, the node fails to start. Always set this value, because you can't change it for an existing cluster.

The cluster name protects you from joining an incorrect cluster, but you need to supply an additional configuration to join the cluster correctly. Let's take a closer look at how you provide the seeds so that a node on startup knows who to contact to join the cluster.

9.1.2   Seeds

When you built your cluster in chapter 2, you confronted one of the first dilemmas in distributed systems: how do nodes know about other nodes? Scylla solves this problem conventionally; you provide a seed node—the address of an already-running Scylla node—to a newly joining node on startup.

When you built your cluster using Docker containers, you passed in the seed node's address via the command line. When starting `scylla-2`, you told it to use `scylla-1` as a seed:

```
$ docker run --name scylla-2  ... --seeds=scylla-1
```

When a fresh node starts up, it contacts the seed node to learn about the cluster's topology. Via the seed, the new node learns the addresses of other nodes and their positions on the hash ring. Once the new node has learned this information, it no longer needs a seed; it can receive this information via the cluster's typical gossip mechanisms. If the node is the first node in a new cluster, it needs to list itself as a seed, which triggers Scylla bootstrapping a new cluster.

In scylla.yaml, the seeds are represented as addresses in a comma-delimited string, as shown in figure 9.1. You're not limited to IP addresses; hostnames are also acceptable, as you saw when using `scylla-1` earlier. The following excerpt is from the Docker container's scylla.yaml file. When you pass in a `seeds` argument to `docker run`, it overrides the configuration defined here.

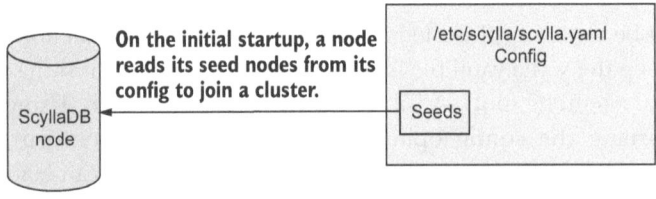

Figure 9.1   Seeds in the config file tell a new node what nodes to contact.

```
# seed_provider class_name is saved for future use.
# A seed address is mandatory.
```

```
seed_provider:
    # The addresses of hosts that will serve as contact points for
    # the joining node. It allows the node to discover the cluster
    # ring topology on startup (when joining the cluster). Once
    # the node has joined the cluster, the seed list has no function.
    - class_name: org.apache.cassandra.locator.SimpleSeedProvider    ◄─────────┐
      parameters:                                                               │
          # In a new cluster, provide the address of the first node.            │
          # In an existing cluster, specify the address of at least one         │
          # existing node. If you specify addresses of more than one            │
          # node, use a comma to separate them.                                 │
          # For example: "<IP1>,<IP2>,<IP3>"                                    │
          - seeds: "127.0.0.1"    ◄─────────┐               There's only one seed provider,
                                             │                but it is defined here in case
            A seed is a comma-delimited      │              additional providers are added.
               string of addresses.
```

Scylla's configuration file explains what each configuration parameter does; it says here that seeds are only used on new nodes and that you should provide the address of an existing node (unless it's the first node in the cluster). Because the first node in a cluster needs to have itself as a seed, the Docker containers default to 127.0.0.1—the local internal IP address—as the seed in its configuration. To build a cluster, you can either update this configuration or override the configuration via the command line. By telling `scylla-2` and `scylla-3` to use `scylla-1` as the seed, they can join the cluster, as opposed to creating individual separate clusters.

> **NOTE** The protection from setting the cluster name described earlier in the chapter also comes into play here. If you specify an incorrect cluster name in your configuration, the seed node will reject the new node's attempt to join.

Seeds work by reaching out to another node at its specified address. The given seed node's scylla.yaml file contains information about how it listens for requests via its address configuration. Let's look at how a ScyllaDB node configures how it responds to traffic.

9.1.3 Addresses

In order for a ScyllaDB node to correctly listen to requests, you're required to specify the node's IP address in the configuration so that other nodes can connect to it. By default, Scylla sets this value to `localhost`. This choice is good for a single-node testing cluster, but any production cluster needs to update it; if you leave the value as `localhost`, every node will say that it communicates via `localhost`, and every node will only be able to talk to itself. That's not a recipe for a working cluster.

There are two configuration values to set so your cluster works correctly:

- `listen_address`
- `rpc_address`

`listen_address` says what address this node uses to listen for user requests. Callers must use this IP address to receive a response from Scylla. `rpc_address` lists what

address the internal remote procedure call (RPC) service binds to. To correctly configure your cluster, you should set these to be the underlying node's IP address. Figure 9.2 illustrates this relationship.

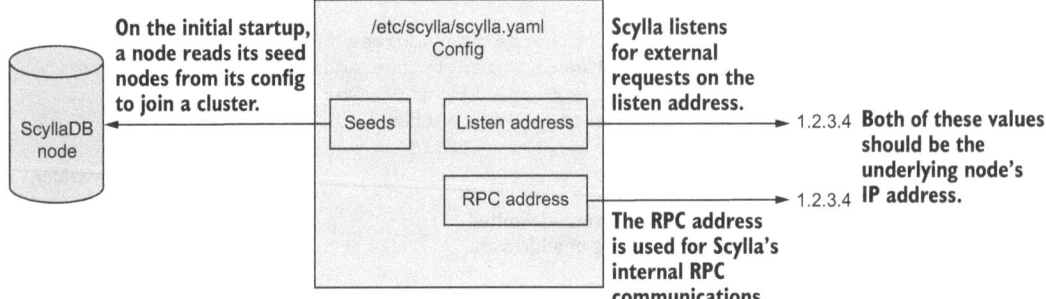

**Figure 9.2   The address config values define what address Scylla listens on so that it can serve both external
and internal traffic.**

> **WARNING** You should not make `rpc_address` publicly available to the inter-
> net (the configuration file also reminds you to avoid this behavior). The RPC
> service implements many administrator-level operations; `nodetool` uses it.
> Keep it behind a firewall!

You can also set these addresses to `0.0.0.0` to listen on every network interface on your
node, but then you need to set the corresponding `broadcast_` configs—`broadcast_`
`address` and `broadcast_rpc_address`—to the node's actual IP address. By default,
the values for these configs are the values of their nonbroadcast versions, but they're
required to be set to a different value if either of their base configs is set to `0.0.0.0`.

Because Scylla is a distributed system, it performs operations over the network. As
you've learned in previous chapters, a single CQL command can delete rows, drop
tables, and delete keyspaces. These operations are powerful, but you'd prefer to limit
them to people you trust. Although firewalling the traffic can help prevent malicious
external actors, there are other measures you can provide to help protect your cluster.
Let's look at how authentication can limit operations to trusted users only.

9.1.4 *Authentication*

Authentication is a key component in securing systems. Being able to validate that
you're a user with the right credentials to access the database provides a baseline
degree of security to your database. To support authentication, ScyllaDB maintains
three authenticators to authenticate connections (although, as you'll see, only one of
them truly does authentication):

- `AllowAllAuthenticator` is the default and allows all connections, regardless of
  any credentials.

- `TransitionalAuthenticator` exists to facilitate turning on authentication without downtime, allowing the user to create credentials and connect using them, but also allowing anonymous logins.
- `PasswordAuthenticator` enforces all connections to present a valid user and password before connecting.

When you think about authentication in ScyllaDB, `PasswordAuthenticator` is what you're envisioning; users can't connect without valid credentials. That transition can be drastic; if you turn on password authentication suddenly, connections from an application without a valid password will immediately break. To solve this problem (as illustrated in figure 9.3), ScyllaDB supports `TransitionalAuthenticator`, which accepts users' connections and validates them if they have credentials but still allows them to log in anonymously without credentials, allowing for a smoother transition.

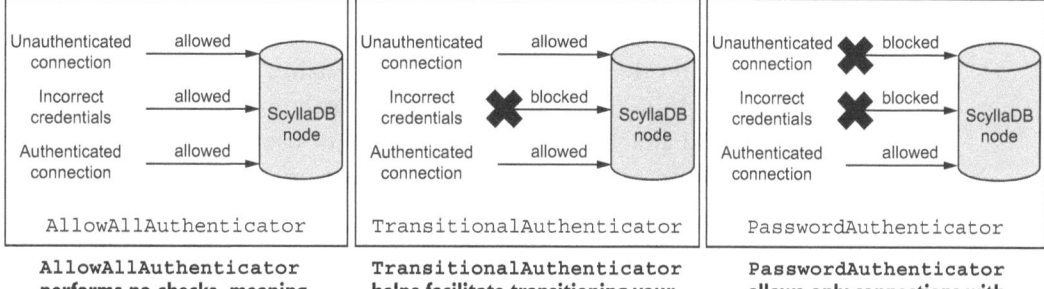

Figure 9.3 In your Scylla cluster are three authenticators: one to allow everything, one that allows only valid users with correct credentials, and one to facilitate transitioning to authentication without downtime.

The default option is `AllowAllAuthenticator`, which you can observe in your scylla.yaml file. Although it's commented out in the config, this option is the default:

```
# Authentication backend, identifying users
# Out of the box, Scylla provides
# org.apache.cassandra.auth.{AllowAllAuthenticator,
# PasswordAuthenticator}.
# - AllowAllAuthenticator performs no checks - set it to
#   disable authentication.
# - PasswordAuthenticator relies on username/password pairs to
#   authenticate users. It keeps usernames and hashed passwords
#   in system_auth.credentials table. Please increase system_auth
#   keyspace replication factor if you use this authenticator.
# - com.scylladb.auth.TransitionalAuthenticator requires
#   username/password pair to authenticate in the same manner as
#   PasswordAuthenticator, but improper credentials result in
```

```
#    being logged in as an anonymous user. Use for upgrading
#    clusters' auth.
# authenticator: AllowAllAuthenticator
```

> **WARNING**   Note the callout with `PasswordAuthenticator`. When turning on this option, you should also increase the replication factor of your `system_auth` keyspace to be the total number of nodes in your cluster. Otherwise, node unavailability may prevent you from logging in. We'll discuss this change more in the next chapter.

In chapter 10, we'll discuss using and setting authentication in your cluster when you learn about connecting to ScyllaDB from your application. It's hard to talk about authentication without mentioning its partner: authorization. Let's see how you can configure Scylla not only to authenticate a connection but also permit it to perform only certain actions.

9.1.5   *Authorization*

If authentication validates that you are who you say you are, authorization validates that you can do what you want to do. Defining authorization allows you to specify certain permissions and attach them to specific roles or users in the database. Perhaps one user is an admin or superuser, whereas other users can only `SELECT` from tables.

Enforcing authorization suffers from the same challenge as authentication; connections without authorization will break if the database is told to enforce that. Just like authentication, ScyllaDB supports three authorizers in its configuration:

- `AllowAllAuthorizer` is the default and allows all connections, regardless of any credentials.
- `TransitionalAuthorizer` exists to facilitate turning on authorization without downtime, enforcing the users' permissions if any are associated, and blocking them otherwise.
- `CassandraAuthorizer` enforces permissions assigned to a user or role, denying the rest.

You begin with `AllowAllAuthorizer` and switch to `TransitionalAuthorizer` when migrating to enforcing authorization. Just as with authentication, `TransitionalAuthorizer` will enforce permissions if there's something to enforce. Once your system is completely configured, you switch to `CassandraAuthorizer`.

Just like authentication, the default option is `AllowAllAuthorizer`, as seen in your scylla.yaml file:

```
# Authorization backend, implementing IAuthorizer; used to limit
# access/provide permissions
# Out of the box, Scylla provides org.apache.cassandra.auth.{
# AllowAllAuthorizer,CassandraAuthorizer}.
#
```

```
# - AllowAllAuthorizer allows any action to any user - set it to
#   disable authorization.
# - CassandraAuthorizer stores permissions in system_auth.permissions
#   table. Please increase system_auth keyspace replication factor if
#   you use this authorizer.
# - com.scylladb.auth.TransitionalAuthorizer wraps around the
#   CassandraAuthorizer, using it for authorizing permission
#   management. Otherwise, it allows all. Use for upgrading clusters'
#   auth.
# authorizer: AllowAllAuthorizer
```

> **WARNING** When switching the authorizer to `CassandraAuthorizer`, you also need to increase the replication factor of your `system_auth` keyspace to be the total number of nodes in your cluster so that authorization works when your cluster is partially offline.

As you've seen, authorization is handled similarly to authentication both in ScyllaDB and in other products; they're almost always referred to together as "authentication and authorization" and abbreviated as *authn* and *authz*. In the next chapter, you'll learn how to configure both and connect as a user with permissions from an application. Continuing the tour of configuration, let's see how you define a cluster's topology, which is critical for a well-functioning Scylla cluster.

9.1.6 *Snitches*

Earlier in the book, you learned that ScyllaDB groups nodes into datacenters and racks, analogous to an on-premises datacenter where servers live in a rack in the datacenter. For each keyspace, you configure a replication setting that determines how data is replicated for each datacenter in your cluster. In chapter 5, when creating the `reviews` keyspace, you told the keysapce to use the preferred `NetworkTopologyStrategy`, which considers racks when placing data for replication, and to replicate each row to three nodes in `datacenter1`:

```
cqlsh> CREATE KEYSPACE reviews WITH replication = {
    'class': 'NetworkTopologyStrategy', 'datacenter1': '3'};
```

Recall that when using `NetworkTopologyStrategy`, Scylla assigns data to a node based on the owning node for the data's position in the hash ring. Scylla then replicates the node to the next node with a rack that hasn't been replicated to for this data, only replicating to an already-used rack if it has exhausted other options. Datacenters and racks are key for data replication and therefore are also key to preserving Scylla's uptime and fault tolerance.

To configure datacenters and racks and define Scylla's topology, you begin with the *snitch*, a piece of ScyllaDB functionality that defines the topology of the cluster and uses it to help route requests. Like authenticators and authorizers, Scylla provides several types of snitches, but I want to concentrate on three of them.

The most basic of these snitches is `SimpleSnitch`. It should only be used in single-datacenter deployments because it groups everything into a single datacenter and rack. This snitch is the default option, and although you may think it is a good starting point for a cluster, changing the snitch requires a full cluster shutdown. You should therefore avoid this option, preferring more flexible ones, even if you think you're going to have only one datacenter. Your Docker cluster currently uses `SimpleSnitch`, but that's its best use case—small, simple development clusters.

Several snitches support automatically determining your clusters' datacenters and racks. If running in AWS, Google Cloud Platform, or Azure, Scylla provides snitches that infer the datacenter and rack based on the underlying instance's region and zone, such as `Ec2MultiRegionSnitch` for AWS, which, if running in `us-west-2` in zone `b`, will set your datacenter to `us-west-2` and rack to `b`. Although your datacenters and zones will always be named following this scheme when using these snitches, Scylla allows you to add suffixes to the datacenter name to differentiate them if you have multiple datacenters in a region. I'll show you how to add these suffixes momentarily.

The last snitch to discuss is `GossipingPropertyFileSnitch`. Instead of automatically determining the cluster's topology, you define it yourself on each node in a cassandra-rackdc.properties file. Right now, each node in your Docker cluster is running in `datacenter1` and `rack1`. When using `GossipingPropertyFileSnitch`, your explicitly defined topology would look like the following file, which lives on every node at /etc/scylla/cassandra-rackdc.properties.

> **Listing 9.1   cassandra-rackdc.properties file**

```
dc=datacenter1
rack=rack1
```

> **TIP**   If you want to set the suffix name when using the cloud-provider snitches, it is also configured in this file via a `dc_suffix` property.

When building production clusters, you should prefer either the appropriate cloud-provider snitch or `GossipingPropertyFileSnitch`. If you're running on-premises, you clearly won't be able to use `GoogleCloudSnitch` effectively. However, even if you're running in the cloud, `GossipingPropertyFileSnitch` is a very strong option as it gives you complete control over your datacenter and rack names, although you'll have to set them manually.

Picking your snitch, like every other config option you've seen thus far, is done via the scylla.yaml file:

```
endpoint_snitch: SimpleSnitch
```

You want to pick the right snitch for your cluster before you start building it, as switching the snitch requires taking the cluster offline to change it. Prefer either `Gossiping-PropertyFileSnitch` or your cloud provider's snitch, if supported, and you'll be well on your way to a well-built production cluster.

The snitch is key to your cluster's topology; deciding where nodes live is critical to building a production-ready cluster. That's only one piece of the puzzle, however. Not only do you have to decide how many nodes you need, but what resources do each of those nodes require? How do you build a cluster that can stand up to production traffic? In the next section, you'll learn how to answer these questions and design your first production cluster.

9.2 Building your cluster

Three Docker containers on a single computer make for an excellent learning tool, but they aren't typically what you'd run in production. A production Scylla cluster consists of multiple servers, usually distributed in some manner to encourage and facilitate ScyllaDB's desired fault tolerance. In this section, you'll learn about two key components of building a cluster: the cluster's topology and its resources.

9.2.1 Designing your cluster topology

Imagine that you're running a real-life physical datacenter (not the ScyllaDB abstraction), and in that datacenter, you're running ScyllaDB on several servers. You've chosen to place every instance of ScyllaDB on the same rack in the datacenter—an approach that leaves you open to disastrous scenarios. If a clumsy coworker trips over the plug (this hypothetical scenario also ignores some basic workplace safety rules) and knocks out power to the rack, suddenly your entire cluster is offline, breaking ScyllaDB's fault-tolerance goals.

Although this is a bit of a contrived scenario, an effective distribution of nodes is key to building a production-ready Scylla cluster. You want to run multiple nodes distributed across racks in a datacenter or zones in a cloud provider to minimize the chances of a wide-scale disruption. If, in your imaginary datacenter, you had spread ScyllaDB between multiple racks, the clumsy employee might not have cost any downtime for your cluster, as long as it was able to maintain a quorum—and your application was performing quorum-consistency reads.

Accordingly, a production-ready ScyllaDB cluster's architecture sticks to the following principles:

- It contains at least three nodes so that it can reach a quorum.
- It distributes its nodes across zones in a cloud provider or across racks in an on-premises datacenter, if possible.
- It contains enough resources to handle the traffic and load your database expects to receive.

Saving the resource utilization piece to discuss later, the first two principles affect the quantity and placement of nodes. You need to have at least three nodes, which, as you've learned about with consistency and quorums, allows losing one node while still maintaining uptime in the cluster. You can, of course, have more than three nodes as well.

The node distribution question is more complicated. When running a production-level system, you want to balance safety and resources. A node having downtime in a cloud provider is rare, but happens occasionally. Losing an entire zone is even more rare, but if not planned for, it can have a gigantic effect on your cluster's uptime. For resiliency, I recommend building your cluster to tolerate at least a zone- or rack-level outage.

Each cloud provider snitch assigns racks to its underlying instance's zone. If a node is running in the `us-east` region in zone c, it gets a datacenter value of `us-east` and a rack value of c. Because the `NetworkTopologyStrategy` replication strategy attempts to replicate data in a rack-aware fashion, running in multiple zones distributes data across multiple zones. If your number of racks in a datacenter is at least equal to the configured replication factor, you can lose an entire zone or rack and suffer no downtime if you're using quorum consistency in your queries, as shown in figure 9.4.

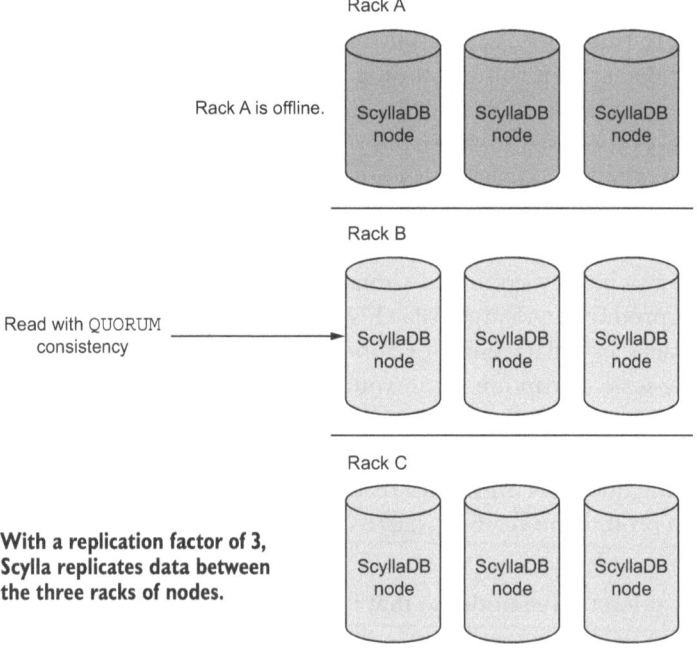

Rack A

Rack A is offline.

Read with QUORUM consistency

Rack B

With a replication factor of 3, Scylla replicates data between the three racks of nodes.

Rack C

Reads with QUORUM consistency can still succeed even with an entire rack offline.

Figure 9.4   By running your Scylla cluster across multiple racks, you can tolerate the loss of an entire rack and still preserve quorum consistency.

Running clusters where the replication factor is less than or equal to the number of racks simplifies operations on the cluster. Each rack holds at most a single copy of the data, and because you can tolerate the loss of a single rack, you can in theory take an entire zone offline at once and suffer no ill effects. Still, the right nodes being down (if your replication factor is 3, one node from two zones) can break the quorum, causing downtime. Although this risk is present in any design, it's important to know your weaknesses.

What about multiple datacenters?

The discussion so far has focused on multiple racks, but there's not much point in defining datacenters if you can only have one. Therefore, ScyllaDB supports multiple datacenters.

When defining your replication factor for a keyspace, you define it per datacenter. Being able to have different replication factors per datacenter can unlock several use cases:

- A standby datacenter to fail over to in the event of a very big incident
- A smaller datacenter with a lower replication factor to run analytics queries against
- A datacenter in a different region to serve traffic to globally distributed services

Scylla handles replicating data to multiple datacenters and, as you saw when learning about consistency options in the last chapter, considers datacenters when calculating quorums. Not every cluster needs multiple datacenters, but for those that do, the option is there for you.

With these factors in mind, my recommended cluster topology approach is as follows:

- A replication factor of 3
- Running nodes in at least three zones or racks

TIP I also prefer using `GossipingPropertyFileSnitch` to have absolute control over datacenter and rack names. Although the cloud provider snitches (which aren't even available to you if you're running on-premises) can automate this behavior, changing the snitches requires complete cluster downtime, so I prefer to do slightly more work to configure the snitch file and keep my options open versus letting the snitch automate the process for me. Additionally, if you need to migrate between clouds when using a cloud-provider snitch, you'll have to switch snitches as part of the migration.

The layout of your nodes isn't the only decision to make when designing your cluster; you must also to choose how many nodes you need and what components those nodes will have. Let's see how you can pick the right compute options for your cluster.

9.2.2 Computing your nodes

You've determined your cluster topology, running in multiple zones with a replication factor of 3, but that's the easy part of designing your cluster. The hard questions await: how many nodes should your cluster have, how big should their disks be, and how many CPU cores do they need?

I am going to let you in on a secret: I don't have a magic formula. There's no magic equation that, when you plug in the variables, gives you the perfect cluster that's exactly sized to fit your needs. In this section, we'll discuss some recommendations and principles you can use to determine the correct resources for your cluster.

The key to determining your cluster's resources is testing. Although I'll give you some guidelines in the next section, at the end of the day, the best way to know if your clusters can stand up to the rigors of production traffic is to send it consequence-free production-level traffic and see what happens. Determining how to build your cluster can be tricky. It's a multidimensional problem; you need to account for disk space, CPU cores, memory, network bandwidth, and—finance teams find this metric very important—cost. Every cluster and every use case is different, and designing a cluster is only the first step on the road to having a production cluster serving traffic. The goal isn't to build a perfect cluster immediately but to provide a baseline that you can tune to build the cluster that meets your needs.

Disk space is the most straightforward decision: take your current (or estimated) storage used, multiply it by your replication factor, and then double that to leave room for uncompacted data and application growth. If you anticipate that your new application will use a terabyte of data, and if it has a replication factor of 3, your cluster needs to allocate 6 TB worth of disk space across all nodes. Additionally, the disks need to be fast enough to meet the needs of the cluster; Scylla prefers local SSDs to achieve optimal throughput, although your cluster may be able to get away with a less speedy option, depending on your use cases.

For CPU cores, Scylla's shard-per-core architecture estimates that each shard can handle 12,500 operations against a kilobyte of data per second. You may be tempted to use the smallest possible machine if your anticipated workload is less than this threshold, but remember that Scylla needs to process other operations beyond user requests: repairs, compactions, gossip, etc. You also want to leave your application room to grow.

Memory in ScyllaDB is important, as it uses a large amount of the available memory to create and maintain the in-memory cache. If the cache is too small, more reads will go to disk, slowing your reads. The suggested threshold to stay above is keeping your RAM-to-disk storage ratio above 1:100; for every 100 GB on disk, you should have at least 1 GB of RAM. The suggested optimal ratio is 1:30, but of course, your application's ideal ratio may vary in the wild.

Network bandwidth is simple; you need enough to satisfy your cluster. The official recommendation is that your network and instances should support at least 10 Gbps.

The desired number of nodes adds additional complexity to your cluster's topology. The total number of nodes you choose to run can be partly driven by the previously described variables, but other requirements often come into play. Perhaps your design tells you that each zone needs 112 cores, but you can only get machines with cores in powers of two, making the closest options machines with 128 or 64 cores. Instead of choosing to run two 64-core machines or one 128-core machine, you may choose to run seven 16-core machines to optimize their cost, as shown in figure 9.5.

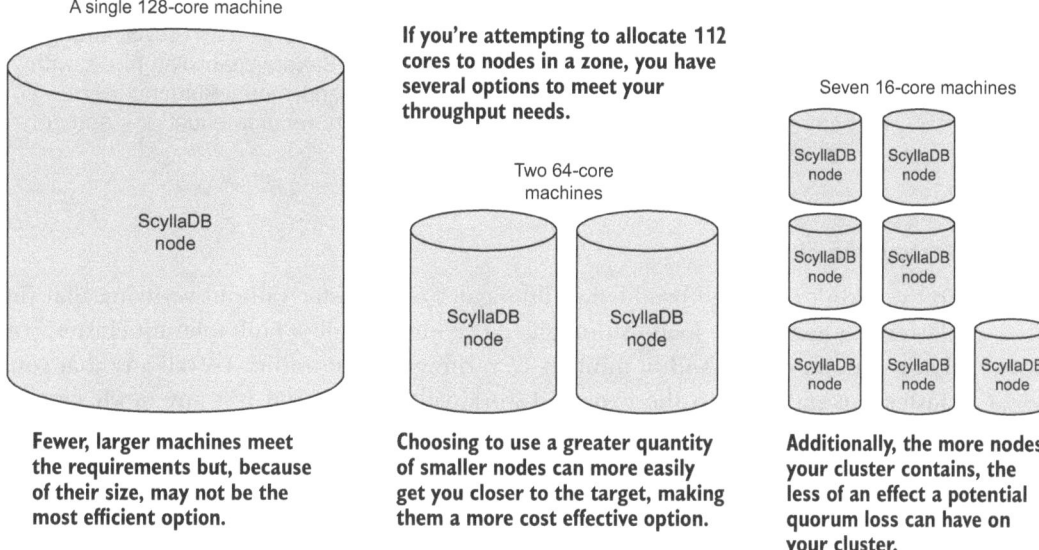

Figure 9.5 **Using smaller nodes in your cluster can be a cost-effective way to meet your throughput goals, as well as increase your cluster's availability if you were to lose a quorum.**

Figure 9.5 shows another factor to consider when calculating node quantity: your application's resilience. If you happen to lose a quorum, with quorum consistency, M/N of the requests to your cluster will fail, where M is the number of nodes down in a zone and N is the total size of the zone. If you run one node per zone, that's all-or-nothing in the event of quorum loss. You may choose to run more nodes to have additional resilience.

As you can see, building a cluster isn't an exact science. Because ScyllaDB scales per-shard—per-core—you can shift resources to fit your needs; there's little difference between four 8-core machines and two 16-core machines. It may sound like a tricky problem, but at the end of the day, the right answer is simple: the most effective ScyllaDB cluster is the one that meets all users' needs.

With these guidelines, you can put together a Scylla cluster. Mixing your topology with your desired configuration gives you a ScyllaDB cluster. But before you run it in production, you should validate that it can handle the expected workloads, which you can accomplish by testing your cluster.

> **After building your nodes**
>
> You explored configuration via the scylla.yaml file, but that file mostly describes the cluster's behavior: how it should handle authentication, authorization, node discovery, etc. It's only the tip of the configuration iceberg, as Scylla also needs to configure the underlying node: setting up the filesystem for where it stores data (Scylla strongly prefers XFS), initializing its CPU configuration so that Seastar can play nicely with other applications that may be running on the node, and more. Running `scylla_setup` before starting the node will walk you through its recommendations and get your node ready to serve production traffic.

9.2.3 *Testing the cluster*

You wouldn't open the production floodgates to a cluster without verifying that the cluster can handle the load. Although you've ideally built a fault-tolerant cluster, you don't want an outage within minutes of turning on the traffic. To validate that your cluster can stand up to the expected workloads, you should test any newly created cluster.

To see your cluster in action without the responsibilities of serving user-facing traffic, you have several options. The most straightforward choice is a synthetic load test, which generates imaginary traffic and sends it to your cluster. Using a tool called `cassandra-stress`, you can stress-test a cluster, providing a benchmark for how many requests it can handle. You'll learn more about this approach in chapter 11. You may also have a different preferred load-testing tool that can work at the application level, sending requests to your application, which, in turn, sends queries to your Scylla cluster.

Although `cassandra-stress` is easy to use because it generates its own traffic, it may not be representative of what workloads your cluster may see. To remedy this gap, you have two potential—and not mutually exclusive—options: controlled rollouts and shadowing.

With a controlled rollout, you send increasing amounts of traffic to your cluster until the database has a problem or successfully handles all traffic. If you run into scaling problems, you can pause at your current level and adjust your cluster to add additional resources, such as changing the CPU cores per instance or adding additional nodes. This rollout can even be your production rollout; it's good to ramp traffic to Scylla incrementally! We'll discuss this approach in greater detail in chapter 12, when you learn about migrating data and bringing a cluster online.

Another testing approach is *shadowing*, where you operate ScyllaDB as a secondary datastore for a currently existing workload (figure 9.6). Imagine that you're using PostgreSQL as a database, and you're working on migrating to ScyllaDB. You build a ScyllaDB cluster, and you want to see if it can stand up to your production traffic. One neat thing you can do in your application is asynchronously send production traffic to ScyllaDB. You can read and write data but not return it to users. You can also get the value of live traffic against what is soon to be your main datastore, validating that it can handle your current workloads. Shadowing works best with a full dataset to most closely mimic production workloads. Just like controlled rollouts, we'll discuss migrating data and how it unlocks shadowing via dual writes and dual reads for you in chapter 12.

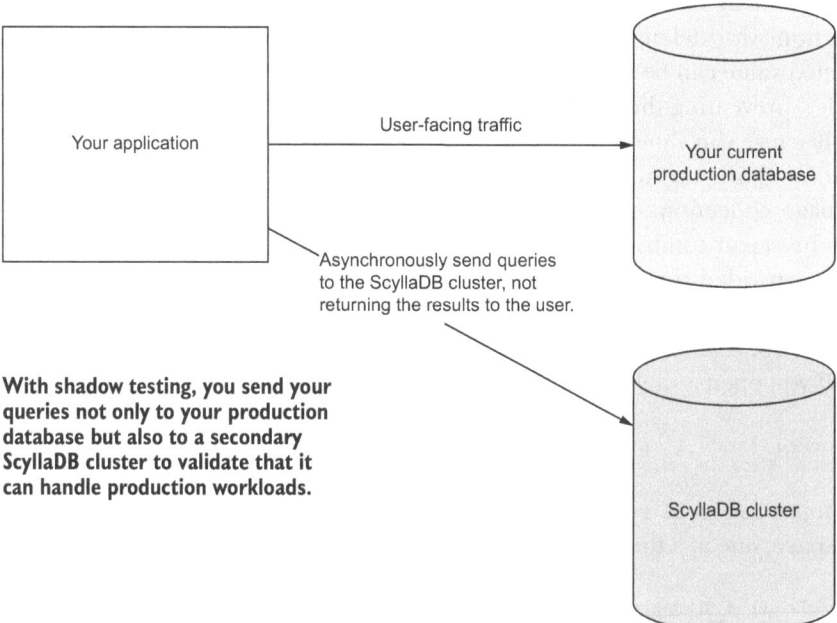

Figure 9.6 Shadow testing uses actual production traffic to validate that your ScyllaDB cluster is correctly sized.

Testing your cluster gives you confidence that when it's live and taking user traffic, it won't fall over due to the volume of queries. It would be awkward to turn traffic onto your cluster and immediately have an outage; testing helps prevent that. The day you turn on your cluster, any problems will need to be fixed immediately. When that day comes, you'll have to operate your cluster differently; avoiding downtime is much more important when there's traffic going to the cluster. Performing operations on a live ScyllaDB cluster is something you'll need to do as an operator, and in the next section you'll learn the most common operations, why they're important, and how to execute them safely.

9.3 Managing the cluster

When a cluster is live in production, you are faced with a new layer of problems: you must keep the cluster up and running. A healthy cluster is mostly hands-off, but you'll sometimes need to intervene to nudge Scylla back to the happy path. In this section, you'll learn how you can further use your old friend `nodetool` to perform tasks in the cluster, improving its health and diagnosing problems.

9.3.1 *Repairing a node*

As discussed in the previous chapter, ScyllaDB reconciles its dataset through repairs, synchronizing data to make sure the cluster is consistent. Repairs also serve a critical function with deleted data. If a node is missing a tombstone from a deletion, the deleted value can be resurrected. Repairs ensure that tombstones are replicated to all nodes, preventing this problem from occurring.

Because you should always run repairs at least once within the `gc_grace_seconds` window (and you still need to run them regularly if using repair-based tombstone garbage collection, or you won't clean up tombstones) or configure your table to use the repair tombstone garbage-collection mode, it's best to schedule them with a Scylla-provided tool called Scylla Manager, which I'll cover in a moment. However, Scylla also supports running ad hoc repairs via `nodetool` and—you guessed it—the `repair` command.

If you open a shell in your `scylla-1` node, you can see a repair in action:

```
$ docker exec -it scylla-1 /bin/bash
```

Running `nodetool repair` begins a repair for that node, kicking off a repair of each keyspace, one at a time:

```
(scylla-1) $ nodetool repair
```

The repair begins by repairing the `system_auth` keyspace, continuing through each of the keyspaces until it finishes with `reviews`:

```
[2023-12-14 14:00:35,999] Starting repair command #1, repairing 1 ranges
➥ for keyspace system_auth (parallelism=SEQUENTIAL, full=true)
[2023-12-14 14:00:36,086] Repair session 1
[2023-12-14 14:00:36,086] Repair session 1 finished
[2023-12-14 14:00:36,094] Starting repair command #2, repairing 1 ranges
➥ for keyspace system_traces (parallelism=SEQUENTIAL, full=true)
[2023-12-14 14:00:42,211] Repair session 2
[2023-12-14 14:00:42,212] Repair session 2 finished
[2023-12-14 14:00:42,328] Repair session 3
[2023-12-14 14:00:42,328] Repair session 3 finished
[2023-12-14 14:00:42,337] Starting repair command #4, repairing 1 ranges
➥ for keyspace system_distributed_everywhere
➥ (parallelism=SEQUENTIAL, full=true)
[2023-12-14 14:00:45,438] Repair session 4
[2023-12-14 14:00:45,438] Repair session 4 finished
[2023-12-14 14:00:45,447] Starting repair command #5, repairing 1 ranges
➥ for keyspace reviews (parallelism=SEQUENTIAL, full=true)
[2023-12-14 14:01:15,558] Repair session 5
[2023-12-14 14:01:15,558] Repair session 5 finished
```

WARNING `nodetool repair` only operates on a single node. To repair all nodes, you need to run `nodetool repair` on every node.

It took about 40 seconds to repair the data, but in a production system with much more data, it would take longer, probably on the order of hours. You can speed up the parallelism by adding threads via the `--job-threads` argument, which will increase the throughput of the repair at the expense of increased load on the cluster.

You can also narrow the scope of the repair. If you look at the `help` command when applied to `repair`, you'll see that it supports an optional keyspace and table:

- If you want to repair only the `reviews` keyspace, you can run `nodetool repair reviews`.
- If you want to repair only the `authors` table in the `reviews` keyspace, you can run `nodetool repair reviews authors`. `nodetool repair` can take any number of tables as an argument.

By running `nodetool repair`, you've only repaired a single node in your cluster, so you would need to repeat this across every node to completely repair your cluster. The preferable option is to instead utilize a tool called Scylla Manager to automate your repairs, which supports this cluster-wide repair orchestration. It takes the cluster's token ranges and repairs them in parallel, allowing you to control the intensity of the repairs against your cluster, as repairing your data so quickly that it takes your cluster offline isn't desired behavior. Scylla Manager also handles the scheduling piece of running repairs, allowing you to specify when your repairs should run and at what frequency.

Unfortunately, the Scylla Docker image doesn't include the necessary pieces to run Scylla Manager locally; Scylla Manager communicates using an agent process running on your node. You can learn more about Scylla Manager and how to run it in your production environment at https://manager.docs.scylladb.com/stable.

If you run repairs regularly using Scylla Manager, when should you choose to use `nodetool repair`? If you elected not to run Scylla Manager, you would need to use `nodetool repair` to repair each of your nodes. Another scenario is when you need to immediately trigger a repair. If your tables are using repair-based tombstone garbage collection, as discussed in the previous chapter, tombstones can only be removed after a repair. You may choose to run a repair off-cycle to trigger garbage collection of partitions with lots of tombstones and thus alleviate slow queries caused by the number of tombstones. You'll learn more about detecting these scenarios in chapter 11.

TIP You can mimic Scylla Manager's repair functionality by running a repair on a specific token range, allowing you to narrow a repair to a single partition by providing the `--start-token` and `--end-token` flags.

Repairs are critical functionality in ScyllaDB, and `nodetool` allows you to run them whenever you want, making their scopes as narrow as needed to fit your uses. They must be run regularly for an effective and healthy ScyllaDB cluster. Another critical operation you need to run regularly is some sort of backup process to protect your cluster in the event of a catastrophe, which we'll examine in the next section.

9.3.2   *Backing up your cluster*

You wouldn't put your data in a database that you couldn't restore if something disastrous happened. Backups are critical for your database and for business continuity, and Scylla supports a couple of ways of backing up a cluster.

The first is via `nodetool`: the `snapshot` command. When you run `nodetool snapshot`, it generates a hard link to each SSTable in a keyspace, storing it in the data directory (/var/lib/scylla/data). Each snapshot lives in a specific snapshot folder in the appropriate folder for the keyspace and table. You can upload these snapshots to another storage location, such as Amazon S3, saving them separately from your database to provide resilience in the event of a disaster. To restore the database, you copy the snapshots back into the SSTable directory and start Scylla.

> **NOTE**   These snapshots aren't automatically cleaned up, so you must remove them manually when they're no longer needed.

Typically, however, you won't be working at this granularity when performing these operations. Just like repairs, Scylla Manager can handle backups and restores for you.

The second technique is to use disk backups by snapshotting the disk. Cloud providers offer the ability to automatically take a snapshot of a disk on a regular schedule. With this functionality, you're able to easily take backups of an entire cluster at approximately the same moment in time. These snapshots also integrate with the cloud provider's disk-creation functionality; it's easy to create new disks from a snapshot.

Whichever option you choose—Scylla snapshots or disk snapshots—it's incredibly important that you regularly test your backups. They're useless if they don't work; you should spin up a set of backups monthly and verify that you can restore them into a functioning ScyllaDB cluster. Hopefully, you'll never need to actually spin up from backups. You should reserve this procedure for a truly catastrophic situation because the backups originate from a past point in time, meaning you will lose data. If some number of nodes (fewer than the replication factor) become unrecoverable, you should instead follow the node-replacement procedure to have the other nodes in the cluster recover their data by replicating to them, which you'll learn more about later in the chapter.

Backups are critical and must be run regularly; not doing so is negligent (don't forget to test restoring them!). Other disk operations, such as compactions, run regularly without you doing anything. Let's look at how `nodetool` provides information about compactions and how a seemingly innocuous command it provides can be a trap.

9.3.3   Compacting a node

Throughout normal operations, ScyllaDB is continuously compacting data according to your desired compaction strategy. You can see this in action by using `nodetool compactionstats`, which gives you information about ongoing compactions in the cluster. This command tells you which keyspaces and tables are being compacted per each compaction operation, as well as how much data Scylla is currently compacting.

`compactionstats` is most useful as a quick high-level view into what data the cluster is compacting. Doing lots of compactions continuously or having a large backlog of compactions can affect your cluster's performance. `compactionstats` lets you quickly view the state of compactions on a given node.

> **Running a major compaction**
>
> Similar to repairs, Scylla supports running a compaction manually via `nodetool compact`. However, this operation should be used with caution. In this major compaction, Scylla compacts all data for a table, pushing it to the highest tier in the compaction strategy. This operation consumes resources and also makes the table harder to compact in the future because all the old data is compacted together, preventing incremental gain when new data is added and goes through a minor compaction. As chapter 8 taught you, running a major compaction often means you'll need to keep running major compactions in the future because minor compactions against that data can be less effective.

`compactionstats` is an excellent troubleshooting tool; if the cluster is spending time compacting, it's spending time not reading data. Although compactions by themselves are okay, if your cluster is running slowly, compactions can be a culprit. Let's take a further look at how you can use `nodetool` to help troubleshoot problems in your cluster.

9.3.4   Troubleshooting tables

`nodetool` can also provide information about tables and queries, helping you understand what's happening in your cluster. I want to discuss a few `nodetool` commands that give detailed information about your cluster's state.

`nodetool tablestats` provides statistics about the data stored in a table. It's a lot of information, but it quickly gives you a view into each of the tables in your cluster. Maybe a table you expected to be tiny is taking up lots of disk space due to tombstones, or perhaps read latency is very high. I've found this view helpful when I know the cluster is unhappy but I'm unsure *why* it's unhappy.

Another quick diagnostic tool is `nodetool tablehistograms`, which prints a histogram of latency and partition size for a given table. By running `nodetool tablehistograms reviews authors`, Scylla will tell you various percentiles of latency and partition size for the `authors` table. It's much easier to find this in your monitoring tooling, which you'll use in chapter 11, but sometimes this command is useful when you're already connecting to the node.

Finally, `nodetool toppartitions` can help you solve your most common problem: hot partitions. When a single partition gets more traffic than the shard can handle, it can slow operations across the cluster that hit that shard. To identify and mitigate the problem, you need to figure out which partition is getting that traffic. It might be a malicious user you need to block, or maybe it's a bug in your application, such as accidentally loading every article for every author of an article when a user loads an article.

`nodetool toppartitions` samples your traffic, telling you the top partitions being queried in your cluster during the sampling period. You can further scope it down to a specific keyspace or table. By continuously querying for Reginald's author row (33a753de-704c-11ee-b962-0242ac120002), you can see data in the `toppartitions` output:

```
(scylla-1) root@scylla-1:/# nodetool toppartitions reviews authors 10000
WRITES Sampler:
  Cardinality: ~0 (256 capacity)
  Top 10 partitions:
    Nothing recorded during sampling period...

READS Sampler:
  Cardinality: ~1 (256 capacity)
  Top 10 partitions:
    Partition                                                Count +/-
    (reviews:authors) 33a753de-704c-11ee-b962-0242ac120002     39 0
```

These monitoring commands can be a bit rough to use. `tablestats` can drown you in information, whereas `tablehistograms` doesn't show you how data has changed over time. You'll almost always prefer using the monitoring stack that you'll set up in chapter 11, but it's important to know about these options for, at worst, a backup plan. `toppartitions` is more useful for identifying the sources of heavy traffic that may be hitting your cluster, and `nodetool` is more immediately useful for performing high-level operations on your cluster. Let's look at how you can use `nodetool` to manage your cluster's lifecycle.

9.4   Managing the node lifecycle

Although your cluster is made up of multiple nodes, it's not made up of multiple nodes that remain with the same count serving traffic forever. Sometimes they need to be offline to apply an update or otherwise undergo maintenance. In this section, you'll learn to safely perform operations on your cluster's nodes, adding them and removing them with ease.

9.4.1   Stopping and starting a node

Imagine that there's a new version of ScyllaDB out, and you'd like to upgrade your cluster. You'll need to install the new version and restart Scylla for it to take effect, but if you are not careful, your upgrade procedure can become an outage. To take a node offline safely, you need to remove it from gossip and mark it as down so that your application and other nodes in the cluster stop connecting to it. You can accomplish this goal with another `nodetool` command: `drain`. With `nodetool drain`, you tell a node to stop listening to connections. It flushes its memtable to disk and stops listening for connections.

> **WARNING** Of course, you want to avoid taking multiple nodes offline and breaking the quorum in your cluster!

You can see it in action by running `nodetool drain` on `scylla-1`:

```
(scylla-1) root@scylla-1:/# nodetool drain
```

It returns almost immediately, logging nothing. If you look at `nodetool status` on `scylla-2` though, you see that `scylla-1` is marked as `DN`:

```
(scylla-2) root@scylla-2:/# nodetool status --resolve-ip
Datacenter: datacenter1
=======================
Status=Up/Down
|/ State=Normal/Leaving/Joining/Moving
--  Address   Load     Tokens  Host ID                                Rack
UN  scylla-3  3.34 MB  256     6db8eb45-77c3-4c9b-b6f7-aacbf0f378b2  rack1
UN  scylla-2  3.42 MB  256     d7625f75-3cba-4d09-9a30-babc9bce02bf  rack1
DN  scylla-1  3.36 MB  256     80233e5f-2acc-455f-98ab-527c05f4791a  rack1
```

Additionally, the logs for `scylla-1` show that it emitted a `DRAINED` message:

```
INFO  2023-12-17 13:39:43,266 [shard 0] storage_service -
    entering DRAINED mode
```

At this point, there's no turning back. Once the node is drained, you've committed to stopping it. To stop the node, you can run `supervisorctl stop scylla`, which tells the supervisor process in Docker to stop the `scylla` process:

```
(scylla-1) root@scylla-1:/# supervisorctl stop scylla
scylla: stopped
```

> **NOTE** If you're running outside of Docker in a production cluster, you'll be using Systemd and not Supervisor, changing your restart command to `sudo systemctl stop scylla-server`.

You've successfully stopped Scylla; it's no longer running. You may be able to guess how to bring it back online—by changing the `stop` to `start`:

```
(scylla-1) root@scylla-1:/# supervisorctl start scylla
scylla: started
```

If you run `nodetool status` again on `scylla-2`, `scylla-1` is once again marked as `UN`:

```
(scylla-2) root@scylla-2:/# nodetool status --resolve-ip
Datacenter: datacenter1
=======================
Status=Up/Down
|/ State=Normal/Leaving/Joining/Moving
--  Address    Load     Tokens   Host ID                                Rack
UN  scylla-3   3.34 MB  256      6db8eb45-77c3-4c9b-b6f7-aacbf0f378b2   rack1
UN  scylla-2   3.42 MB  256      d7625f75-3cba-4d09-9a30-babc9bce02bf   rack1
UN  scylla-1   3.36 MB  256      80233e5f-2acc-455f-98ab-527c05f4791a   rack1
```

TIP   Process managers such as Supervisor and Systemd offer a combined
`stop` and `start` operation: `restart`. Instead of separately stopping and starting, you can run `supervisorctl restart scylla`, which does both. Don't forget to drain the node first!

Restarting a node contains the basics of every cluster operation. You drain the connections, allowing the node to stop gracefully, and then you stop and start Scylla. Let's further expand on this operation by showing how you can replace a node.

9.4.2   *Replacing a node*

Replacing a node is very similar to stopping and starting a node, except you're starting
a different node than you're stopping. You might choose to replace a node when its
underlying hardware is degraded or you're changing instance types in a cloud provider. You begin by stopping the node by draining it and stopping the Scylla process.
When you replace a node, it becomes responsible for the previous node's token
ranges. This stopped node mustn't return to the cluster after this point, so you should
consider disconnecting or stopping the underlying server to avoid this return.

   Next you provision your new replacement node, setting your desired config. Additionally, you add one more parameter to your scylla.yaml file: `replace_node_first_`
`boot`. When running `nodetool status`, you'll see that each node has a host ID. For
example, in the following output, `scylla-2` has a host ID of `d7625f75-3cba-4d09-`
`9a30-babc9bce02bf`:

```
(scylla-2) root@scylla-2:/# nodetool status --resolve-ip
Datacenter: datacenter1
=======================
Status=Up/Down
|/ State=Normal/Leaving/Joining/Moving
--  Address    Load     Tokens   Host ID                                Rack
UN  scylla-3   3.34 MB  256      6db8eb45-77c3-4c9b-b6f7-aacbf0f378b2   rack1
UN  scylla-2   3.42 MB  256      d7625f75-3cba-4d09-9a30-babc9bce02bf   rack1
DN  scylla-1   3.36 MB  256      80233e5f-2acc-455f-98ab-527c05f4791a   rack1
```

This host ID uniquely identifies a node in the cluster. When replacing a node, you
have to tell Scylla that the newly joining node is replacing a specific host in the cluster,
which you do by setting the `replace_node_first_boot` parameter in scylla.yaml to the
old node's Host ID, as shown in figure 9.7.

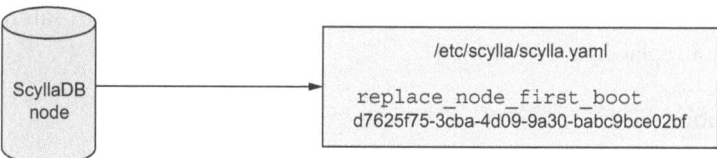

The `replace_node_first_boot` **argument
tells a node when joining the cluster to join in place
of the specified node using the old node's host ID.**

Figure 9.7   By specifying a host ID in the `replace_node_first_boot`
**parameter, a Scylla node joins the ring and becomes responsible for the old
node's token ranges.**

The following example shows how a new node might replace `scylla-2`, which, in this
hypothetical scenario, you can pretend you have already taken offline:

```
replace_node_first_boot: d7625f75-3cba-4d09-9a30-babc9bce02bf
```

On startup, instead of joining new places in the ring, the newly added node takes over
the previous node's token ranges. Bootstrapping otherwise occurs as normal, where
nodes begin sending data to the newly added node—only this time, it's the same data
the previous node was responsible for. Another operation you may choose to do is to
scale up your cluster by adding nodes. Let's look at adding nodes and the further
tweaks the procedure requires.

9.4.3   *Adding a node*

You added nodes to the cluster way back in chapter 2 when you built your Docker-
based cluster, and you have just learned about adding a node as a direct replacement
for another node. Scaling up a cluster—adding nodes without replacing old ones—is
also a common operation. Sometimes you need to add capacity to meet your applications' needs. To scale up your cluster, you start up additional nodes with their desired
configuration, but you should follow these guidelines:

- Add one node at a time to reduce load on the cluster, waiting for it to be UN in
  `nodetool status` before continuing.
- Add nodes to the cluster in a balanced fashion, making sure all racks have
  equivalent numbers of nodes.
- When you're finished, run `nodetool cleanup` on all nodes in the cluster to
  remove data transferred to a new node.

Running `nodetool cleanup` is very important; if you forget to clean up the data that is
handed off to the new nodes, if an old node ever becomes responsible for that token
range again, you can end up with resurrected data from long, long ago. It also saves
on disk space, so anytime you can improve your cluster and avoid a very gnarly bug,
it's a win-win! This scenario can occur when you remove a node, which also has its own

quirks to allow it to run safely and successfully. Let's examine how to safely remove nodes without a replacement.

9.4.4   *Removing a node*

In my experience, you're more likely to expand a cluster, but sometimes you need to remove a node from it. Perhaps your cluster is overprovisioned, or you're removing a no-longer-needed datacenter. Removing a node from the cluster without a replacement shrinks the number of nodes in the ring, meaning it needs to somehow hand off its data to the rest of the cluster. Scylla supports two methods of removing a node from the cluster:

- Using `nodetool decommission` instructs the currently connected-to node to stream its data to the rest of the cluster and leave the ring once streaming data away is complete.
- Using `nodetool removenode` forcefully removes a host ID it from the ring and instructs the rest of the cluster to rebalance data to satisfy the desired replication strategy.

Of these options, using `decommission` is strongly recommended and preferred. Imagine a world where you inserted data with a consistency level of ONE. A node can have data that the other replicas don't know about. Because `removenode` doesn't stream data from the departing node but instead uses the rest of the ring to share its data with the remaining nodes, you have the potential of losing data that only the removed node knows about. By requiring the departing node to stream its data away, `decommission` avoids this problem.

To remove a node, you run `nodetool decommission` on the node you want to remove. In `nodetool status`, you'll see the status change to UL for "leaving." Once the departure process is complete, you'll no longer see the node in `nodetool status`.

With that, you're ready to operate a production Scylla cluster. You've learned how to configure it, size it, and perform operations against it. The next chapter covers another critical step in using ScyllaDB in production: connecting applications to it.

Summary

- A production-ready cluster contains sufficient resources to handle the traffic it receives.
- Configuring your cluster is done predominantly through the scylla.yaml file.
- Setting `cluster_name` in your configuration prevents nodes from accidentally joining the incorrect cluster.
- By specifying a seed node, you provide a contact point for a newly launched node so that it can join the cluster and learn about other nodes.
- Nodes need to set their `listen_address` and `rpc_address` to listen to traffic and receive traffic from other nodes.

- To authenticate connections, Scylla allows you to enable `PasswordAuthenticator`, blocking connections with incorrect credentials.
- Similarly to the authenticator, `CassandraAuthorizer` rejects operations that a user doesn't have permissions to execute.
- The snitch defines the cluster's topology, using it to help route requests in the cluster. I prefer `GossipingPropertyFileSnitch`, which gives you complete control over these definitions, but the various cloud-provider snitches, which automate some of the work for you, can also be a good fit.
- A production-ready cluster contains at least three nodes and distributes its nodes across zones in a cloud provider or across racks in an on-premises datacenter.
- Determining cluster resources isn't the result of a magic formula but is about determining a starting point, testing, and adjusting.
- `nodetool repair` and `nodetool snapshot` perform critical operations on a node, but you should prefer using Scylla Manager to orchestrate them across your cluster.
- When running in production, you must be careful to maintain a quorum in your cluster when performing operations.
- To safely stop a ScyllaDB node, run `nodetool drain` to drain connections before stopping it.
- You can replace a node by taking the old node offline and starting a new one with `replace_node_first_boot` set to the old node's host ID in scylla.yaml.
- You can remove a node from the cluster by executing `nodetool decommission` from the node you wish to remove.

Application development with ScyllaDB

10

This chapter covers

- Creating a Flask application to connect to your cluster using the Scylla driver
- Building an API that executes queries against ScyllaDB
- Tuning the driver's consistency, load-balancing, and query retry behavior
- Authenticating and authorizing connections to the cluster

On top of every database is at least one application that interacts with it. Maybe it's an API, or perhaps a data analytics system. An API needs to provide an interface for users to create, store, and remove data via HTTP requests. A data analytics system may query the entire database—you'll see how to approach this problem in chapter 12—to transfer data into another system for further aggregation. By building an application on top of the cluster, you allow a database to provide its benefits beyond people who understand its schema and how to write a database query.

In this chapter, you'll learn how to use ScyllaDB in an application. By using the *database driver*, a software library for connecting to a database, you'll build a small Python application that queries ScyllaDB by exposing an API. Along the way, you'll learn how to best configure the driver for production systems and how to tackle some real-world application and database concerns: authentication and authorization. However, before you can connect to your database, it's time to set up the application.

10.1 Your application

Thus far, you've designed a schema for a restaurant review application. You'll be shocked to read that, in this chapter, you'll be building a small API for your restaurant reviews. As this book is about using a database and not API design, you won't be building a complete API here, but you'll build something that's extendable to production applications.

In building an API, you'll create some *endpoints*, Python functions reachable by making an HTTP request to a specific URL or path, such as /authors. This path, which you'll add later in the chapter, is linked to a function that loads all authors in the database. First up: ensuring that Python is set up and ready to go.

> **NOTE** The focus of this chapter is showing how to connect an application to Scylla with a database driver. Some Python constructs or specific error-handling cases have been intentionally omitted to focus on connecting to the database. In a real-world system, make sure you validate that the values which you don't want to be `None` or `null` aren't actually `null`!

10.1.1 Python

You'll write your application in this chapter in Python using a lightweight web framework called Flask. I've chosen to use Python here because of its popularity and simple syntax.

> **Installing Python**
>
> If you don't have Python 3 installed on your system, the following website has quality instructions for adding it for each operating system: https://realpython.com/installing-python.
>
> The usage of Python here should be mostly straightforward, but if you're unfamiliar with it and want to learn more, Python's documentation has a quick tutorial: https://docs.python.org/3/tutorial/index.html.
>
> Of course, Manning Publications has several Python books, such as *The Quick Python Book* (by Naomi Ceder, www.manning.com/books/the-quick-python-book-fourth-edition) to aid your learning as well!

Before proceeding, make sure you have Python 3 installed on your system. The minor version isn't as important here, but you want at least 3.7, which was released in June 2018:

```
$ python3 --version
Python 3.11.5
```

10.1.2 *Virtual environments*

Before installing any dependencies, you need to be sure you have `pip`, the Python packager manager, installed. Python contains an `ensurepip` module that will install it if it's not already installed on your system:

```
$ python3 -m ensurepip
```

Third-party packages in Python are globally installed, which can wreak havoc on your local developer environment if you're working on multiple projects on the same machine. If two projects nccd two versions of a dependency, and both are incompatible with each other, you're in a pickle.

To prevent this problem, Python provides functionality called *virtual environments* so you can specify a specific version of Python and have separate dependencies per project. To use a virtual environment, you need to install one dependency globally: `virtualenv`. You can install it via `pip` to ensure that you're using your Python 3's `pip`:

```
$ pip3 install virtualenv
```

You'll see a stream of messages as it collects the dependencies for `virtualenv`. On completion, you'll see a message telling you the installation succeeded:

```
Successfully installed distlib-0.3.8 filelock-3.13.1 platformdirs-4.1.0
➥ virtualenv-20.25.0
```

Make a folder for your application in a directory of your choosing. You will create the application in this directory:

```
$ mkdir scylladbia-app
```

Open the directory in your terminal so that you can create the virtual environment in it:

```
$ cd scylladbia-app
```

It's finally time to create your virtual environment. You'll tell Python to create a virtual environment using the `venv` module, calling it `scylladbia-env`. Go ahead and run the following command:

```
$ python3 -m venv scylladbia-env
```

Once the command returns, if you run `ls` against the directory, you'll see a new folder for your environment:

```
$ ls
scylladbia-env/
```

You've successfully created your virtual environment, but you're not using it yet. To use the virtual environment, you must activate it in your terminal session. For activation, you need to run the `activate` script in scylladbia-env/bin/. This script switches your Python executable and environment to be the one in the virtual environment:

```
$ source scylladbia-env/bin/activate
```

Your terminal prompt should change to indicate that you're in the virtual environment; but even if it doesn't, you can verify that you're using your new environment by checking where the `python3` executable is located using `which`:

```
(scylladbia-env) $ which python3
.../scylladbia-app/scylladbia-env/bin/python3
```

With your virtual environment created, you're ready to set up Flask and begin building your application.

10.1.3 *Flask*

Flask is a web framework in Python that makes it easy to build a web application in Python. Although it can be used in very large applications, it's also straightforward enough to use in a book that wants to spin up a quick web application to teach using ScyllaDB.

You first need to install Flask in your virtual environment:

```
(scylladbia-env) $ pip3 install flask
```

> **NOTE** The code samples for this chapter include a `pip` requirements file that you can install using `pip3 install -r requirements.txt` to install all the dependencies needed. You can also install them as you go through the examples in the chapter.

With Flask installed, you can finally start building your application. You'll begin by creating a slight variation on Flask's version of the traditional "hello world" program. A web application wants to listen for HTTP requests on a given path and route those requests to a specific method. Your application listens for requests to / and returns the string `ScyllaDB in Action!`, which Flask automatically returns as an HTTP response. Figure 10.1 shows how this approach is the first building block for your API: you'll create an endpoint, and later you'll use the database driver to query the database and return responses to the user.

Create a new file named app.py, and add the code shown in listing 10.1. This initial version of the app returns the name of the book if you load its base route.

> **NOTE** The listings from this chapter can also be found in the chapter's code samples repo.

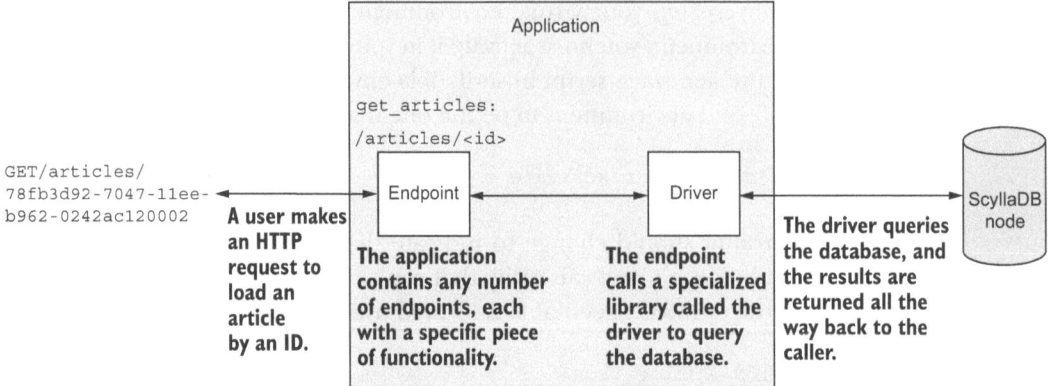

Figure 10.1 Your application will listen for HTTP requests and use the driver to query the database for rows returned to the user.

```
Listing 10.1    Initial version of the app
```

```
from flask import Flask                    ◁──┤ Imports Flask into
                                                 your application.

app = Flask(__name__)              ◁───────  Creates a Flask app based
                                             on the name of the file.

@app.route('/')                    ◁────────
def hello_world():                           Routes HTTP
    return 'ScyllaDB in Action!'   ◁──┐      requests to /
                                             to this function.
        Returns the name of the book. Flask
        automatically converts the value into
                    an HTTP response.
```

There are no Scylla connections yet, but it's always good to work iteratively, making sure the less complex pieces work before adding more to your apps. To make requests against your application, you need to start it using `flask run`, which starts the server and makes it available at 127.0.0.1:5000:

```
(scylladbia-env) $ flask run
 * Debug mode: off
WARNING: This is a development server. Do not use it in a production
    deployment. Use a production WSGI server instead.
 * Running on http://127.0.0.1:5000
Press CTRL+C to quit
```

Using cURL or your browser, make an HTTP request to http://127.0.0.1:5000, and you'll see the name of the book you're reading:

```
$ curl http://127.0.0.1:5000/
ScyllaDB in Action!
```

And with that, you've got the beginnings of your application! With a brand-new virtual environment and a very basic Flask app, you're ready to connect to your cluster and run queries from an application. Let's drive on and learn how to connect your application to ScyllaDB.

10.2 Querying Scylla

Connecting to Scylla from an application involves using a specific software library: the database driver. Whether you're using Postgres, MongoDB, or Scylla, you connect via the client driver in the language of your choice. Scylla supports Python, Java, Go, C/C++, and Rust. Because you've written a Python application thus far, it would be madness to switch to Java for this section; you'll integrate the Python driver into your app.

> **NOTE** You can also use a Cassandra driver library to connect to ScyllaDB, because Scylla is compatible with Cassandra's drivers and wire protocol. But if you do, you won't be able to take advantage of some Scylla-specific features that you'll learn more about later in this chapter.

To use the driver, you first need to install it. Just like Flask, you can use `pip` to install the dependency `scylla-driver` locally. I've also pinned the driver's version to 3.26.4 to avoid any version discrepancies:

```
(scylladbia-env) $ pip3 install scylla-driver==3.26.4
...
Successfully installed geomet-0.2.1.post1 pyyaml-6.0.1 scylla-driver-3.26.4
    six-1.16.0
```

You've got an application and installed driver; you're ready to connect to ScyllaDB. Now you need the ScyllaDB piece. Let's set up a new cluster that better meets your needs for this chapter.

10.2.1 A new Scylla cluster

Up to this point, you've been working with your three-node Docker cluster. Because the three containers share a network, they easily communicate with each other using DNS. When you started your cluster, you were able to pass `scylla-1` as a hostname as opposed to an IP address.

However, this topology complicates things for this chapter. To make ports in a container accessible on your local machine, Docker requires you to forward a port on your local machine to make the desired port in the container reachable. To access the CQL port from your application in each container, you need to designate a specific port on your machine for the CQL port on `scylla-1`, with separate ports for `scylla-2` and `scylla-3`. This approach clashes with the Scylla driver, which assumes that all nodes it's connecting to use the same port. Although there are ways to make this topology work, they're complicated and can vary based on your machine; so to proceed, you're going to choose a simpler option: spinning up a single-node Scylla cluster. This approach is illustrated in figure 10.2.

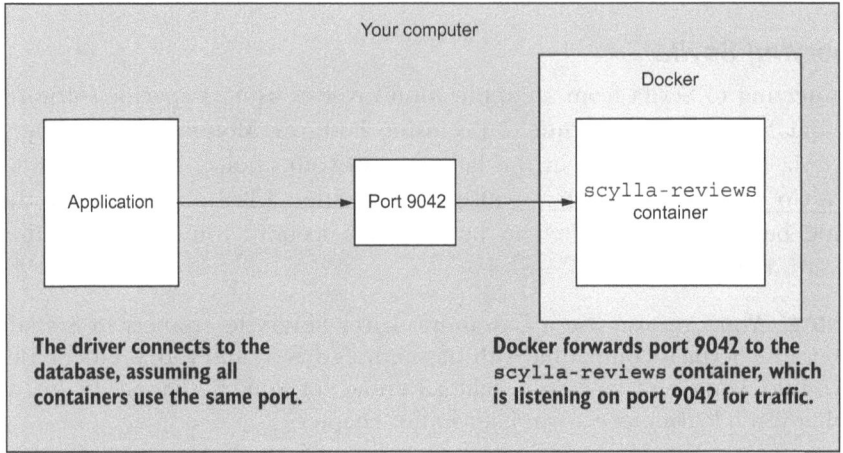

Figure 10.2   The database driver assumes that all Scylla instances use the same port, which conflicts with your previous Scylla cluster. A new `scylla-reviews` cluster powers your work in this chapter.

NOTE   You may be wondering, "What about my data in the old cluster?" As in chapter 7, I've included a dataset here, which you'll set up soon.

A single-node cluster is not something you want in production. But it can work great for local development because it lessens the resources required to run your app. First you need to create the cluster.

The `docker run` command is very similar to the one in your previous clusters. In addition to the name change—hello `scylla-reviews`—you have the addition of the `-p` flag, which forwards ports on the local machine to ports in your container. Here, you've forwarded three ports: the CQL port, another special CQL port I'll explain later in the chapter, and a third port I'll discuss in the next chapter.

Go ahead and run this command to create your second Scylla cluster:

```
$ docker run --name scylla-reviews --hostname scylla-reviews \
  --network scylla-network --detach -p 9042:9042 -p 19042:19042 \
  -p 9180:9180 scylladb/scylla:5.4
```

Cleaning up after yourself
If you like, you can delete your old Scylla containers by running `docker rm --force`, deleting the container and its data:

```
$ docker rm --force scylla-1
```

> Repeat the process for `scylla-2` and `scylla-3` if you'd like to free up resources for your machine. If you prefer to keep them around (maybe you added some additional data), you can stop the containers with `docker stop <container name>`.

You can connect to your new single-node cluster via `cqlsh`, just like you did with your previous cluster:

```
$ docker exec -it scylla-reviews cqlsh
```

As in chapter 7, I've included in the code samples for this chapter (www.manning .com/books/scylladb-in-action and https://github.com/scylladb-in-action/code) the schema and dataset you'll be using in your application. If you copy the contents of ch10/1_schema.cql and ch10/2_dataset.cql into your `cqlsh` session, you'll have the data you need for your app. Because you'll be running a single-node cluster, I've already set the replication factor to 1 for the keyspace:

```
cqlsh> DESCRIBE reviews;
CREATE KEYSPACE reviews WITH replication =
{'class': 'NetworkTopologyStrategy', 'datacenter1': '1'}
AND durable_writes = true;


...
```

After creating the schema and inserting the dataset, you should be able to query the `authors` table and see your old friends Alice and Reginald:

```
cqlsh> USE reviews;
cqlsh:reviews> SELECT id, name FROM authors;

@ Row 1
------+--------------------------------------
 id   | 33a753de-704c-11ee-b962-0242ac120002
 name | Reginald Reviewer

@ Row 2
------+--------------------------------------
 id   | eff9bd01-4a73-11ee-8863-c02b3f99d2b2
 name | Alice Author

(2 rows)
```

With your new cluster up and running, along with your schema and dataset, you're finally ready to connect to Scylla from your application.

10.2.2   *Connecting to the cluster*

Before running any queries, you should validate that you can successfully connect to the cluster. Instead of connecting to port 9042 like `cqlsh` does, you'll connect to a special port that provides greater performance: 19042. This port—the *shard-aware port*—routes requests directly to their owning shard in the node, speeding up your queries. Update your app.py file with the code in the following listing. It imports the Cluster object from the Scylla driver and opens a connection to your new scylla-reviews cluster, connecting to the reviews keyspace.

Listing 10.2   Using the Scylla driver to connect to your cluster on startup

```
from cassandra.cluster import Cluster          ◁——  Imports the cluster from the Scylla
                                                     driver (which uses the Cassandra API).

from flask import Flask, g          ◁——  Imports the Flask global context.

def create_app():          ◁——
    app = Flask(__name__)                  You need to perform additional setup for the
                                           app, so you extract the creation into a function.

    with app.app_context():          ◁——
        get_db_session()                   To access the global context, you need to
                                           ensure that you're in the Flask application
    print('Connected to Scylla!')          context. It's a Flask thing required to share
                                           your database session across requests.

    return app

def get_db_session():          ◁——  Initializes the session if it's not already set up,
    if 'db' not in g:                   letting you retrieve the database in an endpoint.
        cluster = Cluster(["127.0.0.1"], port=19042)          ◁——
                                                                    Creates a Cluster
        session = cluster.connect('reviews')          ◁——          object with Scylla's
                                                                    address (localhost)
        g.db = session          ◁——                                and port.
                                     Saves the database
    return g.db                      session in the Flask      Connects to a specific
                                     global context.           keyspace on the cluster.

app = create_app()          ◁——
                                  Calls your create_app function to
...                               create a Scylla connection, leaving
                                  the following code unchanged.
```

Run flask run again, and you'll see your Connected to Scylla! message printed in the terminal:

```
$ flask run
Connected to Scylla!
...
```

Are you having trouble connecting?

If there's an error, make sure the following things are true:

- Your new cluster is up and running with the arguments specified, especially the -p ones. Without port forwarding, your application will be unable to connect to the cluster.
- You created the schema with the reviews keyspace in the previous section.

With a successful connection, you're ready to query Scylla from your application.

10.2.3 *Your first application query*

For your first query, you can perform the query you used to test the newly created cluster: loading authors. You'll add a new endpoint to your API to load all authors, which will retrieve your database session and execute the query, returning the result to the caller.

Before setting up the endpoint, you need to make a configuration change to the driver to make the rest of the chapter much easier. By default, Flask returns any objects that are lists or dictionaries (Python's name for a map data structure) as their JSON equivalents. The driver-returned values (*named tuples*, if you're curious) are converted to lists by Flask if returned directly. There are many ways to handle this conversion—making the driver return dictionaries, converting to a data class, etc.—but in this book, I've chosen to have the driver return a dictionary for ease of use.

First you need some new imports. To make the driver return a dictionary, you need to set an *execution profile*, which is a series of options in your driver. If you import ExecutionProfile (along with a couple of other associated objects), you'll have access to it in your code (listing 10.3).

Listing 10.3 Importing execution profiles

```
from cassandra.cluster import Cluster, ExecutionProfile,
   EXEC_PROFILE_DEFAULT

from cassandra.query import dict_factory

from flask import Flask, g
...
```

Importing the execution profile allows you to override the cluster's options.

dict_factory instructs the driver to return rows as dictionaries.

With ExecutionProfile imported, you can use it by setting the dict_factory option to return rows as dictionaries and passing your created ExecutionProfile to the Cluster object to specify the options you want the driver to have.

Listing 10.4 Passing the execution profile to the cluster

```
def get_db_session():
    if 'db' not in g:
        profile = ExecutionProfile(
            row_factory=dict_factory
        )

        cluster = Cluster(
            ["127.0.0.1"],
            port=19042,
            execution_profiles={EXEC_PROFILE_DEFAULT: profile}
        )

        session = cluster.connect('reviews')

        ...
```

Lets you override the driver's behavior.

Tells the driver to return rows as a dictionary.

Passing the profile to the cluster applies the options specified in your profile.

EXEC_PROFILE_DEFAULT is the default profile used.

With that configuration out of the way, you're ready to set up your new endpoint. You can make reading all authors available at /authors. This endpoint retrieves the database session and loads all authors, obtaining a special object called a *result set*, which contains the retrieved rows. This result can be iterated over, allowing you to extract the rows. Finally, you return the retrieved rows to the caller; Flask converts them to a JSON list. Add the endpoint in the following listing to your app.py file.

Listing 10.5   /authors endpoint that reads every author from the database

```
app = create_app()

@app.route('/authors')
def authors():
    db = get_db_session()              ◁── Retrieves the
                                            database.
                                                           Executes the
    result_set = db.execute('SELECT * FROM authors')    ◁── query, returning
                                                           a result set.
    authors = []
                                    Iterates through the
                                    result set and adds the
    for row in result_set:      ◁── authors to a list.
        authors.append(row)
                                    Returns the retrieved authors,
    return authors        ◁──      which Flask automatically
                                    converts to JSON.
```

With the endpoint created, you're finally ready to run a query from your application. Use flask run again to start up your local server. Request /authors, and you'll see the authors again!

```
$ curl http://127.0.0.1:5000/authors
[
  {
    "bio": "Reginald is a food enthusiast who loves to review food",
    "id": "33a753de-704c-11ee-b962-0242ac120002",
    "image": null,
    "name": "Reginald Reviewer"
  },
  {
    "bio": "Alice loves writing about food",
    "id": "eff9bd01-4a73-11ee-8863-c02b3f99d2b2",
    "image": null,
    "name": "Alice Author"
  }
]
```

Formatting tip

For you cURL users out there, you can pretty-print the JSON by piping it to a tool like jq or Python's own json.tool:

```
$ curl localhost:5000/authors | python -m json.tool
```

Your request returns the authors you've used in previous chapters. Take a moment and acknowledge how far you've come! You've learned about Scylla, designed a schema, and read and written data. Now you've created an application and are querying your cluster from it.

Of course, as you've learned while studying Scylla's performance, exposing an API to query across all partitions is not a best practice. It does make a great example endpoint, however. In the next section, you'll learn how you can read data efficiently in your application by using more practical read queries. Let's see how your application can do parameterized reads.

10.3   Reading data

Your application wants to run practical queries; multipartition reads are typically something to avoid on a production system. You'll be reading against a single partition, passing in a partition key and optional clustering keys to find the data you're looking for. These queries present a challenge: how do you handle input and set parameters in your queries? To solve this challenge, let's see how you can use a database-driver technique that brings both performance and safety.

10.3.1   Prepared statements

When you try to read an article from the database, you write a query that specifies the columns you want to read (or a wildcard), the table name, and the ID of the article. Your query is then converted into a request to the database, which returns a response containing the matching rows.

A query in an application isn't used just once; you read articles from the database frequently as users navigate to them. Without any optimization, this conversion from query to request happens each time you want to load an article. To save on parsing the query, database drivers support a feature called *prepared statements*, where they cache the parsed form of the query. After preparing a statement, queries to the database can reuse that statement, only passing in the parameters to *bind*, or use, in the query.

To load an article, its prepared statement is created from the query `SELECT * FROM articles WHERE id = ?`. The `?` indicates the parameter to bind. Each time you load an article, you pass the ID to the prepared statement. The driver replaces the `?` in the query with your supplied ID. Figure 10.3 illustrates the relationship between your query strings, the prepared statements, and the bound statements you execute to get results from the cluster.

This replacement has an additional benefit: security. If you were passing input to a query, you might think string concatenation or some form of templating would work great. But this approach leaves you open to a common security vulnerability: SQL injection. In a SQL injection (for Scylla, it's really a CQL injection) attack, an adversary takes advantage of naive query parsing by including extra commands in a query. As I'm talking about SQL injection, I'm professionally obligated to share the popular

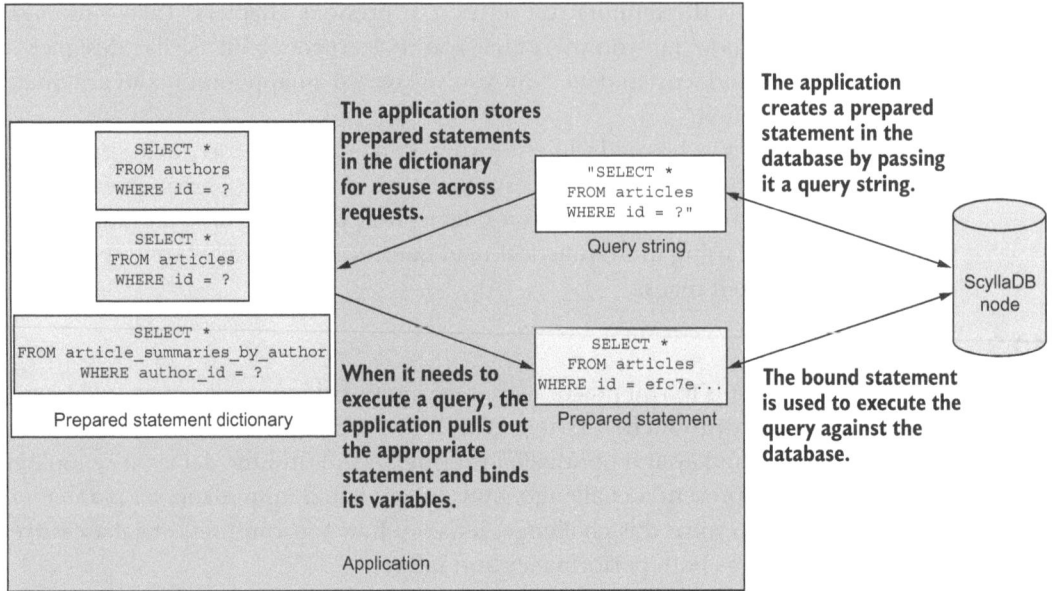

Figure 10.3   Using prepared statements in your application lets you reuse queries across requests, binding parameters for each use.

web comic xkcd's famous SQL injection strip: https://xkcd.com/327/. If your database is vulnerable to this kind of attack, a malicious user can drop tables, read unauthorized data, and wreak havoc.

Prepared statements prevent this vulnerability. In addition to caching the parsed query, they ensure that parameters parsed to it are correctly sanitized, stopping these attacks from adding commands. You should use prepared statements in your applications, so let's replace your existing "all authors" query with a prepared statement.

> **TIP**   Prepared statements are stored in a cache on the server. If the cache fills up, an existing prepared statement can be evicted and then reprepared (the driver handles this for you). Only prepare statements that need to run many times—not one-off commands—to minimize this risk.

First create two top-level variables, as shown in the next listing. The first is an empty dictionary that you'll use to store the prepared statements so you can access them during a request. The second value is a constant that you'll use as a key for your query that loads all authors.

Listing 10.6   Creating a dictionary for prepared statements

```
...
from flask import Flask, g
```

```
PREPARED_STATEMENTS = {}
ALL_AUTHORS = 'all_authors'

...
```

Store prepared statements in this dictionary to use them in your queries.

Saves the keys for the dictionary as a constant.

Next you need to prepare those statements so you can store them in your dictionary. In your `get_db_session` method, call `session.prepare()` with your query, storing the result in your `PREPARED_STATEMENTS` dictionary.

Listing 10.7 Creating a prepared statement from a query

```
def get_db_session():
    if 'db' not in g:
        profile = ExecutionProfile(row_factory=dict_factory)

        cluster = Cluster(
            ["127.0.0.1"],
            port=9042,
            execution_profiles={EXEC_PROFILE_DEFAULT: profile}
        )

        session = cluster.connect('reviews')

        PREPARED_STATEMENTS[ALL_AUTHORS] = session.prepare(
            'SELECT * FROM authors'
        )

        g.db = session

    return g.db
```

Inserts prepared queries into the dictionary when initializing the database.

To prepare a statement, you need a query string.

The last thing you need to do is use your prepared statement. Update your `authors` endpoint to pass the prepared statement, replacing the query string. The driver will use the prepared statement to execute the query.

Listing 10.8 Passing the prepared statement to execute the query

```
@app.route('/authors')
def authors():
    db = get_db_session()

    result_set = db.execute(PREPARED_STATEMENTS[ALL_AUTHORS])

    authors = []
    for row in result_set:
        authors.append(row)

    return authors
```

To use a prepared statement, pass it to the session's execute method.

Running `flask run` again starts the app with your prepared statement. If you send a request to /authors, the database driver uses the prepared statement to read the authors from the database. Pretty cool!

```
$ curl http://127.0.0.1:5000/authors
[
  {
    "bio": "Reginald is a food enthusiast who loves to review food",
    "id": "33a753de-704c-11ee-b962-0242ac120002",
    "image": null,
    "name": "Reginald Reviewer"
  },
  {
    "bio": "Alice loves writing about food",
    "id": "eff9bd01-4a73-11ee-8863-c02b3f99d2b2",
    "image": null,
    "name": "Alice Author"
  }
]
```

This shows how to set up prepared statements and integrate them into your application, but you haven't bound any parameters yet, and you're still doing a multipartition read. Let's dive further in and load an article from the database using these newfound prepared statements.

10.3.2 Reading articles

Setting up the prepared statement for reading an article follows a similar workflow:

1 Get your query.
2 Set up a constant name for it.
3 Prepare the statement from your query.
4 Use the prepared statement where needed.

Getting your query is easy. You've used it throughout the book: SELECT * FROM articles WHERE id = ?. Next, set up the constant name GET_ARTICLE for it.

Listing 10.9   `GET_ARTICLE` constant

```
PREPARED_STATEMENTS = {}
ALL_AUTHORS = 'all_authors'
GET_ARTICLE = 'get_article'
```

Just like before, you prepare the statement from the query, as shown in listing 10.10. Load every column but `images` from the `articles` table. Recall from chapter 4 that `images` is a collection type containing your `image` user-defined type. You skip `images` because it's a nested type, and Flask makes it much more complicated to serialize as JSON. This approach requires some extra attention: it's straightforward to serialize and deserialize strings, but how do you handle a set of images? You'll learn more about querying user-defined types (UDTs) in your application later.

Listing 10.10 `GET_ARTICLE` query

```
def get_db_session():
    if 'db' not in g:
        ...

        session = cluster.connect('reviews')

        PREPARED_STATEMENTS[ALL_AUTHORS] = session.prepare(
            'SELECT * FROM authors'
        )

        PREPARED_STATEMENTS[GET_ARTICLE] = session.prepare(
            """
            SELECT id, author_id, date, restaurant_name, review,
                score, title
            FROM articles
            WHERE id = ?
            """
        )

        g.db = session

    return g.db
```

Adds a prepared statement to load an article.

Skips loading images for now to simplify the example.

The prepared statement allows you to get an article, but the easy part stops here. You now have an additional challenge: how to pass the article ID from a request into your application so you can use it in the prepared statement. You have a variety of options: you can make it part of the path of the URL, you can make it a query parameter, or you can even put it in the body of the request (but that's a tremendously awkward approach). REST-ful API design suggests it should be part of a path, making the request look something like `/articles/a04db1e8-be37-11ee-a506-0242ac120002`.

Flask supports this pattern: include the ID in your path in brackets, and you can use it as a parameter in your `route` function. You'll then be able to pass it to your prepared statement, passing the parameters to bind in your query in a list. Note that you'll also need to convert the ID to a UUID so it will use the correct type that the database expects—an article ID in your schema is a version 1 UUID (don't forget to `import uuid`!).

As before, your query returns a result set containing a list of results. However, you only expect a single result (or nothing) because you've queried by the primary key—the article ID. You can extract the single row after verifying its existence and return it to the caller. Update app.py with the changes in the next listing.

Listing 10.11 Binding parameters with prepared statements to enable reuse

```
...

from flask import Flask, g, abort

import uuid
```

```
...

@app.route('/articles/<id>')
def articles(id):
    db = get_db_session()

    result_set = db.execute(
        PREPARED_STATEMENTS[GET_ARTICLE],
        [uuid.UUID(id)]
    )

    if result_set is None:
        abort(404)

    row = result_set[0]

    return row
```

By including id in brackets, you're able to access it as a method parameter.

Executes the prepared statement to read the article.

Passing in the ID (and converting it to a UUID) binds the ID to the ? parameter in the prepared statement.

If you find nothing, return a 404.

There should be only one row in the result set because you're querying by the full primary key.

If you load the review for Main Street Tacos—78fb3d92-7047-11ee-b962-0242ac120002—you're in for a surprise. Unfortunately, it returns an error!

> **TIP** Instead of manually typing this value, it's easier to SELECT * FROM articles in cqlsh and grab the ID.

```
$ curl http://127.0.0.1:5000/articles/78fb3d92-7047-11ee-b962-0242ac120002
<!doctype html>
<html lang=en>
<title>500 Internal Server Error</title>
<h1>Internal Server Error</h1>
<p>The server encountered an internal error and was unable to complete
your request. Either the server is overloaded or there is an error in
the application.</p>
```

That's not ideal. Looking at the output for your server, you see a large stack trace and an additional error message: TypeError: Object of type Date is not JSON serializable. This error brings us to a common problem in both programming and database drivers: they use data types that are specific to the database and not necessarily suited for other purposes, such as easy serialization in a web application. Whether you're using a Scylla Python driver or a Java MySQL driver, you'll often need to convert data types in your results to use them elsewhere in your application.

Here, you need to convert this date from a Cassandra date into a serializable Python date. The driver library supports this conversion, providing a handy .date() method to do just that. The following listing walks you through this conversion, safely converting the Cassandra date to a Python date.

Listing 10.12   Serializing the date to fix the error

```
@app.route('/articles/<id>')
def articles(id):
    ...
```

```
row = result_set[0]                    ┌─ Skip this logic if
                                       │  there's no date.
if row.get("date") is not None:    ◄───┘
    row["date"] = row["date"].date().strftime('%Y-%m-%d')   ◄──┐
                                                               │
return row                   Converts the database's date into a │
                             date string that serializes correctly.
```

If you `flask run` and try your request again, it works:

```
$ curl http://127.0.0.1:5000/articles/78fb3d92-7047-11ee-b962-0242ac120002
{"author_id":"eff9bd01-4a73-11ee-8863-c02b3f99d2b2",
"date":"2023-10-24",
"id":"78fb3d92-7047-11ee-b962-0242ac120002",
"restaurant_name":"Main Street Tacos",
"review":"Homemade tortillas make the difference...",
"score":85,"title":"Good Tacos at Main Street Tacos"}
```

Your application successfully serializes the review and returns it to you. With that, you've hooked up your first parameterized prepared statement. Next, let's examine how you can use prepared statements to write data.

10.4 Writing data

At a high level, writing data isn't too dissimilar from reading it. You've already learned how to read and write to the database; writing to the cluster in an application also uses prepared statements. The complexity of writing data lies not in its statements but in its surrounding context. You need to pass the data you want to write to your service, validate it, retrieve related data, and ultimately write to the database (figure 10.4).

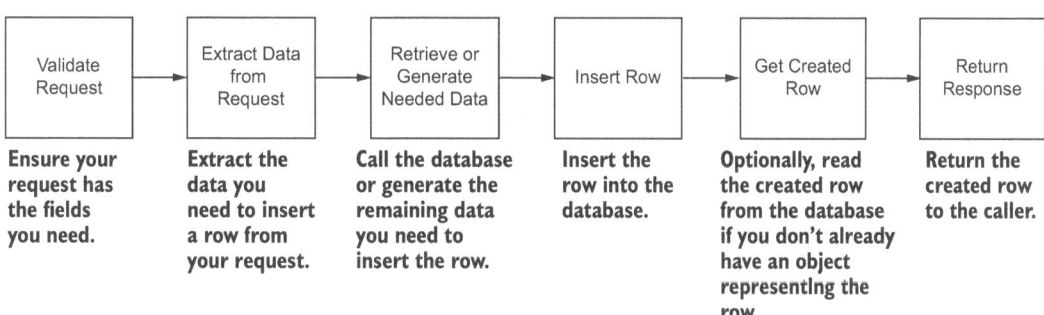

Figure 10.4 Executing a write query against the database is straightforward, but the surrounding operations to prepare for it add complexity.

To examine writes from an application, you'll set up the batch writes on inserting an article and adding its summary to the three summary tables. Before writing any code, let's get a refresher about what data you need to insert.

10.4.1 *The necessary data*

As you read from the database in the last section, an article consists of the following fields:

- `author_id`
- `date`
- `id`
- `images`
- `restaurant_name`
- `review`
- `score`
- `title`

Several of these fields are used in the article summary:

- `author_id` (partition key for `article_summaries_by_author`)
- `author_name`
- `date`
- `date_bucket` (partition key for `article_summaries_by_date`)
- `id`
- `image` (taken from the list of images)
- `score`
- `title`

When an application writes data, it typically receives that data from a request, but that approach doesn't fit all fields. What happens if you pass the author's name in a request to the application to use in an article summary? Is there any guarantee that it matches an existing author or the author ID that you'll also need?

Additionally, you decided back in chapter 5 to use a bucketed date as your partition key. If the date passed in doesn't match its associated bucket, that's likely to lead to further bugs elsewhere in your application. For these properties, it makes sense not to directly set them via user input but instead to compute them in your application.

Another good choice for the computation approach is the article ID. Sure, you can generate a TIMEUUID and pass it into your application, but programming languages have libraries that will do the same thing. You can use the `uuid` module in Python to generate a unique ID, taking the burden away from callers of your API.

This computation for the date bucket and ID is simple: you do some quick calculations. To validate the author, however, you need to load the author with the supplied ID and retrieve their name to use in the summary. This approach adds another query to your application.

When you make a request to your application, you know what data to pass it (you'll soon learn how) but what do you expect to get back? You can return the created article. However, recall from chapter 6 that Scylla doesn't return the written data when you insert a row. You need to do an additional read for your newly created article to return it to the user.

Although the write statements themselves are often simple, the act of writing data from an application is often complicated. Validation, computation, additional queries—it's rarely as straightforward as "insert this row" in the real world. Let's begin adding your write path by laying all the groundwork: importing dependencies and preparing statements so that you can write your write endpoint.

10.4.2 Laying the write groundwork

You need to import a few new modules to batch-write articles into Scylla. First you need the `BatchStatement` class from the Scylla driver—the key to your plans. To calculate the date bucket for `article_summaries_by_date`, you also need to import the `datetime` module, which contains functions to give you the current date. Finally, you'll import the `request` class from Flask, which gives you access to the local request object. You'll eventually pass data to your `route` function via an HTTP request; the `request` class will let you use this data. Add these imports to app.py.

Listing 10.13 Adding imports to batch-write articles to the cluster

```
...                                    BatchStatement allows you to perform
                                               batch writes to the cluster.

from cassandra.query import BatchStatement, dict_factory    <—
from datetime import datetime                         <—     datetime is imported to
from flask import Flask, abort, g, request            <—     help calculate summaries'
                                                            date buckets.
...              The request is also imported from
                 Flask to access the response body.
```

With those imports knocked out, next up is declaring your constants for the prepared statements. Remember, you need to support inserts into four tables:

- `articles`
- `article_summaries_by_author`
- `article_summaries_by_date`
- `article_summaries_by_score`

Additionally, you need to load an author to retrieve the author's name, as discussed previously. The following listing adds the constants to use as keys in your prepared-statement dictionary. I've also included an additional constant: the beginning date for bucket calculations. You'll use this value soon to determine which date bucket an article belongs in.

Listing 10.14 Constants to use as keys

```
GET_AUTHOR = 'get_author'
GET_ARTICLE = 'get_article'
INSERT_ARTICLE = 'insert_article'
```

```
INSERT_ARTICLE_SUMMARIES_BY_AUTHOR = 'insert_article_summaries_by_author'
INSERT_ARTICLE_SUMMARIES_BY_DATE = 'insert_article_summaries_by_date'
INSERT_ARTICLE_SUMMARIES_BY_SCORE = 'insert_article_summaries_by_score'

BUCKET_START_DATE = datetime(2023, 10, 1)
```

With these constants, you're ready to create the prepared statements and insert them in the dictionary. The catch is that because you're inserting multiple values, you need a ? for each.

Listing 10.15   Inserting prepared statements in the dictionary

```
def get_db_session():
    if 'db' not in g:
        ...

        PREPARED_STATEMENTS[GET_AUTHOR] = session.prepare(
            'SELECT * FROM authors WHERE id = ?'
        )
        PREPARED_STATEMENTS[INSERT_ARTICLE] =
    ⇒       session.prepare(
            """INSERT INTO articles(
                id, author_id, date, images, restaurant_name, review,
                score, title
            ) VALUES (
                ?, ?, ?, ?, ?, ?, ?, ?
            )"""
        )
        PREPARED_STATEMENTS[INSERT_ARTICLE_SUMMARIES_BY_AUTHOR] =
    ⇒           session.prepare(
                """INSERT INTO article_summaries_by_author(
                    author_id, id, author_name, image, score, title
                ) VALUES (
                    ?, ?, ?, ?, ?, ?
                )"""
            )
        PREPARED_STATEMENTS[INSERT_ARTICLE_SUMMARIES_BY_DATE] =
    ⇒           session.prepare(
                """INSERT INTO article_summaries_by_date(
                    date_bucket, id, author_name, image, score, title
                ) VALUES (
                    ?, ?, ?, ?, ?, ?
                )"""
            )
        PREPARED_STATEMENTS[INSERT_ARTICLE_SUMMARIES_BY_SCORE] =
    ⇒           session.prepare(
                """INSERT INTO article_summaries_by_score(
                    score, id, author_name, image, title
                ) VALUES (
                    ?, ?, ?, ?, ?
                )"""
            )
```

Avoiding the tedium of binding everything

You may be familiar with an *object-relational mapper* (ORM) when using a database from within an application. Originally used with relational databases (hence the name), an ORM maps an object or class in the language of your choice to a row in the database. Although there are great debates to be held about balancing ease of use and masking performance concerns, I'm choosing to sidestep that discussion and only point out that they can provide a friendlier interface to developers as opposed to having to write a query with 10 question marks.

Many Scylla drivers support some sort of ORM functionality. In the Python driver, this function is implemented by the Object Mapper. You can define a class that sub-classes `cassandra.cqlengine.models.Model`, containing fields corresponding to your columns:

```
import uuid
from cassandra.cqlengine import columns
from cassandra.cqlengine.models import Model


class Author(Model):
    id = columns.UUID(primary_key=True, default=uuid.uuid1)
    name = columns.Text(required=True)
    ...
```

By extending `Model`, your application can make queries using the model:

```
result = Author.objects(id='eff9bd01-4a73-11ee-8863-c02b3f99d2b2')
```

At this point, you may be wondering, "Why not teach querying from the application this way?" How each driver handles this interface is idiomatic to the language: the Rust driver, for example, takes a different approach than the Python driver. In this chapter, I want to communicate the core concepts of using a database driver from an application and not rely on language-specific constructs. My goal is for you to be able to take the concepts taught from learning how the driver works and apply it in your language—whether it's Python, Go, C++, or Java.

Now that you've defined the prepared statements, there's one bit of refactoring to knock out. At the end of the function, you should return the article you've created. Although you can already load an article, that logic currently lives in the /articles route. Go ahead and extract it into its function so you can load an article without calling the `route` method.

Listing 10.16 Breaking out the article load functionality

```
...

@app.route('/articles/<id>')
def articles(id):
    return get_article(uuid.UUID(id))
```

```
def get_article(id, db=None):
    if db is None:
        db = get_db_session()

    result_set = db.execute(
        PREPARED_STATEMENTS[GET_ARTICLE],
        [id]
    )

    if result_set is None:
        abort(404)

    row = result_set[0]

    if row.get("date") is not None:
        row["date"] = row["date"].date().strftime('%Y-%m-%d')

    return row


...
```

Defaulting db to None allows you to pass in an already-existing session if you have one.

The following code has been extracted from the articles function.

Having refactored loading articles, you're ready to build your article-creation route. You'll use your prepared statements and the imported batch functionality to insert articles into the main table and the three associated summary tables. Let's begin!

10.4.3 *Batch-writing articles*

With the prepared statements created, you're ready to dive into the complexity that comes with inserting data in an application. When you read an article earlier, the only value you needed to provide was the article's ID. However, when inserting an entire article plus its summaries, you have to supply each of the fields in your request. To do that, you send JSON in your HTTP request. Additionally, you change the type of the HTTP request from GET (the implicit default) to POST, which is the traditional request type to use when sending data in the body of the request to create something on the server. These tweaks unlock the ability to pass typed data in the request body to your endpoint, which you can read, convert, and insert into your tables.

To begin, create a new route for /articles, but this time specify that you'll be using a POST HTTP request. Once the route is complete, you'll send the data you create as a JSON blob in your request, reading it in your route and passing it to your batched insert statements. To access your request data, use the imported request from before, which gets the json data from the request, giving you a dictionary with the request's JSON data. The next listing shows you how to create the route for your new POST request to create an article.

> **Listing 10.17   Sending JSON data in a POST request to /articles**

```
@app.route('/articles', methods = ['POST'])
def create_article():
    data = request.json
```

Now that you've got your hands on the data, you can begin parsing it and computing the necessary fields to insert into the database. The first step is to load the author so you can get their name for the article summary. You'll extract the author's ID from the request—data['author_id']—and convert it to a UUID as you did when loading an article, allowing you to read that author from the database. On executing that query, if you don't find the author, you should return an error to the caller; you can't continue with an author-less article! Finally, save the author's name into a variable for later use.

Listing 10.18   Loading the author using the supplied ID

```
def create_article():
    ...
    author_id = uuid.UUID(data['author_id'])      ⟵ Converts the author
                                                      ID from the request
                                                      into a UUID.

    db = get_db_session()                 ⟵
    author_result_set = db.execute(            Retrieves the
        PREPARED_STATEMENTS[GET_AUTHOR],       author so you can
        [author_id]                            get their name.
    )

    if author_result_set is None:       ⟵  If the author doesn't exist,
        abort(404)                          returns an error to the caller.

    author_name = author_result_set[0]['name']
```

After retrieving the author's name, you can continue collecting the rest of the data you need, extracting the date, restaurant name, review, score, and title from your request. To calculate the date bucket, use your constant from earlier—BUCKET_START_DATE—and determine the number of months that have elapsed since that point. Once again, I've marked the image fields as placeholders. You'll see how to write using a UDT in the next section when you add inserting images. For now, they're left as their default values. Finally, you need an ID for the article, which you can generate via the uuid module.

Listing 10.19   Remaining fields to insert an article

```
def create_article():
    ...
                                            Calculates the date bucket by
                                         determining the number of months
                                              since the bucket start date.
    date = data['date']
    restaurant_name = data['restaurant_name']
    review = data['review']                 Converts the date into a
    score = data['score']                    datetime to prepare to
    title = data['title']                    calculate the bucket.

    article_date = datetime.strptime(date, '%Y-%m-%d')    ⟵

    date_bucket = (article_date.year - BUCKET_START_DATE.year) * 12 + \   ⟵
        article_date.month - BUCKET_START_DATE.month
```

```
images = []                        ◁──┐  Adds placeholders
summary_image = None                  │  for now.

id = uuid.uuid1()           ◁──── Generates an article ID.
```

With all the data gathered, you're ready to insert the articles. You construct a special `batch` statement that will hold each of your prepared statements, which you add to the batch. Executing the batch performs the batch write, inserting rows into the article table and its associated article summary tables. Finally, you read the article from the database and return it to the user. Add the following code, and you'll finally be ready to execute the insert.

Listing 10.20   `BatchStatement` to perform a batch write to the database

```
def create_article():
    ...
                                           To perform a batch query, construct
                                           a batch statement and add your
    batch = BatchStatement()        ◁──┘   prepared statements to the batch.
    batch.add(
        PREPARED_STATEMENTS[INSERT_ARTICLE],
        [id, author_id, date, images, restaurant_name, review, score, title]
    )
    batch.add(
        PREPARED_STATEMENTS[INSERT_ARTICLE_SUMMARIES_BY_AUTHOR],
        [author_id, id, author_name, summary_image, score, title]
    )
    batch.add(
        PREPARED_STATEMENTS[INSERT_ARTICLE_SUMMARIES_BY_DATE],
        [date_bucket, id, author_name, summary_image, score, title]
    )
    batch.add(
        PREPARED_STATEMENTS[INSERT_ARTICLE_SUMMARIES_BY_SCORE],
        [score, id, author_name, summary_image, title]
    )

    db.execute(batch)          ◁──┐  Once all queries have been added,
                                  │  you're free to execute the batch.

    article = get_article(id, db=db)    ◁──┐  Loads the article from the
                                           │  database to return to the user.
    return article
```

TIP   One obvious optimization is to skip reading the article after inserting it. After all, if you have enough data to insert an article, you've got enough data to return an article to the user. But reading the article proves that you successfully inserted an article.

With the endpoint written, you can finally call it. Using your browser here, unless you've got some sort of add-on, won't work. You need an HTTP client like cURL (which is what I'm using in the terminal) to execute a POST HTTP request. Use `flask run` again to start your development server with the new endpoint.

Alice Author (id `eff9bd01-4a73-11ee-8863-c02b3f99d2b2`) has written a new review for Pie Palace, giving it a 9.5 out of 10 (you're multiplying scores by 10 in the database, as described in chapter 4, so you'll insert `95`). She says that "Pies at Pie Palace are to pie for" (insisting that the pun is not a typo) and has titled her review "Pies Fit for a King." This information gives you the necessary data to insert a review. First, let's assemble the JSON payload for your request:

```
{
    "author_id": "eff9bd01-4a73-11ee-8863-c02b3f99d2b2",
    "date": "2024-01-31",
    "restaurant_name": "Pie Palace",
    "review": "Pies at Pie Palace are to pie for...",
    "score": 95,
    "title": "Pies Fit for a King"
}
```

You can insert this payload via cURL and see your newly inserted review! You need to specify three arguments to your command:

- `-X POST` to indicate that you're making a `POST` request
- `-H "Content-Type: application/json"` to set the `Content-Type` header, indicating that your request body is JSON-encoded
- `-d '{"author_id":…}'` for the body of your request

You get back the review with a fresh new ID. For mine, it's `f235832a-c088-11ee-bacd-ba235f449265`:

```
$ curl -X POST http://127.0.0.1:5000/articles -H "Content-Type:
    application/json" \
    -d '{"author_id":"eff9bd01-4a73-11ee-8863-c02b3f99d2b2",
    "date":"2024-01-31","restaurant_name":"Pie Palace",
    "review":"Pies at Pie Palace are to pie for...","score":95,
    "title":"Pies Fit for a King"}'
{
  "author_id": "eff9bd01-4a73-11ee-8863-c02b3f99d2b2",
  "date": "2024-01-31",
  "id": "f235832a-c088-11ee-bacd-ba235f449265",
  "restaurant_name": "Pie Palace",
  "review": "Pies at Pie Palace are to pie for...",
  "score": 95,
  "title": "Pies Fit for a King"
}
```

Plug that ID into the article-loading endpoint, and you'll get the same response.

> **WARNING** You will have a different ID than me, so don't copy my ID in and expect to get the same results.

```
$ curl localhost:5000/articles/f235832a-c088-11ee-bacd-ba235f449265
{
  "author_id": "eff9bd01-4a73-11ee-8863-c02b3f99d2b2",
```

```
    "date": "2024-01-31",
    "id": "f235832a-c088-11ee-bacd-ba235f449265",
    "restaurant_name": "Pie Palace",
    "review": "Pies at Pie Palace are to pie for...",
    "score": 95,
    "title": "Pies Fit for a King"
}
```

You're 99% done with inserting an article. You've prepared the statements, inserted the row, and read the response, but you still have the images to contend with. Let's wrap up writing data from the application by integrating UDTs into the flow.

10.4.4 *Working with user-defined types*

A UDT brings additional complexity to your application. By default, your driver knows how to serialize basic types—integers, strings, lists, etc. When you create a UDT, however, the driver needs to know how it should serialize and deserialize that type for you. To read and write the image UDT you created in chapter 5, you need to tell the driver about it, which you do by creating a *dataclass*, a custom Python class that has some built-in functionality to make your life simpler. For example, it automatically defines the `init` function (Python's version of a constructor).

To use a dataclass, you first need to import it.

Listing 10.21   Importing a dataclass

```
from dataclasses import dataclass
```

With the `dataclass` decorator imported, you're ready to define a custom class for your UDT. Recall that in your schema, your image consists of two fields: `path` and `image`. Your application's class to represent the UDT will contain both these fields. Define each of them in a new `Image` class annotated as a dataclass. Create this class after your imports.

Listing 10.22   Defining a dataclass in app.py to match the UDT in your schema

```
@dataclass
class Image:
    path: str
    caption: str
```

Now you need to tell the driver about your UDT's dataclass so it knows how to convert from your application's class to the database's UDT (and vice versa). Additionally, you need to update your article query; you previously weren't loading images because you hadn't gotten the UDT up and running yet. The following listing shows you how to register your new dataclass with the cluster, mapping the keyspace's UDT directly to the new class you've defined in your application.

Listing 10.23 Mapping the UDT to your dataclass

```
def get_db_session():
    if 'db' not in g:
        ...

        cluster = Cluster(
            ["127.0.0.1"],
            port=9042,
            execution_profiles={EXEC_PROFILE_DEFAULT: profile}
        )

        cluster.register_user_type('reviews', 'image', Image)    ◁

        ...

        PREPARED_STATEMENTS[GET_ARTICLE] = session.prepare(    ◁
            """
            SELECT *
            FROM articles
            WHERE id = ?
            """
        )

        ...
```

> To serialize and deserialize the UDT, you need to register your dataclass with the driver.

> You can query for all columns now that you know how to handle your image UDT.

There's one more piece of preparation to tackle before you can begin updating your article-creation route: you need to update the `get_article` function to correctly deserialize the set of images. Because they're stored as a set and not as a list in Scylla, the driver loads them as a set. Unfortunately, Flask won't automatically serialize the sorted set you get back from the database, so you need to cast it to a list to return it on the response. This casting is similar to how you handle dates, where you convert them into a string. The next listing checks whether there are any images in the row, and if some are found, converts that set into a list.

Listing 10.24 Serializing the images correctly

```
def get_article(id, db=None):
    ...

    row = result_oct[0]

    if row.get("date") is not None:
        row["date"] = row["date"].date().strftime('%Y-%m-%d')

    if row.get("images") is not None:
        row["images"] = list(row["images"])

    ...
```

After registering the UDT and updating the query, you next need to extract the image data from your HTTP request and translate it into your dataclass so you can insert it into the database. Previously you inserted placeholder values into the database, but you can now use the actual ones!

When the request comes into your application, it is a JSON array because you store a set of the image UDTs in Scylla. To parse it into a dataclass, iterate through the list, taking your UDT's fields out of each map in the list, passing them to your dataclass's constructor, and appending it to a new map of images. For the summary's image, grab the first image from your list of dataclass images, if you have any. Figure 10.5 shows how your JSON image data ultimately becomes a value in your database.

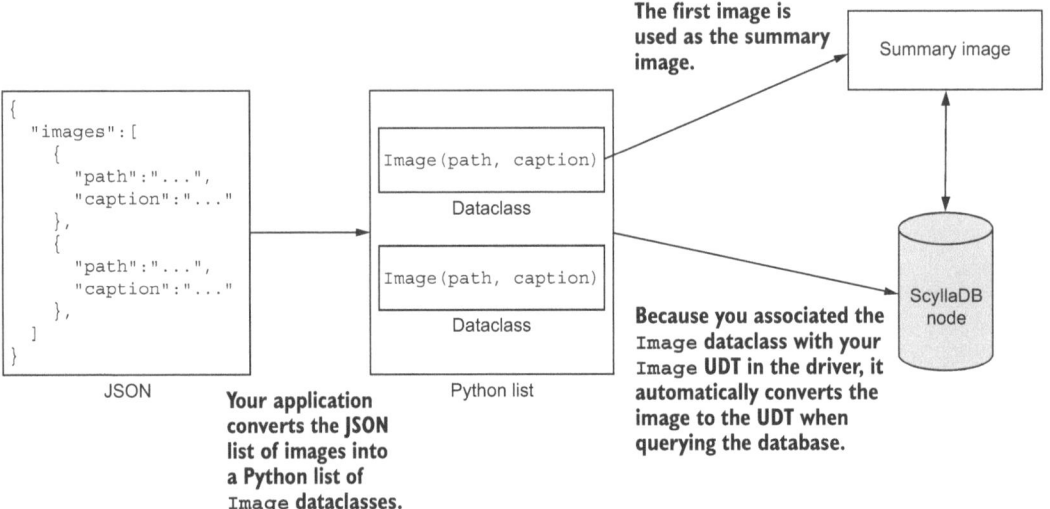

Figure 10.5   Converting the JSON image data into your dataclass lets the driver know to treat the dataclass as the official type for the Image UDT.

Finally, I've included a small tweak to the article ID calculation to enable reusing an existing ID and updating a row. Add the following changes to your `create_article` function, and you'll be ready to add images to an article.

Listing 10.25   Converting images from your request correctly

```
@app.route('/articles', methods = ['POST'])
def create_article():
    ...

    images = []

    image_data = data.get('images')            If you have image data in
                                                your request, you need to
                                                convert it to the dataclass.
    if image_data is not None:
        for image in image_data:
            path = image['path']
```

```
            caption = image['caption']
            images.append(Image(path=path, caption=caption))

    summary_image = images[0] if len(images) > 0 else None    ◁────────────┐

    if data.get('id') is None:    ◁───────┐   Updates ID              The summary
        id = uuid.uuid1()                     generation so you        image can be the
    else:                                     can pass in an existing  first image if
        id = uuid.UUID(data['id'])            ID, allowing you to      one exists.
                                              update an article.
    ...
```

Adding the ability to update an article previews your next task: updating Pie Palace's review to add an image. You need to add the ID and the `images` array to your previous request data. Pass that in, and you'll get back your updated article—with the images:

```
$ curl -X POST http://127.0.0.1:5000/articles -H "Content-Type:
    application/json" \
    -d '{"author_id":"eff9bd01-4a73-11ee-8863-c02b3f99d2b2",
    "date":"2024-01-31","restaurant_name":"Pie Palace",
    "review":"Pies at Pie Palace are to pie for...","score":95,
    "title":"Pies Fit for a King","images":[{"path":"pie.jpg",
    "caption":"Amazing strawberry rhubarb"}],
    "id":"f235832a-c088-11ee-bacd-ba235f449265"}'
{
  "author_id": "eff9bd01-4a73-11ee-8863-c02b3f99d2b2",
  "date": "2024-01-31",
  "id": "39495054-c375-11ee-a2fb-ba235f449265",
  "images": [
    {
      "caption": "Amazing strawberry rhubarb",
      "path": "pie.jpg"
    }
  ],
  "restaurant_name": "Pie Palace",
  "review": "Pies at Pie Palace are to pie for...",
  "score": 95,
  "title": "Pies Fit for a King"
}
```

You've written a lot of code! This chapter has been action packed so far; you've set up a Python app, hooked it up to a Scylla cluster, and built an API that reads and writes data to your database. This pattern, if Python isn't your language of choice, can be extrapolated to other languages. If you're writing in Java or Rust (or anything else), you'll also connect to the database via a driver. I've focused thus far on this basic read-and-write path, but there's much more to cover. For example, I haven't even discussed how consistency works with the driver! Let's look at how you can further configure the driver to make your application's queries as performant as possible.

10.5   *Configuring the driver*

Although the queries your application executes are important, the driver's behavior also plays a critical role in your app. With a weaker consistency level, you may see stale data. If you send every request to a slow Scylla node, your application will respond more slowly. Correctly configuring the driver has a big effect on your application; to learn what you need to do for a well-functioning production system, let's look at how you can configure consistency in the driver.

10.5.1   *Consistency*

As you've learned throughout the book, query consistency is key to Scylla's goals. Weaker consistency options allow you to better tolerate failure, whereas stronger options help enforce data correctness. My recommendation hasn't changed since chapter 8: prefer quorum consistency. It ensures that a majority of nodes see every write and gives some room in your cluster for fault tolerance.

You won't be able to see the benefits of quorum consistency here, as your application is running against a single-node cluster, but you can still change the consistency of your queries. Consistency is a query-level property; accordingly, you set it on a query's statement.

Prepared statements help facilitate this configuration: if you set consistency on a prepared statement, the driver will use that consistency level for all invocations of the statement. The following listing loops over the statements in the prepared statements dictionary, setting each of their consistency levels to LOCAL_QUORUM.

> **Listing 10.26   Setting the consistency level on a prepared statement**

```
from cassandra import ConsistencyLevel

...


def get_db_session():
    if 'db' not in g:
        ...

        PREPARED_STATEMENTS[INSERT_ARTICLE_SUMMARIES_BY_SCORE] =
➥ session.prepare(
                """INSERT INTO article_summaries_by_score(
                    score, id, author_name, image, title
                ) VALUES (
                    ?, ?, ?, ?, ?
                )"""
            )

        for statement in PREPARED_STATEMENTS.values():
            statement.consistency_level = ConsistencyLevel.LOCAL_QUORUM

        ...
```

You can also override the consistency level for specific query executions by first binding your fields, which generates a `BoundStatement`. You can then set the `consistency_level` property on that bound statement and execute it:

```
def get_article_default_consistency(id, db=None):
    ...

    result_set = db.execute(
        PREPARED_STATEMENTS[GET_ARTICLE],
        [id]
    )

    ...

def get_article_override_consistency(id, db=None):
    ...

    statement = PREPARED_STATEMENTS[GET_ARTICLE].bind([id])
    statement.consistency_level = ConsistencyLevel.LOCAL_ONE
    result_set = db.execute(statement)

    ...
```

Uses the default consistency for the prepared statement.

Overrides a single query's consistency.

Setting the consistency level on the prepared statement allows you to consistently use the same option, but the driver gives you the flexibility to override it by letting you update it on the bound statement. When building a production application, don't forget to set this value, or you may see some expected results. Next up, let's examine how you can configure the driver to load-balance queries around your cluster.

10.5.2 *Load balancing*

Although Scylla encourages balancing its load by sharding its dataset across the cluster, it's still possible to have imbalanced traffic. Imagine that you have three racks: a, b, and c. If your application sends requests only to b, that rack can potentially be overwhelmed because the traffic is imbalanced. To help share the load, Scylla's drivers contain *load-balancing policies* to algorithmically determine which nodes a query is sent to. There are two policies to be aware of:

- `TokenAwarePolicy` routes queries directly to the shard that owns them by being aware of the token ranges in the cluster.
- `DCAwareRoundRobinPolicy` rotates through all nodes in the datacenter and falls back to other datacenters if necessary (there is also a variant—`RoundRobinPolicy`—that uses all nodes in the cluster).

You don't have to pick between these two options; the best choice is to use them both together. The `TokenAwarePolicy` "wraps" another policy, applying token awareness first and then using the secondary option to pick a replica to ultimately send the query to, as shown in figure 10.6. When `TokenAwarePolicy` is used in combination with connecting to port 19042—which you set earlier in the chapter—the driver can not only direct requests to an owning replica but also go directly to the owning shard.

SELECT * FROM authors WHERE id = 123

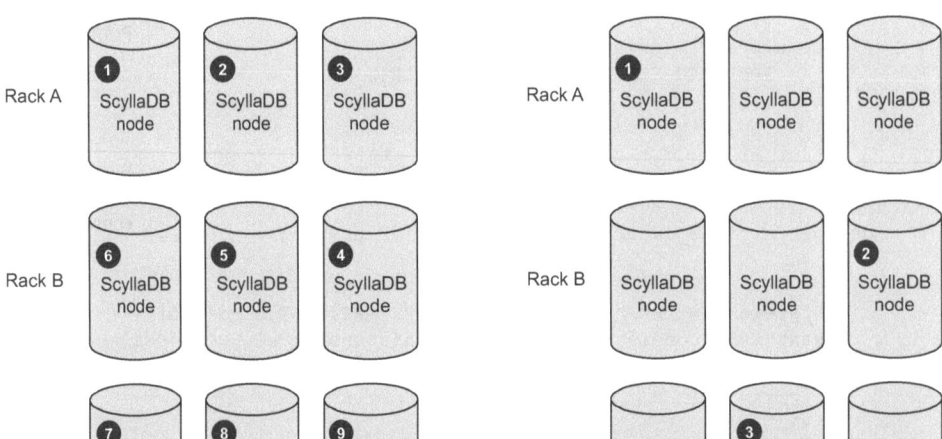

Round-robin routing

Round-robin routing rotates through every node in the cluster, sending requests to each node in turn.

Token-aware routing + round-robin routing

By wrapping round-robin routing with token-aware routing, the driver can send requests directly to the shard that owns the relevant partition, rotating among the replicas.

Figure 10.6   Round-robin routing rotates through the nodes in the cluster, whereas token-aware routing can send requests directly to the shard that owns the partition.

TIP   Some of the Scylla drivers (not Python) support an additional relevant option: latency-aware routing. With this approach, the driver tracks query latencies and prefers sending queries to nodes that respond faster. If you're seeing performance problems with the default, using latency-aware in non-Python drivers can sometimes be a helpful optimization.

The load-balancing policy is part of the cluster's execution profile. To use token awareness and round-robin routing together, you first need to import each of the policies. The execution profile contains a `load_balancing_policy` argument, which you override by first specifying `TokenAwarePolicy` and passing to it as an argument the `DCAwareRoundRobinPolicy`.

Listing 10.27 Using `TokenAwarePolicy` and `DCAwareRoundRobinPolicy`

```
from cassandra.policies import TokenAwarePolicy, DCAwareRoundRobinPolicy

...

def get_db_session():
    if 'db' not in g:
        profile = ExecutionProfile(
            row_factory=dict_factory,
            load_balancing_policy=
    ⇒   TokenAwarePolicy(DCAwareRoundRobinPolicy())        ◁──  Rotates between the
        )                                                       shards that own the
        ...                                                     given partition.
```

After applying this change, you won't notice much of a difference for two reasons:

- This policy combination is the default.
- Your cluster has one node.

If nothing changes, why bother setting the policy? First, it's a good way to explain how to set the configuration and show how Scylla routes requests. Second, you may need to further configure your policy. If you have multiple datacenters, you might prefer traffic to go to a datacenter you've designated in your application as the primary. Additionally, if your driver supports latency-aware routing, such as in the C++ implementation, you should consider enabling that property to further optimize performance.

Continuing the tour of driver configuration, let's next look at how you can use it to automatically retry queries. If unfortunate events occur, a query may time out or fail. The Scylla driver can aid in the situation by reexecuting queries when it's safe to do so. Let's examine how the driver can preemptively refresh your queries.

10.5.3 *Retrying queries*

We've all been on the internet and seen a slowly loading page. You refresh, and it loads instantly. Everyone thinks, "Why didn't it work the first time?" The same thing can happen with a database. Perhaps a connection is dropped by the network, or a database node's underlying server is degraded. The follow-up request hits a different node, and the request returns immediately and successfully.

Instead of users pressing the refresh button in that scenario, the database driver can retry queries through a feature called *speculative retries*. After a certain amount of time has elapsed without the query completing, the driver speculates that a query won't be successful. It can then reissue the query, which ideally executes faster. Speculative retries try to exchange increased load for a faster response time. If your cluster is overwhelmed by traffic, it will not help the situation, because it will retry queries. On the other hand, it does a great job of mitigating ephemeral failures. If a node is down but gossip hasn't figured that out yet, a speculative retry can mitigate those consequences while the cluster discovers the failure. Figure 10.7 illustrates this process.

```
SELECT * FROM authors WHERE id = 123
```

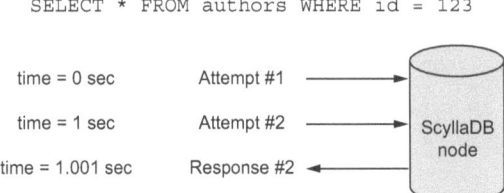

After the configured time has elapsed, the
driver speculatively retries the query.

**Figure 10.7 Speculatively retrying
queries helps the application mitigate
the effects of a query not returning.**

To speculatively retry a query, it first must be marked as idempotent—executing the
query repeatedly must always produce the same state on the cluster. As you learned in
chapter 4, operations like appending to a list or generating an ID via `uuid()` are not
idempotent. If you repeatedly add a value to a list, you'll have multiple copies of that
value in the list. Idempotency is not an implicit state in speculative retry's eyes; each
query must be set individually.

At this point, you may be worried about that first query. What if you've decided to
speculatively retry, but then suddenly the first query returns? You're not stuck waiting
for the retry to succeed; the driver stops waiting for the second query to return and
returns the first query. Think of it like a race where the racers start at different times:
the winner is the first one across the finish line.

> **WARNING** This race demonstrates a different potential performance con-
> cern: if you're too aggressive with speculative retries, your nodes will perform
> unnecessary duplicate work.

To enable speculative retries, you need to set a speculative execution policy on the
execution profile, just like with load balancing. Currently there are two possible policies: `NoSpeculativeExcutionPolicy` (it does what it says) and `ConstantSpeculative-
ExecutionPolicy`. The constant version retries a query after a specified time interval
up to a configured number of reattempts.

The first configuration value is the retry interval: how long should Scylla wait
before retrying? For your small reviews application, I would expect a query to return
in 100 milliseconds or not at all. In practice, I'd expect it to be even faster, considering
the minuscule number of rows and that it's running locally on your machine, but I'd
like to use a value that's plausible in a production system. If you're setting it on your
own application in the wild, examine your query performance and metrics (as you'll
see in the next chapter) to pick an effective retry interval that isn't hit by a "normal"
slow query.

> **TIP** The 99.9 percentile latency value is a great starting point for determin-
> ing your application's speculative retry value, implying that you only want to
> speculatively retry 0.1% of requests. Using this value generally balances the
> cluster's workload and saves speculative retries for when they're most useful.

Nonspeculative retries

The Scylla driver also supports waiting for a request to return before performing any retries to mitigate server-side errors, supporting a few retry policies. These policies apply only if specific server-side errors occur; a client-side timeout does not trigger them. In these instances, Scylla communicates information about the failure to the driver, which can choose to retry the request.

The default policy retries a request when the coordinator detects either a node timeout or an unavailable node. It retries any read or a logged batch write.

The downgrading consistency policy retries requests with a lower consistency level on the follow-up request. When at least one node responds to the request, the driver retries the request, assigning it a lower consistency level—such as going from ALL to QUORUM. You should use this policy with caution (it's not the default); in times of errors, you can break your application's consistency expectations. I've only used it when testing via dual writing to a completely separate secondary Scylla cluster that I was trying to keep in sync with a primary for comparison purposes; more on this technique in chapter 12.

Finally, you can use the fallthrough policy—telling Scylla you'll handle any retries yourself—or do nothing with them.

The second configuration value you need is the maximum number of attempts. This value includes the initial attempt, so you should set it to at least 2. I prefer using 2 in production systems; if it doesn't succeed after the second attempt, chances are very low that it will succeed after the third. Each retry brings diminishing returns on success and potentially increases the load in your cluster.

Listing 10.28 Speculative retries applied to an idempotent query

```
from cassandra.policies import ConstantSpeculativeExecutionPolicy, \
    TokenAwarePolicy, RoundRobinPolicy

...

SPECULATIVE_RETRY_INTERVAL_SECONDS = 0.1
SPECULATIVE_RETRY_MAX_ATTEMPTS = 2

IDEMPOTENT_QUERIES = {ALL_AUTHORS, GET_ARTICLE, GET_AUTHOR}

def get_db_session():
    if 'db' not in g:
        profile = ExecutionProfile(
            row_factory=dict_factory,
            load_balancing_policy=TokenAwarePolicy(RoundRobinPolicy()),

            speculative_execution_policy=
                ConstantSpeculativeExecutionPolicy(
                    SPECULATIVE_RETRY_INTERVAL_SECONDS,
                    SPECULATIVE_RETRY_MAX_ATTEMPTS
```

Lists queries to be marked as idempotent after creating their prepared statements

Retries queries once if they haven't returned in 100 ms

```
        )
    )
    ...

    for key in IDEMPOTENT_QUERIES:
        PREPARED_STATEMENTS[key].is_idempotent = True

    g.db = session
```

> **By iterating over the idempotent queries, you can access their prepared statements and mark them as idempotent.**

WARNING You may have noticed that I only marked the read queries as idempotent in listing 10.28. You may also be thinking that the write queries themselves are idempotent: they don't use the result of functions nor manipulate lists, and they insert the same values every time. Well, they are. I chose not to mark the writes as idempotent to indicate that not every query in your application is idempotent. Although the insertions here are idempotent, I don't want you to copy and paste this approach and inadvertently mark every query in your application as idempotent. If you had non-idempotent operations, you could potentially add extraneous or confusing data.

When you start up the application, you won't see any difference. If a retry happens, it will manifest as a slightly slower request to the user. The driver, however, will emit a metric that you can observe in your observability solution. The retry policy exists if a request is slow, waiting in the background to help you out.

Now that you've got an application with a driver, it also unlocks playing with more Scylla features. In chapter 9, you learned how Scylla lets you configure authentication and authorization for your cluster. To see this in action, let's set it up and configure your application to correctly use a username and role.

10.6 *Authentication and authorization*

As discussed in chapter 9, authentication and authorization help provide security to your Scylla cluster by limiting permissions and access to designated users with specific permissions. In this section, you'll create a user for your reviews application and give it specific permissions. You'll then update the application to connect with these credentials. Before you can begin creating users and passwords, you need to enable authentication and authorization in your Scylla configuration. Without this step, Scylla will reject your creation attempts. Let's turn on the authenticator and authorizer.

10.6.1 *Enabling authentication and authorization*

The usage of the authenticator and authorizer is driven by the config file—your friend scylla.yaml. You don't need to worry about uptime, so you can skip the transitional versions and go directly to `PasswordAuthenticator` and `CassandraAuthorizer`. This approach is also facilitated by Scylla: it provides a default superuser with credentials, which you'll get to use in a moment.

First you need to copy scylla.yaml out of the container to edit it locally. Docker supports a copy operation—`cp`—similar to the traditional command-line copy. Local paths work the same as usual, but container paths are prefixed with the container name followed by a colon (`:`). To get your scylla.yaml config file locally, you can execute the following command, which copies /etc/scylla/scylla.yaml from your `scylla-reviews` container and saves it locally with the same name—scylla.yaml:

```
$ docker cp scylla-reviews:/etc/scylla/scylla.yaml
```

Open that file in a text editor. If you search for `authenticator` and `authorizer` (they're lines 251 and 263 for me, running Scylla 5.4), you see two commented-out lines that set the authenticator to `AllowAllAuthenticator` and the authorizer to `AllowAllAuthorizer`—the default values. To use authentication and authorization, you need to do the following three things:

1 Uncomment the authenticator and authorizer.
2 Set the authenticator to `PasswordAuthenticator`.
3 Set the authorizer to `CassandraAuthorizer`.

Following these steps adds these configs to your scylla.yaml file:

```
...
authenticator: PasswordAuthenticator
...
authorizer: CassandraAuthorizer
...
```

But these changes are only on your local machine at the moment. You need to re-add them to the container by copying the scylla.yaml file back. Perform the reverse of your previous copy operation:

```
$ docker cp scylla.yaml scylla-reviews:/etc/scylla/scylla.yaml
```

Finally, you need to restart Scylla to pick up your changes. Open a shell in your container:

```
$ docker exec -it scylla-reviews /bin/bash
```

In `scylla-reviews`, use `nodetool drain` to drain the connections and prepare Scylla for restart, and then restart Scylla with `supervisorctl restart scylla`:

```
(scylla-reviews) root@scylla-reviews:/# nodetool drain
(scylla-reviews) root@scylla-reviews:/# supervisorctl restart scylla
```

With that, Scylla is up and running with the authenticator and authorizer initialized. Look closely at the logs, and you'll see that it has performed some updates on startup and created a superuser for you:

```
INFO  2024-02-03 19:55:31,178 [shard 0:main] password_authenticator -
Created default superuser authentication record.
```

Now that this functionality is enabled, you're ready to create roles. Let's roll on over and do just that.

10.6.2 *Implementing role-based access control*

If you try to cqlsh into your node like you always have, you run into an error:

```
$ docker exec -it scylla-reviews cqlsh
Connection error: ('Unable to connect to any servers', {'172.18.0.2:9042':
AuthenticationFailed('Remote end requires authentication')})
```

Because you turned on PasswordAuthenticator, you have to connect with a username and password. You'll be creating roles, so you need to connect as a superuser with sufficient permissions. The default superuser is cassandra, which is what you'll log in as. To log in with the correct credentials, supply the --username flag (or -u) and specify cassandra:

```
$ docker exec -it scylla-reviews cqlsh --username cassandra
Password:
```

You're immediately prompted for the password. By default, it's the same as the username: cassandra. Enter cassandra as your password, and you'll be authenticated as the cassandra superuser.

> **TIP** If running in production, you should change the cassandra user's password.

Scylla's authorization paradigm is designed around role-based access control. Clients connect as a role, and that role has permissions. For example, you might create an application role (guess what you're going to do in a moment) that lacks the full permissions that a superuser has. Roles can also inherit the permissions of other roles: you could then create a role that's specific to each application you run that inherits the application permissions and potentially other permissions if needed—such as if you wanted to run database migrations, which require additional capabilities that an API doesn't need.

You've turned on authentication and authorization, and your priority is to get your application connected to your cluster again. The first step is to create your application role: application. This role is created through a CREATE ROLE statement. Although this statement has some optional arguments that you'll see in action soon, you can run it with just the role name to create a role with that given name:

```
cassandra@cqlsh> CREATE ROLE application;
```

Run the LIST ROLES command to list roles, and you'll see your newly created role and the existing cassandra role:

```
cassandra@cqlsh> LIST ROLES;

@ Row 1
---------+------------
 role    | application
 super   | False
 login   | False
 options | {}

@ Row 2
---------+------------
 role    | cassandra
 super   | True
 login   | True
 options | {}

(2 rows)
```

Note that `application` isn't marked as `super`, nor is `login` set to true. You can't log in as `application`, nor does it have any permissions by default; you explicitly need to grant them. Granting permissions is accomplished via a `GRANT` statement. In a `GRANT` statement, you grant something to a role. That "something" can be another role or a specific permission on a resource. You'll see how to grant a role to a role in a bit, but first you need to give `application` some permissions that it can grant to another role.

When granting permissions, the `GRANT` statement takes the form `GRANT (permission | "ALL PERMISSIONS") ON resource TO role`. In that statement, you know what a role is, but what exactly is a permission or a resource? A *permission* is a single word describing the actions it grants. Table 10.1 describes what each permission grants.

Table 10.1 Scylla's permissions enable you to grant access to specific actions on resources.

Permissions	Allowed actions
CREATE	Create a table or a keyspace.
ALTER	Alter a table or a keyspace.
DROP	Drop a table or a keyspace.
SELECT	Select data from a table.
MODIFY	Insert, update, delete, or truncate on a table.
AUTHORIZE	Grant and revoke permissions.
DESCRIBE	List roles.

These permissions are granted to a role that will be applied to a resource. A resource can be a keyspace, table, or role, taking the following forms, where parentheses indicate the name of a Scylla resource such as the keyspace `reviews` or the table `articles`:

- KEYSPACE (name)
- (keyspace).(table)

- All keyspaces via ALL KEYSPACES
- (role)
- All roles via ALL ROLES

For example, DROP applied to all keyspaces lets a role drop any keyspace or tables, whereas applying DROP to reviews.authors only allows the role to drop the authors table in the reviews keyspace.

Considering the possibilities for permissions and resources, what permissions should the application role have? Generally, you want a role to have the minimum necessary permissions. The application role should be scoped to the reviews keyspace because it doesn't need to perform any actions against the internal Scylla keyspaces. It shouldn't need to create or alter a table, nor does it need to explicitly grant roles. What it does need to do is select and modify data—the SELECT and MODIFY permissions. Putting these together, you need to grant two permissions:

- SELECT ON KEYSPACE reviews
- MODIFY ON KEYSPACE reviews

You're now ready to grant these permissions to application. Combining the previous permissions with the GRANT ROLE statement gives you the entries in the following listing.

Listing 10.29   Granting SELECT and MODIFY to the application role

```
cassandra@cqlsh> GRANT SELECT ON KEYSPACE reviews TO application;
cassandra@cqlsh> GRANT MODIFY ON KEYSPACE reviews TO application;
```

If you run the LIST ALL command on application to list permissions, you see your newly granted permissions:

```
cassandra@cqlsh> LIST ALL OF application;

@ Row 1
-----------+--------------------
 role       | application
 username   | application
 resource   | <keyspace reviews>
 permission | MODIFY

@ Row 2
-----------+--------------------
 role       | application
 username   | application
 resource   | <keyspace reviews>
 permission | SELECT

(2 rows)
```

Before you can log in, you need a role to log in as. You can create a new role—reviews_api—and give it both login capabilities and a password.

```
cassandra@cqlsh> CREATE ROLE reviews_api WITH PASSWORD = 'password'
➥ AND LOGIN = true;
```

Just like before, this newly created role has no permissions associated with it. Instead of explicitly assigning the same permissions, you can grant a role to another role. Some permissions schemes allow you to grant permissions to a group and assign users to a group, giving them the group's permissions. Scylla's scheme doesn't explicitly have this mapping, but you can create roles that represent users and roles that represent groups. By granting a role to a role, you can mimic the group and user behavior.

To give a role another role's permissions, you use the GRANT statement again. This version is simpler, however. You GRANT application TO reviews_api, only using the role names. Executing this command lets the reviews_api role inherit the permissions of the application role, giving you a role that you can authenticate as and that is authorized to query the tables it needs.

```
cassandra@cqlsh> GRANT application TO reviews_api;
```

List the permissions for reviews_api, and you'll see that the new role has the permissions from reviews:

```
cassandra@cqlsh> LIST ALL OF reviews_api;

@ Row 1
------------+--------------------
 role       | application
 username   | application
 resource   | <keyspace reviews>
 permission | MODIFY

@ Row 2
------------+--------------------
 role       | application
 username   | application
 resource   | <keyspace reviews>
 permission | SELECT

(2 rows)
```

With these permissions granted, you're ready to authenticate as the new reviews_api role. Let's update your app and get it connected again!

10.6.3 *Authenticating via the app*

In theory, everything in your app will work if you only supply it with a username and password. Without that, the driver will fail to connect to Scylla, and your app won't start. Use `flask run`, and the driver will report connection errors:

```
cassandra.cluster.NoHostAvailable: ('Unable to connect to any servers',
{'127.0.0.1:9042': AuthenticationFailed('Remote end requires authentication'
)})
```

To fix that, your driver needs to authenticate with the database, so you must give your application credentials to a valid role: the `reviews_api` role you created in the previous section. To pass the credentials to the driver, you need to import the driver's `PlainTextAuthProvider`, which takes in the credentials as strings.

> **NOTE** "Plain text" in the context of authentication may sound scary, but it refers to the fact that the arguments to the class are strings. It contrasts with other providers that use specific protocols, such as the `SaslAuthProvider`. In production, they shouldn't be strings hard-coded into your application; you should retrieve them from a secure secret provider.

After importing the auth provider, you're ready to initialize it. You need to pass it two arguments, which are exactly what you hope: the username and password. Pass the auth provider to the cluster by setting its `auth_provider` argument. The next listing demonstrates this process, providing the code to log in.

Listing 10.32   Providing the driver with correct credentials for the cluster

```
from cassandra.auth import PlainTextAuthProvider

...

def get_db_session():
    if 'db' not in g:

        ...

        auth_provider = PlainTextAuthProvider(          ⟵ PlainTextAuthProvider
            username='reviews_api', password='password')     works with the
                                                             PasswordAuthenticator
        cluster = Cluster(                                   in Scylla.
            ["127.0.0.1"],
            port=19042,
            execution_profiles={EXEC_PROFILE_DEFAULT: profile},
            auth_provider=auth_provider      ⟵ Passing the auth provider to the
        )                                       cluster allows you to log in using
                                                the provider's credentials.
```

Run `flask run` one more time, and you'll see your application successfully connect. Your queries work as they did before, but now you can't sneak in a `DROP KEYSPACE reviews`.

With that, you've built a well-configured application that connects to your ScyllaDB cluster. Presumably, some sort of front-end client will use your API to read and write reviews. In the meantime, you'll work on making your cluster even better. In the next chapter, you'll expand on building a production-ready application by learning how to monitor and observe your database. Monitoring is critical to operating any database; your application is useless if the database is down. Stay on alert as you get ready to learn about monitoring and alerting!

Summary

- Applications connect to ScyllaDB using a database driver library.
- Scylla has database drivers for many popular programming languages.
- To connect to the database with the Python driver, you construct a `Cluster` object with the hostname and port of a Scylla node and connect to a given keyspace.
- The driver is configured via an `ExecutionProfile`, which allows you to change how it returns rows, load-balances queries, and many more behaviors.
- To query the database, your connection returns a session, which can execute queries and return rows.
- Passing data to a query should always use prepared statements to correctly sanitize inputs and prevent injection attacks.
- A prepared statement is created once and data is bound to at query-time, allowing it to be reused across requests.
- Prepared statements replace `?` in queries with the data the statement is asked to bind.
- Across all programming languages, the types used in the database often aren't the types you want to return to a user. Applications often need to perform type conversions to meet these contracts.
- A `batch` statement allows you to perform a batch query against Scylla
- Not all data comes directly from a request; you can also compute data from your request data by querying additional rows or calculating a property.
- To deserialize a UDT into a concrete type, that type must be registered with the driver.
- Consistency is a statement-level property. It can be set on a prepared statement, or it can be overridden after binding variables.
- Token-aware routing routes queries directly to the shard that owns the partition.
- Round-robin routing rotates queries through all nodes in the cluster. The `DCAwareRoundRobinPolicy` variant attempts to do this routing in a datacenter.
- By wrapping round-robin routing with token-aware routing, you can rotate between the owning shards for a partition.
- Speculative retries can retry idempotent queries that haven't been completed after a specified time.

- ScyllaDB authorizes requests by granting permissions to a role.
- Roles are created with a CREATE ROLE statement.
- Permissions are granted via a GRANT statement and can be applied to specific keyspaces, tables, or roles.
- Roles can be granted another role directly, inheriting that role's permissions.
- Authenticating via the driver requires you to provide an auth provider with the relevant credentials.

Monitoring ScyllaDB

This chapter covers

- Configuring the Scylla monitoring stack against your cluster
- Using Prometheus to collect metrics
- Viewing dashboards and visualizations of your cluster's performance using Grafana
- Load-testing via `cassandra-stress`
- Diagnosing and remediating common incidents

To run a database in production, you need to know if it's actually running. The rest of the book is about using Scylla in a way that minimizes the chances of an alert happening, but this chapter is about monitoring your cluster. Not monitoring a database is a great way to never get paged in the middle of the night, but it's also highly frowned on by users, managers, and about every best practice out there. Here, you'll learn how to monitor Scylla, observe its performance and generate alerts to clue you in on problems in your cluster.

Ideally, your cluster never has a problem, and you're never paged. You'll learn how to load-test Scylla to help determine how much traffic your database can handle, compare it against your expected traffic volume, and size the cluster appropriately.

Additionally, a load test is a great way to see the monitoring tools in action; they generate load on the cluster that you can see in dashboards.

Finally, you will eventually be paged for an incident with Scylla. Although every page will be different and specific to your use cases, you'll learn about the most frequent problems a Scylla cluster has and how you can mitigate and solve them for your systems. But before you can solve a problem, you have to know that there is one—hence, the monitoring stack.

11.1 *The monitoring stack*

Monitoring solutions abound; every job I've worked has used a different one. As we discuss monitoring Scylla here, you may see technologies you're unfamiliar with; that doesn't mean your current monitoring stack can't monitor ScyllaDB. To support monitoring the database, Scylla provides a combined set of tooling preconfigured to work with Scylla that I'll cover in this chapter (figure 11.1):

- Prometheus ingests metrics from the database nodes.
- Alertmanager alerts you when a metric crosses a configured threshold.
- Grafana provides dashboards from the metrics.

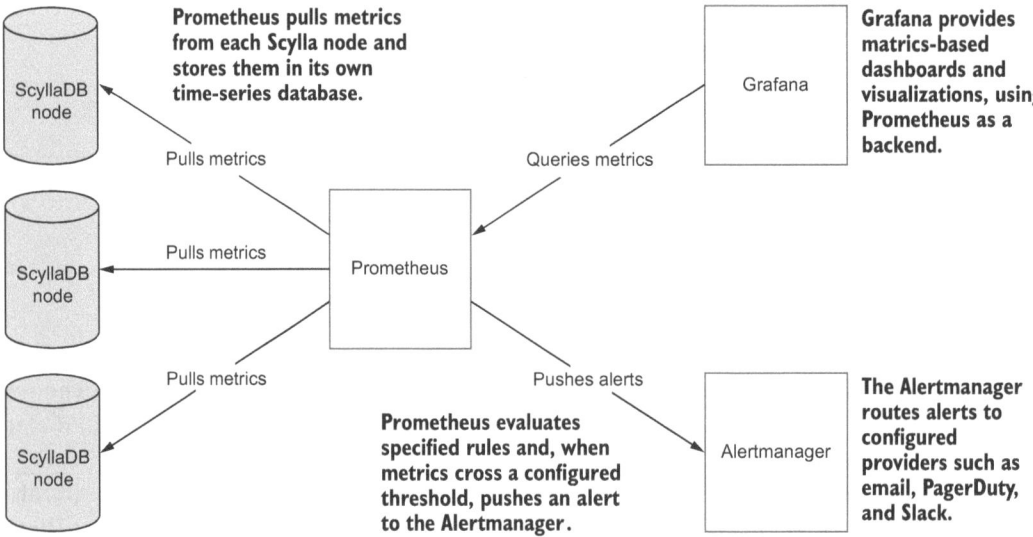

Figure 11.1 **Prometheus pulls metrics from your database nodes, which are used by the downstream components to provide visualizations and alert notifications.**

These pieces are open source and not made by Scylla, nor are they unique to Scylla; you may be using some of them in your own monitoring stack today. Just like your database nodes, you run these in Docker using Scylla's blessed monitoring stack configuration, which preconnects the components to get the end-to-end flow working. Let's start monitoring.

11.1.1 Deploying monitoring

To begin, you need to download the monitoring stack files—a variety of folders, scripts, and configuration files. Make a directory, download the monitoring files, and unpack them:

```
mkdir scylla-monitoring
wget -O scylla-monitoring.tar.gz https://github.com/scylladb/
➥ scylla-monitoring/archive/refs/tags/4.7.2.tar.gz
tar -xzf scylla-monitoring.tar.gz -C scylla-monitoring \
    --strip-components=1
```

You need to create a couple of files in this directory. First you have to tell Prometheus where your Scylla nodes live. You'll continue using `scylla-reviews` from the previous chapter. You'll learn more about Prometheus in the next section, but at a high level, Prometheus takes a list of server hosts and calls a designated metrics endpoint on each of them, reading their provided metrics and ingesting them.

Change your working directory to the scylla-monitoring folder, and save the file shown in the following listing in prometheus/scylla_servers.yml. This configuration file will be pulled in when you start up the monitoring stack, letting Prometheus know hosts it needs to pull metrics from.

> **NOTE** As usual, the code listings in this chapter can also be found in the book's code repo.

Listing 11.1 Importing execution profiles

```
- targets:              ◁——┐  The targets block
    - scylla-reviews        takes a list of hosts.
  labels:              ◁——   The labels block applies the
    cluster: cluster1        following labels to those targets
    dc: dc1                  and their metrics.
```

> **WARNING** Double-check the path here; if it doesn't match, Prometheus won't be able to find the file or your nodes.

Next you need to generate additional Prometheus configuration via the `prometheus-config` script in the folder. This script replaces some templated arguments in the included config files:

```
$ ./prometheus-config.sh --compose
```

After updating your Prometheus configuration, you also need to update Grafana's so that it can pull data from Prometheus and display it in dashboards. The following script updates the configuration to use the Prometheus container as a data source for Grafana:

```
$ ./grafana-datasource.sh --compose
```

The next script generates Grafana's dashboards. Because you're only testing, pass the -t flag to indicate that it should create the data locally. The -v flag specifies the Scylla version to use; you're using 5.4:

```
$ ./generate-dashboards.sh -t -v 5.4
```

> **WARNING**   You may see some errors as this script executes, but they're safe to proceed with.

To start the monitoring stack, you'll use docker compose, an easy way to launch multiple containers together. It takes a compose.yml file and launches the containers in it together, setting the appropriate configuration options as defined in the file.

The compose file you need is nearly 100 lines of YAML. Arguing the benefits and drawbacks of various configuration files is a Classic Debate in software engineering, but in my opinion, the biggest drawback of YAML is its whitespace sensitivity. Because of the length of this file, and to encourage you not to attempt to write it out manually and possibly run into whitespace errors, I've opted not to include it directly in the book. To continue, pull the compose.yml file out of the ch11 directory in the book's code repo (www.manning.com/books/scylladb-in-action or https://github.com/scylladb-in -action/code) and save it in your scylla-monitoring folder.

The compose.yml file supports spinning up the relevant pieces of the monitoring stack as containers; launching Prometheus, Grafana, and the Alertmanager as their own containers in your previously configured Docker scylla-network; and allowing them to communicate with your scylla-reviews cluster. Included in the configuration are various arguments to map configuration files in the monitoring stack folder to their appropriate homes in each container to power these connections.

With the file created as compose.yml, you're ready to start up the monitoring stack. docker compose takes the up command to apply a compose.yml file. You additionally add the --detach argument so it can run in the background, just like your scylla-reviews container:

```
$ docker compose up --detach
```

After running this command, you'll see the three containers start:

```
[+] Running 3/3
 ⠿ Container aalert    Started 0.6s
 ⠿ Container agraf     Started 0.8s
 ⠿ Container aprom     Started 0.8s
```

> **NOTE**   The monitoring stack shortens the name of the Alertmanager, Grafana, and Prometheus containers to aalert, agraf, and aprom.

Let's now look at each of these and show how they work together to build a cohesive monitoring solution.

11.1.2 Prometheus

Each node in your database is continuously measuring hundreds of metrics: the read latency on the database, the size of the commit logs, and the number of entries in the cache, among many others. Scylla makes these metrics available by default on port 9180 at /metrics. If you point your browser at localhost:9180/metrics, you'll find yourself drowning in all the numbers Scylla is tracking. I've included a sample of one metric, the number of partitions inserted into the cache:

```
# HELP scylla_cache_partition_insertions total number of partitions
added to cache
# TYPE scylla_cache_partition_insertions counter
scylla_cache_partition_insertions{shard="0"} 77
scylla_cache_partition_insertions{shard="1"} 2
scylla_cache_partition_insertions{shard="2"} 7
scylla_cache_partition_insertions{shard="3"} 4
scylla_cache_partition_insertions{shard="4"} 8
```

These metrics are the foundation of monitoring Scylla. By ingesting them into a system that can query them, you can answer questions like these:

- What is the 95th-percentile latency of reads to the database?
- How many reads are in progress?
- How many compactions is a given node doing relative to yesterday?

These questions are important things to know about your database. The 95th-percentile read latency tells you how slow the worst 5% of queries are—a helpful question for putting yourself in your users' shoes and assessing your database performance. Knowing how many reads are currently in progress can help explain why the read latency has gone through the roof. Perhaps you've just rolled out a new feature that's doing way more reads than intended. Compactions are another potential source of a latency increase; knowing that they've increased relative to yesterday helps evaluate changes you've made—for good or for bad.

Enter Prometheus: a metrics aggregator. Prometheus scrapes this metrics endpoint (or any—Prometheus isn't specific to Scylla) over a configured interval of time (20 seconds by default in the Scylla monitoring stack) and ingests the retrieved metrics into its own specialized time-series metrics storage. Each of these metrics is associated with a point in time; Prometheus allows you to query these metrics to observe their change over time (figure 11.2).

Prometheus comes with a web UI, allowing you to explore its stored metrics and configuration. Point your browser to http://localhost:9090, and you'll be dropped at Prometheus's query window. This view supports using Prometheus's special query language—*PromQL*—to query metrics from the system.

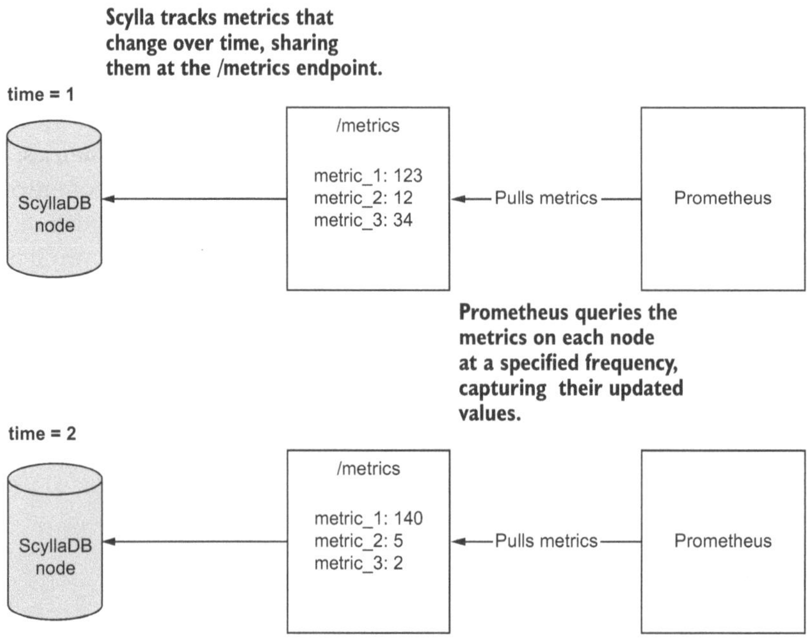

Scylla tracks metrics that change over time, sharing them at the /metrics endpoint.

time = 1

ScyllaDB node

/metrics

metric_1: 123
metric_2: 12
metric_3: 34

←— Pulls metrics —

Prometheus

Prometheus queries the metrics on each node at a specified frequency, capturing their updated values.

time = 2

ScyllaDB node

/metrics

metric_1: 140
metric_2: 5
metric_3: 2

←— Pulls metrics —

Prometheus

Figure 11.2   Scylla tracks metrics that change over time, which Prometheus ingests at a specified frequency.

You'll come back here in a moment, but first you should verify that everything is configured correctly by navigating to http://localhost:9090/targets. You can also reach this page via the Status dropdown at the top of the window, by selecting Targets.

The Targets view shows three components:

- `node_exporter` exports host-level metrics about an underlying node (CPU, memory, etc.).
- `prometheus` scrapes metrics from itself to query its performance.
- `scylla` is your `scylla-reviews` node.

NOTE   Each of these should be green and indicate that all targets are online. If not, verify that your `scylla-reviews` cluster is running and that you copied the compose YAML file correctly.

Returning to the graph view, Prometheus allows you to query metrics and see how they change over time—although there's a better tool for this job, as you'll see in a moment. To see this behavior in action, you can put together a query with PromQL to view your database's average read latency, a critical value for assessing your systems' performance. You can do some really neat things with PromQL: smooth out spiky graphs, predict future values, and much more. Although it's powerful, you're only going to dip your toes into it today to see how it works.

TIP   If you're using Prometheus as part of your monitoring solution when using ScyllaDB in production, I highly recommend reading the Prometheus docs on querying: https://prometheus.io/docs/prometheus/latest/querying/basics.

First, generate some traffic for your database. If you're still running the application from the last chapter, feel free to send your app some requests to /authors and send a few requests to individual authors. Otherwise, connect to cqlsh (don't forget to use authentication!) and run some queries.

To view the read latency in Prometheus, you may think, "I need to view the read latency metric." Unfortunately, it's slightly more complicated (figure 11.3). If you start typing "read latency" into the expression search bar, you'll see Prometheus begin to autocomplete metrics for you. Eventually you'll end up with a few options, but of these, two are the most notable:

- scylla_storage_proxy_coordinator_read_latency_count
- scylla_storage_proxy_coordinator_read_latency_sum

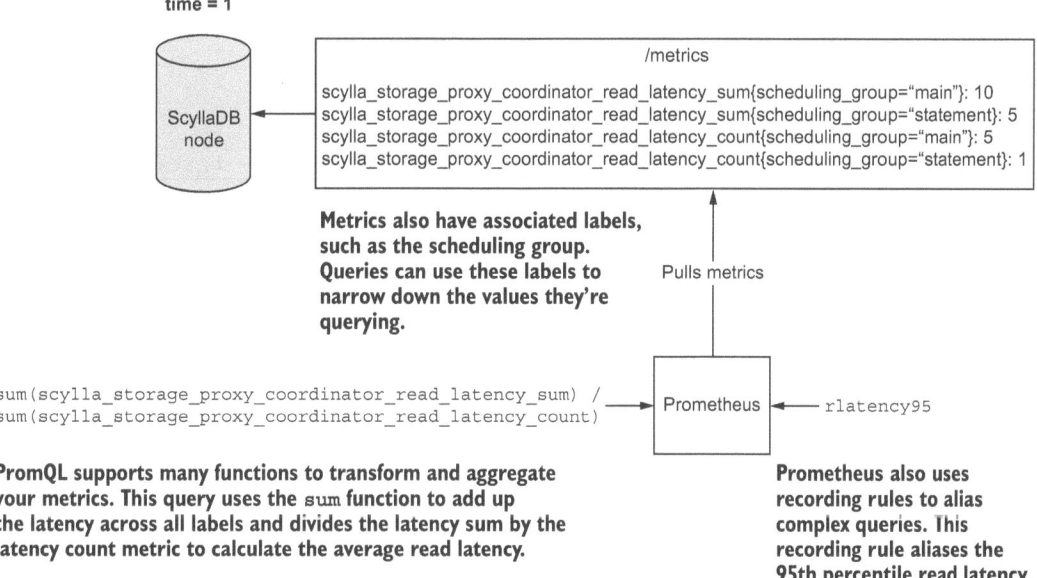

Figure 11.3   PromQL combines metrics, labels, functions, and recording rules to help you query and transform ingested metrics.

Although Scylla doesn't maintain an explicit "This is the current read latency of the database" metric (there is something similar, but it's a composite of multiple metrics that you'll learn more about in a moment), these two values can be combined to give you that view. If you have the total combined read latency across all requests and the total number of requests, you can divide the sum of all latency by the total number of requests to determine the average latency. To do this calculation in Prometheus, you first need to query the `scylla_storage_proxy_coordinator_read_latency_sum` metric:

```
scylla_storage_proxy_coordinator_read_latency_sum
```

When you query this metric, you see multiple values. Scylla tracks latency per *scheduling group*: a Seastar construct used to schedule tasks and allocate workloads in a shard. You'll see a few groups here; the `statement` group tells you the total latency for query execution, and the `streaming` group tells you the latency for maintenance operations such as bootstrapping the node or building a materialized view. Prometheus calls these descriptive properties *labels*; they're used to further define and filter a metric.

Because you're looking for the total read latency, you need a way to aggregate these labeled metrics. Fortunately, Prometheus supports applying a function to metrics. If the average read latency is the total latency across all requests divided by the sum of the total number of requests, you need to combine these metrics to give you the actual total—add them up! Prometheus supports a `sum()` function that adds all labeled metrics to which it's applied. Wrap your metric in the `sum()` function, and you'll see that you have a single line on your graph:

```
sum(scylla_storage_proxy_coordinator_read_latency_sum)
```

With the total latency calculated, you can now investigate the request count metric. Adding `scylla_storage_proxy_coordinator_read_latency_count`—the total number of requests—presents a challenge similar to the total latency metric: it's labeled by scheduling groups. Just as you did before, `sum()` these values together.

You now have the two components of the PromQL query needed to see your cluster's read latency. Divide the total latency by the number of requests, and you'll see your cluster's average read latency, calculated in microseconds:

```
sum(scylla_storage_proxy_coordinator_read_latency_sum) /
⇒ sum(scylla_storage_proxy_coordinator_read_latency_count)
```

When the monitoring stack wants to calculate read latency, it does so via a Prometheus *recording rule*: an aliased query that provides a shortcut to this calculation. Scylla's read-latency query, which you'll see in Grafana later in the chapter, is more nuanced, considering specific scheduling groups and calculating per shard. You can see it in action by querying for `rlatency95` to see the database's *95th-percentile read latency*—the latency value that 95% of reads are less than or equal to.

By ingesting metrics, Prometheus can tell you what's going on with your cluster and when something's wrong. But you're not going to find yourself diving deep into Prometheus often, frantically writing queries to inspect your cluster's state. Instead, the monitoring stack provides other tooling on top of Prometheus to make its metrics easier to work with. This knowledge is important, however, because without understanding PromQL, you won't be able to expand and add alerts and visualizations that fit your application. Next up, let's look at Grafana and how it uses Prometheus as a data source to provide helpful dashboards and visualizations.

11.1.3 Grafana

Grafana is an open source data-visualization tool; it works by pulling metrics from a variety of potential data sources and displaying them via graphs and other visual-based widgets. The Scylla monitoring stack includes Grafana and preconfigures it to work with the other pieces, using Prometheus as a data source to provide several dashboards to you.

Point your browser to localhost:3000/dashboards and click the General tab in the middle of the screen, and you'll see several dashboards:

- Advanced shows detailed information about the scheduling groups, internal I/O queues, and commit logs.
- Alternator shows data about Scylla's Alternator API: the DynamoDB-compatible API.
- Detailed goes in depth about your cluster's performance, looking at reads, writes, compaction, tombstones, and more.
- Keyspace displays high-level metrics for each table in a given keyspace.
- OS Metrics looks at the performance of the underlying node.
- Overview provides a very high-level overview of your cluster, focusing on traffic, latency, and availability.
- Scylla CQL gives information about query volume and performance.

Ignore the default sorting order and the temptation to click the first entry in the list. You'll come back here and look closer at the graphs later in the chapter when doing some load tests, but for now, look at the Scylla CQL dashboard.

> **NOTE** If it's been a few minutes since you ran queries to generate metrics, run some read queries against your cluster to get some traffic.

Looking at this dashboard, you see a variety of graphs, many without data right now. In a production system, they'll be populated, but because you've only done a couple of bursts of manual queries since setting up your monitoring, they're pretty sparse. However, from your reads, you'll see a spike in the CQL Reads graph (figure 11.4).

> **NOTE** If the value is higher than you expect, check out the units on the y axis. Scylla defaults these graphs to operations per second, but Grafana will sometimes do milli-operations per second (mops/sec). For example, 800 milli-operations per second is 0.8 operations per second.

Looking at graphs is a helpful part of understanding how your database operates, and you'll return to Grafana multiple times later in the chapter to check out some graphs.

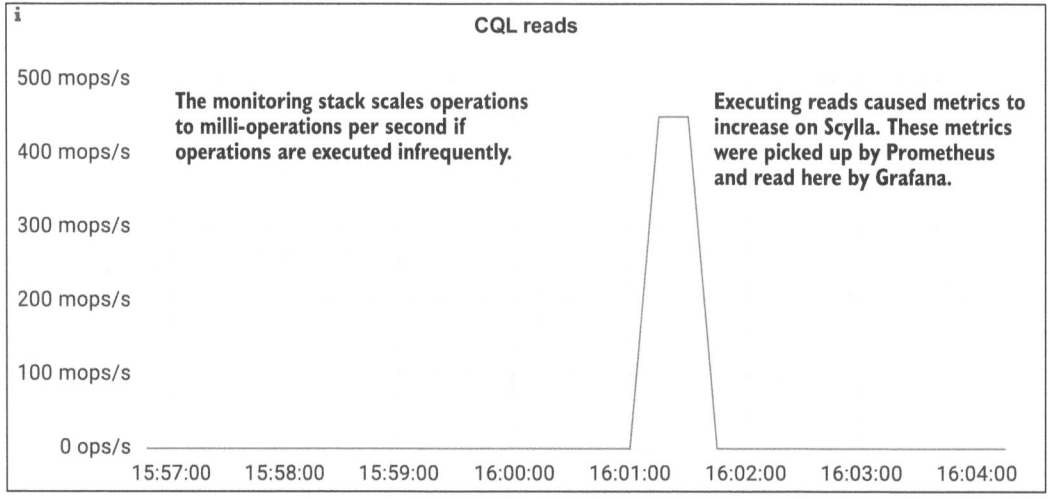

Figure 11.4   Metrics from your queries are visible in Grafana, allowing you to assess your cluster's performance.

For now, let's step away from Grafana and look at how Prometheus powers yet another component of the monitoring stack: the Alertmanager.

11.1.4 Alertmanager

Alerting is the bane of an on-call engineer's existence and the bedrock of any monitoring strategy. Continuously staring at graphs and waiting for something to go wrong is both boring and inefficient. In the monitoring stack, the Alertmanager handles this notification need. Prometheus is configured with a special set of queries called *alerting rules* that compare metrics against a threshold. If the metric's value is outside the acceptable range, that rule is considered *alerting*; for each of these alerts, Prometheus pushes a notification to the Alertmanager. For each alert that it gets, the Alertmanager knows how to handle it: perhaps it pages someone via PagerDuty or, if it's low priority, sends a message to your favorite chat system (figure 11.5).

Open http://localhost:9093 to see the Alertmanager's UI. You may see some alerts already firing. Due to how Docker mounts filesystems on different operating systems, a `tooManyFiles` alert may appear (figure 11.6). Each alert is sourced from Prometheus evaluating a rule and contains two elements: *labels*, which provide key-value data to route and filter alerts and look and behave just like the labels you saw in Prometheus, and *components*, which contain more detailed information such as a summary and description used to format the alert notification. When the Alertmanager sends a notification to the configured notification provider, it uses these labels and annotations to format the message. However, in the UI, the Alertmanager displays them both together, not making any difference. You'll see their distinction in a moment when you see how the alert is defined. In a real production system, you'd

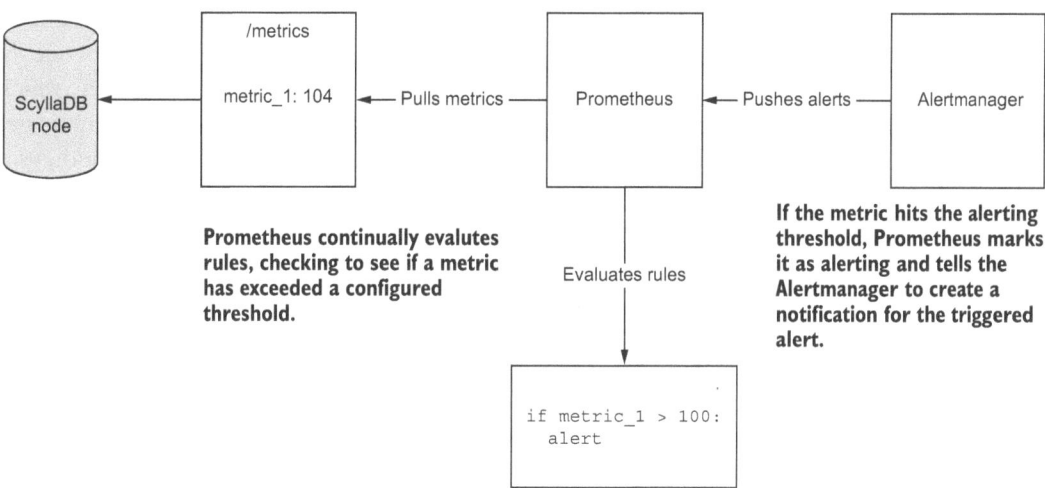

Figure 11.5   Prometheus is responsible for determining what alerts, whereas the Alertmanager is responsible for forwarding alert notifications.

tune this alert or remove it if it was always a false positive, but because this is a book, it's a good demonstration (if it's happening for you) of how the Alertmanager works.

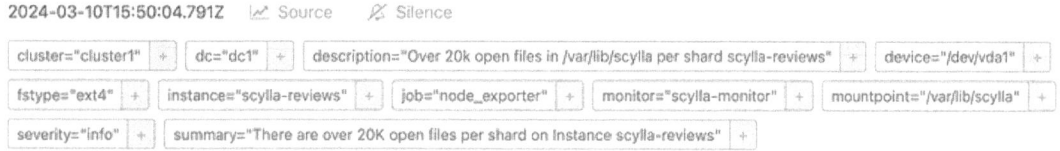

Figure 11.6   Alertmanager's UI lists Prometheus's firing alerts, showing the labels associated with each alert.

The monitoring stack defines a set of alerting rules in prometheus/prom_rules/ prometheus.rules.yml. For example, the following code block shows how Prometheus can detect a dead node in the cluster. Note the usage of the labels and annotations, which are merged in the UI in figure 11.6:

Alert's name.

```
- alert: InstanceDown
    expr: up{job="scylla"} == 0
    for: 30s
    labels:
      severity: "error"
    annotations:
      description: '{{ $labels.instance }} has been down for more
  than 30 seconds.'
      summary: Instance {{ $labels.instance }} down
```

Expression to evaluate for the alert, which runs a query and checks the result.

The Alertmanager can use labels to route alerts.

The Alertmanager can use annotations to add specific info to its notifications.

Prometheus is continuously evaluating these alerting rules; you can see them defined in Prometheus under the Alerts tab at http://localhost:9090/alerts. When one of these alerts fires, Prometheus sends a message about it to the Alertmanager, which looks at its labels and routes it to one of the configured senders. The Alertmanager only handles routing alerts; the bulk of the logic and work is actually in Prometheus.

Grafana, Prometheus, and Alertmanager provide a lot of functionality for a monitoring stack: visualization, metrics collection, and alerting. You'll go far on these alone, but to truly monitor a ScyllaDB cluster, you need to add components. Let's discuss what else can help you best understand your cluster's performance.

11.1.5 *Other monitoring needs*

Throughout this book, you've started both Scylla clusters and your Python application. When you're running up to three Scylla nodes or a single instance of an application, it's easy to look at their logs and correlate what they're doing. When your application begins printing errors, you can look to see if Scylla's logging anything interesting. As you grow, the scale of things you need to manually correlate grows as well. *Log aggregation*, the collection of logs in a centralized store to enable searching and correlation, becomes critical.

Grafana Loki (https://grafana.com/oss/loki/) is a technology designed to meet this need and fit in the Prometheus and Grafana ecosystem (as its name suggests, it's made by the same organization that makes Grafana). If you're starting from scratch, it's a tool worth considering. However, the best option is an existing tool that your team or organization is already using.

Another helpful monitoring piece isn't Scylla-focused but will greatly help you understand your systems: *application traces*. By measuring the length of time an application spends communicating with other services, you can not only gain a visual understanding of a single request's performance but also aggregate these calls together and see which systems are more heavily utilized. You can even track partition keys in traces, identifying the hotspots in your database.

Tracing is the monitoring tool I've found most helpful when diagnosing Scylla problems. Being able to trace increased latency directly to an increase in traces to a specific endpoint or specific partitions, illuminates the path forward to fixing an incident. If you're looking to add tracing to your application, check out Jaeger (www.jaegertracing.io), which is an open-source distributed tracing platform.

These tools help you diagnose problems and understand your cluster's behavior, but if there's no traffic going through your cluster, that's already a trivial thing to do. To see how ScyllaDB looks in action, you'll set up some load tests in the next section using a Scylla load-testing tool with a somewhat confusing name: `cassandra-stress`.

11.2 *Causing stress with cassandra-stress*

Load-testing is a helpful technique for determining how much traffic a system can handle. You start by sending some traffic, and then you send more until you stop seeing performance gains. Scylla supports load-testing through a tool—as its name suggests—inherited from Cassandra: `cassandra-stress`.

With `cassandra-stress`, you can find the limits of your cluster by seeing how much traffic it can support. Although it supports running tests via a generic schema by default, you can pass it your schema, tell the tests how to query it, and `cassandra-stress` will perform those load tests using your schema. The generic schema can tell you the approximate throughput from your underlying infrastructure, but you'll get a more accurate answer if it's accurately simulating your workloads. Let's set that up and send a bunch of traffic to our cluster to see what happens.

11.2.1 Setting up cassandra-stress

Before you configure `cassandra-stress`, I've included an updated copy of the schema to apply. Because the load tests generate data, you may want to avoid polluting your existing `reviews` keyspace. In the code samples for this chapter, I've included a copy of the schema in a new `stress` keyspace. Copy the contents of ch11/1_schema.cql into `cqlsh`, and you'll be ready to go.

> **NOTE** For ease of use and teaching, I've removed the image user-defined types from this stress schema.

YAML continues its relentless march as a configuration option: you configure `cassandra-stress` to use your schema with a YAML file. I'll walk you through building this file, but as always, a copy is included in the chapter's code samples (stress.yaml).

You run `cassandra-stress` against a single table at a time, so you need to provide both the keyspace and the table. If you want to run against multiple tables, you have to run multiple copies of `cassandra-stress` concurrently or use a more sophisticated load-testing tool. The following code block begins your config file, which you can name stress.yaml. You'll use the new `stress` keyspace and test the `article_summaries_by_date` table:

```
keyspace: stress
table: article_summaries_by_date
```

When run, `cassandra-stress` generates data for the `articles` table and inserts it into the database. If you're going to the trouble of running it against a table, however, you also want to make sure the data it generates is representative of what it will be for users. There are three properties to tune per column to generate accurate data:

- The *size* controls how large the value is.
- The *population* limits how many possibilities there are for a given value.
- The *cluster* limits the number of values per partition key.

By default, `cassandra-stress` limits the size between four and eight: for example, TEXT fields will be between four and eight characters. It considers up to 100 billion possible values and defaults the clustering to 1. Recall from the earlier chapters the columns in `article_summaries_by_date`:

- date_bucket SMALLINT
- id TIMEUUID
- author_name TEXT
- score TINYINT
- title TEXT

To have your tests use representative values, you need to override the defaults for some of these columns. By default, `cassandra-stress` uses large random numbers for `date_bucket` (both positive and negative), but your design says that `date_bucket` groups articles by the month they were published, starting from zero. To override these values, you need to redefine in the config file how your tests should generate data for these columns.

Begin by adding a `columnspec` key, followed by your column's name as a child of that key. You'll have a child for every overridden column:

```
columnspec:
  - name: date_bucket
    ...
```

Let's say you'll run against 20 years of buckets—up to bucket 240. That's a nice, big, round number. To limit to only the buckets from 0 to 240, you need to constrain the available values to `date_bucket`, which, as you learned earlier, is controlled by the `population` field. Each field takes a *distribution* defining its range of values. The easiest option is `uniform(min..max)`, which uniformly distributes values over the supplied range.

> **NOTE** `cassandra-stress` supports other distributions, including `fixed` (always use the same value), `exponential`, and `gaussian`, which distributes data according to a normal distribution with a mean and standard deviation.

To limit the date buckets to the ones you've specified, set the `population` to `uniform(0, 240)`:

```
columnspec:
  - name: date_bucket
    population: uniform(0..240)
```

Continuing through your columns, `id` works out of the box just fine; `cassandra-stress` understands how to generate a valid TIMEUUID. However, the load tests will attempt to generate thousands of rows and give massive buckets; you can constrain this behavior by setting the `cluster` property to limit the number of articles per bucket. Let's imagine that the reviews business is going strong, and you're doing between 10 and 25 articles per month:

```
columnspec:
  ...
  - name: id
    cluster: uniform(10..25)
```

The author names are a little short, considering that the default size of a text field in your stress tests is between four and eight characters. You can increase the size of the generated author names by updating their size; let's say author names are typically between 5 and 20 characters (I made up these numbers). Adding this restriction to the config file makes that data more representative of the real world:

```
columnspec:
  ...
  - name: author_name
    size: uniform(5..20)
```

score runs into the same challenges the date bucket ran into; by default, cassandra-stress chooses numbers from all possible integers, not ones that necessarily fit your data. Constrain score to the appropriate values, between 1 and 100:

```
columnspec:
  ...
  - name: score
    population: uniform(1..100)
```

Finally, you have the article title. By this point, you're a pro at setting field sizes. I'll say that article titles are between 20 and 50 characters, but you're the one writing data into the config file, so it's up to you!

```
columnspec:
  ...
  - name: title
    size: uniform(20..50)
```

Before you can finally run your tests, you need to tell cassandra-stress how to query your data. Define a query specification to execute in the YAML, give it a query to run, and tell it how to generate the fields in the query:

```
queries:                          Query for the load test to run.        CQL query your load
  read:                           You can have multiple of these.        tests will execute.
    cql: SELECT * FROM article_summaries_by_date WHERE date_bucket = ?
    fields: samerow
                                          When generating fields for the query, use values
                                          from the list of already-generated keys.
```

Combined, you have the following YAML config file:

```
keyspace: stress
table: article_summaries_by_date
```

```
columnspec:
  - name: date_bucket
    population: uniform(0..240)
  - name: id
    cluster: uniform(10..25)
  - name: author_name
    size: uniform(5..20)
  - name: score
    population: uniform(1..100)
  - name: title
    size: uniform(20..50)
queries:
  read:
    cql: SELECT * FROM article_summaries_by_date WHERE date_bucket = ?
    fields: samerow
```

To access this file for your tests, you need to copy it into your `scylla-reviews` container:

```
$ docker cp stress.yaml scylla-reviews:/stress.yaml
```

In the next section, you'll execute this load test, observing its effects not only from its output but also how it makes the graphs go up and to the right in Grafana.

11.2.2 *Examining performance*

With your config file uploaded, you're ready to start the test. `cassandra-stress` works by slowly increasing the number of threads making queries. You'll execute a *user test*, running against a user-supplied schema (as opposed to its included default benchmarking schema). The load tests also allow you to specify the ratio of reads to writes in your tests. Because users will read articles much more frequently than you can write them, I've specified the tests to execute 1,000 read queries for every write. I've also shortened the time it takes to run the tests; by default, the entire operation can take many minutes.

Execute the following command in your `scylla-reviews` container to kick off the test.

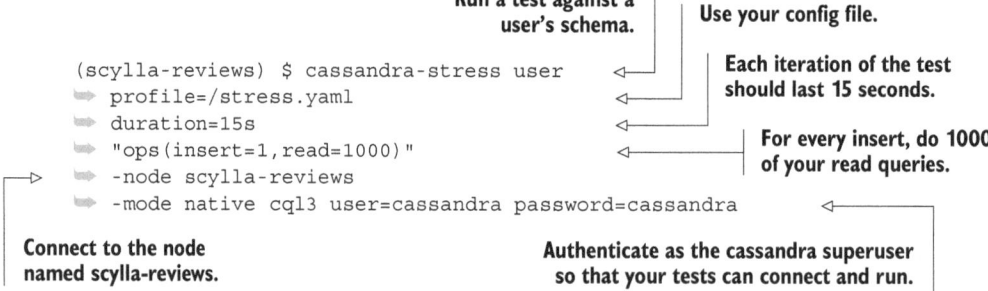

With that command, your load tests begin. `cassandra-stress` spins up some worker threads and sends increasing amounts of traffic to the database. As long as the database's throughput keeps growing, the load tests will add more threads after each run. You'll see a lot of numbers stream by as the tests run, but the important ones are the post-run summaries:

```
Results:
Op rate                       :    5,476 op/s [insert: 6 op/s, read: 5,470 op/s]
Partition rate                :    5,476 pk/s [insert: 6 pk/s, read: 5,470 pk/s]
Row rate                      :  136,851 row/s
➥ [insert: 103 row/s, read: 136,761 row/s]
Latency mean                  :    0.7 ms [insert: 1.0 ms, read: 0.7 ms]
Latency median                :    0.6 ms [insert: 0.9 ms, read: 0.6 ms]
Latency 95th percentile       :    1.2 ms [insert: 1.7 ms, read: 1.2 ms]
Latency 99th percentile       :    1.8 ms [insert: 2.1 ms, read: 1.8 ms]
Latency 99.9th percentile     :    4.5 ms [insert: 2.1 ms, read: 4.5 ms]
Latency max                   :   34.7 ms [insert: 2.1 ms, read: 34.7 ms]
Total partitions              :    86,286 [insert: 80, read: 86,206]
Total errors                  :          0 [insert: 0, read: 0]
Total GC count                : 0
Total GC memory               : 0.000 KiB
Total GC time                 :    0.0 seconds
Avg GC time                   :    NaN ms
StdDev GC time                :    0.0 ms
Total operation time          : 00:00:15
```

These summaries give you an overview of the test run, telling you how many partitions `cassandra-stress` was able to query per second (nearly 5,000) and how the latency looked—a 99.9th percentile of 4.5 milliseconds. The tests will keep running, 15 seconds at a time, adding further threads and measuring the output. As you may expect, a later test run improves on these benchmarks:

```
Results:
Op rate                       :   24,619 op/s
➥ [insert: 20 op/s, read: 24,600 op/s]
Partition rate                :   24,619 pk/s
➥ [insert: 20 pk/s, read: 24,600 pk/s]
Row rate                      :  615,323 row/s
➥ [insert: 334 row/s, read: 614,989 row/s]
Latency mean                  :    7.0 ms [insert: 4.8 ms, read: 7.0 ms]
Latency median                :    4.8 ms [insert: 4.4 ms, read: 4.8 ms]
Latency 95th percentile       :   21.0 ms [insert: 9.6 ms, read: 21.0 ms]
Latency 99th percentile       :   33.0 ms [insert: 13.8 ms, read: 33.0 ms]
Latency 99.9th percentile     :   44.9 ms [insert: 19.3 ms, read: 45.0 ms]
Latency max                   :  112.6 ms [insert: 19.3 ms, read: 112.6 ms]
Total partitions              :   383,198 [insert: 306, read: 382,892]
Total errors                  :          0 [insert: 0, read: 0]
Total GC count                : 0
Total GC memory               : 0.000 KiB
Total GC time                 :    0.0 seconds
Avg GC time                   :    NaN ms
StdDev GC time                :    0.0 ms
Total operation time          : 00:00:15

Improvement over 121 threadCount: 13%
```

By sending more traffic, this later test can push the database to 25,000 partitions per second, a 5× improvement over the first test. Latency does get worse; the 99.9th percentile here is approximately 45 milliseconds. `cassandra-stress` also tracks the improvement over the most recent run, telling you that it's 13% better than the previous one.

Because you're querying Scylla, these load tests also appear in your dashboards. Open Grafana's dashboards (http://localhost:3000/dashboards) again and choose the Overview dashboard, which gives you an overview of your cluster. You can see your load tests' effect: reads, writes, and their accompanying latency are all growing (figure 11.7).

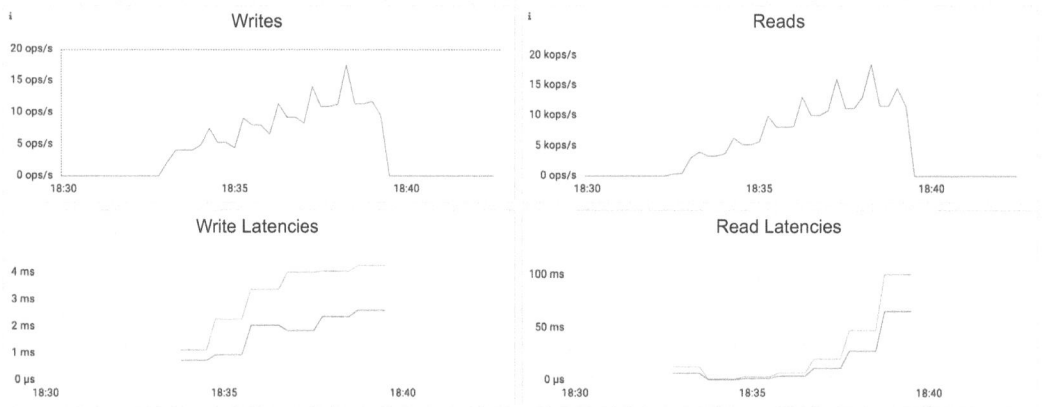

Figure 11.7 You can observe the effects of the load tests on your cluster by looking at the number of queries and their latency in Grafana.

Load tests aren't just a neat trick for adding some load to your cluster to view in dashboards; they're also helpful in understanding how much traffic your database can handle. In addition, you can use these values to right-size your cluster. I've found that you generally should keep read latency below 10 milliseconds. If you have an estimation of traffic coming into the database and your load tests tell you that your read latency is too high for that traffic, you'll probably want to expand your cluster.

By using `cassandra-stress` and its outputs, you can help prevent incidents where the database gets overwhelmed. However, sometimes you won't get the balance exactly right, and Prometheus will notice your latency is too high and tell the Alertmanager to page you and tell you to take a look. I want to close out this chapter by examining what happens when the pager goes off: remediating and recovering from a Scylla incident.

11.3 Common incidents

With monitoring applied, you're able to observe your cluster's behavior. Knowledge is only half the battle; the other half is dealing with problems when something in your cluster breaks. Although I can't provide exact remediations, as every incident will be unique to your application, I'll share what the most common incident looks like, as well as some general troubleshooting steps. First, let's look at the most common Scylla incident: a hot partition.

11.3.1 A hot partition

As Scylla's data distribution doesn't guarantee an even traffic distribution, some shards on a node receive more traffic than others. When one shard receives more traffic than it can handle, degrading its performance, the cluster is said to have a *hot partition*. The database gets a lot of traffic to a specific partition key, and that shard is unable to serve requests in a timely fashion.

How can you diagnose this problem? The telltale images of a hot partition have outliers in read latency. In read latency per node, you'll see outliers equivalent to your replication factor (figure 11.8). When looking at read latency per shard (the superior view because it gives you more specific information about what's causing the slowdown), you'll see your replication factor's worth of elevated shards, as well as that same shard on unaffected nodes elevated to a lesser degree.

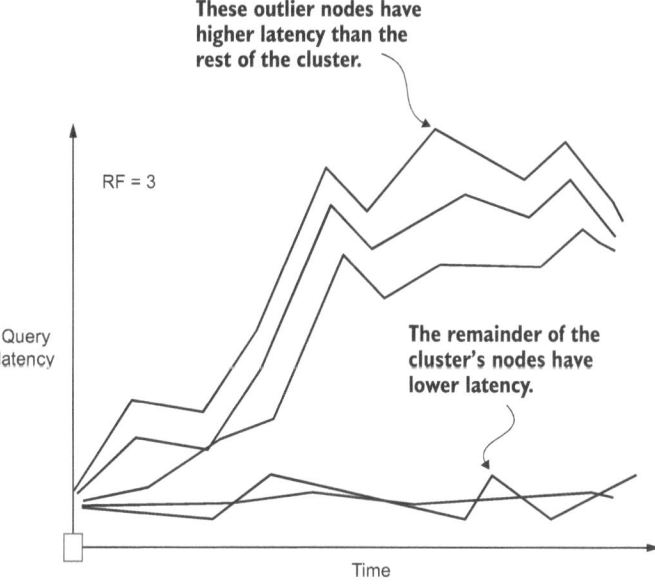

These outlier nodes have higher latency than the rest of the cluster.

RF = 3

Query latency

The remainder of the cluster's nodes have lower latency.

Time

If you see a number of outlier nodes equal to your replication factor, that's a strong sign that your database is suffering from a hot partition.

Figure 11.8 When Scylla gets more queries to a partition than it can handle, latency on the shard and node increases.

Although diagnosis is straightforward, finding the problematic key and fixing it can be tricky. Chapter 9 taught you about a tool that's helpful here: `nodetool toppartitions` can help find the most-queried partitions on a given node. Another tool to use is upstream monitoring: request logs from an application or application traces can also help you find the potential offender.

Knowing what is causing the hot partition is helpful but doesn't necessarily fix the situation. Stopping a database from being overwhelmed by queries is ultimately an economics problem: you need to either increase supply or reduce demand. Increasing supply by expanding the cluster is a slower solution, so you're almost always best off reducing demand.

Shards don't get hot by themselves; performance degradation happens due to a change in upstream traffic. The first thing you should check is whether this problem is caused by a recent code change. Perhaps there's a recently deployed pull request ominously titled "Inefficient Database Access Part 1" (roll it back immediately!).

However, if it's due to a specific traffic pattern, finding ways to limit the traffic to the database can help the cluster recover. Rate limits are helpful here; allowing your application to throttle traffic to protect the database keeps the system up and running for everyone. Tuning the rate limit will help you today and going forward.

> **TIP** The data generated by `cassandra-stress` can be an excellent starting point for rate limits, as it tells you the maximum capacity of a given table.

Scylla also supports per-partition rate limits on a given table, specifying the maximum number of reads and writes a partition is allowed to execute. However, these limits aren't precisely applied; the replication factor and Scylla's internal implementation details can lead to inaccurate counting of traffic for these rate limits. It's recommended to set the rate limits to an order of magnitude higher than your desired limits, as shown here:

```
ALTER TABLE reviews.articles WITH per_partition_rate_limit = {
    'max_reads_per_second': 10000,
    'max_writes_per_second': 100
};
```

Another technique to limit traffic to a hot partition is to avoid sending that traffic to the database by reading it from elsewhere. If a hot partition is frequently reading data that isn't frequently updated, you might consider caching that data in your application or even storing it temporarily in an external cache like Redis.

A hot partition is the most frequent incident you'll see as a Scylla operator, but its solutions are common to almost any system you run. Code changes, which mutate the system, are prime suspects in a novel incident. Load shedding via rate limits and caching will protect any downstream systems—Scylla, Postgres, internal APIs—from more traffic than they can handle.

The next incident you'll see is similar to a hot partition. Instead of one shard on a few nodes being on fire, however, when the database is overwhelmed, everything's on fire.

11.3.2 *An overwhelmed database*

An overwhelmed database is a lot like a hot partition, except enough partitions are hot to overload the nodes in the cluster. This can be a much more critical situation for the cluster; instead of one degraded partition, your entire cluster is overloaded with traffic. Just as with a hot partition, your options are to either increase supply or reduce demand. If this volume of traffic is expected in the future, expanding your cluster is the way to go. However, as before, expanding the cluster takes time, so to fix the immediate problem, you need to reduce traffic.

The same solutions also apply:

- Check for recent code changes that add large amounts of query fanout.
- Tune rate limits to reduce traffic to the database.

Find ways to reduce traffic to help your systems recover, and expand further in the future if this traffic is the new normal. Although every situation is different, and a book is limited to sharing general advice, I can safely say that being partially down is better than being completely down. In that spirit of partial failure, let's look at what happens when you can't satisfy a query's desired consistency: quorum loss.

11.3.3 *Failing to meet consistency requirements*

Scylla supports tunable consistency levels, but there's always some point at which enough nodes are offline that the consistency level can't be met. At this point, your application's in trouble because a sizable percentage of requests will be unable to succeed.

The solution is straightforward: bring the nodes back online. Perhaps it's due to an underlying failure in your cloud provider or on-premises infrastructure; if so, consider changing your cluster's topology to make it more failure-tolerant, as discussed in chapter 9.

Quorum loss can be due to an unsafe database operation. Although mistakes happen, you should endeavor to make quorum loss as difficult to occur as possible. These principles can help you safely perform operations:

- Automate as much as you can, codifying safety in your procedures.
- Perform operations on a single node at a time. The more nodes offline at a time, the greater the chance of quorum loss.
- When performing cluster-wide operations, validate a node's health before continuing to the next node.

These guidelines won't prevent all incidents but will minimize their occurrences when you're running ScyllaDB. Sometimes you'll need to replace a node with a degraded disk or to upgrade Scylla. Following these principles makes it a safer operation for the cluster and an unnoticed—and therefore successful—operation for users.

Running ScyllaDB in production can be complicated; you have many nodes, each taking lots of traffic. The monitoring stack helps you observe your clusters' behavior and performance, and load-testing can help you find its limits before your users do. When that happens, you've got some steps you can take to recover from those pesky alarms.

In the final chapter of this book, you'll learn how you can access data in bulk with ScyllaDB. Whether it's transferring it into another database for analysis or copying data into (and potentially also out of) Scylla, you'll learn about the tricks and tools needed to get the job done.

Summary

- Scylla provides a preconfigured monitoring stack to monitor your cluster by providing tooling for metrics ingestion, alerting, and visualizations.
- Prometheus ingests metrics from your Scylla cluster (or any other system it's configured to watch), serving as a backend for other systems by allowing you to query, transform, and aggregate metrics from different nodes at different points in time using its query language, PromQL.
- By configuring targets to scrape metrics from, Prometheus knows which hosts have metrics for it to read.
- Metrics in Prometheus have associated labels used to further filter and define a metric; Scylla, for example, tracks latency per scheduling group, a Seastar construct used to schedule tasks and allocate workloads in each shard.
- The monitoring stack defines recording rules that provide a shortcut for complex calculations, such as computing the 95th-percentile read latency of your database.
- Grafana provides dashboards and visualizations built atop the metrics stored in Prometheus, using the defined recording rules and other preconfigured queries to let you provide premade views of your cluster's performance.
- Prometheus uses its metrics to evaluate configured alerts, telling the Alertmanager to send a notification when an alerting threshold is triggered.
- Each alert sent to the Alertmanager uses labels to route and filter alerts, and annotations to include detailed information about the alert to include in the notification.
- When running Scylla in production, your monitoring solution should also include log aggregation, letting you query and correlate log entries from multiple nodes and application traces to track and understand the lifecycle of a request throughout your system to see where it spends the most time.
- You can use `cassandra-stress` to load-test your cluster against your schema, helping you see how much traffic your cluster can tolerate without becoming too slow.
- `cassandra-stress` lets you tune the size of values, the number of distinct values, and the number of values per partition for each column in your schema via a configuration file.

- The most common incident you'll see running Scylla is a hot partition, where one partition in the database gets more traffic than it can easily handle. To mitigate this incident, you need to reduce traffic to the database to let it recover.
- Solving database incidents often involves reducing demand via tuning rate limits or rolling back recent code changes to lessen traffic on the database.
- If your entire cluster is overwhelmed because each node is handling too many requests, in the short term you need to find a way to reduce traffic. But if this is a desired amount of traffic, you'll eventually need to expand your cluster.
- If you suffer quorum loss, the priority is to restore your quorum so that requests can once again succeed at their desired consistency.
- Investing in automation and encoding safety into your operations makes losing quorum less likely by stopping operators from making manual decisions that inadvertently make unsafe changes.

12

Moving data in bulk with ScyllaDB

This chapter covers

- Reading an entire table efficiently via token-range queries
- Tracking changes to a table using change data capture
- Using tooling to migrate data into ScyllaDB
- Validating data via dual-reading to verify a data migration

Throughout the book, your queries have assumed the upstream user's perspective: inserting a row at a time (or maybe multiple, if using a batch write) and reading a single partition of data. A database, however, isn't only queried by a user-facing API. Your company may extract data for analysis into a centralized data warehouse, combining the Scylla data with other sources to query together. Alternatively, maybe you're working to migrate some legacy data into Scylla; your options are wider than writing rows to two places.

In this final chapter, you'll learn how to work with Scylla's data at database scale. You'll learn about the techniques that work best for bulk reading and writing data with Scylla and how you can apply them to your use cases. First, let's examine how you can export data from Scylla through bulk reading and how to choose options to balance your reading speed while not breaking other traffic on the database.

12.1   *Extracting data from ScyllaDB*

As time goes by, your application will insert data into your database and read it out no more than a few rows at a time. These lightweight patterns are great if you're running a review application where readers want to read one article at a time. A common secondary use case for databases is extracting the data into another system that aggregates data from multiple sources. Perhaps you want to see if lower or higher-scoring articles generate more advertising revenue or which day of the week gives you the most page views. These questions can't be completely answered by your existing schema and often require data from other systems.

To fulfill these analytics use cases, you often need to extract data from Scylla and copy it into a specialized data store, such as AWS Redshift or Google Cloud's BigQuery. In this section, you'll see how you can extract lots of data as fast as you can without swamping the database. You'll learn some querying and configuration tools to export your data, as well as how to throttle the performance to ensure you're not breaking existing user-facing traffic. First, let's see how you can utilize the hash ring to export data.

12.1.1   *Using token ranges*

Let's say that time has passed, you now have thousands of articles (the reviews business is booming!), and every night you want to export the contents of the `articles` table into your data warehouse for further analysis and aggregation. How can you efficiently query the entire table?

A `SELECT` statement without a `WHERE` clause will be extremely slow, so that's a no-go. You need multiple queries, but how should you subdivide your table? Because the primary key of `articles` is a `TIMEUUID`, you may think a primary key-based slicing scheme is the way to go—dividing the articles into time-based slices and running each of them. However, consider how data is replicated across the cluster. Each primary key is hashed to a token, and these tokens are used to distribute data. If sorted by their IDs, two articles may be next to each other, but if you consider their token values, they're likely to be located on separate nodes. Therefore, if you try to subdivide the primary key space and query using that, each query is likely to involve many, if not all, nodes in your cluster—not very efficient (figure 12.1).

The hash ring distribution hints at how you solve this dilemma; you query by the token ranges, as shown in the contrasting option in figure 12.1. Because a token range is owned by a node and replicated to the succeeding nodes in the hash ring, you can use this distribution to efficiently query your entire table. Recall from chapter 8 that ScyllaDB supports the `TOKEN` function, allowing you to get the hashed token for a given value. Similarly, Scylla supports using the token function in the `WHERE` clause. By doing a query for data with a token range, you can get all rows that have a token in the range:

```
cqlsh> SELECT * FROM articles WHERE TOKEN(id) >= ... AND TOKEN(id) < ...;
```

```
SELECT * FROM table WHERE id > ??? AND id < ???    SELECT * FROM table WHERE TOKEN(id) >= ??? AND TOKEN(id) < ???
```

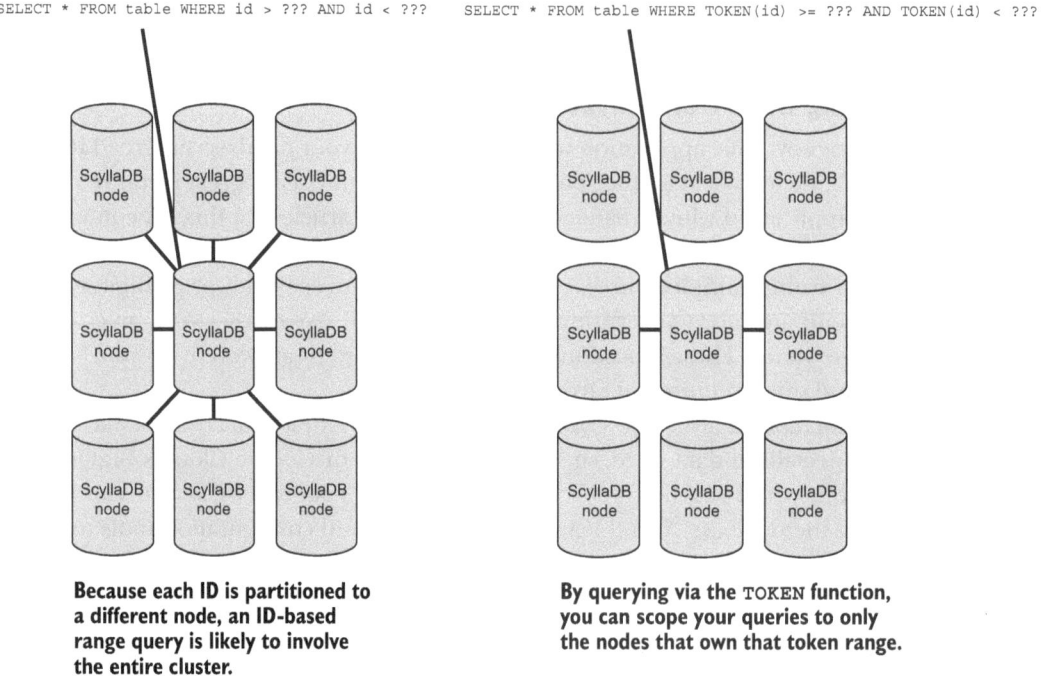

Because each ID is partitioned to a different node, an ID-based range query is likely to involve the entire cluster.

By querying via the TOKEN function, you can scope your queries to only the nodes that own that token range.

Figure 12.1   Attempting to export data via performing range queries using the partition key is an inefficient pattern that adds unnecessary load to your cluster, but you can use the TOKEN function to narrow these large queries to a single token range.

If you're querying by token ranges, what should those ranges be? You don't want to query by more nodes than necessary, so the boundaries of the vnodes in the hash ring are as big as your slices should be. To find the vnodes where ownership shifts, you can use the `nodetool describering` command, which prints out the token range for a given keyspace:

```
(scylla-reviews) $ nodetool describering reviews
Schema Version:bf868c5f-4f72-3a5c-bcb9-494cdf538889
TokenRange:
    TokenRange(start_token:8988086067483717526,
    ➥ end_token:8994847225697856081, endpoints:[172.18.0.2],
    ➥ rpc_endpoints:[172.18.0.2], endpoint_details:[EndpointDetails(
    ➥ host:172.18.0.2, datacenter:datacenter1, rack:rack1)])
    TokenRange(start_token:8806240936801133673,
    ➥ end_token:8855640390092123302, endpoints:[172.18.0.2],
    ➥ rpc_endpoints:[172.18.0.2], endpoint_details:[EndpointDetails(
    ➥ host:172.18.0.2, datacenter:datacenter1, rack:rack1)])
    ...
```

Although the output isn't sorted, you can see the start and end tokens, as well as the endpoints for which nodes own that token range. Because `scylla-reviews` has only one node, the token range specifies only one endpoint. You can pull this data from your driver or parse the `describering` output to pass the list of token ranges to your queries and limit your queries to only one node and its replicas.

> **TIP** The Python driver stores this information internally at `cluster.meta-data.token_map.tokens_to_host_by_ks`, which maps the end of a token range to its owning hosts for each keyspace in the cluster.

The goal when performing data extractions is to do it as fast as possible without breaking other traffic. It's easy to index on speed and not on remaining friendly to other workloads. When executing these workloads, you need to perform some tuning around just how much of the token range you query at a time, your concurrency, and how to back off and retry queries that may time out—for example, if you hit a very large partition. It may take some dialing-in to strike the right balance. You may even go so far as to spin up a second datacenter solely for these workloads to lessen traffic on your primary datacenter.

This token-range scanning approach is comprehensive, but with the balancing act not to break existing workloads, it can be expensive. Provisioning additional compute to support a daily workload may be expensive, or you may have terabytes of data that take a very long time to query. Scylla supports another method of doing this extraction, but instead of doing large queries of the entire database, it spreads that cost over each write you do to the database by capturing the changes made to each row and summarizing them in a specialized log table. Let's look at how Scylla can track changes over time and how that can be used to extract data from other systems.

12.1.2 Change data capture

Scylla supports a feature called *change data capture* (CDC), which tracks changes to tables when configured, surfacing them in a specific table to give you a history of the changes made. If you modify an author's bio, for example, you'll see a row in the table representing the act of updating that author's bio. CDC groups these changes using a special partition key, allowing you to efficiently query for every change made to a table.

Why is change-tracking valuable? Querying an entire table to export to another system is not only an expensive operation; it also gives you the given values for that table only at the moment your queries execute. Imagine if you had a massive multipetabyte table that you wanted to export. Instead of querying the entire data set regularly for export, you could use CDC to track the changes over time to your table and apply those changes in that secondary data store.

CDC isn't just valuable for data exports. Because it tracks the history of changes to your database, you can also use it to build a history of changes to data. Imagine that you wanted to track who changed what in an article over time by adding an `edited_by` column to the `articles` table that you set on each write. With CDC, you could see which fields were changed and which editor changed them, ingesting those updates into another system to build a timeline of article changes.

Let's see it in action by enabling it and trying it out. CDC is enabled on a per-table basis via the `cdc` property:

```
cqlsh:reviews> ALTER TABLE reviews.authors WITH cdc = {'enabled': true};
```

> **NOTE** Similar to other table properties, you can also enable it when creating the table.

If you describe the `reviews` keyspace, you see that Scylla has created the CDC table:

```
cqlsh:reviews> DESCRIBE reviews;
...

CREATE TABLE reviews.authors_scylla_cdc_log (          ◀──  The table name always has the
    "cdc$stream_id" blob,                                    form of the original table name
    "cdc$time" timeuuid,                                     appended with scylla_cdc_log.
    "cdc$batch_seq_no" int,
    bio text,                                          ◀──  Columns from the original
    "cdc$deleted_bio" boolean,                              table appear here with
    "cdc$deleted_elements_image" frozen<set<smallint>>,    their updated values.
    "cdc$deleted_image" boolean,                       ◀──  The CDC table also
    "cdc$deleted_name" boolean,                             contains a column to track
    "cdc$end_of_batch" boolean,                            if a column was deleted.
    "cdc$operation" tinyint,
    "cdc$ttl" bigint,                                       The table is partitioned by the CDC
    id timeuuid,                                            stream (more on this in a moment)
    image frozen<image>,                                   and is uniquely identified by the time
    name text,                                             and batch sequence number.
    PRIMARY KEY ("cdc$stream_id", "cdc$time", "cdc$batch_seq_no")  ◀──┘
) WITH CLUSTERING ORDER BY ("cdc$time" ASC, "cdc$batch_seq_no" ASC)
...
```

To see CDC in action, insert a new author—Charlie Change:

```
cqlsh:reviews> INSERT INTO authors(id, name, bio)
    VALUES (
        8f635bb1-e3a0-11ee-bd5f-fbf866e91d30,
        'Charlie Change',
        'Charlie Change helps track changes over time'
    );
```

Query the CDC table, and you'll see the insertion reflected there:

```
cqlsh:reviews> SELECT * FROM reviews.authors_scylla_cdc_log;

@ Row 1
----------------------------+-----------------------------------------------
 cdc$stream_id              | 0x967ccccccccccccd21ac560b50000181
 cdc$time                   | 8f61b986-e3a0-11ee-a485-a3784fa2eb37
 cdc$batch_seq_no           | 0
 bio                        | Charlie Change helps track changes over time
 cdc$deleted_bio            | null
 cdc$deleted_elements_image | null
```

```
cdc$deleted_image           | null
cdc$deleted_name            | null
cdc$end_of_batch            | True
cdc$operation               | 2
cdc$ttl                     | null
id                          | 8f635bb1-e3a0-11ee-bd5f-fbf866e91d30
image                       | null
name                        | Charlie Change
```

(1 rows)

To see how a change appears, update Charlie Change's bio:

```
cqlsh:reviews> UPDATE authors
  SET bio = 'Charlie Change helps track changes over time. Change is good!'
  WHERE id = 8f635bb1-e3a0-11ee-bd5f-fbf866e91d30;
```

When you query the CDC table again, you'll see output for two rows. One row represents your initial insert, and the second row represents the bio update. Pay attention to the name rows: you set the name in your initial insert, so the name appears in the first CDC row. But because you didn't update the name in your UPDATE statement, the name field is set to null in the second row:

```
cqlsh:reviews> SELECT * FROM reviews.authors_scylla_cdc_log;

@ Row 1
---------------------------+-----------------------------------------------
 cdc$stream_id             | 0x967ccccccccccccd21ac560b50000181
 cdc$time                  | 8f61b986-e3a0-11ee-a485-a3784fa2eb37
 cdc$batch_seq_no          | 0
 bio                       | Charlie Change helps track changes over time
 cdc$deleted_bio           | null
 cdc$deleted_elements_image | null
 cdc$deleted_image         | null
 cdc$deleted_name          | null
 cdc$end_of_batch          | True
 cdc$operation             | 2
 cdc$ttl                   | null
 id                        | 8f635bb1-e3a0-11ee-bd5f-fbf866e91d30
 image                     | null
 name                      | Charlie Change

@ Row 2
---------------------------+-----------------------------------------------
 cdc$stream_id             | 0x967ccccccccccccd21ac560b50000181
 cdc$time                  | f823de7c-e3a0-11ee-f1b3-00cbcac7af95
 cdc$batch_seq_no          | 0
 bio                       | Charlie Change helps track changes over time.
                        ⇒ Change is good!
 cdc$deleted_bio           | null
 cdc$deleted_elements_image | null
 cdc$deleted_image         | null
 cdc$deleted_name          | null
```

```
cdc$end_of_batch              | True
cdc$operation                 | 1
cdc$ttl                       | null
id                            | 8f635bb1-e3a0-11ee-bd5f-fbf866e91d30
image                         | null
name                          | null

(2 rows)
```

This behavior is critical to understanding CDC: it tracks the changes to a table over time, not the state of individual rows after a query. The CDC table describes changes; because you didn't change the name, it's set to null in the second update. To determine the full state of a row, you need to ingest all changes over time.

Take a closer look at the CDC table, and you'll see that a different value is used to partition the data: the *CDC stream*, which is a method of grouping changes to a given partition and providing ordering. Because the data is partitioned by the stream ID, you should query for a given stream at a time. When a Scylla cluster's topology changes, such as when you add a node, the *CDC stream generation* updates. For each generation, Scylla maintains some number of stream IDs. When you write to a table with CDC enabled, Scylla maps the partition key of that query to a stream ID. This isn't a unique mapping; many partitions can share a stream ID. This mapping is consistent: in a generation, each partition key always maps to the same stream ID. Figure 12.2 shows this relationship between partition keys and stream IDs.

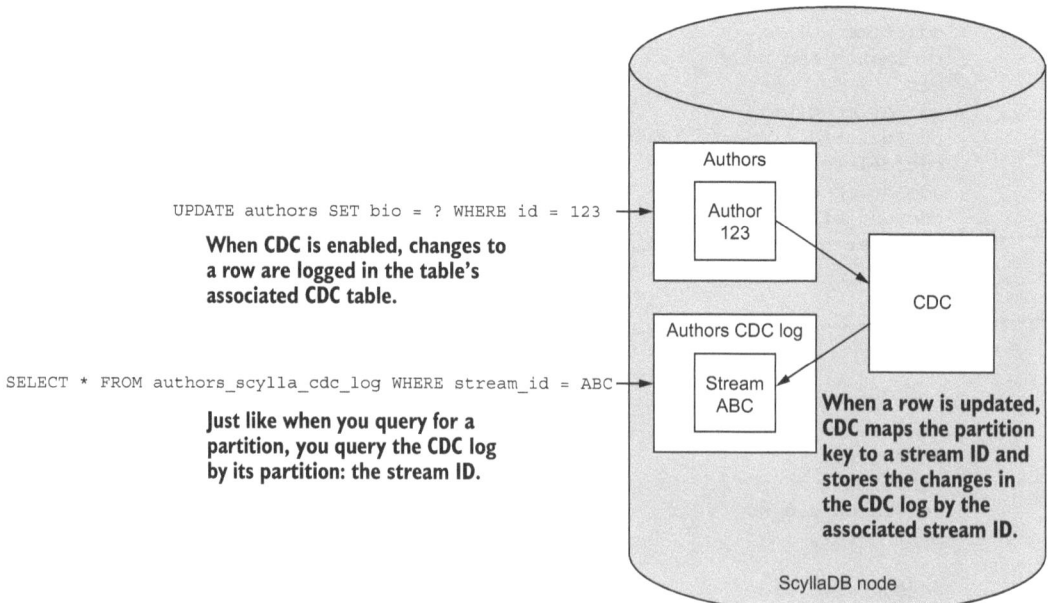

Figure 12.2   Each entry in the CDC logs maps to a stream ID, which may be shared with other partitions.

> **NOTE** Under the hood, Scylla uses a custom partitioner to ensure that both the data partition and the CDC partition are stored on the same shard to make it easier for the cluster to perform updates.

Although the full-table scan works well when you have two rows, it falls apart as the table grows. Querying by stream ID is a three-step process.

1 Get the current CDC generation timestamp.
2 Retrieve the stream IDs for the current generation using the timestamp.
3 Query the CDC table for each stream ID.

To get the current CDC generation timestamp, you need to grab the highest value from the `cdc_generation_timestamps` table, which resides in the `system_distributed` keyspace:

```
cqlsh:reviews> SELECT time
FROM system_distributed.cdc_generation_timestamps
WHERE key = 'timestamps'
LIMIT 1;

@ Row 1
------+----------------------------------
 time | 2024-02-27 23:13:34.444000+0000

(1 rows)
```

> **NOTE** If you're following along, your timestamp will be different than mine.

Truncate this timestamp to millisecond precision, and use it to query the `cdc_streams_descriptions_v2` table. This query will return lots of rows, each containing a list of hexadecimal stream IDs:

```
cqlsh:reviews> SELECT streams
FROM system_distributed.cdc_streams_descriptions_v2
WHERE time = '2024-02-27 23:13:34.444+0000';

@ Row 1
---------+----------------------------------------------------------------------
streams | {0x7fc67f250274c9d864cef00888000001,
➥ 0x7fc999999999999a061c8edf9c0000001, 0x7fccccccccccccccd9ba28e1758000001,
➥ 0x7fd0000000000000dbea7f9354000001, 0x7fd33333333333346dce9f6718000001}

@ Row 2
---------+----------------------------------------------------------------------
streams | {0x8103c12036e975f2df91f7e9c0000011,
➥ 0x8106666666666667db22d9eaf4000011, 0x810999999999999aa80217d9a4000011,
➥ 0x810ccccccccccccd17a18f0414000011, 0x8110000000000000eeab23f6cc000011}
```

Collect all of the stream IDs for each row, combining them into one big list. If you query your CDC tables with every one of these stream IDs, you can load all of the data stored in the CDC tables. Bulk extracts use the `token` function, but Scylla provides a separate grouping with these stream IDs, allowing efficient access to the entire CDC table by giving you a query to get the stream IDs that together encompass the entirety of the CDC table.

As mentioned earlier, the stream generation—and therefore the stream IDs used to query—updates when your cluster topology changes. The preceding steps illustrate a happy path that demonstrates how to find the stream IDs, but in practice you should find all generation IDs in the CDC window: those timestamps that fit between the CDC time to live (TTL) and now. Most of the time, you'll only have one timestamp in `cdc_streams_descriptions_v2`. But if you expand the cluster, you will potentially have multiple timestamps in the CDC TTL and will need to query for each of their stream IDs to get a full picture of the changes in your cluster (figure 12.3).

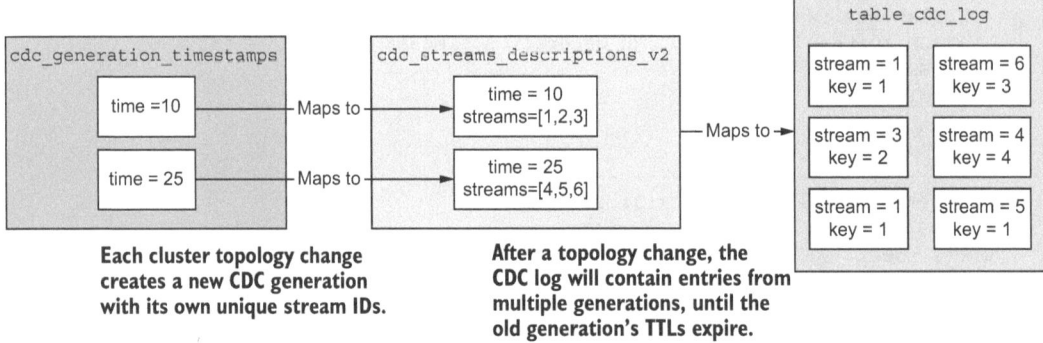

Figure 12.3   Topology changes mean any CDC queries need to be aware of multiple generates in the CDC log.

Although CDC can feel like it requires a complicated series of queries to work, like many things in software, it's made easier through abstractions. Scylla provides client libraries to help applications use CDC instead of requiring you to build your own bespoke implementation, such as the Go client (https://github.com/scylladb/scylla-cdc-go) and the Rust client (https://github.com/scylladb/scylla-cdc-rust).

CDC tracks each change to a table, so you may be concerned about the growth of the log table if you're performing frequent updates. Scylla protects against rampant, uncontrolled CDC growth by writing each update with a TTL—24 hours by default. This property has an important implication: if you're using CDC for data replication, you need to pull from it more frequently than its TTL. If not, you'll miss updates!

Although CDC can give you an entire picture of how your data changes over time, it does assume that you have a baseline to track changes from, whether it's initialized on an empty table or via an exported table through token-range reads that you can use to track CDC changes after a point in time. As mentioned earlier, CDC only stores changes for a configured time. If you don't pull every change, you will have out-of-sync data and missed updates. If you happen to miss a large amount of data and that sizable mismatch is crucial to your use cases, it may be worth declaring "CDC bankruptcy," reexporting data via token-range reads, and starting your CDC process over again.

With CDC, you can use Scylla to track changes to your data over time. It can stop you from running expensive queries against a massive data set—and at any scale, it allows you to ingest each change to a table, unlocking a world of possibilities. Whether it's tracking edits or duplicating your data elsewhere, it's a powerful tool in your data toolbox. The complications lie in tracking this data. When using CDC, you must build it to be tolerant of new stream generations due to topology changes; and because this data is TTL'd, missing any updates can have critical downstream effects, depending on your use cases.

Exporting data from Scylla can be challenging: you need to move a lot of data without breaking the database. Through token-range reads and CDC, you have two varying approaches that you can mix and match to meet your needs. Just like you need to read a lot of data from the database, sometimes you need to write a lot of data, such as when migrating existing data into Scylla. In the next section, you'll learn how to efficiently write a lot of data and how the process frequently faces the same challenges as bulk reads: doing it as fast as you can without breaking anything.

12.2   Migrating to ScyllaDB

At a high level, migrating data into ScyllaDB is very straightforward. You have data that lives elsewhere, and you put it in ScyllaDB. The job is done, and you're on to a different project. Alas, like almost everything, the devil is in the details. Data migrations involve several challenges in order to complete the procedure efficiently and correctly.

If you're migrating data to Scylla—or any other data store—you're choosing to do so because the recipient database has some desirable characteristics or features that the previous one doesn't. To take advantage of the new database, you'd like to complete the migration as quickly as possible. To speed up a migration, you need to increase either the throughput at the source or at the destination. However, you can't turn the dial too far up; there is some level of traffic at which either database becomes degraded—as you saw during your load tests in the previous chapter.

Taking either the source or destination offline from user traffic can simplify the procedure, but that's often not an option. Not only can you not break existing traffic to the database, but while you're migrating, that source database is frequently taking new writes, adding more data that you need to migrate. Any migration strategy must account for this additional data written during the procedure.

Just because you've migrated the data doesn't mean the data is correct. Perhaps data is missing, or perhaps the data changed subtly between the two data stores (timestamp precision has bitten me several times). Simply moving the data from one database to another isn't enough; you need to validate its correctness.

In this section, you'll learn about some techniques and tools you can use to migrate data into ScyllaDB. First you'll learn about a critical part of any data migration: ensuring that new data is written to both your source and destination database.

12.2.1 Dual writing

During a migration, you often need to keep your source database online and receive traffic. Because of this requirement, you'll likely update data that you've already migrated. If you don't somehow account for this missed update, you'll have unmigrated data in your destination ScyllaDB after the migration is complete. To avoid this problem, you should update your applications to *dual-write* data, writing to both the source and destination databases to avoid missed updates (figure 12.4).

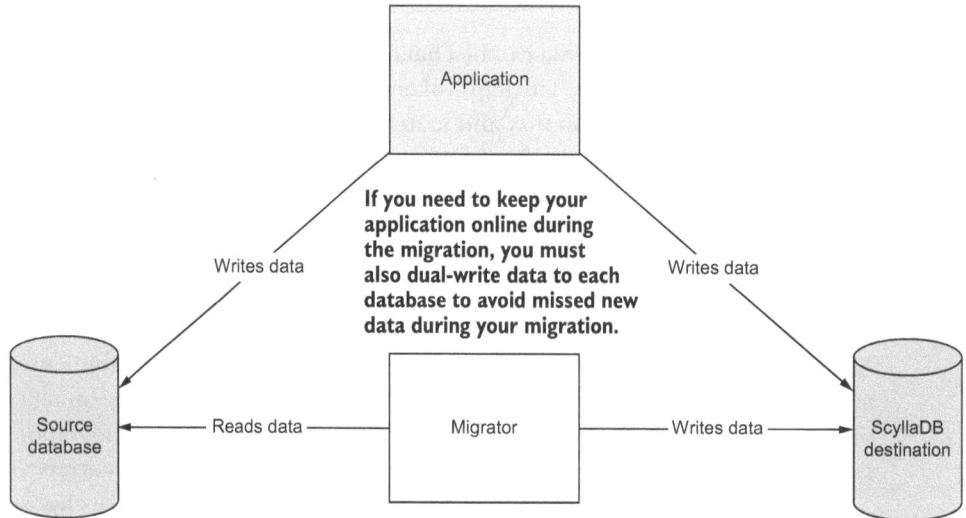

Figure 12.4 **If you need to keep your application online during a migration, you must also dual-write data to avoid missed writes.**

It's not as straightforward as sending the requests to both databases; there are nuances to consider as you orchestrate these requests. Writing to two databases invites consistency problems; you only want to write to the secondary or destination database if the write to the primary source database succeeds. A write only in the destination but not the source is extra data that would suddenly appear in your system after you cut traffic over to the freshly migrated ScyllaDB.

The parallel of this relationship is that you want writes that succeed on the primary to also succeed on the secondary. Consider using the Scylla driver's downgrading consistency options, which retry writes with increasingly weaker consistency options until a write succeeds, relying on Scylla's repair and replication options to correctly replicate the data to its owning nodes.

This dual-writing approach is critical for all online data migrations. You'll learn about a few migration options in this chapter; each of them should be paired with dual-writing from your application to safely migrate data from a source database that remains online. First, let's look at the most straightforward option: Scylla's SSTable-Loader. Although it's limited to migrating from Cassandra or older Scylla clusters, it does things in an easy-to-understand way: it copies the SSTables.

12.2.2   SSTableLoader

Recall from chapter 9 that you can use nodetool's snapshot functionality to generate hard links to SSTables for a given keyspace. At this point, you may be thinking that it would be convenient to use these SSTables to migrate data into Scylla. As you may expect in a section about data migration, Scylla supports that operation via its SSTableLoader.

The tool provides a simple interface: you pass it the directory where the SSTables for a given table live. The SSTableLoader makes few assumptions: it assumes the SSTables live in a directory similar to the existing /var/lib/scylla/data, where there is a directory for each keyspace and each keyspace directory has subfolders for its tables. Additionally, it assumes the schema for these SSTables has already been created and is ready and waiting for the migrated SSTables.

For example, if you snapshotted your `reviews` keyspace and want to restore your `articles` table, you need to move those snapshotted SSTables into a directory called reviews/articles. After moving the SSTables to the location where the SSTableLoader expects them, you can point the SSTableLoader at the directory to load them into Scylla. The SSTableLoader then scans each SSTable, converting its contents to CQL statements that it executes on the destination cluster (figure 12.5).

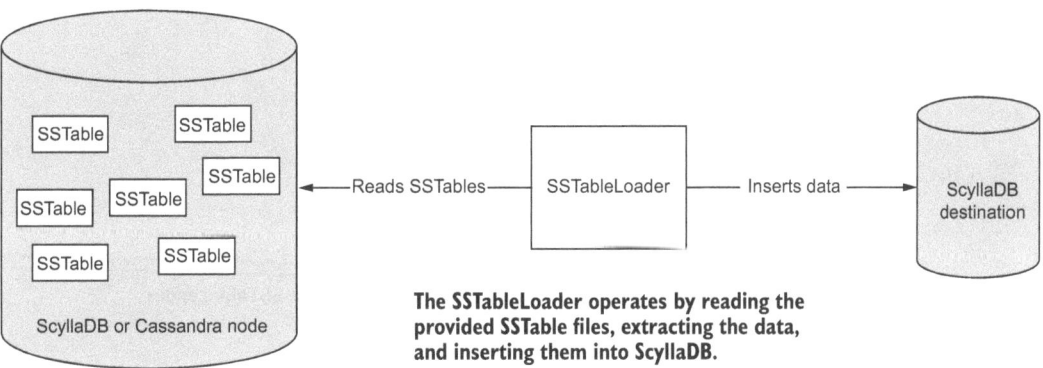

Figure 12.5   The SSTableLoader, as its name suggests, migrates data by reading a set of SSTables and inserting their contents into Scylla.

If you have existing SSTables from Cassandra or Scylla, Scylla's SSTableLoader is a natural fit, but that's also a narrow use case. If you're not using Cassandra or Scylla, this option is immediately ruled out. The SSTableLoader is also limited in another respect: its scalability is orchestrated solely by you. You can speed it up by running more SSTableLoaders concurrently, but you can only parallelize it per database table, giving you an upper bound of data that it can migrate at once.

To deal with this scalability challenge, Scylla supports a second migration option: the Spark Migrator. By using a data-processing engine—Apache Spark—Scylla can easily utilize multiple processes to migrate from Cassandra or Scylla. Let's look at how Spark works and how the Spark Migrator uses it as a foundation to move data into Scylla.

12.2.3 *Spark Migrator*

Spark is a distributed data-processing platform; you provide it with some machines to run as Spark nodes, give it a data-processing job to do, and let it run. ScyllaDB has written a migrator that runs using Spark, dividing a table into slices and giving each Spark node that slice to migrate. The more machines you run, the more work you can do in parallel—assuming you don't run into any bottlenecks in the source or destination. Figure 12.6 demonstrates this scalability.

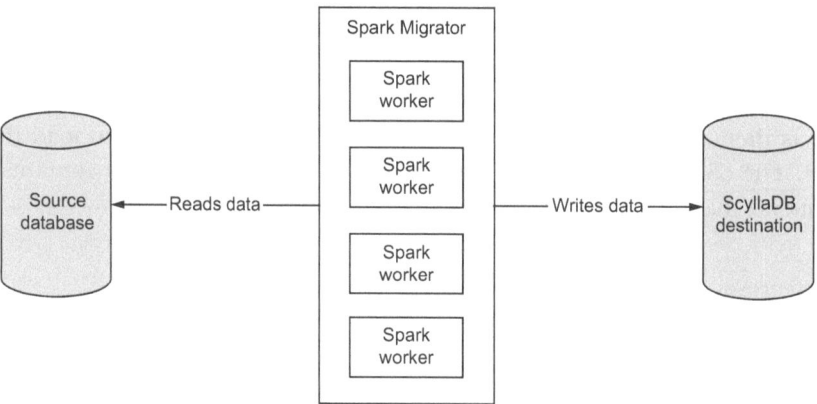

The Spark Migrator uses Apache Spark to empower finer control of your migrator's scalability, allowing you to add more workers that each migrate a token range at a time.

Figure 12.6   The Spark Migrator offers greater scalability than Scylla's SSTableLoader.

Spark's included parallelism makes it easy to scale, but it's also a potentially unfamiliar technology that you need to set up and run. Because it runs on multiple machines, you have to provision them, install Spark, and install the migrator (https://github .com/scylladb/scylla-migrator) before you can begin running the migration. If you're running in a cloud provider, Google Cloud's Dataproc or AWS's EMR makes it easier to set up Spark and run jobs. Otherwise, you're on your own.

The Spark Migrator improves on the SSTableLoader's scalability, but it does inherit the SSTableLoader's primary weakness: it's predominantly used with Cassandra and ScyllaDB, although it does also support Amazon's DynamoDB and Apache Parquet, a columnar file format. If you're running Postgres and trying to migrate to ScyllaDB, this tool isn't a match. If the Spark Migrator only works for these limited cases and is complex to set up, why would you use it?

The most immediate answer is that you're migrating from a compatible datastore and you need its scalability. The Spark Migrator, because of its elasticity, can migrate data much faster than the SSTableLoader; it's not limited by table, only by the bandwidth of each of your databases and the compute of the migrator. The Spark Migrator also has a few more bells and whistles. It supports filtering your data via a WHERE clause, only migrating data that matches it, and checkpointing, enabling you to pause progress and resume from where you stopped.

Earlier, we discussed how data correctness is key to performing a migration. Although I believe there is a better way to validate a migration (you'll learn more about it soon), the Spark Migrator has an included validation function, which compares a Cassandra source's data to the Scylla destination's. You can validate that after completing your migration, Spark's view of the data in the source matches its view of the destination. For pesky things like timestamp equality, the migrator even supports changing the accepted tolerance for what makes two values equal.

If you're migrating from a compatible database, the Spark Migrator, despite its initial complexity, is helpful. The initial setup effort isn't trivial, but it allows you to fire-hose data into Scylla from a source data store. If you're not using a compatible data store, though, you're blocked from using the Spark Migrator, but that doesn't mean you're blocked from migrating data. Next, I want to cover an option that's customizable to any use case or database: writing your own migrator.

12.2.4 *Writing a migrator*

I acknowledge that writing about how the Spark Migrator is complex to set up and then following up by discussing how you write your own migrator is potentially incongruous, but bear with me for a moment. Everyone's data sets and use cases are unique. The previous migration tools are each generic; they're designed to support migrating data from Cassandra or Scylla as well as possible. Let's imagine that you're migrating data from a relational database like MySQL. The SSTableLoader and the Spark Migrator aren't an option; you need to blaze your own trail to copy data from that relational database into Scylla.

Let's assume you have some queries you can run against your source database to extract data, but you now need to insert that data into ScyllaDB. Recall from chapter 6 that every value in the database gets an associated write timestamp. In the event of a conflict, the value with the higher timestamp wins—"last write wins." If you're not careful with your write times, your migration can wreak havoc on your destination database.

If two editors update the same article concurrently, the most recent update wins. When migrating data, your migrator also becomes a potential source of concurrent updates. With dual-writing going on during your migration, you can observe the following sequence of events if you're unlucky:

- The migrator reads an article and prepares to insert it into the database.
- Concurrently, an editor updates the article, changing the title and dual-writing it to the source and destination databases.
- The migrator inserts the article into the source database.

If the editor's update has a lower timestamp than the migration's insert, the migration can overwrite this updated data. Figure 12.7 illustrates this risk.

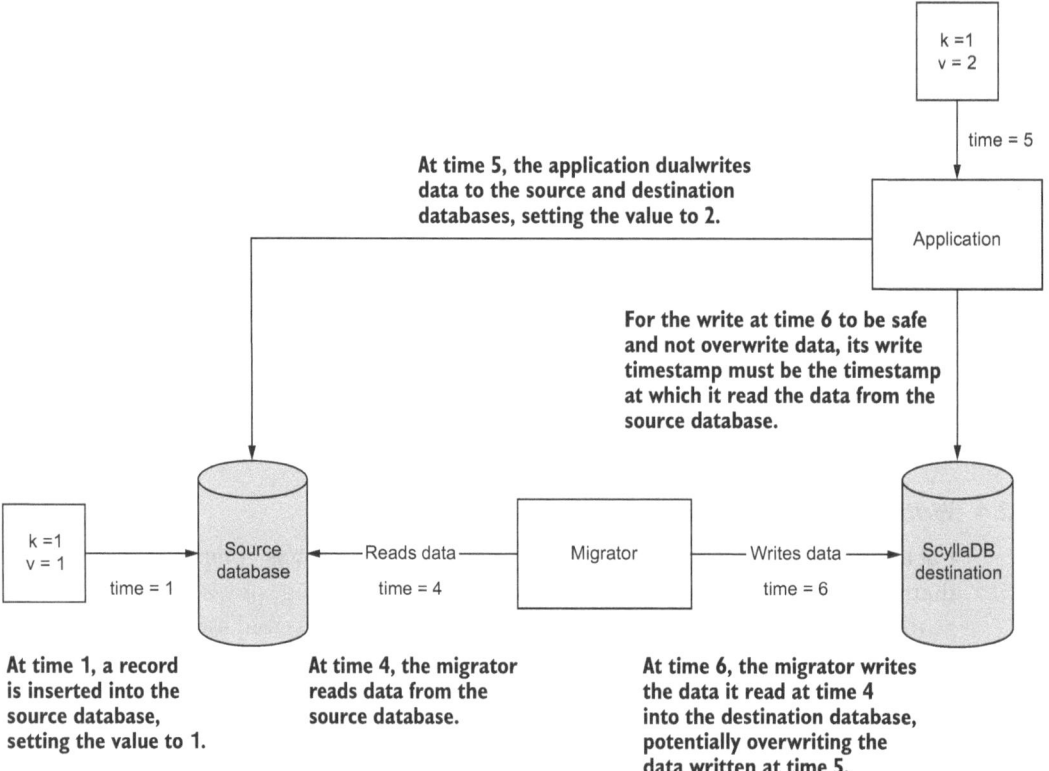

Figure 12.7   If a dual-write updates a value that your migration has recently read but not updated, you can overwrite newer versions of data in your source application.

When writing data with your migrator, you should use a USING TIMESTAMP clause to specify the insertion statement's write time. That value should be no later than the moment in time you begin your read queries.

TIP Prefer using the source database's representation of that write time-stamp, whether it's an actual Cassandra or Scylla write timestamp or a modified timestamp in a relational database. Following these guidelines helps your migration not to stomp data.

Your migrator also needs to consider the characteristics of your source database. A distributed database like Cassandra or a Postgres database with several read replicas can give you potentially greater throughput than a smaller single MySQL instance serving heavy traffic regularly. Generally, your migrator should run as fast as it can without negatively affecting either the source or destination data stores.

Your source database also clearly affects how you migrate your data. Whereas Scylla neatly divides the data space into token ranges (the approach described earlier in the chapter is very useful here), a relational database may only have a list of IDs that you can grab in (large) handfuls. Because of these differences, your migrator should include some form of *progress checkpointing* to enable pausing and resuming. Migrating a large data set isn't always a linear path; you may need to pause to scale up the destination or throttle the intensity you're querying your source. If you have to start over every time you need to change something, you can make a migration take much longer than expected. Checkpointing doesn't have to be sophisticated. You can store the token ranges you've migrated in a table in your source or destination databases, for example.

Writing your own migrator isn't an out-of-the-box approach, but it gives you full control over the most critical part of your application: your data. For a successful migration, you need to ensure that the migrated data is correct. Data validation is just as important as data migration; let's examine how you can validate your migration's success.

12.2.5 *Validating migrations*

Data validation encompasses two dimensions: comprehensiveness and correctness. You should ensure that you migrated all the data and that you migrated them correctly. Some migrators support this validation: the Spark Migrator can compare the source and destination databases for you. It's especially useful for the comprehensiveness check to ensure that all data in the source is present in your destination ScyllaDB. Ultimately, though, the best way to determine the validity of the migration is through your application. You shouldn't throw caution to the wind and immediately start using the destination database; instead, probabilistically validate your correctness via dual-reading.

When evaluating correctness, the ultimate measure of success is whether the migration introduces any negative behavior in upstream applications. Differing results from your source and destination databases can bubble up to become showstopping client bugs. Just like you dual-write data to send new updates to both the source and the destination, you should dual-read requests to both your source and destination databases. This dual-reading isn't just sending every query to the destination—although that behavior does help load test your destination, ensuring that it can handle the full amount of traffic—it adds validation logic.

Given a read to the primary source database, you should also send it to the secondary and compare their results. If they are equivalent, great! If not, try checking again. Frequently updated rows may be updated between the two reads, so doing a follow-up read can reduce mismatch noise. If the two reads don't converge to the same value, your application thinks they're unequal. You can log the query that produced the mismatch and investigate. Figure 12.8 illustrates this dual-read validation.

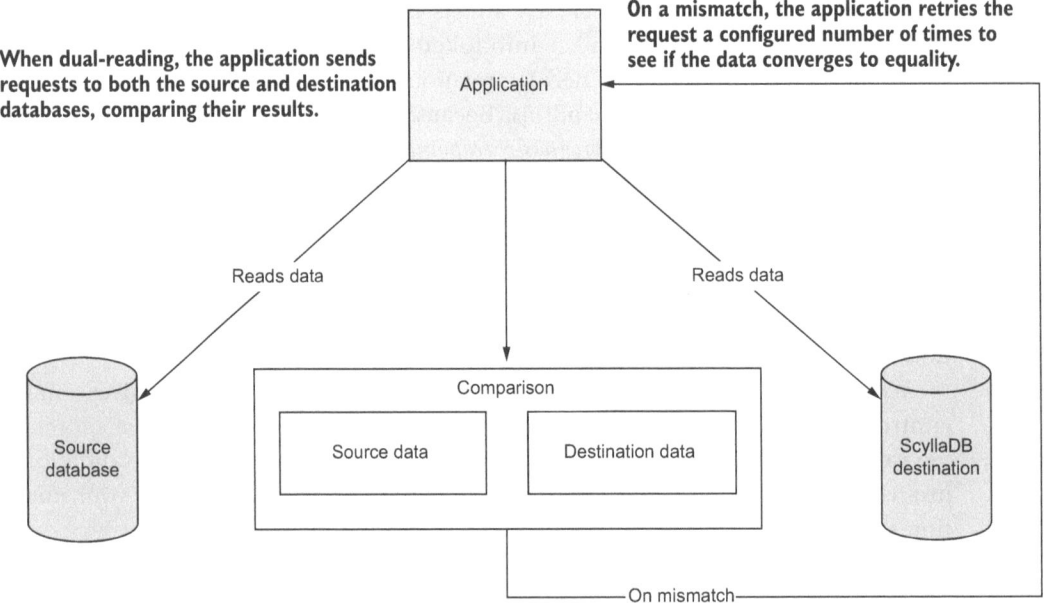

Figure 12.8   By dual-reading your application's request, you can check for mismatches and verify the correctness of your migration.

There are two scenarios for a mismatch:

- The data is different but functionally equivalent. For example, one timestamp is in milliseconds, while the other is in microseconds.
- The data is meaningfully different: missing some fields or even the entire row.

Migrating to Scylla should be invisible to users, so you should investigate, explain, and potentially fix any problems.

I recommend doing this dual-read validation probabilistically: send some percentage of your requests through this flow. First, because you retry mismatches, if there are many of them or there is a bug in your mismatch-checking logic, you can multiply the traffic to your source database by the number of retries. Increasing the percentage as you observe fewer mismatches helps increase your confidence in the migration without accidentally taking your databases offline by drowning them in traffic.

If it's possible, another solution is to do *two-way scanning*: checking that every row present in the source database is also present in your destination and then repeating the procedure in the other direction. This tells you that there are no rows only in one database. You can also do this analysis probabilistically, grabbing random token ranges or slices of data and checking either side.

Once you're confident in your migration after testing and analysis, you're ready to switch traffic over. When you decide to use ScyllaDB as your new primary database, you should continue dual-writing just in case. After your validation, it's unlikely that you'll find something new that causes a problem severe enough to switch back, but it's helpful to preserve that option just in case.

When migrating data, you have a few options. The SSTableLoader is the easiest to set up, but it only works with Cassandra and Scylla, doesn't support checkpointing, and you're limited to one table at a time. The Spark Migrator allows easier scalability and checkpointing, but it has the same source data-store limitations and is complex to set up. Writing your own migrator isn't a trivial effort, but it allows you to use any data source—such as Postgres or MySQL—and gives you control over the entire process. You'll still need to dual-write data to ensure that you're migrating the latest written data. And finally, no matter which option you pick, validating your migration via dual-reading is paramount.

Summary

- Databases frequently need to support exporting data into other systems for aggregation and analysis.
- To query across multiple partitions for data exports, use the hash ring's token ranges to query a large chunk of data on a single node.
- The `nodetool describering` command tells you which token ranges are owned by which nodes.
- Change data capture (CDC) writes each update to the table's corresponding CDC table that describes the changes made to each row over time.
- If a value isn't updated in a statement, it's not reflected in the CDC table entry, even if the underlying value exists, because CDC tracks changes, not the state of the row.
- CDC maps changes to a given partition to a specific stream ID, which is created per stream generation. To query changes in CDC, you should query by the stream IDs, which you can obtain from the stream generation table.
- Migrating data into Scylla must balance speed and availability while achieving correctness.
- When migrating data from a database that must take user-facing traffic during the migration, you should also dual-write data from your application to the source and destination databases to prevent missed writes.

- The SSTableLoader can migrate SSTables from Cassandra or ScyllaDB, but it can only be parallelized per table.
- The Spark Migrator uses Apache Spark to run an elastic amount of workers, allowing you to tune your migrator's scalability when migrating data from Cassandra or Scylla.
- If you can't use either of these migrators, writing your own gives you control over the migration process.
- When writing a migrator, you should be careful to specify a write timestamp for your migrated data that won't overwrite recently written new data.
- Dual-read validation helps provide the ultimate test of correctness: is the data equivalent in your application's eyes?
- Two-way scanning helps verify that no data is missing on either side of your migration.

appendix
Docker

Running ScyllaDB requires a Linux-based operating system and several configuration steps. We discuss configuration in this book, but for ease in getting started quickly, you'll use *Docker* to run your clusters. Docker allows you to run packaged Linux applications in virtualized environments. In this appendix, you'll learn how to install and configure Docker to run Scylla locally.

A.1 *Linux*

Docker is written for Linux, and other operating systems' implementations require running a virtual machine (which Linux handles for you in the background) to run Docker, so it should be straightforward. On the other hand, there are so many flavors of Linux that installing Docker becomes slightly more involved. To install Docker, go to the link for your distro and follow the instructions:

- *Ubuntu*—https://docs.docker.com/engine/install/ubuntu
- *CentOS*—https://docs.docker.com/engine/install/centos
- *Debian*—https://docs.docker.com/engine/install/debian

A.2 *macOS*

To install Docker on macOS, you first need to be aware of its license restrictions. As of August 31, 2021, using Docker Desktop on a Mac on an enterprise machine (with a company larger than 250 employees or $10 million in revenue) requires a license. Otherwise, it's free for personal use. If you want to install it on a work Mac, I suggest doing so on a personal computer or investigating an open source equivalent like Podman.

Running Docker on a Mac entails installing Docker Desktop, which handles provisioning a virtual machine to run your containers. To install, follow the instructions at https://docs.docker.com/desktop/install/mac-install. Make sure you select the correct version for your CPU architecture—Intel or Apple Silicon.

A.3   *Windows*

Running Docker on Windows entails the same license complications as macOS, so if you're running the Desktop version, you should run it only on a personal computer. Additionally, Docker for Windows requires virtualization support to be enabled in the BIOS settings, which the standard install instructions will guide you through. To install Docker for Windows, follow the steps at https://docs.docker.com/desktop/install/windows-install.

If you want to avoid Docker Desktop, you can install Docker directly on Windows Subsytem for Linux, which lets you run Linux alongside Windows. This approach is somewhat off the beaten path, but you can find several blog posts online that will walk you through setting it up.

A.4   *Running ScyllaDB on Docker*

In this book, we discuss how to run ScyllaDB specifically on Docker. You'll learn how to launch a container, build a cluster, run queries, and much more. For a broad overview of running ScyllaDB on Docker, you can look at Scylla's documentation (https://mng.bz/6YNe), which touches on many of the topics we discuss throughout the book.

index

RELATED MANNING TITLES

DuckDB in Action
by Mark Needham, Michael Hunger, and
Michael Simons
Foreword by Mark Raasveldt and Hannes Mühleisen

ISBN 9781633437258
312 pages, $59.99
July 2024

Apache Pulsar in Action
by David Kjerrumgaard
Foreword by Matteo Merli

ISBN 9781617296888
400 pages, $49.99
October 2021

Acing the System Design Interview
by Zhiyong Tan
Forewords by Anthony Asta and Michael Elder

ISBN 9781633439108
472 pages, $59.99
January 2024

*Azure Storage, Streaming, and Batch
Analytics*
by Richard L. Nuckolls

ISBN 9781617296307
448 pages, $49.99
October 2020

For ordering information, go to www.manning.com